G Lemmie

THE REVELATION OF BAHÁ'U'LLÁH
'Akká, The Early Years: 1868–77

By the same author

TRUSTEES OF THE MERCIFUL
(Bahá'í Publishing Trust, London, 1972)

THE REVELATION OF BAHÁ'U'LLÁH
Baghdád 1853–63

THE REVELATION OF BAHÁ'U'LLÁH
Adrianople 1863–68

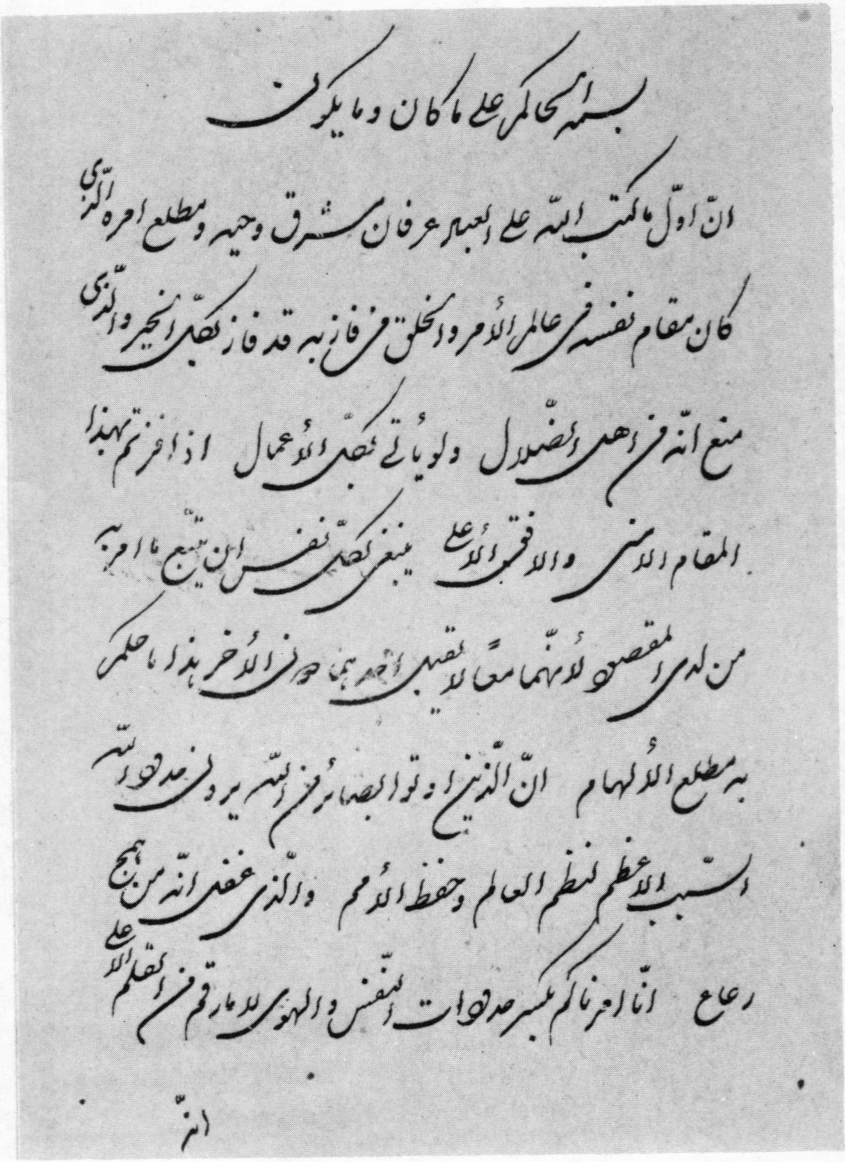

بسمه الحاكم على ما كان و ما يكون

ان اوّل ما كتب الله على العباد عرفان مشرق وحيه و مطلع امره الّذي
كان مقام نفسه في عالم الأمر و الخلق من فاز به قد فاز بكلّ الخير و الّذي
منع انّه من اهل الضّلال و لو يأتي بكلّ الأعمال اذا فزتم بهذا
المقام الأسنى و الأفق الأعلى ينبغي لكلّ نفس ان يتّبع ما امر به
من لدى المقصود لأنّهما معاً لا يقبل احدهما دون الآخر هذا ما حكم
به مطلع الإلهام انّ الّذين اوتوا البصائر من الله يرون حدود الله
السّبب الأعظم لنظم العالم و حفظ الأمم و الّذي غفل انّه من همج
رعاع انّا امرناكم بكسر حدودات النّفس و الهوى لا ما رقم من القلم الأعلى

انّ

THE FIRST PAGE OF THE KITÁB-I-AQDAS

In the handwriting of ‘Abdu’l-Bahá

THE REVELATION OF Bahá'u'lláh

'Akká, The Early Years 1868~77

Adib Taherzadeh

GR

GEORGE RONALD
OXFORD

GEORGE RONALD, Publisher

46 High Street, Kidlington, Oxford OX5 2DN

Reprinted 1984

ISBN 0-85398-143-4 (cased)

Typeset in Garamond by Sunrise Setting, Torquay, Devon
Printed in England by Billing & Sons Ltd., Worcester

To those brilliant souls
the Bahá'í Pioneers and Teachers in every land
who have expended their lives and their substance
in the path of Bahá'u'lláh

CONTENTS

ILLUSTRATIONS

NOTES AND ACKNOWLEDGEMENTS

The extracts from the Writings of the Báb and Bahá'u'lláh contained in this book are from the matchless translations by Shoghi Effendi, the Guardian of the Bahá'í Faith, and those carried out under the auspices of The Universal House of Justice. Published sources are acknowledged in the references and bibliography. There are many other quotations from Persian manuscripts and publications, and these I have translated, unless otherwise indicated. Most quotations had to be edited prior to translation. The footnotes to these quotations, however, are mostly mine, and this is indicated explicitly where confusion may arise. Verses taken from the *Qur'án* are numbered in accordance with the Arabic text, although their numbering may differ from that given in English translations. Persian and Arabic names are transliterated in accordance with the system adopted for books on the Bahá'í Faith, but quotations are reproduced in their original form.

The early followers of Bahá'u'lláh seldom sought to be photographed. Occasionally group photographs were taken, from which it has been possible to obtain many of the individual photographs which I have included, in the belief that their historical interest outweighs the fact that some are faded and out of focus. I am deeply indebted to the Audio-Visual Department of the Bahá'í World Centre for supplying most of these photographs. I should like to thank Mr Ruhi Shakibai for his excellent reproduction of some of the photographs printed in this book.

I wish to acknowledge with sincere thanks the co-operation of the Bahá'í Publishing Trust, London, and the Bahá'í Publishing Trust, Wilmette, Illinois, in permitting me to quote from their publications.

I desire to record my warm appreciation to Dr May Ballerio for her untiring efforts in helping me to speed up the preparation of the manuscript and for her skilful editing, and for the making of the index. My thanks go to Miss Eithne Earley for typing the manuscript from my original scribbled notes, many of which were illegible and often difficult to decipher, and to Mrs Corrine Alexander for additional typing assistance. I am also grateful to Mr Harold Boyce for his careful reading of the proofs.

Although I consider this work to be a very insignificant contribution to the great wealth of Bahá'í knowledge, nevertheless it has taken me a very long time to produce this volume. The main reason has been lack of time on my part. I have had to work during my free hours at home, usually in the late evening, and consequently the pace has been very slow. And probably the same situation will apply to Volume 4. However, in all my work I am deeply indebted to my wife Lesley for her constant support and encouragement.

Adib Taherzadeh

FOREWORD

The arrival of Bahá'u'lláh in 'Akká, signalizing the long-awaited fulfilment of the prophecies of the advent of the Lord of Hosts in the Holy Land, opens a new chapter of glorious consummation in the Revelation of Bahá'u'lláh. The momentous events associated with this period surpass those of the earlier days of His ministry. The final acts of the proclamation of His Message to individual kings, rulers and ecclesiastics, the revelation of the laws of His Dispensation regarded as the warp and woof of His World Order, the reversing of the tides of misfortune and misrepresentation into those of honour and public reverence, the revelation of countless Tablets bringing to a mighty climax all that had been revealed in the past, and the release of vast spiritual energies destined to regenerate human society and create a new race of men, all these characterize this period of Bahá'u'lláh's ministry in 'Akká and later in Bahjí.

This volume, covering the first nine years of the ministry of Bahá'u'lláh in 'Akká, is an attempt to catch a glimpse of this mighty Revelation. But how puny and feeble are the mind and vision of man, how poorly they equip him to venture into the arena of Divine Revelation which is far above his ken. It is obvious that we are unable to fathom this deep ocean of the Word of God in this age. We can only pass over the surface.

The aim of this volume is to describe some of the contents of the Tablets of Bahá'u'lláh. To achieve this, the author has followed the same pattern as in the two preceding volumes. He has outlined some of the main topics of a Tablet and elaborated on certain points which are in his opinion helpful for understanding some basic truths of the Faith. The aim has not been, however, to write a book of history. It is only to provide a background to the revelation of the Word of God that the author has dwelt at some length on the life of Bahá'u'lláh, the circumstances of His imprisonment in the barracks and later in 'Akká, and has also given brief accounts of the lives of some of the early believers involved.

The study of the Writings of Bahá'u'lláh is a never-ending spiritual experience; the many significances contained in His utterances and the power of His words are inexhaustible. The reader, therefore, will discover in this book only a drop out of the ocean, for only through a deeper study of the Writings of Bahá'u'lláh can we see the immensity of the Knowledge of God which Bahá'u'lláh has bestowed upon us in this day, a knowledge which will continually expand and unfold itself with the passage of time.

'AKKÁ IN THE NINETEENTH CENTURY

1

Bahá'u'lláh's Arrival at 'Akká

The journey of Bahá'u'lláh from Adrianople to 'Akká, described briefly in the closing chapter of the former volume, was laden with enormous hardship and suffering. It once again high-lighted the abasement to which Bahá'u'lláh and His companions were subjected, and the indignities heaped upon Him by the actions of His enemies. And when He arrived in the prison of 'Akká, these sufferings were intensified to such an extent that He designated that city as the 'Most Great Prison'. Referring to the first nine years of His exile in 'Akká, the Pen of the Most High in one of His Tablets has recorded these moving words:

> Know thou that upon Our arrival at this Spot, We chose to designate it as the 'Most Great Prison.' Though previously subjected in another land (Ṭihrán) to chains and fetters, We yet refused to call it by that name. Say: Ponder thereon, O ye endued with understanding![1]

One of the fascinating features of the life of Bahá'u'lláh is the contrast between His glory and majesty born of God, and the imprisonment and abasement to which He was subjected by His enemies. We may observe with amazement that Bahá'u'lláh, the Supreme Manifestation of God, One who held the powers of earth and heaven in His hands, the movement of whose pen could revolutionize the lives of all men, whose words were endowed with such potency as to subdue His adversaries; such a Being submitted Himself with utter resignation to those who had arisen with all their might and authority to take His life and extinguish the light of His Cause.

He did not exercise His God-given spiritual powers to stay the hands of the oppressors persecuting Him. He could have—as He Himself attests in many of His Tablets—conquered the hearts of His enemies with the utterance of one word, had He so wished. But this was not to be. For God has created man and has given him free will to choose between good and evil, to follow the Truth or tread the path of error.

If the Manifestations of God were to reveal fully the signs and tokens of their power, if they were to overwhelm and destroy their persecutors through the force of their spiritual might, such a revelation would run counter to the principle of free will which God has bestowed upon man. Because no one, whether good or bad, deserving or undeserving, when confronted with the manifold evidences of the overwhelming power of the Manifestation of God, would have any choice but to acknowledge His authority and accept the authenticity of His message. In such a case man would be reduced to a mere puppet who loses control over his actions, and those who have no spiritual merit would become equal to those who have.

This is why the Manifestations of God hide their powers from the eyes of men in general and occasionally (and to a certain extent) reveal them to a few who are endowed with spiritual qualities.* For instance, Christ enabled some of His disciples to witness the signs of His glory, but the great majority of the people in the Holy Land, their religious leaders and their rulers, were not affected by these. He did not use His spiritual ascendancy to prevent His own crucifixion.

The powers of the Manifestation of God remain hidden behind the veil of His human temple. He lives like the rest of the people and is subject to all the limitations which this imposes on Him. He has to eat and sleep in order to survive. He feels pain if He is afflicted with sufferings, He becomes ill at times and eventually dies. Indeed, He comes as if camouflaged by His mortal frame. And this prevents most of His contemporaries from recognizing His station. His actions

* see vol. 2, p. 83, and p. 300 below.

also prove to be great barriers and stumbling blocks for those who come into contact with Him. The way He lives is similar to the life of His countrymen. He speaks the same language, obeys the same laws, and practises the same customs. He does not appear to know the future, has to be informed of the news of the day, and even some of His teachings and words may cast doubt into the minds of many who are veiled from His glory. Those intellectuals and men of learning who are spiritually blind, and who weigh His utterances with their own standards, will often find fault with His sayings and reject His message outright.

All these human characteristics which the Manifestation of God displays act as a thick cloud hiding the splendours of the light of His Revelation from the eyes of men. For He does not reveal Himself in His naked glory. Only those with spiritual eyes may penetrate through and witness the radiance of the Sun of Truth behind this cloud. Man has to make an effort in order to find the truth. This is an irrevocable law of creation, and through it man's free will is preserved. This free will is bestowed upon man by God. He has given him authority to rule over this world. Man has the power of life and death in his hands. He can lead a peaceful life and build a united world, or he can kindle the fire of enmity and bring destruction and death to great multitudes. And although God has sent His Messengers from time to time to show the way to the human race, and has thrown light upon its path, yet He has left man free to choose for himself. In each Dispensation a considerable number of people have been led to follow the path of truth by their own free will, whereas the majority of the peoples have rejected the call of God and followed the dictates of their own selves.

In this age humanity has strayed far from the path of truth, and the call of Bahá'u'lláh to recognize Him as the viceregent of God on earth has fallen on deaf ears. But a careful study of His writings leads us to believe that His Revelation, being the culmination of past Revelations and one which has ushered in the Day of God Himself, will exert such a potent influence upon mankind as a whole that eventually all the peoples of the world will recognize His station of their own free will and embrace His cause of their own volition. And this in turn will bring about, in the distant future, the appearance of a new race of men whose noble character and spiritual virtues we, in this age, are unable to visualize.

With this basic principle in mind that the Manifestations of God hide their glory from the eyes of men, we can appreciate more clearly the manner in which they have appeared and acted among the peoples of the world. We observe that they have always submitted themselves to their enemies, and yet through the power of God they have succeeded in firmly establishing the foundation of their Cause among men. The sufferings which were inflicted on Bahá'u'lláh by His enemies throughout His forty-year ministry and the forbearance and resignation with which He endured these, demonstrate this principle. This becomes especially apparent in 'Akká where those in authority inflicted on Him tribulations more severe than at any other period in His ministry.

Although Bahá'u'lláh submitted Himself to a hostile enemy who made Him a prisoner and condemned Him to solitary confinement for the rest of His life, yet no one could rob Him of His majesty and glory. Even those who had no spiritual eyes and who were blind to His divine authority were forcibly struck by the outward manifestations of His eminent and august personality.

As with other incidents in His life when people came face to face with Him, not one of the officials accompanying Bahá'u'lláh on His journey to 'Akká, nor others who either in the course of duty or for other reasons came into His presence, could fail to recognize His greatness. One such was a young man by the name of Constantine, a Christian, who went aboard the ship at Alexandria in Egypt and attained His presence. This young man was one of the characters in an important incident during Bahá'u'lláh's journey to 'Akká.

The Alexandria Incident

Towards the end of His stay in Adrianople, Bahá'u'lláh sent Nabíl-i-A'ẓam to Egypt on a mission. The Iranian Consul-General in Cairo, Mírzá Ḥasan Khán-i-Khú'í, was an inveterate enemy of the Faith. As soon as he learnt of Nabíl's visit, he approached the Egyptian authorities, brought false accusations against him and urged his arrest. Consequently Nabíl was sent to a prison in Cairo and later transferred to one in Alexandria. Completely unaware of the fate of Bahá'u'lláh and his imminent exile to 'Akká, Nabíl spent his days in Alexandria prison, which was located close to the sea where ships used to anchor.

As we have already stated in a previous volume,* a certain Christian physician, a Syrian by the name of Fáris, who had been put in the same prison for financial reasons, became attracted to Nabíl. At first the former tried to convert the latter to Christianity. But instead Nabíl gave his companion the tidings of the coming of the Father and the advent of the Day of God. He disclosed to his eyes the light of the new-born Faith and imparted to him the knowledge of His revelation.

Soon, as a result of Nabíl's teaching work inspired by his spirit of detachment from this world, and aided by his profound and intimate knowledge of the message of Bahá'u'lláh, Fáris became assured of the truth of the Cause. The fire of faith began to burn fiercely in his heart, and the love of Bahá'u'lláh possessed his whole being. He was filled with joy and ecstasy, the gloom of the prison life vanished and he found himself for the first time in the midst of paradise.

While Nabíl was in Cairo prison, one night Bahá'u'lláh appeared to him in a dream and assured him that after eighty-one days the hardships of prison life would come to an end. That day fell on Thursday, 27 August 1868, and it was on that day that the significance of Nabíl's dream came to light.†

* vol. 1, pp. 203–4.

† According to the shipping records the Austrian Lloyd steamer was due

Around the time of sunset he went on the roof of the prison and began to watch people passing by. Not long after he had settled in a corner on the roof, to his amazement Nabíl sighted Áqá Muḥammad Ibráhím-i-Náẓir (caterer) among the passers-by, escorted by a guard. Áqá Muḥammad Ibráhím used to do the work of catering for Bahá'u'lláh and His companions in Adrianople. Now in Alexandria he had left the ship to purchase provisions for the journey. Not knowing anything about Bahá'u'lláh's exile to 'Akká, the astonished Nabíl called out to Muḥammad Ibráhím who succeeded in persuading his guard to allow him to visit his friend in the prison. There he told him of the fate of Bahá'u'lláh and His companions and pointed to the ship which carried the exiles and could be seen from the prison.

This amazing incident caused great agitation in the heart of Nabíl, for he found himself so close to his Beloved and yet so far. When Fáris Effendi was informed, he too became highly excited but frustrated at not being able to attain the presence of His Lord.

That night neither of the two could sleep. Both decided to write a letter to Bahá'u'lláh and the next morning Fáris Effendi made arrangements with a certain Christian youth, Constantine, who was a watch-maker in the city, to deliver their letters to Bahá'u'lláh on board the ship. They both stood on the roof of the prison to watch the ship, turned their hearts to Bahá'u'lláh and communed with His spirit with much devotion and love.

After a short while they were heart-broken to see the ship steaming away before Constantine could gain admittance. But amazingly, after a few minutes the ship stopped and Constantine, who was in a rowing boat, reached it and went

---

to leave Gallipoli on 21 August 1868 and was due in Alexandria on Wednesday 26 August early in the morning. Bahá'u'lláh and His companions transshipped to another steamer of the same company in Alexandria bound for Cyprus via Haifa, which sailed on Friday 28 August.

aboard. He handed the envelope to one of the attendants who took it to Bahá'u'lláh. The news of Nabíl's whereabouts, and especially the letter of Fáris, which was read aloud by Bahá'u'lláh to those who had assembled in His presence, created great excitement on board the ship. Bahá'u'lláh revealed a Tablet in honour of Nabíl in which He bestowed His bounties and blessings upon Fáris, and assured him that soon he would be released from the prison. He then called the messenger to His presence, and handed him the Tablet with loving kindness and affection. 'Abdu'l-Bahá and the Purest Branch also sent some gifts to Nabíl.

This short visit made an abiding impression upon Constantine. Having come face to face for a brief period with the Supreme Manifestation of God, and seen a glimpse of His glory, he left the ship overwhelmed and awestruck. When he came to deliver the parcel to Fáris Effendi, he was in such a state of excitement that he was heard shouting aloud, 'By God, I have seen the face of the Heavenly Father.' In a state of ecstasy and rapture Fáris embraced Constantine and kissed his eyes which had gazed upon the countenance of his Lord.

The Tablet of Bahá'u'lláh was in the handwriting of His amanuensis Mírzá Áqá Ján in the form of 'Revelation Writing'.* It imparted a new spirit of love and dedication to Fáris; it fanned into flame the fire of faith which had been ignited in his heart by Nabíl in that gloomy prison. As promised by Bahá'u'lláh, Fáris was released from prison three days later. After his release he arose in the propagation of the Faith among his people. Nabíl was also freed soon after, but being ordered to leave Egypt he proceeded to the Holy Land in pursuit of his Lord.

In more than one Tablet Bahá'u'lláh has Himself described the episode of Fáris in Alexandria as a token of the power of God. In a Tablet[2] revealed soon after His arrival in 'Akká and addressed to Raḍ'ar-Rúḥ,† a devoted follower from Man<u>sh</u>ád

* see vol. 1, pp. 24–5, 35–7.

† see vols. 1 and 2. The date of his martyrdom is not clearly known but

who died as a martyr, Bahá'u'lláh relates the story of His banishment from Adrianople, and the outpouring of the revelation of the Word of God in the course of that journey; he declares that the breezes of the revelation of the Words revealed in that period wafted over the entire planet. Referring to Himself as the 'Most Great Ocean', He describes in majestic language His boarding the ship and sailing upon the sea, while every drop of its waters was exhilarated and from it could be heard that which no one is capable of hearing.

Perhaps the highlight of this Tablet concerns the story of Fáris. Bahá'u'lláh relates that while the ship was anchored in Alexandria, He received from the hand of a Christian messenger a mighty letter from which He could inhale the fragrances of holiness. It was written by one who had detached himself from worldly ties and embraced His Cause. Bahá'u'lláh states that He wished Raḍ'ar-Rúḥ had been present to hear the soul-stirring Voice of his Lord as He read aloud to His companions on board the ship the letter of supplication and declaration of faith. This letter, written in Arabic, is indicative of a passionate faith in the Cause of Bahá'u'lláh, a deep understanding of His Revelation and a true recognition of His station. Bahá'u'lláh became so happy on receiving this moving letter that He wanted to share it with the believers. On His instructions, therefore, part of Fáris's letter was copied and sent to some individuals in Persia, that they might read and ponder upon the creative power of the Word of God which is capable of transforming the human heart and leading it to the world of the spirit.

This is a summary of part of Fáris's letter:

> O Thou the Glory of the Most Glorious and the Exalted of the Most Exalted! I write this letter and present it to the One who has been subjected to the same sufferings as Jesus Christ . . . It is incumbent upon us to offer praise and

---

was probably around the time that Bahá'u'lláh arrived in 'Akká and sent him the above Tablet.

thanksgiving to God, the All-glorious, the All-bountiful. And now I beseech Thee to grant me and my kindred a portion of the ocean of Thy bounty, O Thou who art the Ever-living, the Self-subsisting and the Wellspring of Purity and Sanctity.

I entreat Thee by the mystery of Thy most joyful Being, by Thy Prophet who conversed with Thee (Moses), by Thy Son (Jesus), by Thy Friend (Muḥammad) and by Thy Herald (The Báb) who for the love of Thee offered up His life in Thy path, not to deprive me and my family, these poor ones, from beholding the glory of Thy countenance.

O Thou who hast endured for our sake sufferings and tribulations. Strengthen our faith, choose us for Thy service and accept us as martyrs in Thy path so that our blood may be shed for the love of Thee. We are weak and ignorant, confer upon us Thy glory so that we may not be among the losers. Grant us the distinction of love and faith, and cleanse our hearts from whatsoever runs counter to Thy good pleasure. Aid us to forget our own selves so that we may seek no rest in Thy service except by Thy leave and pleasure.

O Thou who knowest the secrets of the hearts! Art Thou sailing in an ark made of wood? O how I long to be a part of that vessel, for it is blessed to be a carrier of the Lord. O, the surging sea! is thy restlessness because of the fear of the glorious Lord? O Alexandria! art thou grief-stricken because He who is the Ever-living, the All-wise, is leaving thy shores? O, the desolate city of 'Akká! Thou art clapping thy hands in fervent joy and art in a state of rapture and ecstasy, for the Lord in His great glory will bless thy land with His footsteps . . .

In the aforementioned Tablet to Raḍ'ar-Rúḥ Bahá'u'lláh makes an important statement which confirms one of the fundamental verities of the Cause of God. Referring to Fáris's recognition of His station, Bahá'u'lláh states that God transformed his heart and created him anew, and that such a creation is greater in the sight of God than the creation of earth and heaven. We may appreciate this statement when we reflect that the soul of man is the most precious reality in this creation, bestowed upon him by God. There is a spiritual and mysterious force of attraction between the soul and the Creator.* It is this love relationship that Bahá'u'lláh refers to in the *Hidden Words* when He says:

> O Son of Man! I loved thy creation, hence I created thee. Wherefore, do thou love Me, that I may name thy name and fill thy soul with the spirit of life.[3]

But the soul becomes attached to this world and it is this attachment which becomes a barrier between the soul and its Creator. If the barriers are removed, however, the soul will draw nearer to God, will recognize Him, will acquire the spirit of faith† and become a new creation. The soul thus fulfils the purpose for which it was created, and this is the most meritorious event in the sight of God and more important than all that is, in this physical creation. It is in this connection that we can appreciate the exhortations of Bahá'u'lláh with regard to teaching His Faith‡ which result in bringing a soul to its God. It is not surprising that Bahá'u'lláh has enjoined upon every believer the duty of teaching His Cause and has regarded it as 'the most meritorious of all deeds'.

Fáris was probably the first Christian to embrace the Faith of Bahá'u'lláh. Through the radiance of Nabíl's indomitable faith, and helped by his own knowledge of the Arabic language and of the Bible, Fáris became a faithful believer with a deep understanding of the station of Bahá'u'lláh. That Fáris and Nabíl should have met in the prison of Alexandria is no accident. God works in mysterious ways. When He is manifested to man, He attracts souls that are detached from this world to Himself. During the ministries of the Báb and Bahá'u'lláh, great numbers were led to the Fountain-head of God's Revelation in mysterious ways—through dreams and

* In this context we are not referring to 'Creator' as the Essence of God, but God manifested to man.

† see vol. 1, pp. 73–4.

‡ see vol. 2, pp. 91–4; and below, p. 331.

visions, through intuition or even through miraculous circumstances. This is because the Manifestation of God was living among men and those who were pure in heart were drawn to Him.

> By the righteousness of the one true God! If one speck of a jewel be lost and buried beneath a mountain of stones, and lie hidden beyond the seven seas, the Hand of Omnipotence would assuredly reveal it in this Day, pure and cleansed from dross.[4]

Fáris devoted his time to teaching the Cause among his own people. The *Lawḥ-i-Aqdas** (The Most Holy Tablet) otherwise known in the West as the 'Tablet to the Christians', is reputed to have been revealed in his honour, but this cannot be substantiated. Up till now, it has not been possible to ascertain for whom this Tablet was revealed.

After this extraordinary contact which was made at Alexandria between Bahá'u'lláh and the two Bahá'í prisoners, the steamer headed towards its destination,† and after three days it arrived at Haifa in the early morning of Monday 31 August.

The Most Great Prison

Bahá'u'lláh and His companions—seventy in all—disembarked from the ship and were taken ashore in sailing boats. All their belongings were also ferried across with them. There, the prisoners were all counted and handed over to government officials.‡ A few hours later they were all taken

* Published in *Tablets of Bahá'u'lláh*, pp. 9–17. Not to be confused with the *Kitáb-i-Aqdas*, the Most Holy Book.

† According to the shipping records, the Austrian Lloyd steamer was due to leave Alexandria at 11 a.m. on Friday, arriving at Port Said on Saturday at 5 p.m., at Jaffa on Sunday at 6 p.m., at Haifa on Monday at 8 a.m., and at noon two days later at Cyprus.

‡ It was here that four of Bahá'u'lláh's followers were not allowed to

aboard a sailing vessel which took them to 'Akká in the afternoon of the same day. As there were no landing facilities at 'Akká, the men had to wade ashore from the boat and it was ordered that the women were to be carried on the backs of men. But at 'Abdu'l-Bahá's insistence the women were carried ashore one by one sitting in a chair which He Himself procured.

When Bahá'u'lláh arrived in 'Akká, that city was a penal colony. Its population in the 1880s was estimated to be about nine thousand. The Turkish Government had consigned to it from its vast empire a great number of criminals, murderers, political detainees and every type of troublemaker. The inhabitants, whom Bahá'u'lláh had stigmatized as 'The Generation of Vipers', had sunk to a very low level. Among these people wild rumours and false accusations were circulating concerning Bahá'u'lláh and His followers as they were about to arrive. The company of exiles, those God-intoxicated heroes who had accompanied their Lord to this most desolate of cities, were considered to be evil men, criminals of the worst type who deserved to be treated most cruelly. It is no wonder, therefore, that great numbers from among the inhabitants of 'Akká had assembled at the landing site to jeer at them and at their Leader whom they referred to as 'the God of the Persians'.

Yet among the crowd there were some endowed with a measure of spiritual perception. These, as they gazed upon the countenance of Bahá'u'lláh, were struck by His majesty and witnessed a glory they had never seen before. Among them was a certain Khalíl Aḥmad 'Abdú, a venerable old man who used to say to the inhabitants of 'Akká that he could see in the face of Bahá'u'lláh signs of greatness and of majesty and truthfulness. He often said that the people of 'Akká should rejoice and be thankful to God for having ennobled their

---

land and were taken to Cyprus instead, and here that one of them, 'Abdu'l-Ghaffár, threw himself into the sea. See vol. 2, p. 411.

homeland by the footsteps of this great Personage. He prophesied that through Him the inhabitants would be blessed and prosper, and this of course literally came to pass.

Another man in the crowd watching the arrival of the exiles was known as 'Abdu'lláh Ṭuzih. He saw the radiance, the power, and the glory of Bahá'u'lláh's countenance and was drawn to Him. He later became a believer and his daughter (who was born on the same day that Bahá'u'lláh arrived in 'Akká) was some years later joined in wedlock with Ḥusayn-i-Á<u>sh</u><u>ch</u>í, a cook in Bahá'u'lláh's household and one of His devoted servants.*

How incomparable is the difference between the vision of those assembled at the sea gate of 'Akká to jeer at and demonstrate their hostility towards the company of exiles and their Leader, and the vision of Bahá'u'lláh Who a few years before, in the Tablet of Sayyáḥ† foreshadowing His arrival in the city of 'Akká, disclosed to those who were endowed with spiritual insight a vastly different spectacle:

> Upon Our arrival We were welcomed with banners of light, whereupon the Voice of the Spirit cried out saying: 'Soon will all that dwell on earth be enlisted under these banners.'[5]

The attitude of these onlookers, blind to the world of the spirit and the all-encompassing vision of Bahá'u'lláh, is characteristic of man's attitude to the Revelation of God in every age. Over one hundred years have passed since Bahá'u'lláh uttered these words. The majority of mankind, its rulers and wise men, have so far failed to recognize their truth. They either remain unaware of the coming of the Lord or turn a deaf ear to His voice. But those who have embraced His Cause can believe in the vision of their Lord that 'soon will all that dwell on earth be enlisted under these banners'.

The history of the rise of every religion demonstrates a similar situation. When Christ was on the cross He saw the

* see vol. 2, pp. 169, 404.

† see vol. 2, p. 213.

vision of His Cause spreading to the far ends of the world, while humanity, represented by His contemporaries in the Holy Land, was insensitive to such a vision. It saw in Christ only a man captive and helpless, dying on the cross. But it did not know the power of the Holy Spirit, a power which brought millions under the shadow of the Christian Faith.

When Muḥammad and His disciples were on one occasion completely surrounded and greatly outnumbered by hosts of His enemies, and when there was no hope of survival among His followers, the Prophet is reported to have stood on a rock and forcefully struck it with His staff saying, 'I have conquered the Roman Empire,' and repeating the same act, 'I have conquered the Persian Empire' . . . Even some of His followers at that time did not have the vision to comprehend these words but soon they witnessed their fulfilment.

Thus the enemies of Bahá'u'lláh, unable to discern the power of the Almighty which was animating His Cause and the person of His own Manifestation, imagined that by confining Him to the prison they could succeed in putting out His light and destroying His Cause. It was for this reason that the authorities had been ordered to impose the harshest restrictions upon Him and His followers.

In the masterly language so characteristic of his divinely guided writings, Shoghi Effendi, the Guardian of the Bahá'í Faith, has briefly touched upon the significance of Bahá'u'lláh's arrival in 'Akká. He writes:

> The arrival of Bahá'u'lláh in 'Akká marks the opening of the last phase of His forty-year-long ministry, the final stage, and indeed the climax, of the banishment in which the whole of that ministry was spent. A banishment that had, at first, brought Him to the immediate vicinity of the strongholds of Shí'ah orthodoxy and into contact with its outstanding exponents, and which, at a later period, had carried Him to the capital of the Ottoman empire, and led Him to address His epoch-making pronouncements to the Sulṭán, to his ministers and to the ecclesiastical leaders of

Sunní Islám, had now been instrumental in landing Him upon the shores of the Holy Land—the Land promised by God to Abraham, sanctified by the Revelation of Moses, honoured by the lives and labours of the Hebrew patriarchs, judges, kings and prophets, revered as the cradle of Christianity, and as the place where Zoroaster, according to 'Abdu'l-Bahá's testimony, had 'held converse with some of the Prophets of Israel,' and associated by Islám with the Apostle's night-journey, through the seven heavens, to the throne of the Almighty. Within the confines of this holy and enviable country, 'the nest of all the Prophets of God,' 'the Vale of God's unsearchable Decree, the snow-white Spot, the Land of unfading splendour' was the Exile of Baghdád, of Constantinople and Adrianople condemned to spend no less than a third of the allotted span of His life and over half of the total period of His Mission. 'It is difficult,' declares 'Abdu'l-Bahá, 'to understand how Bahá'u'lláh could have been obliged to leave Persia, and to pitch His tent in this Holy Land, but for the persecution of His enemies, His banishment and exile.'

Indeed such a consummation, He assures us, had been actually prophesied 'through the tongue of the Prophets two or three thousand years before.' God, 'faithful to His promise,' had, 'to some of the Prophets' 'revealed and given the good news that the "Lord of Hosts should be manifested in the Holy Land."' Isaiah had, in this connection, announced in his Book: 'Get thee up into the high mountain, O Zion that bringest good tidings; lift up thy voice with strength, O Jerusalem, that bringest good tidings. Lift it up, be not afraid; say unto the cities of Judah: "Behold your God! Behold the Lord God will come with strong band, and His arm shall rule for Him."' David, in his Psalms, had predicted: 'Lift up your heads, O ye gates; even lift them up, ye everlasting doors; and the King of Glory shall come in. Who is this King of Glory? The Lord of Hosts, He is the King of Glory.' 'Out of Zion, the perfection of beauty, God hath shined. Our God shall come, and shall not keep silence.' Amos had, likewise, foretold His coming: 'The Lord will roar from Zion, and utter His voice from Jerusalem; and the habitations of the shepherds shall mourn, and the top of Carmel shall wither.'

'Akká, itself, flanked by the 'glory of Lebanon,' and lying in full view of the 'splendour of Carmel,' at the foot of the hills which enclose the home of Jesus Christ Himself, had been described by David as 'the Strong City,' designated by Hosea as 'a door of hope,' and alluded to by Ezekiel as 'the gate that looketh towards the East,' whereunto 'the glory of the God of Israel came from the way of the East,' His voice 'like a noise of many waters.' To it the Arabian Prophet had referred as 'a city in Syria to which God hath shown His special mercy,' situated 'betwixt two mountains . . . in the middle of a meadow,' 'by the shore of the sea . . . suspended beneath the Throne,' 'white, whose whiteness is pleasing unto God.' 'Blessed the man,' He, moreover, as confirmed by Bahá'u'lláh, had declared, 'that hath visited 'Akká, and blessed he that hath visited the visitor of 'Akká.' Furthermore, 'He that raiseth therein the call to prayer, his voice will be lifted up unto Paradise.' And again: 'The poor of 'Akká are the kings of Paradise and the princes thereof. A month in 'Akká is better than a thousand years elsewhere.' Moreover, in a remarkable tradition, which is contained in Shaykh Ibnu'l-'Arabí's work, entitled 'Futúḥát-i-Makkíy-yih,' and which is recognized as an authentic utterance of Muḥammad, and is quoted by Mírzá Abu'l-Faḍl in his 'Fará'id,' this significant prediction has been made: 'All of them (the companions of the Qá'im) shall be slain except One Who shall reach the plain of 'Akká, the Banquet-Hall of God.'[6]

Bahá'u'lláh and His party entered the prison city through the sea gate and were conducted along the narrow and twisting roads of 'Akká to the barracks. The hardships of the long and arduous journey from Adrianople to 'Akká in the burning heat of the midsummer season, with inadequate and primitive facilities on board the ships crowded by so many, had exhausted everyone. And now added to all this were the appalling conditions of their confinement in the barracks, especially during the first night of their arrival there. Bahá'u'lláh was placed in a filthy room completely bare and devoid of any furniture. Later He was moved into a room on the upper floor of the barracks; this room, the interior of which is now kept in good condition and visited by Bahá'í pilgrims, was in the days of Bahá'u'lláh unfit for habitation. He Himself has recounted in a Tablet[7] that its floor was covered with earth, and what plaster remained on the ceiling was falling.

Bahá'u'lláh's followers were huddled into another room, the floor of which was covered with mud. Ten soldiers were posted at the gate to guard the prisoners. The foul air and the stench in the prison, coupled with the sultry heat of the summer, were so offensive that Bahá'íyyih Khánum, the daughter of Bahá'u'lláh entitled the 'Greatest Holy Leaf', was overcome and fainted on arrival.

There was no water for drinking except that in a small pool which had already been used for washing. The water in this pool was so filthy that the mere thought of drinking it would make one sick. That first night, water was withheld from the prisoners. Everyone was thirsty in those hot surroundings and some of the women and children were overcome by thirst. Mothers with suckling babes were unable to feed them, and for hours the children were crying for food and water. 'Abdu'l-Bahá made several appeals to the guards to show mercy to the children and even sent a message to the Governor of 'Akká, but all was without avail. At last in the morning some water was given to the prisoners and three loaves of bread to each as a daily ration: the bread was unfit to eat but after some time they were allowed to take it to the market and exchange it for two loaves of a better quality.

Soon after the arrival of the prisoners the Governor visited the barracks for inspection. 'Abdu'l-Bahá, accompanied by a few believers, went to see him. But the Governor was discourteous and spoke to them in a provocative manner. He threatened to cut the supply of bread if one of the prisoners went missing and then ordered them back to their room. Ḥusayn-i-Áshchí, one of 'Abdu'l-Bahá's attendants, could not bear to remain silent after such insulting treatment. He retorted with rage and hurled back at the Governor some offensive remarks.

'Abdu'l-Bahá immediately chastised Ḥusayn by slapping him hard in the face in front of the Governor and ordering him to return to his room. This action by 'Abdu'l-Bahá not only defused a dangerous situation but also opened the eyes of the Governor to the existence of a real leader among the prisoners, a leader who would act with authority and justice.

Ḥusayn-i-Áshchí, who has recorded this incident in his memoirs, and who prided himself on being chastised by the Master on that occasion, recalls that because of this action the Governor's attitude towards 'Abdu'l-Bahá changed. He realized that, contrary to the wild rumours circulating in 'Akká at the time, 'Abdu'l-Bahá and His family were from a noble background, and not criminals as he had been led to believe. The Governor therefore began to act in a more humane way towards the prisoners. He eventually agreed to substitute the allotted ration of bread with a sum of money and allowed a small party of the prisoners, escorted by guards, to visit the markets of 'Akká daily to buy their provisions.

Three days after the arrival of Bahá'u'lláh and His companions, the edict of the Sulṭán condemning Him to life imprisonment was read out in the Mosque. The prisoners were introduced as criminals who had corrupted the morals of the people. It was stated that they were to be confined in prison and were not allowed to associate with anyone.

In the course of a talk[8] to the friends in Haifa, 'Abdu'l-Bahá has described His being summoned by the Governor of 'Akká to hear the contents of the edict. When it was read out to Him that they were to remain in prison for ever,* 'Abdu'l-Bahá responded by saying that the contents of the edict were

* In Arabic the term used for life imprisonment is often 'prisoner for ever'.

meaningless and without foundation. Upon hearing this remark, the Governor became angry and retorted that the edict was from the Sulṭán, and he wanted to know how it could be described as meaningless. 'Abdu'l-Bahá reiterated His comment and explained that it made no sense to describe their imprisonment as lasting for ever, for man lives in this world only for a short period, and that sooner or later the captives would leave this prison either dead or alive. The Governor and his officers were impressed by the vision of 'Abdu'l-Bahá and felt easier in His presence.

It is interesting to note that some time later, when the Master emerged as the most eminent and the most loved person in 'Akká and the neighbouring lands, when practically all the people of 'Akká, both high and low, turned to Him for help, and when the Governors and high officials sought His advice and sat at His feet to receive enlightenment, the edict of the Sulṭán together with other documents relating to the imprisonment of Bahá'u'lláh and His companions were removed from the government files and presented to 'Abdu'l-Bahá by a government official.

In the meantime, life in the prison of 'Akká in the early days was extremely difficult and tortuous. For three months, the authorities did not allow Bahá'u'lláh to attend the public bath which in those days was the only place where people could take a bath. The guards had been given strict orders not to allow any person to visit Him. Even when a barber came to attend to Bahá'u'lláh's hair, he was accompanied by a guard and was not allowed to talk to Him. 'Abdu'l-Bahá had to live in a room on the ground floor which had been formerly used as a morgue. Its moist air affected His health for the rest of His life. As for the prisoners, the filthy conditions under which they were living, the lack of proper food and hygiene, and the severity of restrictions, took their toll. Shortly after their arrival in the barracks, all but two fell sick. Nine of the ten guards were also struck down by illness. Malaria and dysentery added to their ordeal. The only two unaffected at that stage were 'Abdu'l-Bahá and Áqá Riḍáy-i-Qannád,* although both of them were taken ill at a later time. The Master, helped by this believer, attended to the needs of the sick and nursed them day and night. The authorities did not call for a doctor to administer medicine. With the few provisions at His disposal all that 'Abdu'l-Bahá could do was to cook for them a simple broth and some rice each day. But the hygienic conditions were appalling. The heat was severe during the day and there was no adequate water for washing.

In these circumstances three people died. The first victim was a certain Abu'l-Qásim-i-Sulṭán Ábádí. Then two brothers, Ustád Muḥammad-Báqir and Ustád Muḥammad-Ismá'íl, both tailors by profession, died one evening within a few hours of each other. They were locked in each other's arms as they lay on the floor. Bahá'u'lláh particularly expressed His grief at this tragic death, and stated that never before had two brothers passed away from this dark world and entered the realms of glory in such unity. He, as stated in a Tablet,[9] praised them, showered His bounties upon them, and blessed their parents.

The burial of these three posed a difficult problem for the company of exiles. For the Government refused to allow anyone from among the prisoners to bury them, nor did they provide funds for their burial. The guards demanded payment of necessary expenses for burial before removing the bodies. And as there were very few possessions which could be sold, in order to raise the money Bahá'u'lláh ordered the sale of the only luxury He had, a small prayer carpet used by Him. This was done, and the proceeds were handed to the guards who then pocketed the money and buried the dead in the clothes they wore, without coffins and without the customary Muslim rites of washing and wrapping the bodies in shrouds.

As they were not allowed to be buried inside the Muslim Cemetery they were laid to rest outside it. Some years later

* see vol. 1, pp. 288–9; vol. 2, pp. 403–4.

'Abdu'l-Bahá arranged for one of the believers to build their graves, which are joined together.

After the death of these three men, Bahá'u'lláh revealed a short healing prayer especially for the believers in the barracks and asked them to chant it repeatedly and with absolute sincerity. This the friends did and soon everyone recovered.

The Desolate City

Long before His departure from Adrianople, Bahá'u'lláh had prophesied the impending calamities which were to befall Him in His forthcoming exile to 'Akká. In some of His Tablets revealed in Adrianople He had alluded to that city, in others He had mentioned 'Akká by name as being the next place of His exile. For instance in the *Lawḥ-i-Sulṭán*,* the Tablet to Náṣiri'd-Dín Sháh of Persia, He had clearly prophesied that the next place of His exile would be 'Akká. Concerning that city He writes in that Tablet: 'According to what they say, it is the most desolate of the cities of the world, the most unsightly of them in appearance, the most detestable in climate, and the foulest in water.'[10]

In another Tablet[11] revealed soon before His departure from Adrianople He predicts a new wave of calamities that would soon encompass Him in the fortress of 'Akká. He describes the conditions of the city in similar terms as those in the *Lawḥ-i-Sulṭán*, but declares that soon its climate would improve, because its Builder would enter it and adorn it with the ornament of His Greatest Name.

The foul air of 'Akká was often summed up by the proverb that a bird flying over the city would drop dead. But the climate changed soon after Bahá'u'lláh's arrival. To this the inhabitants of 'Akká testified, and many attributed it to the presence of Bahá'u'lláh. To cite one example: Mírzá Abu'l-Faḍl,† the famous Bahá'í scholar, has, in his well-known

* see vol. 2, ch. 16.

† see below, p. 91.

work *Fará'id*, quoted the testimony of one of the leading men of culture in 'Akká. These are his words:

> In the year AH 1313 (1895–6) when the writer was staying in Syria, Ya'qúb-ibn-Betros of Lebanon, who is a learned doctor of divinity and linguistics in those parts and well known amongst the Christian community of 'Akká, composed the following statements in praise of the Holy Shrine of Bahá'u'lláh in 'Akká and offered this composition to His Holiness 'Abdu'l-Bahá, and presented me with a copy of the composition as a gift.
>
> 'Set betwixt the twin mounts of Lebanon and Carmel is the Bahjí,
> Therein is the resting place of Bahá, the Lord of Bounty and Mercy,
> The Chosen Master, the Lamp of Guidance, Bahá—the Splendour and the Light of the Sun of Truth,
> He Who is the Luminary of all names,
> Therein the true joy, the Desire of all hearts, hearts that seek His lights,
> The Solace of the eyes, the Fulfilment and Realization of all hope,
> By His beneficent presence, the water that springs from the wells of those parts was purified (i.e. of 'Akká) and the air and clime of 'Akká and its environs were changed.'
>
> In these words above there is a definite and clear reference to the transformation that occurred in the city of 'Akká as a result of the presence of Bahá'u'lláh. As this land was well known for its foul water, for its bad weather, for the bitterness and saltiness of its fountains and wells, so much so that it was the prison city for those who had gravely offended the Ottoman Government and it was the penal colony of those condemned to death, its peoples were all usually ill and had a sallow appearance because of its bad weather and climate. But when this territory became the place of exile of Bahá'u'lláh, its bitter waters were changed, its inclement weather transformed.[12]

When Bahá'u'lláh arrived in 'Akká there was no source of

fresh water within the city gates fit to drink. There was a well, situated about ten minutes walk from the city, from which most of the people carried water to their homes. But its taste was very unpleasant. Bahá'u'lláh and His companions used this water, which was carried by the believers to the prison. There was one believer in particular, Áqá 'Aẓím-i-Tafris͟hí, who served Bahá'u'lláh and His companions as a water-supplier. It was a difficult task, as he had to make numerous trips to the well and carry skinfuls of water on his back to the friends in 'Akká. Later he managed to get water with a better taste from springs at Kabrí, which were situated in the same direction as Bahjí and about half an hour's walking distance from 'Akká.

Áqá 'Aẓím was a devoted believer who had first attained the presence of Bahá'u'lláh in Bag͟hdád and become the recipient of His bounties and favours. After some time he returned to Persia where he engaged himself in serving the friends. There he worked as a servant in the household of Mírzá Naṣru'lláh-i-Tafris͟hí and when the latter went to Adrianople in company with his son and with his brother Mírzá Riḍá-Qulí, 'Aẓím also went with the party. Mírzá Naṣru'lláh, who was a brother of Badrí-Ján, one of the wives of Mírzá Yaḥyá Azal,* died in Adrianople. However, 'Aẓím remained in Adrianople in the service of Mírzá Riḍá-Qulí and his nephew.

The main reason for their journey to Adrianople was that their sister had deserted her husband and had taken refuge in the household of Jináb-i-Kalím,† Bahá'u'lláh's faithful brother. In these circumstances the two brothers were summoned to Adrianople to take their sister back to Persia. But soon after the death of Mírzá Naṣru'lláh, Bahá'u'lláh and His companions were exiled to 'Akká; Badrí-Ján, her brother Riḍá-Qulí, and nephew along with Áqá 'Azím were included in the party which accompanied Bahá'u'lláh. As we shall see later, Riḍá-Qulí and his sister joined hands in 'Akká with

* see vols. 1 and 2; and below, p. 235.

† see vols. 1 and 2.

Siyyid Muḥammad-i-Iṣfahání,* the Anti-Christ of the Revelation of Bahá'u'lláh, and were cast out of the community by Bahá'u'lláh; later Riḍá-Qulí was murdered along with two other followers of Mírzá Yaḥyá.†

As to Áqá 'Aẓím, as soon as he discovered the signs of unfaithfulness towards Bahá'u'lláh in his master, he dissociated himself from him and continued to serve Bahá'u'lláh and His companions with great devotion and selflessness. Through his sincerity, faith, and services he acquired the good pleasure of his Lord who continued to shower upon him His blessings till the end of his life.

The water in 'Akká, of which 'Aẓím was a carrier for Bahá'u'lláh and His followers, improved considerably not merely in its quality but became more easily available through the restoration of a disused aqueduct, bringing fresh water to the city. This also happened through the influence of the word of Bahá'u'lláh.

When Bahá'u'lláh was in the house of 'Abbúd, He prophesied to him that God would raise up a person to restore the aqueduct, which had fallen into disuse, and expressed a desire that 'Abbúd might become the one to carry out this project. 'Abbúd was a Christian merchant of great influence in 'Akká and was highly respected by the people. It is said of him that when he walked through the city people stood up and showed their respect to him. But 'Abbúd did not follow Bahá'u'lláh's advice. Soon after this, Aḥmad Big Tawfíq, the Governor of 'Akká who had become aware of Bahá'u'lláh's greatness and had evinced an ardent admiration for 'Abdu'l-Bahá, and who often sat at His feet for instruction and illumination, was allowed an audience with Bahá'u'lláh. It was in the course of that audience when the Governor offered to do some service for Him, that Bahá'u'lláh suggested the restoration of the aqueduct for the benefit of the people of

* see vols. 1 and 2.

† see below, pp. 235ff.

'Akká. To this suggestion, the Governor readily responded and arose to carry it out.

However, the restoration of the aqueduct was not completed until Fayḍí Pás͟há became Governor of 'Akká. He was a great personality in government circles in Istanbul and a man of action. It was he who completed this project, although his tenure of office was very short indeed. Ḥusayn-i-Ás͟hc͟hí has left us with an account, summarized below, concerning the aqueduct.

> When Fayḍí Pás͟há arrived in 'Akká, he noticed that water from the springs at Kabrí was now within easy reach of 'Akká but the work of completing the building of the aqueduct was at a standstill. He remonstrated with those responsible and ordered an immediate resumption of work. Municipal workers were drafted to complete this project . . . with his tremendous drive and personal supervision, a task which would normally have taken at least six months to accomplish was completed within six days. Fresh water arrived in 'Akká and the people of the city rejoiced. One hundred and one cannon shots were fired to celebrate the occasion.[13]

Lawḥ-i-Salmán (Tablet of Salmán)

This is a significant Tablet revealed in honour of S͟hayk͟h Salmán whose life story has been mentioned in the two previous volumes. He is the one who travelled every year between Persia and the places of Bahá'u'lláh's exile, carrying His Tablets for the friends to Persia and bringing their letters and messages back to Him. Salmán has several Tablets in his honour, two of which are known as *Lawḥ-i-Salmán* I and II. The first Tablet is described in volume 2, chapter 13. This is the second. This Tablet was revealed in 'Akká during the early part of Bahá'u'lláh's imprisonment in the barracks, for in it He refers to the believers exiled* to Mosul from Bag͟hdád. This

* see vol. 2, pp. 334–6.

happened in the summer of 1868. Bahá'u'lláh refers to this event also in His Tablet to Náṣiri'd-Dín Sháh of Persia which was written shortly before His departure from Adrianople.

In this Tablet Bahá'u'lláh counsels Salmán to be resigned to the decrees of God and with acquiescence accept tests and trials in His path. He describes His own sufferings, states that although every door is closed to His face and the enemies are at all times at work trying to extinguish His light, yet it shines as brilliant as the sun, shedding light upon all who are in heaven and on earth. He urges Salmán to follow His example and never complain when afflicted by abasement or misery in this life, rather he should focus his attention upon God, and seek no one but Him. In one of His Tablets, Bahá'u'lláh cites His own celebrated utterance: 'He doeth what He pleaseth and ordaineth what He willeth.' He states that anyone who fully believes these words will remain steadfast in His Cause and will find himself possessed of such confidence and certitude that nothing in the world will make him falter or fill him with fear and dismay.

Bahá'u'lláh reminds Salmán that those who look for glory in this world and are proud of their position in it have grievously erred, for soon the messenger of death will bring an end to all earthly attachments.

In a Tablet to Nabíl-i-A'ẓam, Bahá'u'lláh reveals these words concerning the transitory nature of this world:

> By the righteousness of God! The world and its vanities, and its glory, and whatever delights it can offer, are all, in the sight of God, as worthless as, nay, even more contemptible than, dust and ashes. Would that the hearts of men could comprehend it! Wash yourselves thoroughly, O people of Bahá, from the defilement of the world, and of all that pertaineth unto it. God Himself beareth Me witness. The things of the earth ill beseem you. Cast them away unto such as may desire them, and fasten your eyes upon this most holy and effulgent Vision.
>
> That which beseemeth you is the love of God, and the

> love of Him Who is the Manifestation of His Essence, and the observance of whatsoever He chooseth to prescribe unto you, did ye but know it.[14]

When the news of Bahá'u'lláh's banishment from Adrianople reached the people of Persia, the enemies together with the followers of Azal took heart and prophesied the downfall of the Cause and its Author. They fabricated false stories and widely spread them around to demoralize the believers. Among these was the rumour that Bahá'u'lláh and His companions had been drowned on their way to 'Akká. Many believers were alarmed and some even made enquiries about the circumstances of Bahá'u'lláh's banishment through the British Telegraph office in Julfá, the centre of the Christian community in the neighbourbood of Iṣfahán.

It was at this time that some of the teachers of the Cause, those whom Bahá'u'lláh had referred to[15] as the 'learned ones in Bahá', and extolled as 'the billows of the most Mighty Ocean', 'the stars of the firmament of Glory' and the 'standards of triumph waving betwixt earth and heaven', arose with determination to refute these false rumours.

Foremost among them were the erudite Mírzá Aḥmad-i-Azghandí and Mullá Muḥammad-i-Furúghí. We have already referred to the former in a previous volume* and described the extent of his knowledge. We have also mentioned briefly the circumstances which had led the latter,† a survivor of the Fort of Ṭabarsí, to recognize the station of Bahá'u'lláh. In more than one Tablet Bahá'u'lláh has extolled the station of these two men from the Province of Khurásán, and has stated that God had chosen them especially to announce the glad-tidings of His Revelation to the peoples of the world.[16] These two men, who were teaching the Faith and explaining the fulfilment of the prophecies of old concerning the coming of the Promised One of Islám and later of Bahá'u'lláh, were of

* vol. 1, p. 194.
† see vol. 2, pp. 114–15.

especially great help to the believers in this incident. Through their vast knowledge of the prophecies and their depth of understanding, they proclaimed to the friends the falsity of such rumours as the drowning of Bahá'u'lláh in the sea. They made it clear that if such a thing had happened, then all that had been revealed by God in past Dispensations—including the Revelation of the Báb—would have been invalid.

Indeed, Bahá'u'lláh's exile to 'Akká and the establishment of His Throne in the Holy Land is one of the great proofs of the authenticity of the Revelations of the past, which have in numerous passages and in glowing terms foretold the coming of the Lord to that land.

The Templers of Haifa

Significantly, many Bible scholars of the nineteenth century concluded that the second coming of Christ was at hand and that, according to many, it would happen around the year 1844.* Therefore, it is not surprising that a group of Germans known as the Templers left their homes in their enthusiasm to meet the Lord when He should come, and sailed to the Holy Land. They had concluded from the prophecies that the Messiah would appear there, that the people of all races would recognize Him and that He would establish His spiritual throne in that land. They began to arrive at the foot of Mount Carmel in the year of Bahá'u'lláh's Declaration in far-off Baghdád (1863), and built a colony (1868) which was located about a mile to the west of the then village of Haifa. On their doorways still remains the inscription 'Der Herr ist Nahe' (The Lord is near).

How significant it is that when in Haifa years later, Bahá'u'lláh even pitched His tent next door to them: God passed them by and they did not recognize Him. A Tablet was even revealed by Bahá'u'lláh in response to a letter from Georg David Hardegg, the head of the Templers in Haifa. This

* The year of the Declaration of the Báb, the Forerunner of Bahá'u'lláh.

AN AERIAL VIEW OF ‘AKKÁ

The barracks are shown in the centre foreground

THE SEA GATE OF 'AKKÁ

Here Bahá'u'lláh entered the prison city

THE BARRACKS GATE

At the top of the stairway, on the east side of the barracks. Bahá'u'lláh entered the Most Great Prison through this gate

THE CELL OF BAHÁ'U'LLÁH

'THE LORD IS NIGH'

Inscription over the doorway of one of the Templer houses

THE COURTYARD OF THE BARRACKS, *c.* 1920

The waterpool is in the centre. It is probably in this courtyard that the tent was pitched for the washing of the body of the Purest Branch

Tablet, known as the *Lawḥ-i-Hirtík* (Tablet of Hirtík), is in Arabic and appears to have been revealed in the house of 'Údí Khammár (see below, p. 221).

Bearing in mind that the Templers had come to the Holy Land for the sole purpose of witnessing the return of Christ, this Tablet assumes a special significance. Its perusal leads one to think that Hardegg, its recipient, must have been familiar with the language of mystery which is to be found in this Tablet. Bahá'u'lláh states that He had found in Hardegg's letter signs which pointed to his sincerity, and prays that God may assist him to understand the truths hidden in this Tablet, and enable him to hear the melodies of the Divine Nightingale. He urges him to meditate on the word of God, its power as well as its sweetness, reminds him that it was the power of the word of God which attracted the heart of the first believer in Christ, states that it is through their idle fancy and vain imaginings that the majority of the peoples have been kept back from recognizing their Lord, asserts that land and sea in this day are proclaiming the truth of God, and that when the appointed time had come, Mount Carmel became exhilarated by the breezes wafting from the direction of its Lord.

Bahá'u'lláh calls the attention of Hardegg to the days of Christ when the divines, the learned and the philosophers of the time denied Him, while a fisherman devoid of knowledge and learning recognized Him. He assures Hardegg that if he were to meditate sincerely on the history of the past while keeping God in his sight, he would behold the light of God manifest before his eyes. Bahá'u'lláh confirms Hardegg's views about the darkness which has fallen upon the earth and explains that darkness is vain imaginings which have enveloped the peoples and prevented them from turning to the Kingdom of God which is manifested in this Day.

Although Bahá'u'lláh in this Tablet speaks generally about the Revelation of God in this age, of the warbling of the Nightingale, of the flowing of the water of life, of the appearance of the light of God and of His Kingdom, He does not explicitly state His own station nor does He refer to His own person in clear terms. Indeed, He declares that if He were to reveal the sign of the One who is veiled in mystery—meaning Himself—the hearts of the people would be filled with fear and consternation. Perhaps the reason for this is that Bahá'u'lláh, who had already forbidden His followers to teach His Faith to the people living under the rule of the Ottoman Empire, found it unwise to proclaim His station in an explicit manner to the members of the Christian colony living in Haifa.

Furthermore, part of this Tablet is revealed in the language of mystery. For instance, Bahá'u'lláh in a maze of several Arabic letters, and alluding to certain key words from His other Tablets or those of the Báb and even of Islám, constructs His own name. One needs to be well versed in the Holy Writings of these Faiths in order to grasp the significance of these symbolic utterances used by Bahá'u'lláh. Moreover, by employing the technique of using the numerical values of Arabic letters,* He produces the word 'Comforter' which is a reference to His own station in the terminology of the New Testament. It is hard to believe that the recipient of this Tablet would have been able to fathom some of the symbolic and mysterious terms deliberately used by Bahá'u'lláh. Probably it is for this reason that in the beginning of this Tablet, He prays that God may assist Hardegg to understand the significance of what is hidden in His words. He assures him that if he should meditate on what He has advised him and follow His counsels, he will find the truth in this day.

Needless to say, neither Hardegg nor any other member of the Christian colony was able to recognize the truth of the Message of Bahá'u'lláh. This in spite of the fact that from the early days some members of the colony, including Hardegg himself, had been in contact with the believers and with 'Abdu'l-Bahá, and that later, towards the end of His ministry, Bahá'u'lláh Himself visited Haifa and at one time stayed in one

* Each letter of the Arabic alphabet has a numerical value; therefore it is possible to express a word by a number and vice versa.

of the houses belonging to the Templers. That they failed to recognize Him may seem strange to an observer who is unfamiliar with the history of religions—a history which repeats itself every time a new Manifestation of God is revealed to mankind. Almost two thousand years before the German Templers came to the Holy Land, the inhabitants of that same land expected with much earnestness the coming of their Messiah, and yet when He manifested Himself in the person of Christ and appeared in their midst, they rejected Him. These words of Bahá'u'lláh are truly applicable to their case:

> Consider the past. How many, both high and low, have, at all times, yearningly awaited the advent of the Manifestations of God in the sanctified persons of His chosen Ones. How often have they expected His coming, how frequently have they prayed that the breeze of Divine mercy might blow, and the promised Beauty step forth from behind the veil of concealment, and be made manifest to all the world. And whensoever the portals of grace did open, and the clouds of divine bounty did rain upon mankind, and the light of the Unseen did shine above the horizon of celestial might, they all denied Him, and turned away from His face—the face of God Himself . . . [17]

2

'The Cause of God will Flourish through Persecution'

The rejection by man of the Manifestation of God is the most grievous event in human society and one which brings great sorrow and suffering to Him. It was through man's perversity and blindness that Bahá'u'lláh suffered unbearable hardship and tribulation in 'Akká. But all the forces of opposition which were leagued against Him proved ineffective in destroying Him or His Cause. In many Tablets[1] revealed soon after His arrival in the prison of 'Akká, Bahá'u'lláh stated that the Cause of God would flourish through persecutions. He often counselled the believers not to be disturbed or feel sad when they heard the sufferings of their Lord in the Most Great Prison. He urged them not to dwell on the hardships and sufferings of His imprisonment, but rather to rejoice, because the Blessed Beauty, although severely oppressed, was in the utmost joy and contentment. In another Tablet He states:

> Know thou, moreover, that We have been cast into an afflictive Prison, and are encompassed with the hosts of tyranny, as a result of what the hands of the infidels have wrought. Such is the gladness, however, which the Youth hath tasted that no earthly joy can compare unto it. By God! The harm He suffereth at the hands of the oppressor can never grieve His heart, nor can He be saddened by the ascendancy of such as have repudiated His truth.
>
> Say: Tribulation is a horizon unto My Revelation. The day star of grace shineth above it, and sheddeth a light which neither the clouds of men's idle fancy nor the vain imaginations of the aggressor can obscure.[2]

Another theme repeatedly announced in the Tablets revealed in the early days of 'Akká is the invincibility of the Cause of God and the impotence of its enemies to destroy it. In one of these Tablets[3] Bahá'u'lláh assures the believers that tribulations inflicted upon Him in the path of God will never render Him powerless, nor will the winds of trials succeed in extinguishing the lamp of His Cause, a lamp whose radiance, He states, has illumined the whole world. He affirms that no measure of persecution and suffering which the enemy may heap upon Him is capable of depriving Him of His sovereignty and power, and He declares in majestic language the ascendancy of His Cause, an ascendancy such that if all the peoples of the world were to rise up against Him and attack Him with drawn swords from every direction they would be impotent to destroy His Cause. In the midst of the most harrowing afflictions He would proclaim that He was the Glory of God revealed for all who are in the heavens and all who are on earth.

In another Tablet[4] revealed in the same period, Bahá'u'lláh describes how His enemies had placed barriers between Him and His companions in the prison of 'Akká, barriers as feeble as their own vain imaginings. For they thought that they could hide the glory of the Sun behind the clouds of their self and passion, unaware that all created things derided their ignorance and blindness.

And finally, there are Bahá'u'lláh's assuring words in most of these Tablets prophesying that ere long, through the power of God, the doors of the prison would be flung open, and He would come out of it with majesty and glory.

As we shall see later, these prophecies—the invincibility of His Cause, the ascendancy of His Revelation and the release of His own person and His companions from the prison of 'Akká—were all fulfilled.

Lawḥ-i-Ra'ís

In the early stages of His imprisonment in the barracks and

soon after the death of three of His followers, Bahá'u'lláh revealed the momentous Tablet of Ra'ís in Persian, addressed to 'Álí Pás͟há, the Grand Vizír of Turkey, who was His great adversary and the one who had brought about His exile to 'Akká.*

Already, a few months earlier, on His way to Gallipoli, Bahá'u'lláh had addressed to 'Álí Pás͟há a Tablet in Arabic known as the *Súriy-i-Ra'ís*.† In it He had forcefully condemned the actions of the Grand Vizír as the main instigator of His exile to the prison city. Of the significance of this Tablet Bahá'u'lláh declares:

> From the moment the Súriy-i-Ra'ís was revealed until the present day, neither hath the world been tranquillized, nor have the hearts of its peoples been at rest.[5]

Now, in the *Lawḥ-i-Ra'ís*, the second Tablet to 'Álí Pás͟há, written from within the walls of the Most Great Prison, Bahá'u'lláh rebukes him further for his acts of cruelty and inhuman treatment.

The tone of this Tablet is at once moving and tender. In it Bahá'u'lláh refers to 'Álí Pás͟há as one who considers himself to be the most exalted among men and Bahá'u'lláh, the supreme Manifestation of God, as the lowest of all servants. He identifies 'Álí Pás͟há with those who had opposed the Manifestations of the past and had wrongly regarded them to be the cause of discord and dissension in older dispensations. He admonishes him for his ignorance and immaturity, and reveals for him his true status as a person ruled by the most abject of all created things—namely self and passion.

* see vol. 2.

† see vol. 2, pp. 411–17. The two Tablets, commonly designated as the *Súriy-i-Ra'ís* (in Arabic) and the *Lawḥ-i-Ra'ís* (in Persian) are addressed to the same person. In His writings Shoghi Effendi generally referred to these Tablets in this order, although occasionally he used the designation *Súrih* for *Lawḥ* and vice versa.

This thought-provoking statement of Bahá'u'lláh denouncing self and passion as the worst of all human characteristics merits some explanation: we find similar statements in other Tablets also.

There are two contrasting forces working within man, the animal nature and the spiritual one. Self and passion may be described as the expression of the animal nature in the life of man, that nature which tends to drag him down into the abyss of material existence. On the other hand, the soul, which emanates from the spiritual worlds of God, becomes, if illumined with the light of faith, the motive power for the elevation of man into the realms of the spirit. One brings about his perishing on this earth, the other confers eternal life in the realms of God.

These two opposing forces within man are similar to the force of gravity pulling down a bird and the force of its wings lifting it upwards. As long as man turns away from the Manifestation of God—in this day Bahá'u'lláh—his soul is in darkness and devoid of the necessary power to lift itself up from the fetters of this mortal world. The animal nature becomes victor and the soul a bond-slave of self and passion.

In one of His Tablets[6] 'Abdu'l-Bahá states that the word 'courageous' can apply to a person who conquers his own self and passion. For it is easier to conquer whole countries than to defeat one's own self. The purpose of the coming of the Manifestations of God is to endow the soul of man with spiritual qualities and enable him to defeat his greatest enemy—his own self.

Another enemy as dangerous as one's own self and passion is association with the ungodly which will dampen or destroy one's faith. This is Bahá'u'lláh's ominous warning:

> O Son of Dust! Beware! Walk not with the ungodly and seek not fellowship with him, for such companionship turneth the radiance of the heart into infernal fire.[7]

The word 'ungodly' should not be misunderstood. An

ungodly person may profess belief in God, while many who regard themselves as agnostics or atheists may not be ungodly in reality. An ungodly person is one who through his friendship, knowingly or unknowingly, prevents a believer from following the dictates of his faith and becomes a barrier between him and his God.

Returning to the *Lawḥ-i-Ra'ís*, Bahá'u'lláh in that Tablet rebukes 'Álí Pá<u>sh</u>á for his cruelties in committing a number of innocent people including women and young children to the harsh life of a grim prison, expatiates on His own sufferings and those of His companions in that fortress, recounts the inhuman treatment meted out to everyone on the first night of their arrival in the barracks when the guards had refused to give them food or water, thereby causing unbearable hardship especially to mothers and their suckling babes, relates the tragic story of those two of His disciples who as a result of the prison's loathsome conditions were found dead locked in each other's arms, extols the spirit of love and devotion which two of His followers had manifested when they were prevented by the authorities from accompanying Bahá'u'lláh,* describes other cruelties and deprivations to which the prisoners were subjected without any justification, and asserts that no measure of persecution will ever affect the believers, for they long to offer up their lives in the path of their Lord.

Bahá'u'lláh informs 'Álí Pá<u>sh</u>á that if he were to become vivified by the breezes of holiness which were being wafted from the glorious court of His presence, he would become so transformed as to renounce the world and long to dwell in one of the ruined quarters of the Most Great Prison. He narrates for him a story of His childhood, portraying in a dramatic way the instability and futility of this earthly life, counsels him not to rely on his pomp and glory as they will soon be coming to an

* Ḥájí Ja'far-i-Tabrízí, who cut his own throat (see vol. 2, pp. 406–7) and 'Abdu'l-<u>Gh</u>affár, who threw himself into the sea in desperation (see vol. 2, p. 411).

end, reveals to him the greatness of His Revelation, points out the Páshá's impotence to quench the fire of the Cause of God, denounces him for the iniquities he has perpetrated, states that because of his cruelties, the Spirit of God has lamented, the pillars of His Throne have trembled and the hearts of His loved ones been shaken. He emphatically warns him that God's chastisement will assail him from every direction and confusion overtake his peoples and government, and affirms that the wrath of God has so surrounded him that he will never be able to repent for his wrongdoings or make amends.

On this last point, Mírzá Áqá Ján, Bahá'u'lláh's amanuensis, asked Him what would happen if, after all, 'Álí Páshá changed his attitude and truly repented. Bahá'u'lláh's emphatic response was that whatever had been stated in the *Lawḥ-i-Ra'ís* would inevitably be fulfilled, and if all the peoples of the world were to join together in order to change one word of that Tablet, they would be impotent to do so.

On Miracles

Bahá'u'lláh in the *Lawḥ-i-Ra'ís* also states that at Gallipoli He sent a verbal message to the Sulṭán of Turkey through the Turkish officer in charge, who had promised to convey the message. He asked the Sulṭán to meet Him face to face for a few minutes in order that He might demonstrate to him the authenticity of His Mission. Bahá'u'lláh affirmed His readiness to produce anything that the Sulṭán considered to be a criterion for the truth of His Revelation. Should he fulfil this criterion through the power of God, then the Sulṭán should free all the innocent prisoners.

Bahá'u'lláh explains that the only reason for this proposition was that a number of women and children were among the prisoners and had become the victims of tyranny and were afflicted with great hardship and suffering. He reiterates the basic principle that it is not befitting God to justify Himself to any man. For all the peoples of the world have been created to worship and obey Him. However, Bahá'u'lláh had consented in this case to allow the Sulṭán to seek from Him the truth of His Cause, so that the innocent might not suffer. But neither did the Sulṭán respond to this challenge nor did the above-mentioned officer send a report to Bahá'u'lláh.

This was not the only time Bahá'u'lláh offered to establish the validity of His Cause for those who held the reins of power in their hands. A similar challenging proposition was made to Náṣiri'd-Dín Sháh of Persia in the *Lawḥ-i-Sulṭán*,* a proposition which was ignored by him and the divines.

On another occasion, in Baghdád, the divines of Shí'ah Islám requested Bahá'u'lláh to perform a miracle for them. He accepted their demand provided they pledged their allegiance to His Cause should the miracle that they ask for be performed by Him. The divines became fearful and did not pursue the matter any more. We have already described the circumstances of this challenging episode in a former volume.†

On occasions such as this Bahá'u'lláh always stated that it was for God to test His servants and not the other way round. Indeed man will find himself in a sorry plight should he contemplate testing the Manifestation of God.

The question of miracles is one of the most misunderstood subjects concerning the prophets and messengers of God. The followers of most religions attribute miracles to their prophets. The belief in miracles comes from the study of the Holy Books of old religions and through traditions handed down from generation to generation. Religious leaders have endeavoured to emphasize miracles as one of the most important proofs of the authenticity of their faiths. Consequently the followers of a religion regard their own Prophet as one who had a halo of light around his head and carried out supernatural acts to convince people of His station.

The study of the life and teachings of the Prophets and their

* see vol. 2, p. 349.
† see vol. 1, p. 145.

Holy Books shows that the opposite is true. The Manifestations of God have not established miracles as a testimony to their truth. They are the bearers of the Message of God and their mission is to educate the souls of men. Their word is creative and may be regarded as the greatest instrument for the vivification and regeneration of humanity.

The Bahá'í view concerning miracles is that the Manifestations of God derive their power and authority from Almighty God. They are the embodiments of His attributes and the manifestations of His glory in this world. They are therefore able to do what they will, even to change the laws of nature and perform miracles. For it is obvious that God, having established the laws of nature, is Himself able to change them if He so wishes. To entertain doubt that He can do this is tantamount to attributing impotence to Him. The followers of Bahá'u'lláh therefore do not deny the possibility of the performance of miracles by the Prophets and Messengers of God. However, such miracles, even when they have been performed, are valid as proof only for the few who have witnessed them. They cannot be regarded as a conclusive testimony to the authenticity of the message of the Prophet. For no one can prove that a certain miracle attributed to a Prophet has actually been performed. On the other hand, some of the miracles mentioned in the Holy Books such as the raising of the dead, the curing of lepers, or the ascending to heaven have spiritual significance. Bahá'u'lláh has revealed these meanings in many of His Writings and especially in the *Kitáb-i-Íqán*.

There is a great difference between fact and belief. There are things in this life whose existence is proved and no one has ever denied them. For example, the existence of the sea on this planet is a proven fact and no person, including those who have never seen the sea, has ever denied its existence. But having a belief in something with which a number of people may disagree is a different matter. Such a belief may not be used as factual evidence for the simple reason that its authenticity is challenged, even though the belief in itself may be true. Miracles are examples of this. For instance, the followers of Christ believe that He performed many miracles. But since many people have denied the claim, one cannot consider these miracles as a factual reality, although they may well have been performed.

In the earlier days of the Bahá'í Faith when religion was still a vital force in society and exerted a far deeper influence upon the hearts of men than it does nowadays, people asked for religious proofs when they took part in discussion with Bahá'ís. One of the major questions was that of miracles. Many people believed blindly in them and the task of the Bahá'í teacher was to explain the reality and true significance of miracles in religion. But when beliefs are held fanatically a mere explanation is not always successful. This is why some of the old teachers of the Faith, when conversing with a dogmatic person whose religious beliefs bordered on vain imaginings, conducted their discussions in such a way as to enable him to first see the hollowness of his ideas, and then to present him with the Message of Bahá'u'lláh. This often helped those who were sincere and pure-hearted to see the light of truth.

To cite an example, here is the gist of a dialogue between Ḥájí Muḥammad Ṭáhir-i-Málmírí,* one of the early believers, and a Christian missionary in Yazd. The former has recorded his recollections of this dialogue in his memoirs. The following is a translation of a part of this interesting discussion:

> Some years ago a Christian clergyman . . . was touring Persia doing missionary work. While staying in Yazd he used to give public lectures and interview such people as he regarded as prospective converts. He knew the Persian language well and had a fairly good knowledge of Persian life, habits and trends of thought. One morning I, together with a couple of friends, went to see him at the missionary house. He received us very kindly. We exchanged greetings and after indulging in a few minutes of ordinary talk the

* the father of the author; for more information see vol. 1, Appendix II.

subject of religion was broached. So far as I can remember the following is the gist of the conversation that passed between us:

I: What do you know about the Bahá'í Faith?

He: I am afraid I do not know anything about it.

I: What do you know about the Christian Faith?

He: Well, I know almost everything about Christianity.

I: Could you please explain to me some of the things you know about the Christian religion?

He: Oh yes, by all means and with pleasure. But is there anything particular you want me to describe?

I: I would like you to prove for me the authenticity of Christ's message; in other words, how can I be sure that the Christian religion is true and divine?

He: But you already believe that Christ was the Son of God and that Christianity is divine in origin, don't you?

I: Yes, in fact I do; but this belief came to me through the word of Muḥammad, and since you regard him as an impostor, then in that case his word loses its authority altogether and none of his utterances can be trusted to contain truth.

He turned round and reached for a copy of the New Testament which lay on his desk. He then started reading passages concerning miracles performed by Christ—raising the dead, curing the leper, healing the sick, etc. Then after a pause conversation was resumed as follows:

I: I regret to say that your readings did not help to enlighten me on the subject. I shall appreciate it if you will kindly demonstrate for me the truth of Christ's revelation by means of rational proofs.

He: I am sorry we don't have anything other than what is given in the Book.

I: Muslims attribute lots of miracles to their prophet, Muḥammad.

He: There is not a grain of truth in all that they say.

I: The Jews categorically deny all these miracles you ascribe to the person of Christ, as you deny those miracles which Muslims attribute to Muḥammad.

He: You know Jews are our antagonists, and as such you

should not expect them to utter words in praise of our Lord.

I: Muslims also argue the same way. They say since Christians reject Islám as a false religion, therefore the view they hold regarding our Prophet is highly biased and distorted.

He: You ought to be sure that the charges they bring against us are all baseless.

I: Now let us see, if an earnest seeker sincerely wishes to comprehend the reality of Christ's mission, do you think these miracles will lead to the truth?

He: Oh yes, I think these miracles are the greatest proof of His mission.

I: But can anyone regard miracles as conclusive proof without witnessing them?

He: Yes, you ought to be sure that it all came to pass.

I: Can we accept the miracles attributed to Muḥammad as true without any visual evidence?

He: Certainly not.

I: How is it then that in the case of miracles which you attribute to Christ there is no need for evidence, whereas in the case of Muḥammad's it should be substantiated by visual evidence?

He: Because we regard Muḥammad as one of the false prophets and the so-called supernatural acts of his are mere fabrications.

I: The Zoroastrians attribute some miracles to Zoroaster. Can we accept their assertions without any evidence?

He: No. For the simple reason that we do not recognize Zoroaster as a divine messenger.

I: Bahá'ís attribute certain supernatural acts to the Báb, the Forerunner of the Bahá'í Faith, who appeared in Shíráz, Persia. Can we believe what they say?

He: I think Bahá'ís can be trusted, but even so they must furnish evidence in support of their claim.

I: Now let us see, how is it that all the creeds other than Christianity will have to substantiate their assertions by evidence while you maintain that the words written in the Bible ought to be accepted arbitrarily as conclusive proof?

He: As I said, we don't have any proofs greater than miracles, however, if you can produce anything from Bahá'u'lláh superior to those acts of Christ I shall be much delighted.

I: So long as you fail to appreciate the reality of Christ in its true perspective and persist in regarding miracles as the decisive test for a prophet—miracles which you have never seen nor could prove to have occurred in their outward sense—I am sorry to say that you won't be able to know Bahá'u'lláh.

He: Then what is the conclusive evidence other than miracles?

I: We Bahá'ís believe that the proof of Prophethood must be something so convincing, so overwhelming, that no one in the whole world could deny or be able to question its validity.

He: Can you tell me what that proof is?

I: I did not mean to say what that proof is. I simply wanted to point out the essential quality of such a proof. You already know that the Jews, Buddhists and Zoroastrians deny those miracles you attribute to Christ, the same as you reject those which Muslims, Buddhists and Zoroastrians ascribe to their respective prophets. Therefore miracles ought to be dismissed altogether as a conclusive proof, because they fall short of the essential quality such proofs must possess.

He: That sounds right and I agree with you, but is there any proof you could call conclusive?

I: Now, I will tell you something, please see if it stands the test.

He: Very well.

I: I think no one in the whole world would deny the fact that over 1900 years ago there lived a man named Jesus who rose up and declared Himself as one who embodied the Spirit of God.

He: Yes.

I: Well, do you think there is anyone who could deny this fact? Even those who disbelieve in Him admit that He did claim to have been invested with such a mission, though they might say His declaration was a false one.

Is there anyone who could say there is no Christian in the world, that those many millions who bear allegiance to Christianity do not owe their faith primarily to the Word of Christ or that Christ influenced his adherents through acquired knowledge or through material wealth or power?

He: Certainly not.

I: Can you or I or any other human being on this planet, guided by his own impulse, stand up to-day, say the same thing that Christ said and succeed in establishing a new religion without any material means?

He: That is splendid. How about Muḥammad?[8]*

The greatest miracle of the Manifestation of God is that He changes the hearts of people and creates a new civilization merely through the influence of His word. Every word that He utters is creative† and endowed with such potency that all the powers of the world will not be able to resist the world-vivifying forces that are released through it. Like the animating energies of the spring season which are let loose in abundance and penetrate to the core of all living things, the creative Word of the Manifestation of God revolutionizes human society and by its resistless force breaks down man-made barriers of opposition, creating a new race of men and a new civilization.

There can be no miracle greater than this, a miracle that every unbiased observer can witness and the glory of which can never be dimmed by the passage of time. But those who have no spiritual insight and follow their own vain imaginings have opposed the Manifestations of God and one form of this opposition is to demand the performance of miracles.

When Bahá'u'lláh was in 'Akká, four Muslim divines from the village of Man<u>sh</u>ád in the province of Yazd sent a letter to Bahá'u'lláh introducing themselves as followers of Azal in order to test Him. They posed two riddles and promised to

* see vol. 2, pp. 21–2, for the rest of the dialogue.

† see more explanation about the Word of God in vols. 1 and 2.

accept His Cause if He revealed the correct answers. This is a translation of a part of their letter:

> The first question is to inform us of the death of a certain man or woman of Manshád, by predicting the exact hour, and the date of death, the cause of death together with the name of the person, the name of his mother, his address, the description of his relatives and family and altogether every detail of his personal status.
>
> The second question is to inform us of the birth of a certain child, by predicting its sex, the name of the mother, and of the father, and the exact time and date of birth in this year . . .[9]

Man, with his petty mind and narrow vision and in an egotistical mood, stands before his Lord, challenges Him to comply with his trivial and idle fancies and warns the Manifestation of God that unless He produces what is demanded of Him, He will be rejected. How dreadful this seems to anyone endowed with a measure of spiritual insight! The questions put to Bahá'u'lláh on this occasion are as comical as they are pitiful. In answer to this a lengthy Tablet[10] was revealed by Bahá'u'lláh, partly in the words of His amanuensis and partly His own words,* admonishing the writers for their perversity and blindness in testing God. In it He announces the advent of the Day of God, and states that the outpouring of His Revelation has encompassed the world. How grievous then is the plight of those who are seeking proof when the signs of His power and majesty are evident on all sides. This is not the day for asking questions but for hearkening to the call of God and embracing His Cause. He reminds them, by quoting various passages from the *Qur'án*,

* Some Tablets of Bahá'u'lláh are composed in such a way that a part of the Tablet is in the words of His amanuensis, but in fact was dictated by Bahá'u'lláh to appear as if composed by the amanuensis. Every word of the Tablet therefore is from Bahá'u'lláh Himself. For more information see vol. 1, pp. 40–42.

that the unbelievers of a previous dispensation had demanded the performance of miracles from the Prophet of Islám. They asked Him to send down angels from heaven, to make water gush forth out of the earth, to cause the sky to lie shattered in pieces, to produce a house made of gold, to ascend to the heavens and bring back a book and many similar demands. The study of the *Qur'án* makes it clear that Muḥammad's response to these preposterous requests was that the main proof of His Mission was the revelation of the Word of God.

Bahá'u'lláh warns the four clergymen of Man<u>sh</u>ád that by testing God their plight was as grievous as those who denied Him in former dispensations. An interesting aspect of this episode is that since these men introduced themselves as followers of Azal, Bahá'u'lláh addressed them in this Tablet as if they were Azalís. He quoted profusely from the Writings of the Báb in support of His argument. This He did notwithstanding the fact that He knew well who the four were. Apart from His divine knowledge which encompassed all created things, it was well known to Him and even to His disciples that there were no such followers of Azal in Man<u>sh</u>ád. Some of the believers living at that time* in 'Akká were actually from the village of Man<u>sh</u>ád and knew the identity of these men very well!

This is where the Manifestation of God tests man by appearing to be ignorant of the truth. This is where he hides His glory and knowledge from the eyes of men so that the bad may not gain admittance into His Court of holiness and become equal with the good. And this is where man's free will to follow whichever path he may choose is not interfered with, and he is not turned into a puppet manipulated from on high.† By addressing them as if they were the followers of Azal, Bahá'u'lláh put these four men to the test. Actually one of the four was known to have claimed privately to a few Bahá'ís that he was inclined towards the Faith in his heart. This Tablet,

* This was in 1885.

† see also pp. 2–4 above.

however, was a test for him. He failed in it and lost his faith altogether.

Tests and Trials

Test is an integral part of creation. Even in this physical world there are tests. We note that as long as an object is stationary there are no tests, but as soon as there is movement there will be resistance, which is nature's form of test. The faster one moves, the greater the resistance. For instance, a modern aircraft flying faster than sound meets such resistance by its sheer speed that its body becomes red hot.

This is true in a spiritual sense also. God tests His servants. It is stated in the *Qur'án*:

> We will surely prove you by afflicting you in some measure with fear, and hunger, and decrease of wealth, and loss of lives and scarcity of fruits . . .*[11]

In many of His Tablets Bahá'u'lláh speaks of tests, especially in this Day when God, by revealing Himself, has tested even the realities of the Prophets and chosen ones. These are the words of Bahá'u'lláh:

> By the righteousness of God! These are the days in which God hath proved the hearts of the entire company of His Messengers and Prophets, and beyond them those that stand guard over His sacred and inviolable Sanctuary, the inmates of the celestial Pavilion and dwellers of the Tabernacle of Glory.[12]

When the individual embraces the Cause of God he will be tested in many ways, often without realizing it. Each time he is successful in passing a test, he will acquire greater spiritual insight and will grow stronger in faith. He will come closer to

* The Arabic word for 'fruits' is *thamarát*, which also means descendants, or one's children. One could translate this phrase as 'loss of lives and descendants'.

God, will be elevated to a higher level of service and his tests will be more difficult next time. But if through ego, which is the most harmful form of attachment to this world, he fails in this, his faith will be weakened and he could lose it altogether. There were many believers among the outstanding teachers of the Cause who served it with great distinction and ability and defended it against its adversaries; yet when the winds of tests blew, their insincerity and selfish ambitions became apparent and robbed them of the mantle of faith so that they perished spiritually.

But the nature of the tests which confront the believer may vary from age to age. In the days of the Báb, Bahá'u'lláh, and 'Abdu'l-Bahá, tests were mainly in the form of persecution and martyrdom. The believers were often faced with situations in which they had either to recant their faith in public or give their lives. But the hand of divine power had so sustained and strengthened them that the great majority stood steadfast till the end and heroically quaffed the cup of martyrdom.

Today in the Formative Age the tests of the Bahá'ís come mainly from two sources. The first lies outside the Bahá'í community; it is the challenge to live in a Bahá'í way in a world which is corrupt, spiritually bankrupt, and characterized by all the evil influences of a decadent civilization. Within such a world heading swiftly towards destruction, Bahá'ís must learn to be happy and confident, to hold to Bahá'u'lláh's vision of future society, and to adorn themselves with the characteristics of a Bahá'í life. To live in accordance with the teachings of Bahá'u'lláh in a world so weighed down with evil is a severe test in this day, a test which every believer must undergo.

The other source of tests is from within the Bahá'í community. Those who lived and laboured in the Heroic Age did not often suffer these tests as must do the present and future generations, for they had come into direct contact with the Supreme Manifestation of God and the Centre of His Covenant. Intoxicated by the wine of Their utterances, these souls forgot themselves and through their love and attraction became the spiritual giants of this Dispensation. There were less grounds for ill feeling or misunderstanding among the believers, since there were then no community activities as we know them now.

But in this Formative Age, the Bahá'ís work together within communities. Their Administrative Order, now maturing in its embryonic form, throws up many tests, embracing as it does people from every stratum of human society, rich and poor, young and old, learned and uneducated, veteran and newly enrolled, who must work in unity for the progress of the Faith. To work within such a community, the very nucleus and pattern of future world society, is not always free of tests.

Today, then, the greatest tests come to the individual from his inability to work with the right spirit either within the institutions of the Administrative Order, or in relation to them. The basic problem may stem from an inadequate understanding of the nature of the institutions of the Faith. From old religious traditions come the idea that religious institutions are man-made additions to the teachings of the Prophet. Such an idea may act subconsciously as a bias in the mind of the individual when he studies the teachings of Bahá'u'lláh. Consequently he may not appreciate fully that, unlike other religions, the Author of the Faith Himself has brought into being, as part of the religion of God, its administrative institutions, and that the administrative principles of the Faith are on a par with its spiritual principles.

Another contributory factor to this misconception originates from the outside world where man-made institutions have become the focal points of contention and strife within society. Such thoughts, whether originating from old religions or from present-day political and social institutions, are so stamped upon the minds of men that they become as subconscious obstacles to the proper understanding of the Bahá'í Administrative Order. There is need for real deepening in the verities of the Faith before the effect of these ill-judged notions can be completely eradicated.

The institutions of the Administrative Order are inseparable organs of the Faith of Bahá'u'lláh. The main features of this divine order were delineated by Bahá'u'lláh Himself* and by 'Abdu'l-Bahá. It was Shoghi Effendi, the Guardian of the Faith, who erected its foundations and explained its functions. In his masterly description of the birth of the Administrative Order, Shoghi Effendi has summarized its genesis in these words:

> The moment had now arrived for that undying, that world-vitalizing Spirit that was born in Shíráz, that had been rekindled in Ṭihrán, that had been fanned into flame in Baghdád and Adrianople, that had been carried to the West, and was now illuminating the fringes of five continents, to incarnate itself in institutions designed to canalize its outspreading energies and stimulate its growth.[13]

This great and penetrating vision of Shoghi Effendi, the unerring Interpreter of the Word of God, has disclosed in simple terms the relationship between the Revelation of Bahá'u'lláh and the Administrative Order of His Faith. It clearly emphasizes that the institutions of the Cause are not man-made additions, but rather divine channels through which the energies released by the Revelation of Bahá'u'lláh can flow to mankind.

The crowning edifice of the Administrative Order is the Universal House of Justice, its supreme institution. It is essential for a Bahá'í to accept the authority of this august body and to believe that, in the words of 'Abdu'l-Bahá, it is 'the source of all good and freed from all error . . . '[14] This is one of the verities of the Faith which a believer accepts wholeheartedly when he embraces the Cause of Bahá'u'lláh. No faithful Bahá'í will question the authority or infallibility of this supreme body which is under the guidance of the Báb and Bahá'u'lláh.

But tests are often brought about when serving on local or

* see ch. 14.

national institutions. To cite one example: during the consultation period members are often tested, probably without realizing it. The standards of conduct which must govern the motives and actions of the members of assemblies during consultation are noble and very high indeed. The following words of 'Abdu'l-Bahá set out some of these lofty standards:

> The prime requisites for them that take counsel together are purity of motive, radiance of spirit, detachment from all else save God, attraction to His Divine Fragrances, humility and lowliness amongst His loved ones, patience and long-suffering in difficulties and servitude to His exalted Threshold . . . The first condition is absolute love and harmony amongst the members of the assembly. They must be wholly free from estrangement and must manifest in themselves the Unity of God, for they are the waves of one sea, the drops of one river, the stars of one heaven, the rays of one sun, the trees of one orchard, the flowers of one garden . . .[15]

The standards established by 'Abdu'l-Bahá in the aforementioned Tablet are essential requisites for Bahá'í consultation and are not subject to compromise or change.* Failure to apply them may turn the meeting of a Spiritual Assembly into a battle arena for its members, whose faith and steadfastness in the Covenant may be severely tested during consultation. The spiritual battles within the heart begin when the ego comes on to the scene. A believer will bring suffering and test upon himself to the extent that he ignores 'Abdu'l-Bahá's exhortations and allows his selfish interests or un-Bahá'í practices to influence his participation in assembly consultation.

The practice of the spiritual principles of consultation must be genuine and true. The feelings of love, unity, patience, humility, servitude, devotion, courtesy and other virtues called for by 'Abdu'l-Bahá must come from the heart. If not, one has failed to meet the tests, and the spiritual battle has not been won.

* see also below, pp. 317–18.

3

The Prisoner

The edict of the Sulṭán condemning Bahá'u'lláh to solitary life imprisonment and forbidding Him to meet anyone, including His companions, was at the beginning carried out strictly. But very soon the prison authorities became aware of the striking majesty of Bahá'u'lláh, the loftiness of His standards and the exalted character of His person. They were also deeply impressed by the loving disposition of the Master, His divine qualities and virtues; they increasingly turned to Him for advice and guidance. As a result they became lenient and relaxed some of the restrictions.

As time went on the companions of Bahá'u'lláh were allotted rooms in different parts of the barracks. Some of them took on essential duties such as cooking, cleaning, water delivery or shopping and some were able to spend their free time in other useful work. At one stage 'Abdu'l-Bahá engaged a certain Egyptian by the name of Ḥají 'Alíy-i-Miṣrí* to come to the barracks and teach the prisoners the art of making rush mats. As the restrictions were somewhat relaxed the companions were able to communicate with Bahá'u'lláh and even attain His presence.

An important point to bear in mind is that at no time did Bahá'u'lláh break the rules imposed upon Him, either in the prison or in later years. It was the authorities, sometimes encouraged by 'Abdu'l-Bahá, who relaxed the restrictions. The story of His leaving the House of 'Abbúd and taking up

* As a result of coming into contact with 'Abdu'l-Bahá this man was deeply attracted to the Cause, and his son, who was a rebellious youth, was transformed into a new person and became an ardent believer.

residence outside the gates of the city, as we shall see later,* is a clear example of His total submission to the will of His enemies or those who were charged by them to guard His person.

Although the barracks was a depressing place to live in, soon the companions of Bahá'u'lláh, mainly through 'Abdu'l-Bahá's leadership and guidance, organized their daily lives in such a way as to create the best possible conditions for the whole community. Their greatest source of joy was nearness to their Lord, and sometimes Bahá'u'lláh visited them in their quarters where they entertained Him with what meagre food or refreshments they could provide.

Believers in the Holy Land

There is a Tablet[1] revealed by Bahá'u'lláh in the barracks on the ninth day of the Festival of Riḍván.† It was probably revealed during Riḍván 1869, the first of the two Riḍván Festivals that He celebrated in the prison, for in it He mentions the names of several believers who had tried to enter 'Akká and been stopped by the authorities.

In this Tablet Bahá'u'lláh describes how on that day He was invited by one of the believers in the prison to honour his room with His presence and attend the celebration of that great Festival. His companions on that day were truly intoxicated with the wine of His presence. The believer who had invited Bahá'u'lláh entertained Him with the best food he could provide. Bahá'u'lláh refers to this and states that other believers had invited Him to their rooms during the Riḍván period also. Each according to his capacity had provided some food and some had nothing to entertain Him with except a cup of tea.

* see below, pp. 414–17.

† 21 April to 2 May, in commemoration of the twelve days that Bahá'u'lláh spent in the Garden of Riḍván in Ba<u>gh</u>dád in 1863 when He declared His mission to a few companions.

In this Tablet Bahá'u'lláh showers His bounties upon His companions, and prays that they may remain steadfast in His Cause and united among themselves. When the Tablet was revealed there were two Persian believers living in 'Akká itself, there were some who were trying to come in, and some who were staying at Haifa; Bahá'u'lláh refers to them all in this Tablet. The two in 'Akká were Muḥammad Ja'far-i-Tabrízí, entitled Manṣúr, and Mírzá Hádí entitled 'Abdu'l-Aḥad. The latter was the first to arrive in 'Akká. He had been sent there by 'Abdu'l-Bahá some time before Bahá'u'lláh's exile to that city, thus establishing a valuable contact. No one suspected him of being a Bahá'í. Helped by the Persian political agent in that city he had managed to open a shop but did not try to contact Bahá'u'lláh and His companions in the barracks when they arrived. However, the few Bahá'í prisoners who went to the market every day to purchase provisions met him and knew that he was a Bahá'í. Through him, and by other means, the news of Bahá'u'lláh's whereabouts soon reached the believers in Persia and a few of His followers travelled to 'Akká. 'Abdu'l-Aḥad very discreetly helped some of the visitors who had managed to enter the city to approach the barracks. Sometimes he even had to hide the visitors in the back of his shop. The disciples of Bahá'u'lláh, most of whom had walked all the way from Persia, were only able to stand in front of the barracks and watch Bahá'u'lláh wave His blessed hand. This was sufficient to inspire them with faith and courage and uplift them to such heights that they were ready and longing to lay down their lives in His path.

Among those living at Haifa was Mírzá Ibráhim-i-Ká_sh_ání,* a copper-smith by profession, whom Bahá'u'lláh refers to as _Kh_alíl in the forementioned Tablet of Riḍván. He was a devoted believer, on fire with the love of Bahá'u'lláh, and had been among the Bahá'í prisoners sent from Bag_h_dád to Mosul.† Accompanied by some relatives he had managed to

* see 'Abdu'l-Bahá, *Memorials*, pp. 81–2.

† see vol. 2, pp. 334–6.

leave Mosul and settle in Haifa. In those days, entering 'Akká was very difficult for the believers, but he managed to enter frequently by taking some of his copper implements for sale. He thus became an important channel of communication between the believers and Bahá'u'lláh.

Another believer mentioned in the Riḍván Tablet, and one in whose heart the fire of love for Bahá'u'lláh burnt very brightly, was an old man, Ustád Ismá'íl. He was a master builder of wide experience who had worked for the government officials in Persia. When he became known as a Bábí, he had to leave his work. He then went to Baghdád where he was given the honour of carrying out construction work on the house of Bahá'u'lláh.* And when the believers in that city were exiled to Mosul, he managed to travel to 'Akká. In spite of old age he walked all the way until he came and stood in front of the Most Great Prison eagerly waiting to behold the face of his Beloved from across the moat.

But alas, because of his old age and the feebleness of his eyesight he failed to see the hand of Bahá'u'lláh waving from one of the windows of the barracks. This was a pitiful scene. He broke into tears which brought tears also to the eyes of the Holy Family and a few others who were watching the sad plight of that devoted believer. Bahá'u'lláh is reported to have said on that occasion that soon through the power of God restrictions would be relaxed and circumstances would make it possible for the believers to attain His presence.

Of course, not until Bahá'u'lláh left the barracks in 1870 was it possible for the Bahá'í pilgrims to come into His presence freely. However, during the time that He was in the prison, it was officially impossible for any outsider to come in and attain His presence, but as restrictions were gradually relaxed, the officials often turned a blind eye and in some cases they actually helped some of His disciples to enter.

Ustád Ismá'íl eventually succeeded in entering the prison where he stayed for a short while and attained the presence of

* see vol. 1, pp. 211–12.

His Lord. His usual place of residence in the Holy Land was a cave on Mount Carmel. He earned his living as a pedlar, carrying around a small tray on which he set out some needles, thimbles and other trifling articles for sale. He lived in poverty, but in the utmost happiness, his heart filled with the joy of nearness to His Lord.

As he wandered about with his shabby little tray, his heart was in communion with Bahá'u'lláh. Sometimes he would walk around the barracks in order to feel close to his Beloved. On one occasion Bahá'u'lláh was watching him from the prison window. He called His cook Ḥusayn-i-Á<u>sh</u><u>ch</u>í, who was a nephew of Ustád Ismá'íl, and asked him if he had ever seen the tray that his uncle carried around. When he replied that he had not, Bahá'u'lláh in an amusing tone told him that if he were to put on a pair of glasses he might see him in the distance carrying a few rusted needles placed on one side of the tray and a few rusted thimbles on the other! Bahá'u'lláh often praised him for his detachment from this world and his thankfulness to his Lord.

One of those whom Bahá'u'lláh mentions in the Tablet of Riḍván is Nabíl-i-A'ẓam, who travelled to 'Akká but was expelled from the city. After being released from prison in Alexandria, Nabíl hastened to the abode of his Beloved. Although he was disguised* as a man from Bu<u>kh</u>árá, he was nevertheless recognized by two of Bahá'u'lláh's enemies who reported him to the Government authorities and consequently he was expelled. These two men were Siyyid Muḥammad-i-Iṣfahání, the Anti-Christ of Bahá'u'lláh's Revelation,† and Áqá Ján known as Kaj Kuláh.‡ Although they regarded themselves as followers of Mírzá Yaḥyá, they had been condemned to imprisonment in 'Akká, and accompanied

* For fear of being identified as followers of Bahá'u'lláh, most Bahá'ís who attempted to enter 'Akká in the early period of Bahá'u'lláh's banishment to that city adopted some form of disguise.

† see vols. 1 and 2.

‡ see vol. 2, pp. 326, 397, 402.

Bahá'u'lláh and His companions to the barracks. But very soon after their arrival they allied themselves with the authorities who transferred them to a room overlooking the land gate of the city. There they acted as spies and identified the followers of Bahá'u'lláh when they tried to enter.

According to a letter written by Nabíl from 'Akká to the Bahá'ís of Darakhsh in the province of Khurásán, he made the first attempt to enter the city around the end of October 1868. He succeeded in entering and stayed for three days but could not attain the presence of Bahá'u'lláh before being expelled.

He retreated to the caves of Mount Carmel and roamed the countryside for about four months. But he could not endure separation from His Lord. The ardour of his love was increasing day by day until he found it impossible to remain away from the city of his Beloved.

In about the middle of February 1869 he made his second attempt to enter the city. This time he succeeded in remaining for a longer period. He met Mírzá Áqá Ján and a few other believers who had come out of the barracks to purchase provisions. But in his letter Nabíl mentions that at last he achieved his heart's desire of seeing Bahá'u'lláh on the 18th of Muḥarram 1286 (1 May 1869).

Some Early Pilgrims

The first pilgrims to succeed in entering the presence of Bahá'u'lláh were Ḥájí Sháh-Muḥammad-i-Manshádí, entitled Amínu'l-Bayán (Trusted of the Bayán) by Bahá'u'lláh, and Ḥájí Abu'l-Ḥasan-i-Ardikání, entitled Amín-i-Ilahí (Trusted of God) by Bahá'u'lláh. Such were the services of these illustrious Trustees of Bahá'u'lláh that their story demands to be told in detail and will be found in Chapter 4.

Another eminent Bahá'í who came to 'Akká but was recognized and expelled from the city was Mullá Muḥammad-'Alí, surnamed Nabíl-i-Qá'iní by Bahá'u'lláh.* He had known

* Not to be confused with Áqá Muḥammad-i-Qá'iní, entitled Nabíl-i-

Bahá'u'lláh in Ṭihrán some years before the Báb declared His mission. At that time he had recognized the superhuman qualities of Bahá'u'lláh and become an ardent admirer of His person. When Nabíl-i-Akbar returned from 'Iráq to his native town of Qá'in, he began to teach the Cause of the Báb openly to the public. As soon as Mullá Muḥammad-'Alí heard the news of the Báb and Bahá'u'lláh, he became an ardent believer, saying that he had attained the presence of Bahá'u'lláh in Ṭihrán and had been deeply attracted to Him then.

The next time he saw the face of His Lord was in the prison of 'Akká. At first he was driven out of the city. But he made other attempts and eventually plans were made for him to enter the barracks. This he did successfully and was ushered into the presence of Bahá'u'lláh. The glory and majesty emanating from His person so overwhelmed Nabíl-i-Qá'iní that as soon as his eyes beheld Him he fainted and fell upon the ground.

This great man, who had lived many years of his life in luxury and honour and had been held in high esteem by the people of his native town, was now living in such poverty that like Ustád Ismá'íl he too had to sell needles and thimbles as a pedlar to the people of Nazareth. He earned his living in this way for about two years, selling to the women of Nazareth needles at the rate of three for an egg! During this time he succeeded in converting a number of her Christian citizens to the Faith.

Nabíl-i-Qá'iní was a shining example of faith and detachment; he will be always remembered as one who had recognized Bahá'u'lláh's powers prior to the Declaration of the Báb. He passed away in 'Akká.

A devoted follower of Bahá'u'lláh who found his way into the prison in an extraordinary fashion in the early days of Bahá'u'lláh's incarceration in the barracks was a certain

---

Akbar, whose life story may be found in vol. 1, pp. 91–5. Both men were from Qá'in in the province of <u>Kh</u>urásán.

'Abdu'r-Raḥím, a native of Bu<u>sh</u>rú'íyyih, the birthplace of Mullá Ḥusayn, the first to believe in the Báb. His original name was Ja'far, but when he attained the presence of Bahá'u'lláh he was given the name Raḥím (Compassionate). Before his conversion to the Faith, 'Abdu'r-Raḥím had been a fanatical Muslim. Having noticed the growth of the Faith, he once sought guidance from a local clergyman as to his attitude towards the Bahá'ís. 'To fight them', the clergyman said, 'is as meritorious as taking part in the Jihád (holy war), to kill them is praiseworthy in the sight of God, and to be killed is a privilege which bestows upon the individual Muslim the reward of martyrdom and entrance into the highest paradise.'

These words provoked in 'Abdu'r-Raḥím a strong urge to kill some Bahá'ís. Armed with a weapon, he one day confronted an old believer by the name of Ḥájí Bábá, and told him in no uncertain terms that he had come to take his life because he had strayed from the path of truth and had embraced the Faith of the Bahá'ís.

Faced with the threat of death, Ḥájí Bábá displayed unruffled calm and spoke with tenderness such words that the heart of 'Abdu'r-Raḥím was touched. Soon his mood changed. Instead of being an enemy intent upon killing, he now wanted to investigate the truth.

Ḥájí Bábá conducted 'Abdu'r-Raḥím to the home of the sister of Mullá Ḥusayn where the friends often held their meetings for teaching the Cause. That meeting with 'Abdu'r-Raḥím lasted one day and one night, during which time he was most assiduously involved in discussion. At the end of that marathon meeting he recognized the truth of the Cause and became filled with such a new spirit of faith and enthusiasm that he could not rest in his native town any longer. Knowing that the Supreme Manifestation of God was on this earth he could not resist the urge to go and see Him face to face. So he set off on the long journey to attain His presence.

For six months 'Abdu'r-Raḥím travelled on foot until he reached the abode of his Beloved—the prison city of 'Akká. He arrived in the early days of Bahá'u'lláh's incarceration in the barracks when no visitor suspected of being a Bahá'í was permitted even to approach the vicinity of the prison. His arrival coincided with the period when Nabíl-i-A'ẓam was attempting in vain to get a glimpse of his Lord. Nabíl poured out his heart to 'Abdu'r-Raḥím and lamented over his own inability to achieve his purpose. But 'Abdu'r-Raḥím, undismayed, proceeded to attempt to circumambulate the prison.

Before undertaking such a holy mission, he decided that he must wash his clothes which were unclean, as they had been worn throughout the journey. He washed them in the sea and waited until they were dry. When he put them on, however, he looked very odd and shabby as the clothes had shrunk and were torn.

With the utmost devotion and a heart overflowing with the love of Bahá'u'lláh, 'Abdu'r-Raḥím approached the prison and began to circumambulate it. Then to his surprise he noticed that a hand from a window of the prison was beckoning him to come inside. He knew it was the hand of Bahá'u'lláh summoning him to His presence. He rushed to the gate of the prison which was guarded by soldiers. But the soldiers seemed to him to be motionless and without life; they appeared not to see him. They did not even move an eyelid as he went through the gate.

Soon 'Abdu'r-Raḥím found himself in the presence of His Lord, overwhelmed by emotion and carried away into the world of the Spirit, communing with the One who was the object of his adoration and love. Bahá'u'lláh told him that through the hands of power and might He had temporarily blinded the eyes of the guards so that he might attain His presence as a bounty on His part.

It is not clear how many days 'Abdu'r-Raḥím remained in the prison. However, Bahá'u'lláh revealed a Tablet for him while he was there. In that Tablet He confirms that He had closed the eyes of the guards so that 'Abdu'r-Raḥím could enter His presence and witness the glory of His countenance.

THE BARRACKS FROM BEYOND THE MOAT

Bahá'í pilgrims would try to catch a glimpse of Bahá'u'lláh from this distance

MÍRZÁ 'ABDU'R-RAḤÍM

Despite the presence of the soldiers guarding the prison, he went inside the barracks and attained the presence of Bahá'u'lláh

COLONEL AḤMAD-I-JARRÁḤ

Commander of the Guard during Bahá'u'lláh's imprisonment in the barracks. He later became a believer

ḤÁJÍ ABU'L-ḤASAN-I-AMÍN

Trustee of Bahá'u'lláh and one of His Apostles

INTERIOR OF THE PUBLIC BATH IN 'AKKÁ

ḤÁJÍ ÁKHÚND (left) and ḤÁJÍ AMÍN (right)

In the prison of Qazvín. Their feet are in stocks and their necks chained, with the gaoler in attendance

He calls him by the new name Raḥím (Compassionate), showers His blessings upon him, and urges him to recount the experience of his pilgrimage to the friends on his return home.

Before leaving, Bahá'u'lláh entrusted 'Abdu'r-Raḥím with Tablets to be delivered to some believers in Persia. While in Ba<u>gh</u>dád on his way to Persia, the guards saw him one day in the bazaar and became suspicious. They followed him, intending to arrest him. As soon as 'Abdu'r-Raḥím realized this, he took the parcel containing the Tablets of Bahá'u'lláh out of his pocket and as he was walking along threw it into the shop nearest to him. He did this so quickly that the guards did not see it. He took this action because he knew that if the guards had discovered the Tablets of Bahá'u'lláh, not only would they have destroyed or confiscated them, but his own life would have been endangered also.

As he threw the parcel into the unknown shop, he put his whole trust in Bahá'u'lláh, turned to Him in prayer and begged Him to protect these Tablets through His all-embracing power. This is reminiscent of the story of the mother of Moses who placed her babe, as it lay in a box, on the river, trusting that God would take care of it and deliver it into the right hands.

The guards arrested 'Abdu'r-Raḥím and took him into custody. After some investigations into his identity, the authorities were satisfied that he was a man of God and a harmless person. They released him and gave him a small sum of money in compensation. As he looked at the money placed in the palm of his hand, 'Abdu'r-Raḥím could not help complaining to Bahá'u'lláh in his heart saying: 'You took away from me the most precious of all the things in the world—the Tablets—and gave me instead a few coins!' He then returned to the bazaar with much trepidation to see what had happened to the parcel.

At first he strolled up and down the bazaar several times and occasionally stood near the shop and looked inside, but nothing happened. Eventually, toward the end of the day, he went near the shop again. This time there were no customers there and he saw the shopkeeper beckoning him in. He went inside. To his great surprise the shopkeeper came forward, warmly embraced him, welcomed him with the Bahá'í greeting 'Alláh'u'Abhá!' and handed him the parcel. He happened to be one of the few Bahá'ís living in Baghdád. The two men marvelled at the power of God and regarded this incident as a miracle. For there were hundreds of shops in the bazaar, but on that fateful day and at the moment when the guards were approaching him, 'Abdu'r-Raḥím, a complete stranger, happened to be passing in front of the only shop which was owned by a Bahá'í.

The joy and gladness of 'Abdu'r-Raḥím in finding the Tablets knew no bounds. He stayed a few days in the house of the Bahá'í friend, the shopkeeper. Through him he met a few believers in Baghdád, and then departed for Persia. He visited several towns and delivered the Tablets of Bahá'u'lláh to their owners. To each of the believers he recounted the stories of his pilgrimage and spoke of Bahá'u'lláh, of His power and majesty and of the unfailing confirmations which He had bestowed upon him throughout the journey. When 'Abdu'r-Raḥím arrived in his native town he was like a ball of fire ignited by the hand of Bahá'u'lláh. The radiance of his face and the force of his utterance were evident to all. He began to teach the Faith fearlessly after his return from 'Akká, but this action provoked the wrath of the clergy and the fanatic populace who rose up against him and forced him out of his native town of Bushrú'íyyih. He took residence in another town, Fárán.*

Some years later Bahá'u'lláh conferred a great honour upon Mullá Ṣádiq-i-Khurásání, entitled Ismulláh'u'l-Aṣdaq (The name of God, the Most Truthful),† one of the most outstanding followers of the Báb and Bahá'u'lláh, by inviting him to travel

* A new name given by Bahá'u'lláh to the town of Tún in Khurásán.

† see 'Abdu'l-Bahá, *Memorials*, pp. 5–8; also Taherzadeh, vol. 1, pp. 92–3; and below, pp. 252ff.

to 'Akká and attain His presence. But since he was very old, Bahá'u'lláh directed that on his journey to 'Akká Ismulláh'u'l-Aṣdaq be accompanied by a trustworthy man. The Bahá'ís of Mas͟hhad could not agree among themselves who that person ought to be. Therefore they drew lots and 'Abdu'r-Raḥím's name came up. In this way he was given the privilege of attaining the presence of Bahá'u'lláh for the second time. And when he arrived in 'Akká Bahá'u'lláh confirmed that by 'a trustworthy man' he had actually meant 'Abdu'r-Raḥím.

In this life we observe that each individual can progress to the extent of his capacity. The bounties of God reach all created things as the rays of the sun reach every object. But an unpolished rock cannot reflect that light as a mirror could. Similarly man must acquire a greater spiritual capacity by cleansing his heart in order to receive a greater portion of the bounties of God. In a Tablet to Hádíy-i-Qazvíní',* Bahá'u'lláh reveals this basic principle in God's creation:

> From the exalted source, and out of the essence of His favour and bounty He hath entrusted every created thing with a sign of His knowledge, so that none of His creatures may be deprived of its share in expressing, each according to its capacity and rank, this knowledge. This sign is the mirror of His beauty in the world of creation. The greater the effort exerted for the refinement of this sublime and noble mirror, the more faithfully will it be made to reflect the glory of the names and attributes of God, and reveal the wonders of His signs and knowledge. Every created thing will be enabled (so great is this reflecting power) to reveal the potentialities of its pre-ordained station, will recognize its capacity and limitations, and will testify to the truth that 'He verily is God, there is none other God besides Him' . . .
>
> There can be no doubt whatever that, in consequence of the efforts which every man may consciously exert and as a

* One of the Letters of the Living; see vol. 2, pp. 144–5.

result of the exertion of his own spiritual faculties, this mirror can be so cleansed from the dross of earthly defilements and purged from satanic fancies as to be able to draw nigh unto the meads of eternal holiness and attain the courts of everlasting fellowship.[2]

There are many Tablets of Bahá'u'lláh and 'Abdu'l-Bahá in which They state that man's attainments in life depend on his spiritual capacity and perceptiveness. 'Abdu'l-Bahá in one of His talks in 'Akká is reported to have said:

> Pilgrimage should be carried out in a state of utter humbleness and devotion. Otherwise it is not true pilgrimage, it is a form of sight-seeing . . .
>
> Many people used to come and attain the presence of Bahá'u'lláh. They saw His virtuous character, His blessed smile, His magnetic attraction and His infinite bounties, yet they remained unaffected by Him. Some others were instantly transformed by attaining His presence.
>
> Jamál-i-Burújirdí* attained the presence of Bahá'u'lláh in Adrianople. With him were two men from Burújird. One of them was called Mírzá 'Abdu'r-Raḥím.† He was so influenced by the magnetic person of Bahá'u'lláh that he was completely transformed. The Blessed Beauty stated that this man within ten minutes took one step from this mortal world and placed it in the realms of eternity.
>
> It is therefore necessary to acquire spiritual receptiveness. A deaf ear will not enjoy the melody of a beautiful song, and a diseased nostril will be insensible to the perfume of the rose. The sun shines, the breeze is wafted, and the rain falls, but where the land is a salt marsh nothing grows but weeds.
>
> When Bahá'u'lláh was in Baghdád, some of the chiefs of the tribe of Jáf who had become His admirers in the days of Sulaymáníyyih had come to Baghdád by order of the Governor. While there, they would come to the house of Bahá'u'lláh, get permission and then attain His presence in

* see vol. 2.

† Not the believer by the same name whose story is recounted above, pp. 58–63.

the utmost humility and courtesy. Among them was a Kurd who was truly attracted to the Blessed Beauty. He said to me that he wished to see Shaykh Muḥammad (i.e. Bahá'u'lláh) once more, and to gaze upon His luminous Countenance. I realized that he was enchanted by Bahá'u'lláh. Not wanting to keep him waiting, I sent him straight into His blessed room. Bahá'u'lláh received him with loving-kindness and permitted him to sit alongside the chiefs of the tribe. Should, however, all the bounties of God descend upon a person who has no perceptiveness and capacity, there will be no result whatsoever. In the days of Baghdád there was a man by the name Muḥammad-Riḍá who used to attain the presence of Bahá'u'lláh every day in the morning and in the evening . . . When the days of Baghdád came to an end he said proudly: 'I associated with these people for ten years and they could not influence me!'[3]

Citizens of 'Akká

An example of those who had spiritual perceptiveness to recognize the station of Bahá'u'lláh without being taught or approached by the Bahá'ís was Shaykh Maḥmúd-i-'Arrábí, a native of 'Akká. Shaykh Maḥmúd was one of the religious leaders of 'Akká when Bahá'u'lláh was exiled to that city. He was born into a family of devout Muslims. When he was about ten years of age, an old Shaykh, a religious man revered by Maḥmúd's father, had a vision of the coming of the Person of the 'Promised One' to 'Akká. He intimated this to Maḥmúd in the presence of his father and told him that his father and himself were old men and would not live to see that day. But he assured Maḥmúd that he would then be a grown-up person and bade him watch out for the coming of the Lord. He even indicated to Maḥmúd that He would speak in the Persian tongue and reside in an upper room at the top of a long flight of stairs.

Some years passed and the young boy grew up into a strong man, learned and pious, well respected by the community and known as Shaykh Maḥmúd. But he seldom thought of the vision, and when Bahá'u'lláh came to 'Akká it never occurred to him that He might be the One foretold by the old Shaykh. On the contrary, he deeply resented the action of the Government in sending Bahá'u'lláh, whom the authorities had described as an evil man and the 'God of the Persians', to the city of 'Akká. For some time he was in a state of agitation, wanting to do something to rid the city of such a person. It must be remembered that soon after the imprisonment of Bahá'u'lláh in the barracks, the prison authorities relaxed some of the restrictions which had at first been imposed and strictly adhered to. For instance, they agreed to allow a small party of Bahá'í prisoners to visit the city daily for shopping. At times 'Abdu'l-Bahá went out with them and this is how the people of 'Akká came into contact with His magnetic personality and began to unbend towards the company of exiles.

Shaykh Maḥmúd was very perturbed one day to see 'Abdu'l-Bahá in the Mosque. He is reported to have grabbed 'Abdu'l-Bahá by the hand and exclaimed, 'Are you the son of God?' The Master with His characteristic charm pointed out that it was he who was saying it, and not 'Abdu'l-Bahá. He then reminded him of the injunction of Islám as stated in one of the Traditions: 'Be charitable toward the guest even though he be an infidel.'

The impact of these words and the loving personality of the Master affected Shaykh Maḥmúd and he changed his attitude of aggressiveness towards Him. But being a religious leader, he could not remain indifferent to the presence of the group of exiles whom he considered ungodly. He therefore decided to put an end to all this by himself. One day he hid a weapon under his cloak and went straight to the barracks with the intention of assassinating Bahá'u'lláh. He informed the guards at the prison gate that he wished to see Bahá'u'lláh. Since he was an influential personality in 'Akká, the guards complied with his request and went to inform Bahá'u'lláh of the identity of the visitor. 'Tell him', Bahá'u'lláh is reported to have said, 'to cast away the weapon and then he may come in.'* On hearing this Shaykh Maḥmúd was astounded, for he was sure that no one had seen the weapon under his cloak. In a state of utter confusion he returned home, but his agitated mind could not be at rest. He continued in this state for some time until he decided to go to the barracks again, but without any weapons this time. Being a strong man he knew he could take Bahá'u'lláh's life by the mere strength of his hands.

So he went again to the prison gate and made the same request to visit Bahá'u'lláh. On being informed of Shaykh Maḥmúd's desire to meet Him, Bahá'u'lláh is reported to have said: 'Tell him to purify his heart first and then he may come in.'* Perplexed and confused at these utterances, Shaykh Maḥmúd could not bring himself to visit Bahá'u'lláh that day. Later he had a dream in which his father and the old Shaykh appeared to him and reminded him of their vision regarding the coming of the Lord. After this dream Shaykh Maḥmúd went to the barracks again and attained the presence of 'Abdu'l-Bahá. The words of the Master penetrated his heart and he was ushered into the presence of Bahá'u'lláh. The majesty and glory of His countenance overwhelmed the Shaykh and he witnessed the fulfilment of the prophecy of the coming of the Lord to 'Akká. He prostrated himself at His feet and became an ardent believer.

After recognizing the station of Bahá'u'lláh, he arose to serve Him and His Cause. He played a significant part in assisting the believers to enter the city and then harbouring them until they were able to attain the presence of Bahá'u'lláh. On some occasions he even ordered ropes to be lowered so that the Bahá'í visitors might be pulled up the walls which surrounded the city. Another method he sometimes employed was to leave the city and return at night accompanied by one of the believers who would be posing as a servant carrying a

* These are not the exact words of Bahá'u'lláh, but convey the message he is reported to have given.

lantern in front of his master.* After the believer had attained the presence of Bahá'u'lláh, Shaykh Maḥmúd would enable him to leave the city in the same manner that he had entered it. Shaykh Maḥmúd was loved by the Master and served the Cause with great devotion till the end of his life. He made a compilation of the Islámic traditions related to 'Akká and its glorious future.

Well known among those whom Shaykh Maḥmúd assisted to enter 'Akká was Mírzá Ḥasan-i-Mázindarání, who was brought into the city by the sea gate. He stayed at first in the Shaykh's house and later managed to enter the barracks where he stayed for about six months before returning to Persia. Mírzá Ḥasan was a cousin of Bahá'u'lláh and a devoted believer. His father, Mullá Zaynu'l-'Ábidín, was Bahá'u'lláh's paternal uncle. He was among Bahá'u'lláh's kinsmen who had been converted to the Bábí Faith by Bahá'u'lláh Himself in the early days of the ministry of the Báb. He had recognized the station of Bahá'u'lláh and was very devoted to Him. It was this uncle who accompanied Bahá'u'lláh to Ámul† and when He was to be bastinadoed, threw himself on the feet of Bahá'u'lláh as a shield. As a result he was beaten so much that he fainted.

Mírzá Ḥasan, who was much loved by Bahá'u'lláh and 'Abdu'l-Bahá, made several trips to 'Akká and each time he carried back many Tablets for the believers living in the northern cities of Persia. We have already described in a previous volume the story of seventy Tablets that he was carrying on the last of these journeys and the circumstances which led to their disappearance.‡

Another person, a resident of 'Akká who independently recognized the station of Bahá'u'lláh was Aḥmad-i-Jarráḥ, an officer in the Turkish Army. He witnessed the majesty of

* In the old days there was no public lighting and therefore it was necessary to carry a lantern at night. Important people always had servants who performed this service for them.

† see Nabíl-i-A'ẓam, *The Dawn-Breakers.*

‡ see vol. 1, p. 50.

Bahá'u'lláh in the barracks, but it was some years later that his heart was touched, when Bahá'u'lláh (Who was then residing in the house of 'Abbúd) was taken to the Governor's house and kept in custody for about three days. As we shall see later,* this humiliating treatment resulted from the murder of three Azalís in 'Akká. Aḥmad-i-Jarráḥ was one of the officers present in the case and it was then that the majesty and glory of Bahá'u'lláh made a deep impression upon his soul. The mighty and powerful words He uttered on that occasion enabled Jarráḥ to realize that the Prisoner in his custody was not an ordinary man but One endowed with divine authority. After reading some of the Writings and becoming fully conscious of the station of Bahá'u'lláh, he entered the rank of the believers.

Amín Effendi, a brother of Jarráḥ and the head of the municipality of 'Akká, also recognized the truth of the Faith and became a believer. An interesting incident happened which confirmed their faith. One day, Amín and Aḥmad sought permission to attain the presence of Bahá'u'lláh. Permission was granted and they came. They wanted particularly to complain and seek advice about a certain superior officer by the name of Áqásí who was a bitter enemy of theirs. Before they were able to utter a word, Bahá'u'lláh turned to them and said, 'Praise be to God who has rescued you from the evil doings of Áqásí!'† The two brothers were surprised to hear this. Only two days later, the officer was dismissed by the order of the Sulṭán. A third brother of Aḥmad was Khálid. He was a physician, attained the presence of Bahá'u'lláh, and was attracted to Him and to His Cause. He showed much love to the believers and attended them when they were sick.

There were other inhabitants of 'Akká who either embraced the Faith or became admirers of Bahá'u'lláh and His supporters. Ḥusayn-i-Áshchí has recounted the story of some

* see p. 234.

† These are not the exact words of Bahá'u'lláh, but convey the message he is reported to have given.

of these men in his memoirs. The following is a summary of his reminiscences:

> After his recognition of the station of Bahá'u'lláh, Shaykh Maḥmúd went to see a certain Ṣálih Effendi with whom he was very friendly. He reminded him that when they were young, they had both been present at a meeting when the old Shaykh, the religious leader of the father of Shaykh Maḥmúd, had prophesied the coming of the Lord to 'Akká, and had stated that they should both seek Him. Shaykh Maḥmúd conveyed to his friend the glad tidings that the prophecy of the Shaykh had been fulfilled and that he had been led to the Lord in 'Akká and had attained His presence. He thus invited his friend to follow his example.
>
> But Ṣálih Effendi, although he acknowledged the validity of the station of Bahá'u'lláh, did not embrace the Faith because he maintained that he lived a life which was not worthy of the exalted station of Bahá'u'lláh, and his deeds were not in conformity with His teachings. But he always expressed his love for the believers and he did not harm the Faith in any way. Some years later he became ill with tuberculosis, which was incurable in those days, and 'Abdu'l-Bahá provided regular medical help for him till the end of his life.
>
> Another person of note was Shaykh 'Alíy-i-Mírí, the Muftí of 'Akká. He was a somewhat fanatical man. But later he changed as a result of his association with 'Abdu'l-Bahá. For he discovered that his own knowledge and learning was as a drop when compared with the ocean of 'Abdu'l-Bahá's innate knowledge. He therefore showed signs of humility and gradually became friendly.
>
> One day he conveyed to 'Abdu'l-Bahá his desire to meet Bahá'u'lláh as he had some questions and wished to be enlightened. But in those days Bahá'u'lláh did not grant interviews to people, mainly because He did not wish to act against the orders of the Government. However, because of 'Abdu'l-Bahá's pleading, Bahá'u'lláh gave permission and the Muftí of 'Akká attained His presence in the barracks. He was shown to his seat while 'Abdu'l-Bahá stood by the

door. The kitchen in which I was working happened to be opposite the room of Bahá'u'lláh. I could see and hear Him. The Muftí asked some questions and then the Tongue of Grandeur began to speak. At one stage when the utterances of Bahá'u'lláh were still continuing, the Muftí was moved to say something. 'Abdu'l-Bahá gave him an emphatic and commanding signal with his hand that he should not interrupt the words of Bahá'u'lláh. He complied but his pride was hurt.

When the interview was over he left, 'Abdu'l-Bahá accompanying him to the prison gate, but he was annoyed because of the incident, for he was well respected by the inhabitants of the town and as he walked in the bazaars people showed their respect to him and kissed his hands. At that stage he was not aware of the truth of the Cause and the greatness of its Author, therefore he was displeased with the way 'Abdu'l-Bahá had bidden him be silent. But it did not take very long before he realized that in the presence of 'Abdu'l-Bahá he was as utter nothingness. He used to visit the Master and partake of His knowledge and wisdom. He therefore changed his attitude. In the streets and bazaars, whenever he accompanied 'Abdu'l-Bahá he always walked a few steps behind Him and was never found to be walking in front.* When Bahá'u'lláh was moved out of the barracks he used to come regularly to the outer apartment of the house—a room set aside for visitors—and sit at the feet of the Master. He diligently carried out every service that He referred to him.

As time went on the devotion of the Muftí of 'Akká towards Bahá'u'lláh and 'Abdu'l-Bahá increased. He became so attracted that once he intimated to 'Abdu'l-Bahá that every time he stood up to pray, the majestic figure of Bahá'u'lláh appeared before him. 'Abdu'l-Bahá always showered his favours upon the Muftí, as indeed on other prominent people in the land. It is true to say that a time came when the Government of 'Akká used to revolve around the person of 'Abdu'l-Bahá. Every one of the

* In the East it is considered disrespectful to walk in front of an eminent person when accompanying him.

officials was longing to receive His blessings and favours. And because of His qualities and prestige the condition of the believers changed from abasement into honour.

Another person from 'Akká who became a believer was 'Uthmán Effendi. When the exiles were residing in the barracks, he had a grocery shop in town. He used to supply Bahá'u'lláh's daily provisions and was paid on a monthly basis. He was attracted to the Cause by the good deeds and honest dealings of the believers. He embraced the Faith and attained the presence of Bahá'u'lláh who promised him that he would become a wealthy and influential man. Soon 'Uthmán Effendi acquired considerable wealth. He owned half the village of Kasra which is one of the Druze villages. He also became a man of considerable influence well respected in government circles in 'Akká.[4]

4

Trustees of Bahá'u'lláh

Among all those who attained the presence of Bahá'u'lláh while He was in the barracks, the first two were Ḥájí Sháh-Muḥammad-i-Manshádí, entitled Amínu'l-Bayán (Trusted of the Bayán), and Ḥájí Abu'l-Ḥasan-i-Ardikání, entitled Amín-i-Iláhí (Trusted of God). The former was the first trustee* of Bahá'u'lláh, and the latter was appointed to the same position after the death of Hájí Sháh-Muḥammad in 1298 AH (AD 1881). Both men were from the province of Yazd.

In the early days of the Faith Ḥájí Sháh-Muḥammad embraced the Cause and became an ardent believer. He first attained the presence of Bahá'u'lláh in Baghdád. As a result of this he became a new creation on fire with the love of Bahá'u'lláh, a love that sustained him throughout his life and enabled him to render notable services to His Cause.

He owned some farm land in his native village of Manshád, but it did not earn him enough to live on, so he engaged in cattle dealing. He used to buy cattle in the province of Fárs and sell them in Yazd. But after embracing the Faith he gave up this work. He gave a portion of his estate to each of his four daughters, sold the rest, and faithful to the specific injunction of the Báb† to his followers to offer priceless gifts in their possession to 'Him Whom God shall make manifest', he

* One who acted on behalf of Bahá'u'lláh on matters related to *Huqúq'u'lláh* (the Right of God), which is prescribed in the *Kitáb-i-Aqdas*. It is one of the ordinances of Bahá'u'lláh not yet implemented in the West and involves those whose possessions reach a certain value. For more information see *Synopsis*, p.60.

† Bahá'u'lláh abrogated this injunction and absolved the believers from the obligation.

presented the proceeds of the sale to Bahá'u'lláh whom he had recognized as 'Him Whom God shall make manifest'.*

This action, prompted by the purity of his heart and the intensity of his devotion for the Faith, evoked the good pleasure of Bahá'u'lláh, who, while accepting the gift, handed it back to him, conferred upon him the title 'Amín' (Trusted One), and appointed him as His Trustee. In this way, it was made possible for the believers to fulfil their spiritual obligation of Huqúq'u'lláh through him.

Ḥájí S͟háh-Muḥammad used to travel frequently from Persia to attain the presence of Bahá'u'lláh and receive His instructions. He would then set out to carry them out on his return.

As the years went by he discovered in Ḥájí Abu'l-Ḥasan-i-Ardikání (Amín-i-Iláhí) a zealous and devoted co-worker. So, as he became older, he took Ḥájí Abu'l-Haṣan with him on his journeys as an assistant.

It was soon after Bahá'u'lláh's arrival in the Most Great Prison, around the same time that Nabíl-i-A'ẓam was denied admittance to 'Akká by the authorities, that Ḥájí S͟háh-Muḥammad, accompanied by Ḥájí Abu'l-Ḥasan, entered the city. The two had bought a few camels on the way and disguised themselves as Arabs seeking to sell their merchandise which was carried on the camels. This was a common scene in those days. They were not suspected of being followers of Bahá'u'lláh and were admitted.

They succeeded in sending a message to Bahá'u'lláh informing Him of their arrival and expressing their eagerness to attain His presence. Bahá'u'lláh allowed them to see Him in the public bath,† but they were advised to show no sign of

* For more information about 'Him Whom God shall make manifest' see vol. 1, ch. 18.

† As there were no baths in houses in those days, practically everyone had to go to a public bath. These were similar to what is known in the west as Turkish baths—warm with a steamy atmosphere. People would be partly-clad in a cotton towel, as nudity was considered immoral. People often spent hours washing and relaxing in public baths. Certain days of

recognition. On the appointed day the two men entered the public bath. But no sooner did Ḥájí Abu'l-Ḥasan behold the majestic person of Bahá'u'lláh than he was seized by such emotion that his body shook, and he stumbled and fell to the ground. The floor being made of stones, he injured his head very badly and had to be carried out with blood pouring on his face and body.

The two Amíns remained in 'Akká for some time. Ḥájí Sháh-Muḥammad was there when Áqá Buzurg, entitled Badí',* came to 'Akká and as we shall see later, the two met on Mount Carmel as directed by Bahá'u'lláh.

Ḥájí Sháh-Muḥammad rendered notable services to the Faith as the Trustee of Bahá'u'lláh. One of the major missions with which Bahá'u'lláh entrusted him was the transfer of the casket containing the remains of the Báb when its whereabouts in Persia, for several years unknown to the mass of the believers, became public knowledge. The dangers in such a situation were apparent, for the enemies of the Faith, once informed of the casket's location, could have attacked and destroyed it. This transfer of the remains of the Báb from place to place in Persia, covering a period of no less than fifty lunar years, and finally laying them to rest on Mount Carmel is an eventful and moving story. †

In the year AH 1298 (AD 1881) Ḥájí Sháh-Muḥammad was caught up in a massacre by the Kurds of the people of Míyánduáb and fatally wounded. His assistant Ḥájí Abu'l-Ḥasan, who was accompanying him as usual, was shot in the leg but managed to escape. It was after this event that Bahá'u'lláh appointed Ḥájí Abu'l-Ḥasan as His Trustee, and conferred on him the title 'Amín' (Trusted One), in place of Ḥájí Sháh-Muḥammad, Amínu'l-Bayán.

---

the week were allocated to men and certain days to women. The gathering of people in one place created a social atmosphere, and it was possible to meet one's friends and acquaintances there.

* see pp. 182–3 below.

† see Appendix I.

Of Ḥájí Sháh-Muḥammad we have the following eulogy from the pen of 'Abdu'l-Bahá:

> Amín, that is, Sháh-Muḥammad, was honoured with the title of the Trusted One, and bounties were showered upon him. Full of eagerness and love, taking with him Tablets from Bahá'u'lláh, he hastened back to Persia, where, at all times worthy of trust, he laboured for the Cause. His services were outstanding, and he was a consolation to the believers' hearts. There was none to compare with him for energy, enthusiasm and zeal, and no man's services could equal his. He was a haven amidst the people, known everywhere for devotion to the Holy Threshold, widely acclaimed by the friends.[1]

We have already stated that Ḥájí Sháh-Muḥammad and Ḥájí Abu'l-Ḥasan were the first believers to succeed in entering the city of 'Akká and attain the presence of Bahá'u'lláh in the public bath in the early days of His confinement in the Most Great Prison. Ḥájí Abu'l-Ḥasan—or Ḥájí Amín, as he generally became known—is one of the Apostles of Bahá'u'lláh whose life of self-sacrifice and utter dedication to the Cause has left a shining example for posterity to follow. In his youth he was a staunch Muslim. His parents arranged his marriage to the daughter of a merchant in his native town of Ardikán, Yazd. The merchant, who had six sons and one daughter, insisted that Ḥájí Amín, instead of living in the house of his father as was the custom, should live in the bride's home so that she would not live away from her parents. Ḥájí Amín's parents agreed to this request and he took up residence in the home of his father-in-law.

As a result of living in that house, Ḥájí Amín soon discovered that his brothers-in-law were all Bábís. His wife, like himself, was a devoted Muslim and was unaware of her brothers' faith. After lengthy discussions at gatherings of the Bábís, Ḥájí Amín became aware of the truth of the Cause of the Báb and embraced His Faith. He then taught his wife who also became a believer.

Some time later he recognized the station of Bahá'u'lláh and this brought about a mighty transformation in his life, a life totally and completely dedicated to Bahá'u'lláh. So thorough was this transformation of spirit that it is very hard, if not impossible, to attempt to fathom the depth of his dedication to his Lord, or describe in words an adequate appreciation of his outstanding and selfless services to the Cause he loved so much.

No doubt his first attaining the presence of Bahá'u'lláh in the public bath and in such dramatic circumstances as described earlier must have left an abiding impression on his soul and released the necessary forces for the making of one of the greatest spiritual giants of this Faith. His devotion to Bahá'u'lláh knew no bounds and because of this he was truly detached from this world. The flame of love for Bahá'u'lláh that burnt so brightly in his heart illumined the souls of the believers and burnt away the veils of blindness from the faces of the enemies.

He travelled extensively throughout Persia, went to the homes of almost every Bahá'í and poured out so much love and encouragement upon them that they all cherished his companionship. In their homes he was warmly accepted as a true father or brother, one who genuinely cared for the wellbeing and spiritual development of each. Knowing that he was an intimate and loving friend of everyone, parents (who in those days were in the habit of arranging marriages) often turned to him to suggest suitable partners for their sons and daughters.

Detachment from worldly things and utter self-sacrifice in the service of Bahá'u'lláh were among Ḥájí Amín's greatest qualities. Ever since he arose to serve the Cause as the assistant and confidant of Ḥájí Sh̲áh-Muḥammad, and later as the Trustee himself, Ḥájí Amín gave everything he had to the Cause. He kept not a penny for himself; he also made every possible effort to convey to the believers, by word and by deed, that man's most meritorious achievement in life is to offer up everything he has—his time, his labours, his substance and even his life—in the path of God. The Holy Writings fully confirm that there can be no loftier concept of life than this.

God has created two opposing forces within man, the animal and the spiritual. The animal nature inclines him to the material world; self and passion and attachment to earthly things are the characteristics of the animal nature. To subdue these powerful forces, the individual has to develop and strengthen his spiritual qualities so that they can dominate his animal inclinations. Within the human being there is a constant battle between these two forces. If it is left to nature, it is inevitable that the material side will dominate.

This is because the animal characteristics are part of his nature and without any effort on his part will drive him towards the material world. When this happens, man may behave in a manner even worse than an animal.

But the development of spiritual qualities is not controlled by nature. Although the soul aspires to spiritual things, the acquiring of spiritual qualities depends upon effort. It is in this domain that man has been given free will. This is very similar to a bird which in flight must use its wings to counteract the force of gravity. If it fails to do this, it will be pulled down instantly by this force.

The subduing of the animal nature through the ascendancy of the spiritual powers latent within man is the essence of detachment spoken of by Bahá'u'lláh in many of His Tablets. We have already discussed this theme in previous volumes and explained that by detachment is not meant poverty or the living of the life of a mendicant or an ascetic. To become careless of one's personal interests or the affairs of the world is contrary to the teachings of Bahá'u'lláh. Indeed, one may possess the things of this world and its riches and yet remain detached.*

To the extent that man can dominate his lower nature will he

* For further information on this point see vols. 1 and 2, 'Detachment'.

become detached from this world. Not only has he to exert himself to acquire spiritual qualities, but also in subduing his self with all its manifold aspects, he must be prepared to go through pain and suffering and tests. This is only natural, for there is always a reaction when a force is suppressed. Man's material inclinations, when curbed by the dictates of his spiritual being, will undergo some form of deprivation and sacrifice. For instance, one may sacrifice his comfort and material means in order to help the poor and the needy. In so doing, one is rewarded spiritually, but has to give up something of material value instead.

This sacrifice, if carried out in the path of God and for His sake, is most meritorious. It enables the soul to become detached from the material world, and thus brings it closer to God. This is one of the fruits of sacrifice.

It was the realization of this important principle which led Ḥájí Amín to offer up everything he had to the Cause of God. Through the influence of the Word of God revealed by Bahá'u'lláh and the example set by Ḥájí Amín, the believers willingly poured out their substance for the promotion of the Cause. Being the Trustee of Bahá'u'lláh, he was the recipient of the friends' contributions. Although he exhorted the friends generally to sacrifice, he never solicited their giving to the funds, for such soliciting is forbidden in the Faith.

To give to the Bahá'í Fund is an act of devotion to God. It is voluntary and motivated by the desire on the part of the individual to sacrifice something of this material world and spend it in the path of God.

Man is born naked and when dead he is also naked. He brings nothing with him to this world, and when he departs he cannot take anything physical with him to the next. But whatever he has given to the Cause of God while on this earth, his time, his labours, his resources, as well as his services to his fellow human beings, these he can take with him to the spiritual realms. This is one way of transforming something which belongs to the world of matter into the spiritual worlds of God.

The motive for contribution by the believers to the Ḥuqúq'u'lláh or the Bahá'í Funds, whether in the days of Bahá'u'lláh or in any other time, has been and always will be their love for Bahá'u'lláh and His Cause. It is the love of the individual for Him that endows the offering, no matter how small, with a celestial potency through which the Cause of God can be propelled forward. This is why the privilege of giving to the Bahá'í Fund is exclusively vouchsafed to the believers. For the promotion of the Cause of God, whether through teaching or contributing to the Bahá'í Funds, is dependent upon devotion to Bahá'u'lláh and the performance of stainless deeds by the believers. These two factors bring victory to the Cause.

During the days of Bahá'u'lláh, the majority of the believers in Persia were poor, and some needy. But when Ḥájí Amín visited them, they had set aside through sacrifice small sums of money and were able to offer them for the Cause of God. It must be made clear that under Bahá'u'lláh's supervision the funds were spent for the promotion of the Cause, and very little, if any, for His own expenses or those of His companions. The history of the life of Bahá'u'lláh bears ample testimony to this fact. For during the forty years of His ministry He lived for the most part in the utmost poverty. There were days when a mere loaf of bread was not available to Him, and the garments He wore were the only clothes He had. The last few years of His earthly life, although relatively more comfortable, were nevertheless greatly influenced by the austerity that had characterized His life since the days of the Síyáh-Chál in Ṭihrán, when all His possessions had been confiscated and He had been deprived of the means to support Himself and His Family.*

Desire for wealth is non-existent in the person of the Manifestation of God. He abides in a realm which is independent of all creation. And he is detached from all earthly things. Bahá'u'lláh has stated in many of His Tablets that this

* see vol. 1, p. 11.

mortal world is only a handful of dust and as utter nothingness in His sight. For example, in His second Tablet to Napoleon III, Bahá'u'lláh admonishes the monarch for his attachment to this world and states how insignificant this world is in His estimation. These are His words, uttered with authority and might:

> He, for Whose sake the world was called into being, hath been imprisoned in the most desolate of cities ('Akká), by reason of that which the hands of the wayward have wrought. From the horizon of His prison-city He summoneth mankind unto the Dayspring of God, the Exalted, the Great. Exultest thou over the treasures thou dost possess, knowing they shall perish? Rejoicest thou in that thou rulest a span of earth, when the whole world, in the estimation of the people of Bahá, is worth as much as the black in the eye of a dead ant? Abandon it unto such as have set their affections upon it, and turn thou unto Him Who is the Desire of the world.[2]

And in His Will and Testament, the *Kitáb-i-'Ahd*, He has left us these exalted words:

> Although the Realm of Glory hath none of the vanities of the world, yet within the treasury of trust and resignation we have bequeathed to Our heirs an excellent and priceless heritage. Earthly treasures We have not bequeathed, nor have We added such cares as they entail. By God! In earthly riches fear is hidden and peril is concealed. Consider ye and call to mind that which the All-Merciful hath revealed in the Qur'án: 'Woe betide every slanderer and defamer, him that layeth up riches and counteth them.' Fleeting are the riches of the world; all that perisheth and changeth is not, and hath never been, worthy of attention, except to a recognized measure.[3]

It must be pointed out that the same attitude of detachment from earthly things so permeated the souls of 'Abdu'l-Bahá and Shoghi Effendi, the two successive Centres of the Cause of

Bahá'u'lláh, that it was against their nature to turn their affection to the things of this world. They both lived austere lives and followed the example of Bahá'u'lláh. Although they received large contributions from the friends, they authorized their spending strictly for the promotion of the Cause of God and did not have the slightest inclination to spend the funds for their own personal ends. Indeed, similar to Bahá'u'lláh, neither of them had any personal assets, whether monetary or of any other type.

When 'Abdu'l-Bahá travelled to the West to spread the Cause of Bahá'u'lláh and diffuse the divine fragrances in Europe and America, He had to use some of the funds which the Persian friends had contributed to Ḥájí Amín as Huqúq'u'lláh. But He observed such care in spending the absolute minimum for Himself that His companions sometimes felt concerned about the lack of comfort which often resulted.

The renowned chronicler of 'Abdu'l-Bahá's journeys to the West, Mírzá Maḥmúd-i-Zarqání, His devoted secretary and companion, has recorded in his diaries (Badáyi'u'l-Á<u>th</u>ár) that when 'Abdu'l-Bahá and His party were travelling across the United States, the train journey proved to be tiring—especially for 'Abdu'l-Bahá who was nearly seventy years of age. Yet in spite of this, He frequently declined to pay the extra small sum of money for sleeping accommodation on the train. Instead He would sit up all night on the hard wooden seats and close His eyes to rest. But, as demonstrated on that journey, He opened His purse and generously placed coins of silver and gold in the palms of the poor and needy wherever He found them. How different are the ways of God and man!

It was during those same epoch-making journeys that 'Abdu'l-Bahá demonstrated a magnanimity and detachment characteristic of God's chosen ones by declining with graciousness all offers of funds and gifts from friends and strangers.

In his famous diaries Mírzá Maḥmúd recounts a story of

'Abdu'l-Bahá when He was in New York shortly before His departure from the United States:

> . . . that day some of the friends presented 'Abdu'l-Bahá with some funds, but He did not take them in spite of their persistently begging Him to accept them. He said: 'Offer it up to the poor on my behalf. It would be as if I have personally given to them. But for me the best gift is the unity between the loved ones of God, their service to the Cause, the diffusion of divine fragrances and their carrying out the teachings and exhortations of the Blessed Beauty.'
>
> On such occasions the believers became very sad, because their offerings were not accepted by their Beloved. In spite of this the believers in New York, knowing that these were the last few days of His stay in the United States, gathered some presents for the members of the Holy Family* . . . some of the friends had vowed together that they would persist in their request for acceptance of the gifts, that they would cling to the hem of his garment and not leave His presence until He accepted their offerings. They presented their gifts and earnestly pleaded with Him to take them. He then spoke to them in these words:
>
> 'I am very grateful for all your services. Truly you have served me, offered hospitality, rendered your services day and night and persevered in the diffusion of divine fragrances. I shall never forget your devoted services, because you had no other motive but to attain the good pleasure of God, and had desired no station other than entry into His Kingdom. Now you have brought some gifts for my family. These gifts are very praiseworthy, but more exquisite than these are the gifts of the love of God which may be preserved within the treasure-house of the hearts. The former gifts are transitory, but the latter are eternal. These gifts are to be kept in boxes and upon the shelves and will eventually perish, but the other will remain eternally in all the worlds of God treasured within the heart. Therefore I

* Including the wife of 'Abdu'l-Bahá, His sister, daughters and other female members of His household.

carry with me your love to them [i.e. The Holy Family] which is the greatest gift of all. In our house there is no room for diamond rings or other jewellery. That house is devoid of the vanities of this world.

'Now, I accept these gifts, but I entrust them to you to sell them and send the proceeds to Chicago for the construction of the Mas͟hriqu'l-Ad͟hkár [Bahá'í House of Worship].'

The friends, with tearful eyes, were disappointed. 'Abdu'l-Bahá said: 'I want to take with me a gift from you which may remain till eternity, the jewels which belong to the treasure-house of the heart.'

In spite of much persistence and shedding of tears the beloved Master did not accept the gifts and asked the friends to spend them for the Mas͟hriqu'l-Ad͟hkár in Chicago.[4]

Returning to the story of Ḥájí Amín, he lived a long life and was Trustee of the Huqúq'u'lláh during the ministries of Bahá'u'lláh and 'Abdu'l-Bahá and during part of the ministry of Shoghi Effendi. During his long and turbulent life he was a source of inspiration and loving guidance for all the believers. He often visited their homes and urged them to become detached from the things of the world and to follow the path of modesty in all aspects of life. He disliked extravagance, as it would lessen the ability of the believers to contribute all they could to the Cause of God. So much was he against extravagance that whenever the friends invited him to dinner, they knew that Ḥájí Amín would be most unhappy if they entertained him lavishly with various dishes at the table. He insisted that there be only one dish and that it consist of the simplest food. He often urged the host to add some extra water to the pot for his share of the food, and this recipe of adding extra water is widely known among the Persian believers as 'The soup of Ḥájí Amín'!

There are many heartwarming stories about the way he conducted his life and the sacrifices he made in order to serve His Lord. These stories, ranging from trifling anecdotes to highly interesting and instructive comments made by him are entertaining and popular, but must be left out here, because to appreciate them the reader needs to be familiar with the customs and way of life at that time in the Middle East.

Ḥájí Amín suffered many persecutions in his long life of service. Among them was his imprisonment first in Ṭihrán and then in Qazvín in the year AH 1308 (AD 1891) along with Mullá 'Alí-Akbar-i-Shahmírzádí, known as Ḥájí Ákhúnd, one of the Hands of the Cause of God appointed by Bahá'u'lláh. These two heroes of God were imprisoned by the orders of Náṣiri'd-Dín Sháh and his son Kámrán Mírzá, the Governor of Ṭihrán. Their imprisonment in Qazvín lasted about eighteen months, after which Ḥájí Ákhúnd was released but Ḥájí Amín was transferred to a prison in Ṭihrán where he remained for a further year. During this period their feet were kept in stocks and their necks placed in chains. When in the prison of Qazvín, a photographer was specially sent to take their photograph for the monarch to see. This photograph, showing the two in chains sitting with absolute resignation and calm, is widely in circulation among the believers. It was placed by 'Abdu'l-Bahá in the hallway of His house opposite His room. He gazed upon it many times and rejoiced in His heart at beholding the faces of the two who were chained and fettered in the path of Bahá'u'lláh and were the embodiment of steadfastness and faith among the believers.

It was soon after the imprisonment of these two souls in Qazvín that Bahá'u'lláh in the opening paragraph of the *Lawḥ-i-Dunyá** (Tablet of the World) referred to the prison of Qazvín as 'mighty prison' and revealed these exalted words in their honour:

> Praise and thanksgiving beseem the Lord of manifest dominion Who hath adorned this mighty prison with the presence of their honours 'Alí Akbar and Amín, and hath illumined it with the light of certitude, constancy and

* This Tablet was revealed in honour of Mírzá Áqáy-i-Afnán, entitled Núr'u'd-Dín. We shall refer to him and to the Tablet in the next volume.

assurance. The glory of God and the glory of all that are in the heavens and on the earth be upon them.

Light and glory, greeting and praise be upon the Hands of His Cause, through whom the light of fortitude hath shone forth and the truth hath been established that the authority to choose rests with God, the Powerful, the Mighty, the Unconstrained, through whom the ocean of bounty hath surged and the fragrance of the gracious favours of God, the Lord of mankind, hath been diffused. We beseech Him—Exalted is he—to shield them through the power of His hosts, to protect them through the potency of His dominion and to aid them through His indomitable strength which prevaileth over all created things. Sovereignty is God's, the Creator of the heavens and the Lord of the Kingdom of Names.[5]

It is interesting to note that of the two mentioned in the Tablet, only Mullá 'Alí-Akbar had been nominated a Hand of the Cause of God by Bahá'u'lláh. However, Shoghi Effendi, Guardian of the Faith, conferred the same rank upon Ḥájí Amín posthumously. Ḥájí Amín passed away in Ṭihrán in 1928, leaving behind an imperishable memory among the believers. Upon his death Shoghi Effendi appointed Ḥájí Ghulám-Riḍá (entitled Amín-i-Amín), who for several years had been Ḥájí Amín's assistant, to succeed him as Trustee of the Huqúq'u'lláh.

In appreciation of Ḥájí Amín's services, 'Abdu'l-Bahá named one of the doors of the Shrine of the Báb after him.

5

Lawḥ-i-Fu'ád

Fu'ád Pás͟há, Foreign Minister of the Ottoman Empire, had been a close collaborator of the Grand Vizír 'Álí Pás͟há in bringing about the exile of Bahá'u'lláh to 'Akká and His imprisonment there. In 1869 Fu'ád Pás͟há was dismissed from his post and subsequently died in France, at Nice. We have already seen how and in what terms Bahá'u'lláh had addressed the Grand Vizír in the *Súriy-i-Ra'ís* and the *Lawḥ-i-Ra'ís*. Now He revealed the *Lawḥ-i-Fu'ád*, another Tablet of great significance, in which He severely rebukes Fu'ád Pás͟há, declares that God had taken his life as a punishment, and describes in strong terms the agony of his soul in facing the wrath of God in the next life for having inflicted such sufferings upon His Supreme Manifestation. In this Tablet Bahá'u'lláh foreshadows the downfall of 'Álí Pás͟há and the Sulṭán himself in these prophetic words:

> Soon will We dismiss the one* who was like unto him, and will lay hold on their Chief † who ruleth the land, and I, verily, am the Almighty, the All-Compelling.[1]

It did not take long after the revelation of this Tablet until 'Álí Pás͟há was disgracefully dismissed from his post and died in AD 1871. At the same time a process of opposition to the Sulṭán was set in motion in Turkey which culminated in AD 1876 in his dethronement and imprisonment by revolutionaries; a few days later he was killed.

* 'Álí Pás͟há.

† Sulṭán 'Abdu'l-'Azíz.

As we shall see, the *Lawḥ-i-Fu'ád* was to play an important role in the conversion to the Faith of its foremost scholar, Mírzá Abu'l-Faḍl.

Shaykh Káẓim-i-Samandar

The *Lawḥ-i-Fu'ád* was addressed to Shaykh Káẓim-i-Samandar, a native of Qazvín. This great man was one of the Apostles of Bahá'u'lláh and has been described by Shoghi Effendi as a flame of the love of God. His grandfather had met the Báb in Karbilá before His declaration, had witnessed His extraordinary powers of invocation at the time of prayer and become deeply enchanted with the grandeur and majesty of His person. His father Shaykh Muḥammad, entitled Nabíl,* was one of the devoted followers of the Báb and attained His presence in the Fortresses of Máhkú and Chihríq. Later he went to Baghdád and attained the presence of Bahá'u'lláh. He suffered persecution and his home in Qazvín was the centre of the activities of the early Bábís.

Shaykh Káẓim-i-Samandar, born a few months before the Declaration of the Báb, grew up in such a home and from his earliest days associated with the early disciples of the Báb, among them some of the Letters of the Living and the uncle of the Báb. Even in childhood Shaykh Káẓim showed a great enthusiasm for Bábí affairs and when he grew up he was a knowledgeable and devoted believer. Later he recognized the station of Bahá'u'lláh and became one of His outstanding followers, succeeding in diffusing the light of His Faith throughout Persia in general and in Qazvín in particular.

When the news of the Declaration of Bahá'u'lláh and the claims of Mírzá Yaḥyá† reached him, he made an exhaustive study of the Writings of the Báb. His conclusions that Bahá'u'lláh alone was the Promised One of the Bayán were

* Not to be confused with Mullá Muḥammad-i-Zarandí, Nabíl-i-A'ẓam or Mullá Muḥammad-i-Qá'iní, Nabíl-i-Akbar.

† see vols 1 and 2.

clear and unmistakable. In AH 1283 (AD 1866–67) he wrote a treatise in Arabic denouncing Mírzá Yaḥyá's rebellion, refuting his arguments and demonstrating his claims to be utterly false. Bahá'u'lláh refers to this treatise in the *Lawḥ-i-Siráj* * and states that God had inspired Shaykh Káẓim in writing it. It is reported that Bahá'u'lláh conferred the title of Samandar† upon Shaykh Káẓim after the writing of this challenging treatise.

In His Tablets Bahá'u'lláh often commends those who refute the arguments of the enemies of the Faith. In the Tablet of Salmán‡ He exhorts His followers in these words:

> Warn, O Salmán, the beloved of the one true God, not to view with too critical an eye the sayings and writings of men. Let them rather approach such sayings and writings in a spirit of open-mindedness and loving sympathy. Those men, however, who, in this Day, have been led to assail, in their inflammatory writings, the tenets of the Cause of God, are to be treated differently. It is incumbent upon all men, each according to his ability, to refute the arguments of those that have attacked the Faith of God. Thus hath it been decreed by Him Who is the All-Powerful, the Almighty. He that wisheth to promote the Cause of the one true God, let him promote it through his pen and tongue, rather than have recourse to sword or violence. We have, on a previous occasion, revealed this injunction, and We now confirm it, if ye be of them that comprehend. By the righteousness of Him Who, in this Day, crieth within the inmost heart of all created things: 'God, there is none other God besides Me!' If any man were to arise to defend, in his writings, the Cause of God against its assailants, such a man, however inconsiderable his share, shall be so honoured in the world to come that the Concourse on high would envy his glory. No pen can depict the loftiness of his station, neither can any tongue describe its splendour. For whosoever standeth

* see vol. 2, p. 262.

† A legendary bird supposed to live in fire.

‡ see vol. 2, ch. 13.

> firm and steadfast in this holy, this glorious, and exalted Revelation, such power shall be given him as to enable him to face and withstand all that is in heaven and earth. Of this God is Himself a witness.[2]

Shaykh Káẓim-i-Samandar was an outstanding teacher of the Faith. Many early believers of Qazvín in particular owe their allegiance to the Cause to his indefatigable labours in propagating the Message of Bahá'u'lláh. His enthusiasm and faith, his zeal and devotion, deeply affected the hearts of his listeners and made them attentive to the Call of God in this age. He also played an important part in defending the Cause of God from the misrepresentations of the followers of Mírzá Yaḥyá and those who at a later date during the ministry of 'Abdu'l-Bahá were misled by Mírzá Muḥammad-'Alí,* the Arch-Breaker of the Covenant of Bahá'u'lláh. The believers in Qazvín, who from the early days of the Faith were affected by the spirit of division, of controversy and Covenant-breaking, were greatly helped by the presence of Shaykh Káẓim in their midst. Mainly through his steadfastness and perseverance, the community was transformed.

Shaykh Káẓim paid special attention to the education and upbringing of his children. A certain Mullá 'Alí entitled 'Mu'allim' (teacher) whom he had converted to the Faith and who was a man of learning, took up residence in the house and volunteered the work of educating the children.† This he did after reading Bahá'u'lláh's exhortation in the *Kitáb-i-Aqdas*:

> Unto every father hath been enjoined the instruction of his son and daughter in the art of reading and writing and in all that hath been laid down in the Holy Tablet. He that putteth away that which is commanded unto him, the Trustees are then to take from him that which is required for their instruction, if he be wealthy, and if not the matter devolveth

* see vols. 1 and 2.

† In those days people of means often employed a tutor at home for their children's education.

> upon the House of Justice. Verily, have We made it a shelter for the poor and needy. He that bringeth up his son or the son of another, it is as though he hath brought up a son of Mine; upon him rest My Glory, My loving kindness, My Mercy, that have compassed the world.[3]

It was the last sentence which inspired Mullá 'Alí to offer his services as a teacher to Shaykh Káẓim's numerous children. He carried on this work for about thirty-six years. In one of His Tablets,[4] Bahá'u'lláh commends Mullá 'Alí for implementing one of His exhortations and refers to him as the first teacher who has attained the good pleasure of God by carrying out what has been revealed in the *Kitáb-i-Aqdas*. He confers upon him His blessings, declares that the mere mention of him in that Tablet is the greatest reward for his soul, assures him that his name will be immortalized in all the schools throughout the world and intimates that he will send him a gift as a token of appreciation for his work. Bahá'u'lláh later instructed His Trustee, Ḥájí Amín, to send Mullá 'Alí the gift of an 'abá (cloak) on His behalf and added a note that the 'abá should be of very good quality.

Shaykh Káẓim-i-Samandar went twice on pilgrimage to attain the presence of Bahá'u'lláh in 'Akká. Among those who accompanied him on his second pilgrimage in AH 1308 (AD 1891) were Mullá 'Alí 'the teacher', and the Shaykh's son Mírzá Ṭarázu'lláh-i-Samandarí who served the Faith as an eminent Bahá'í teacher for many years. Shoghi Effendi was later to confer upon the latter the rank of Hand of the Cause of God.

The Conversion of Mírzá Abu'l-Faḍl

The dire prophecies in the *Lawḥ-i-Fu'ád*, foreshadowing in clear terms the downfall of the Sulṭán and of 'Álí Páshá, were often the subject of speculation and discussion among the believers of those days. A great many non-Bahá'ís who attended Bahá'í gatherings heard the words of Bahá'u'lláh in this and similar Tablets. They noted His warnings with awe and wonder and some even made their acceptance of the Faith conditional upon their fulfilment. Notable among them was the renowned Mírzá Abu'l-Faḍl, a scholar of great eminence who, after having investigated the Faith, was looking for a conclusive proof to enable him to recognize its truth. He waited for the fulfilment of these prophecies. And when he embraced the Faith he became one of its greatest luminaries and one who defended the Faith from its adversaries with exemplary skill and devotion.

Since Mírzá Abu'l-Faḍl is one of the greatest scholars of the Faith, an apologist of the highest calibre and whose contributions to the literature of the Faith are immense, it is befitting to devote a few pages in this book to his cherished memory.

The story of his encounters with the believers after having come in contact with the Faith is interesting indeed. In the year AH 1293 (AD 1876) when he was at the height of his career as the head of a theological college in Ṭihrán, he was approached by one of his students who asked him to help him reply to some of the arguments put forward by a few Bahá'ís with whom he was in contact. This man used to bring the questions to Mírzá Abu'l-Faḍl and take back his comments to the Bahá'ís.

There was a devoted believer at the time by the name of 'Abdu'l-Karím-i-Máhút Furúsh (draper) who had a shop in the bazaar; his home was a place for the meetings of the Bahá'ís and those who were investigating the Faith. These meetings often lasted till the early hours of the morning. Independently of his student who often brought up the subject of the Bahá'í Faith, Mírzá Abu'l-Faḍl somehow became acquainted with 'Abdu'l-Karím and occasionally used to visit him in his shop. For some time, however, Mírzá Abu'l-Faḍl did not discover that 'Abdu'l-Karím was a Bahá'í. Then a small incident happened which provoked him to encounter a Bahá'í directly.

One Friday afternoon, Mírzá Abu'l-Faḍl, in company with a few mullás, left the city to visit a certain shrine in the countryside in the vicinity of the capital. They were all riding on donkeys. It was customary in those days for the people to leave the city for nearby villages on Fridays (which is a public holiday in Islámic countries) for pleasure as well as visiting holy places.

It so happened that on the way out one of the donkeys lost a shoe, so the party called at the nearest blacksmith for help. Noticing the long beard and large turban of Mírzá Abu'l-Faḍl—indications of his vast knowledge—the blacksmith Ustád Ḥusayn-i-Na'l-Band (shoeing smith), who was illiterate, was tempted to enter into conversation with the learned man. He said to Mírzá that since he had honoured him with his presence, it would be a great privilege for him if he could be allowed to ask a question which had perplexed his mind for some time. When permission was granted he said, 'Is it true that in the Traditions of Shí'ah Islám* it is stated that each drop of rain is accompanied by an angel from heaven? And that this angel brings down the rain to the ground?' 'This is true,' Mírzá Abu'l-Faḍl responded. After a pause, the blacksmith begged to be allowed to ask another question to which Mírzá gave his assent. 'Is it true', the blacksmith asked, 'that if there is a dog in a house no angel will ever visit that house?' Before thinking of the connection between the two questions, Mírzá Abu'l-Faḍl responded in the affirmative. 'In that case', commented the blacksmith, 'no rain should ever fall in a house where a dog is kept.' Mírzá Abu'l-Faḍl, the noted learned man of Islám, was now confounded by an illiterate blacksmith. His rage knew no bounds, and his companions noticed that he was filled with shame. They whispered to him, 'This blacksmith is a Bahá'í!'

* It must be pointed out that the majority of the so-called traditions of Shí'ah Islám are man-made and consist of trivial sayings. However, there are some authentic and weighty utterances by the Holy Imáms which are in conformity with the form and the spirit of the *Qur'án*. And there are certain criteria for assessing the authenticity of such traditions. Bahá'u'lláh, for instance, has quoted many authentic traditions in the *Kitáb-i-Íqán*.

This incident left a deep impression on Mírzá Abu'l-Faḍl. The blacksmith, on the other hand, reported the whole story to 'Abdu'l-Karím and suggested that because his pride had been hurt, Mírzá Abu'l-Faḍl would now welcome an encounter with a Bahá'í teacher in the hope of restoring his superiority. This assessment proved to be correct. For when 'Abdu'l-Karím invited Mírzá Abu'l-Faḍl to take part in a discussion with a certain Bahá'í friend, he accepted the invitation. It appears that even up to this point, Mírzá Abu'l-Faḍl had not realized that 'Abdu'l-Karím himself was a Bahá'í.

The meeting was arranged in the home of 'Abdu'l-Karím. But the Bahá'í teacher whom 'Abdu'l-Karím had invited was a man devoid of learning. He was not an educated man. But his heart was connected to the Source of all Knowledge. Every abstruse subject that Mírzá Abu'l-Faḍl brought up during the discussion and every objection he raised was dealt with in simple terms and in such a manner that he could not question the validity of the arguments put forward by the Bahá'í teacher.

It may seem strange that uneducated people may become the recipients of the knowledge of God. Indeed, one of the proofs of the power of God in this Revelation is that in addition to the many learned people who ranked foremost among the teachers of the Faith, there were those who did not have a proper education and in some cases were even illiterate, but who succeeded in guiding many souls to the Cause of God.

As has been stated in previous volumes,* the knowledge of God and His Manifestations, the power to discover the mysteries of life, to comprehend religious truth, and to understand the reality of man is not dependent upon academic education. This knowledge is bestowed upon the individual by God. And it is the heart of man which receives it and becomes the wellspring of enlightenment, power and understanding.

Bahá'u'lláh has clearly stated that the prerequisite for becoming the repository of such knowledge and understanding

* see vol. 1, pp. 43–4, 98–9, 172–3, 186; vol. 2, pp. 33–4.

is detachment from this world. In the opening paragraph of the *Kitáb-i-Íqán* He declares:

> No man shall attain the shores of the ocean of true understanding except he be detached from all that is in heaven and on earth. Sanctify your souls, O ye peoples of the world, that haply ye may attain that station which God hath destined for you and enter thus the tabernacle which, according to the dispensations of Providence, hath been raised in the firmament of the Bayán.
>
> The essence of these words is this: they that tread the path of faith, they that thirst for the wine of certitude, must cleanse themselves of all that is earthly—their ears from idle talk, their minds from vain imaginings, their hearts from worldly affections, their eyes from that which perisheth. They should put their trust in God, and, holding fast unto Him, follow in His way. Then will they be made worthy of the effulgent glories of the sun of divine knowledge and understanding, and become the recipients of a grace that is infinite and unseen, inasmuch as man can never hope to attain unto the knowledge of the All-Glorious, can never quaff from the stream of divine knowledge and wisdom, can never enter the abode of immortality, nor partake of the cup of divine nearness and favour, unless and until he ceases to regard the words and deeds of mortal man as a standard for the true understanding and recognition of God and His Prophets.[5]

True understanding is the act of perceiving the inner meaning and the significance of a truth. Detachment from this world, a theme which has been constantly repeated and its meaning explained in the Writings of Bahá'u'lláh, is the key to living a life in harmony with the laws of creation. As we have already stated in previous volumes,* detachment from the world does not mean mendicancy, asceticism, poverty or carelessness in worldly affairs. One form of attachment, perhaps the most formidable, is the love of oneself and of one's

* see vols. 1 and 2, 'Detachment'.

accomplishments. In the above passage, Bahá'u'lláh has emphatically closed the door to any alternative by which man may obtain the great gift of understanding, which is not the same thing as scholarly knowledge acquired through learning and study.

A great scholar, a man of learning, may not necessarily be able to understand or discover the inner realities of God's creation and His Revelation. He must become detached from this world, and the greatest attachment for such a man is his knowledge!* Indeed, as Bahá'u'lláh has often stated in His Writings, acquired knowledge may often become a veil for preventing the heart from receiving the light of divine guidance and the gift of true understanding. 'Abdu'l-Karím, who was not educated, and the other uneducated people who were primarily involved in teaching the Faith of Bahá'u'lláh to eminent men of learning such as Mírzá Abu'l-Faḍl, were endowed with the knowledge of God and possessed a great power of understanding. They had acquired these through their faith in Bahá'u'lláh and their detachment from their own ego and passion.

In his first interview with the believers, Mírzá Abu'l-Faḍl was surprised to find himself unable to cope with a Bahá'í who was not a learned man, and could not refute his arguments. However, he requested his host 'Abdu'l-Karím to arrange a meeting in which one of the learned Bahá'ís would take part, for he desired to have an encounter with a person of his own calibre so that he could establish once and for all his own superiority and demonstrate the falsity of the claims of the Báb and Bahá'u'lláh!

The meeting was arranged, but 'Abdu'l-Karím did not invite a learned Bahá'í as Mírzá Abu'l-Faḍl had requested. Although uneducated, 'Abdu'l-Karím in his great wisdom knew that a man who was so proud of his knowledge would be blind to the Message of God. He knew that what Mírzá Abu'l-Faḍl needed most was someone who could expose his real ignorance of true

* see vol. 2, pp. 39–43.

SHAYKH KÁẒIM-I-SAMANDAR

One of the Apostles of Bahá'u'lláh and a devoted teacher of the Cause

USTÁD ḤUSAYN-I-NA'L-BAND

The blacksmith who first encountered Mírzá Abu'l-Faḍl

MÍRZÁ ABU'L-FAḌL

Eminent Bahá'í scholar, Apostle of Bahá'u'lláh and foremost expounder of His Faith

MÁNIKCHÍ ṢÁḤIB

A Zoroastrian envoy who became an admirer of Bahá'u'lláh and received some Tablets from Him. Mírzá Abu'l-Faḍl acted as his secretary for some time and was his link with Bahá'u'lláh (see p. 269)

religion. No one would be better suited to carry out this than a simple believer devoid of academic knowledge but possessed of faith and spiritual understanding.

When Mírzá Abu'l-Faḍl arrived for this meeting he found himself again confronted with uneducated people. In the course of discussion he was utterly confounded by the simple yet brilliant proofs which were put forward in support of the Faith and in answer to his questions. He marvelled at these men who were devoid of learning and knowledge yet possessed such a marvellous understanding of the mysteries of the *Qur'án* and other Holy Books.

In the course of several meetings, discussions between Mírzá Abu'l-Faḍl and his unschooled Bahá'í teachers continued. As anticipated by his host, these discussions had a sobering effect on Mírzá Abu'l-Faḍl. Since his prime motive in coming to Bahá'í meetings was to disclose the absurdity of the claims of the Bahá'ís, he was remarkably humbled by his inability to refute the arguments presented by those few uneducated souls from among the believers, and his pride was badly hurt by the many humiliating defeats he encountered in the course of discussions with them. Later he met with learned Bahá'ís and conversed with them in numerous gatherings, always finding their arguments irrefutable. Once he entered into discussion with the renowned Mullá Muḥammad-i-Qá'iní (Nabíl-i-Akbar).* At the end of that meeting he is reported to have exclaimed in an astonished tone: 'By God! No one could ever be found capable of withstanding the force of argument of this great man of knowledge.'

In one of his writings, Mírzá Abu'l-Faḍl describes his early days of contact with the Faith in these words:

> In the year AH 1293 (AD 1876) when the writer of these pages [i.e. Mírzá Abu'l-Faḍl] was a resident of Ṭihrán and steadfast in the faith of Shí'ah Islám, through some incidents he established association with the people of Bahá. The

* see vol. 1, p. 91.

> prime object of his endeavours was to compel them to surrender and help stifle their growth. For nearly eight months he held many a debate with the learned of this Faith. At the end of this period he found that all his vain imaginings had been broken down and had vanished. He then began to tread the path of search after truth. He exerted all his efforts in investigating the proofs of this Faith, established close association in a spirit of brotherhood with the leaders of all religions, the Jewish, Zoroastrian, Christian, Sunní, Shí'ah and Azalí, made extensive enquiries from both friends and foes concerning the history of the Founder of this Faith, studied the Holy Books attentively, meditated on the words of gnostics and divines most carefully, and prayed in the dead of night and at dawn supplicating the Almighty in a state of utter helplessness and anguish to bestow upon him guidance and grant him a seeing eye—until at last, through the operation of the will of God, he acquired a penetrating insight into revealed religions, and his distressed heart was filled with calm and certitude.[6]

But before reaching the final stage of attaining certitude and embracing the Faith, Mírzá Abu'l-Faḍl went through a great deal of intellectual struggle. His mind was unable to reject the truth of the Cause but his heart was not touched by the light of faith and assurance. During this period of search he read most of the Writings of the Báb and Bahá'u'lláh that were available. The story of his reading the *Kitáb-i-Íqán* for the first time and his reactions are recorded in a previous volume.* That incident is not only highly entertaining: at the same time it reveals the purity of his motive.

When Mírzá Abu'l-Faḍl found himself utterly confounded by the proofs and arguments which his Bahá'í teachers had put forward, he entertained the idea that not until Bahá'u'lláh performed a miracle for him would his heart be satisfied. The Bahá'ís explained to him that miracles could not be regarded as a conclusive proof of the truth of the Messengers of God, for

* vol. 2, pp. 219–20.

they were not capable of being witnessed universally and at all times. They were only meaningful for the few who had seen them. Furthermore it was not for man to test God. But Mírzá Abu'l-Faḍl insisted. He wrote a few questions on a paper, placed it in an envelope, sealed it with his own seal and handed it to 'Abdu'l-Karím for safe keeping. He then placed a blank sheet of paper in another envelope and asked 'Abdu'l-Karím to forward it to Bahá'u'lláh. He stated that if his questions were answered he would entertain no doubt about the truth of the Cause.

'Abdu'l-Karím, accompanied by Mírzá Abu'l-Faḍl, took the blank letter and the sealed envelope to the home of Ḥájí Muḥammad Ismá'íl-i-Dhabíḥ* so that he could forward the letter to Bahá'u'lláh. Mírzá Abu'l-Faḍl later told the story to Ḥájí Mírzá Ḥaydar-'Alí, whose account is summarized in the following translation:

> When we arrived we learnt that the Ḥájí was not at home, but his wife, who knew 'Abdu'l-Karím . . . warmly welcomed us and insisted with such love and hospitality that we went inside . . . We entered a room in which there were books and a case containing Holy Tablets . . . She gave us permission to open the case if we wished and study the Holy Writings. As 'Abdu'l-Karím was unable to read, he asked me if I would read for him. Through courtesy which was characteristic of me I complied.
>
> There was a Tablet written on blue paper addressed to Sulṭán 'Abdu'l-'Azíz.† As I read it, I came upon the story of the 'Show of Sulṭán Salím'‡ and I was fascinated by it. I found the passages to be of the utmost eloquence, lucidity

* see vol. 2, pp. 411–13.

† Ḥájí Mírzá Ḥaydar-'Alí seems to have confused the issue of the Tablets. These were the *Lawḥ-i-Ra'ís* and the *Lawḥ-i-Fu'ád* addressed to 'Álí Páshá and Fu'ád Páshá respectively and not to the Sulṭán, although references are made to the Sulṭán in these Tablets.

‡ As a child, Bahá'u'lláh attended the wedding feast of one of his brothers in Ṭihrán. There He saw a puppet-show which he recounts in the *Lawḥ-i-Ra'ís*.

and sweetness. The more I read it, the more I wanted to read. I had never in all my life come across such wonderful utterances, which captivated my mind and attracted my heart. But I was thinking of everything in my mind except that these were the words of God!

Then I came to these exalted words: 'Soon will We dismiss the one who was like unto him, and will lay hand on their Chief* who ruleth the land, and I, verily, am the Almighty, the All-Compelling.'†

Upon reading this statement I was awe-struck, and plunged into a state of astonishment and wonder. For about half an hour I became speechless. Immersed in my thoughts, I wondered whether it was great magic or sorcery, and certainly it provided a grave test for me.

Eventually I was satisfied in my thoughts that we were entering the 'time of the end' and not until Godlessness spread would the Promised One come. I contended that Bahá'u'lláh had made these statements and prophecies in order to mislead ordinary people and keep a hold on His followers. Otherwise it would not be possible for a person who was a prisoner by the order of a King to address him in such strong language and denounce him in such wrathful terms, especially when He was single and alone, without a helper in a foreign land . . . These vain imaginings and satanic thoughts were flooding my mind and yet I praise God and thank Him for his loving grace that I was never inclined to dislike Bahá'u'lláh or be discourteous to Him.

. . . Anyhow, in order to rescue myself from 'Abdu'l-Karím, I said to him . . . 'To possess the power of life over created things is a miracle the like of which has not been manifested by the Prophets of past' . . . Therefore I took back the sealed envelope and my blank letter addressed to

* Sulṭán 'Abdu'l-'Azíz.

† This is a passage from the *Lawḥ-i-Fu'ád*, see p. 87. From what Ḥájí Mírzá Ḥaydar 'Alí narrates, one concludes that Mírzá Abu'l-Faḍl had first read the *Lawḥ-i-Ra'ís* (revealed in 'Akká) and then the *Lawḥ-i-Fu'ád*. It is reasonable to assume that he read the *Súriy-i-Ra'ís* as well, because the latter (which was addressed to 'Álí Páshá) was revealed in honour of Dhabíḥ in whose house Mírzá Abu'l-Faḍl was.

Bahá'u'lláh and tore them up and declared that for me the fulfilment of these prophecies would constitute the proof and a criterion for truth. I also got a pledge that no one would talk to me about the Faith any more until these prophecies were fulfilled.

I thought to myself that the incident of going to the house of the Ḥájí was not only an act of providence which relieved me of further discussion with the Bahá'ís, but also provided a way by which I would be able to guide these souls and rescue them from going the wrong way. But the believers did not altogether cut off their association with me. They came from time to time to see me and by their discourses . . . tried to rescue me from the fetters of vain imaginings. But I was like a spider. The more they cut the web of my idle fancies the more I continued to make it.

Five or six months passed by [from the day he read the above Tablets]. During this period I often thought of Bahá'u'lláh's prophecy concerning the Sulṭán. Until one day I was passing by the Masjid-i-Sháh (the Sháh Mosque) of Ṭihrán. My eyes fell upon Ḥájí Mírzáy-i-Afnán who was a respectable merchant and one of the illustrious believers of this Most Great Revelation. He was accompanied by Mírzá Ḥaydar-'Alíy-i-Ardistání,* a survivor of the Fort of Shaykh Ṭabarsí.†

These two men were standing in the street and talking together. As I was trying to shun the Bahá'ís and steer clear of them, I pulled my 'abá over my head‡ and began to cross the road away from these two men. But they saw me and called my name, and I had no choice but to respond to their call. They said, 'Now the proof of the Faith of God has been established for you. The news of the dethronement of Sulṭán 'Abdu'l-'Azíz has reached here by telegram.' This news dealt me an enormously heavy blow. Although I knew

* Not to be confused with the renowned Ḥájí Mírzá Ḥaydar-'Alíy-i-Iṣfahání whose chronicles we are quoting in these pages.

† see Nabíl-i-A'ẓam, *The Dawn-Breakers.*

‡ The 'abá was a cloak worn by orientals in those days. It was normally placed over the shoulders, but on cold days it was customary to pull it over one's head.

what they were aiming at, I flared up with rage and shouted at them angrily, 'It is no concern of mine that the Sulṭán has been deposed. I am not a relative of his.' 'Did you not make your acceptance of the truth of this Faith', they reminded me, 'dependent upon this event?' I was so convulsed with rage that I walked away without saying farewell. I did not proceed to where I was intending to go; instead I went back home.

Knowing the immensity of this test, I was overcome with emotion and with tears flowing uncontrollably from my eyes I begged God to assist me so that I might not be misled. While I was in this condition, 'Abdu'l-Karím and two others arrived. I was in no state of mind to invite them in, so I left the house and did not return home until late at night. These friends knew that I could not face them and that I had run away. They waited two to three days and then came. I apologized for my behaviour on that evening, and said to them that we must now wait until the prophecy of 'We will lay hand on their Chief' be fulfilled. I explained that the term 'lay hand on' did not mean natural death, for everyone dies. It signified that he must be killed.

My zeal in finding the truth had by now reached its climax. I visited all the learned men whom I trusted and discussed the principles of religion with them but found them helpless, while the proofs put forward by the Bahá'ís were, in my view, overwhelming and far superior. By this time I found myself able to discover the mysteries and understand the reality and significances of the verses of the *Qur'án*.

A few days passed and the news of the assassination of the Sulṭán was flashed by telegram. I went out of my mind, and was utterly perplexed. I was so agitated that I even aimed blows at myself. At one time I would fight with God, at another I would turn unbeliever, then I would repent and beseech God to assist, guide and protect me. I went through such an ordeal that day and night I could not relieve myself from these thoughts. I could neither eat nor sleep. I could not eat. I only drank tea and smoked and wept.

One night I was roused from my slumber and I began to

admonish myself in these words: 'It is about one year that you have been associating and arguing with these Bahá'ís. These men are illiterate and uneducated, yet they have asserted their ascendancy over you every time, they have adduced proofs and demonstrated the validity of their Cause. Although you consider yourself to be a learned man and a researcher in the Holy Books, commentaries and traditions, yet you know that these men are much more resourceful than you are. It is as if they are inspired and assisted by God, and the Holy Spirit speaks through them. You have also been a witness to their exalted character and heavenly virtues. Why then should you interpret their words as the breathings of the evil whisperer? You remember how enchanted you were when you read the story of the 'Show of Sulṭán Salím' in the *Lawḥ-i-Ra'ís*! How you were attracted by the eloquence and sublimity of those words! Now, you ought to read and investigate the writings of the one who claims to be the revealer of the Word of God with the eye of justice and fairness. If this Cause be untrue, the first to contend it is God. Therefore, its survival is impossible . . .

I arose, performed my ablutions and said prayers. I then took the Tablet of Bahá'u'lláh [*Lawḥ-i-Ra'ís*] which, although it had been in my possession for a long time, I had not been moved to read. I opened it, turned tearfully and with devotion to God, and began to read it. It was then that I heard the voice of God . . . calling me through the mouthpiece of this Manifestation, 'Am I not your Lord?' To that call reaching me from the Beauty of the All-Glorious, I responded with all my heart, 'Thou art, thou art!'* I believed.

I passed from the state of idle fancies and vain imaginings into that of certitude . . . I became highly attracted to the Word of God and carried away by its power. I felt such love and devotion towards the Dayspring of Divine Revelation [Bahá'u'lláh] and experienced such joy and ecstasy in myself that I cannot ever describe it. Words cannot express the

* In Islám, this expression is used as the response of the believer to the call of God when He manifests Himself to him.

heights of spirituality to which I had been transformed . . . I knew that if I served these souls who had become the cause of my guidance to the end of my days, and if I laid down my life in their path, I should never be able to repay them for giving me eternal salvation and spiritual life . . .

With infinite joy I spent that night. Before dawn I hastened to the house of 'Abdu'l-Karím, kissed the threshold of his door, prostrated myself at his feet and manifested such humility and self-effacement towards him that he was highly embarrassed. He told me that my behaviour was not warranted and it was based on my vain imaginings, for God is the one who guides the souls and not man.[7]

After embracing the Faith of Bahá'u'lláh, Mírzá Abu'l-Faḍl became an entirely new creation. He acquired keen spiritual insight and a faith seldom seen among the followers of Bahá'u'lláh. Probably the reason for this, in the first instance, was the purity of his heart which enabled him in his arduous journey of search after truth to battle through and tear up many veils of pride, superstition and vain imaginings, until there was nothing left but a pure spirit attracted to Bahá'u'lláh as a piece of iron would be to a powerful magnet. So complete was this attraction that, like to the iron when it becomes magnetized, he surrendered his will entirely to that of Bahá'u'lláh and as a result became a spiritual giant adorned with such virtues and accomplishments that few, if any, of the Apostles of Bahá'u'lláh have surpassed him in qualities and perfections.

In the second instance, through the influence of the Faith of Bahá'u'lláh, his vast knowledge of religion, history and philosophy acquired a new dimension, a new quality and a new power. The forces of the Revelation of Bahá'u'lláh acted as rays of light, and his knowledge as the eye. The combination of the two brought him new vision. This knowledge, now guided by the light of faith and coupled with detachment from all earthly things, bestowed upon him the gift of true understanding of such magnitude that he became a wellspring of divine knowledge. He used this knowledge as a tool to understand, to the extent that it is possible for man to do, the inner reality of the Revelation of Bahá'u'lláh. Through the knowledge of God, detachment from all earthly things, and living the life, he recognized the station of Bahá'u'lláh and the greatness of this Cause to a degree that perhaps only a few have attained.

The recognition of the Manifestation of God (Bahá'u'lláh, in this day) is the first step towards the spiritual development of the soul. And as this recognition is relative and varies from person to person, it is apparent that those who succeed in recognizing the grandeur of the Revelation of Bahá'u'lláh in depth, and become truly aware of His transcendent glory and awe-inspiring majesty, will be endowed with far greater powers of spiritual understanding. Mírzá Abu'l-Faḍl achieved this to a supreme degree and became the fulfilment of these words of Bahá'u'lláh:

> Whoso hath recognized Me, will arise and serve Me with such determination that the powers of earth and heaven shall be unable to defeat his purpose.[8]

That he had perceived with such penetrating insight the significance and greatness of the Day of God ushered in by Bahá'u'lláh is evident from his writings and the example of his life.

The late Ali-Kuli Khan,* who spent a considerable time with Mírzá Abu'l-Faḍl, has described the ardour with which the latter used to pray, and then comments: 'The reason he prayed with such fervour and such weeping was his concept of the greatness of God and his own nothingness; his belief that his very existence, bestowed on him by Divine mercy, was a sin in this Day "whereon naught can be seen except the

* He rendered notable services to the Faith in the early days of its establishment in the West; among his services were many works of translation.

splendours of the Light that shineth from the face of thy Lord . . .'"[9]

Through these qualities Mírzá Abu'l-Faḍl became a source of divine knowledge and an embodiment of Bahá'í virtues, of humility and self-effacement to such an extent that 'Abdu'l-Bahá in one of his talks[10] after Mírzá Abu'l-Faḍl's passing described him as a 'supreme exemplar for the Bahá'ís to follow'. On another occasion He referred to him as a 'lamp of this Cause', 'the light of guidance', 'a brilliant star', 'a billowing ocean'. When in America, the Master sent a telegram to a friend in Egypt directing him to take great care of Mírzá Abu'l-Faḍl and saying, 'His person is to be regarded as My own self.'

The same Ali-Kuli Khan has described him in these words: 'If I had never seen 'Abdu'l-Bahá and Shoghi Effendi, I would consider Mírzá Abu'l-Faḍl the greatest being I ever laid eyes on.'[11]

Mírzá Abu'l-Faḍl knew the station of Bahá'u'lláh to be so exalted, and himself so unworthy, that he felt unable to seek permission to attain His presence. He was one of the Apostles of Bahá'u'lláh who never gazed upon the face of His Lord. But he attained the presence of 'Abdu'l-Bahá for the first time in 1894 and basked in the sunshine of His love for about ten months. Here he showed such humility and self-effacement that the believers who were present learned from him the meaning of true servitude and utter nothingness. Ali-Kuli Khan has described this so beautifully:

> . . . Yes, but really to know his greatness, you had to watch him when he was in the presence of 'Abdu'l-Bahá. Then his knowledge reduced him to nothingness, and you thought of a pebble on the ocean shore.[12]

Concerning the great bounty of meeting 'Abdu'l-Bahá he has written this account:

> When in AD 1894 the author travelled to the Holy Land and,

through the assistance of the Divine Favors, attained unto the visit of His Holy Threshold, he was amazed to behold in Him all virtues and perfections. These were witnessed during ten months residence in the shelter of His nearness. Many a time we were in His Holy Presence when multitudes of prominent people were there, such as judges, doctors and great military and civil officials of different nationality, religion and language. While He was in their midst large packages of letters from all parts and countries of the world were brought to Him. Although encompassed with insurmountable difficulties, He—Glorified is His Name and Grandeur!—continued to answer questions and requests made by those present, while He wrote replies to each letter. These Tablets and replies were written without meditation, pause of pen, or preliminary rough-copy, and without the help of a scribe. All regions are filled with His Tablets and hearts are attracted through their spread. He has caused the Voice of His Lord . . . to reach the high heavens. Through the words of His widespread epistles, which exhale the purest fragrances of His Utterances, souls are uplifted; and from their verses the fountains of knowledge and wisdom flow onward.[13]

This great man, whom Bahá'u'lláh and 'Abdu'l-Bahá cherished so dearly, and the example of whose life 'Abdu'l-Bahá bade His followers emulate, in memory of whose outstanding services to the Cause is named one of the doors of the Shrine of the Báb, served the Faith of God with distinction mainly because he had detached himself from all earthly things and had the capacity to become the recipient of the bounties and confirmations of Bahá'u'lláh.*

* For an account of Mírzá Abu'l-Faḍl's activities as a Bahá'í teacher, see Appendix II.

6

The World's Most Powerful Rulers

In spite of the severity of the restrictions laid on Bahá'u'lláh in the barracks of 'Akká, He joyously imparted to His followers the glad tidings that soon through the power of the Almighty the gates of the prison would be opened and the spiritual influences of His all-encompassing Revelation would increasingly permeate the whole world. As we survey the succession of events from the day Bahá'u'lláh declared His station in the Garden of Riḍván in 1863 up to the time that He was incarcerated in the Most Great Prison, we note with awe and wonder the momentous happenings which had taken place and the immensity and vastness of His Revelation which had so effectively revitalized the fortunes of the community of the Most Great Name.

During this short period of time covering not quite six years, Bahá'u'lláh, the Supreme Manifestation of God, had unveiled the glory of His Countenance hidden behind 'a myriad veils of light' to a number of His companions in that Garden, when according to His own testimony the whole of creation had been 'immersed in the sea of purification' and the splendours of the light of His Countenance broke upon the world. At that moment the seed of a new world-embracing, world-vitalizing order, divine in origin and possessed of immeasurable potentialities, had been sown in the soil of human society, destined to germinate one decade later with the revelation of the *Kitáb-i-Aqdas* when the laws and ordinances as well as the institutions of that same order would be brought into being.

In the short period of time separating the Declaration of His Mission and His imprisonment in 'Akká, the great majority of the followers of the Báb had embraced the Cause of Bahá'u'lláh, identified themselves with His name, and some had gone as pilgrims, travelling long distances, often on foot, to attain His presence. As a result of their coming into contact with the vitalizing spirit of His exalted Person, most of them became a new creation. They glowed like balls of fire, returned to their homes and radiated the light of His Faith to countless souls in Persia; many of them willingly accepted the crown of martyrdom and laid down their lives in His path.

In that same period, the Cause of God had witnessed a prodigious outpouring of divine revelation for five years in Adrianople, culminating in the historic proclamation of His Message in that land. The *Súriy-i-Mulúk** (Súrih of the Kings) had been revealed in language of authority and power and through it the clarion call of a mighty King had been sounded and His claims fully asserted. The Tablet described by Him as 'The Rumbling' of His proclamation, addressed to Náṣiri'd-Dín Sháh of Persia had been revealed, though not yet delivered.

His first Tablet to Napoleon III had been dispatched. The *Súriy-i-Ra'ís* † in which 'Álí Páshá, the Grand Vizír, had been severely rebuked and about which Bahá'u'lláh had testified that from the moment of its revelation 'until the present day, neither hath the world been tranquillized, nor have the hearts of its people been at rest', had been revealed, and the prophecies it contained had been noted with awe and wonder.

Furthermore, the process of the disintegration and rolling up of the old order had been set in motion when the summons of the Lord of Hosts to the kings and rulers of the world was either rejected or ignored. Also in that short period of time, the breaker of the Covenant of the Báb, Mírzá Yaḥyá, stigmatized by Bahá'u'lláh as the 'Most Great Idol' had been cast out with the hands of power and might from the community of the Most Great Name.

* see vol. 2, ch. 15.

† see vol. 2, p. 411.

Such were the great and momentous events that had marked the opening years of Bahá'u'lláh's ministry since the declaration of His mission in Baghdád, and now, in 'Akká, though confined to a cell and cut off from the body of the believers, the outpouring of Bahá'u'lláh's Revelation did not cease. The Ocean of His utterance continued to surge and the Tongue of Grandeur spoke with authority and might. Behind the walls of the Most Great Prison, the Pen of the Most High directed its warnings and exhortations first to His immediate persecutors and then to some of the outstanding monarchs of the world at that time.

> 'Never since the beginning of the world,' Bahá'u'lláh Himself affirms, 'hath the Message been so openly proclaimed.' 'Each one of them,' He, specifically referring to the Tablets addressed by Him to the sovereigns of the earth—Tablets acclaimed by 'Abdu'l-Bahá as a 'miracle'—has written, 'hath been designated by a special name. The first hath been named 'The Rumbling,' the second 'The Blow,' the third 'The Inevitable,' the fourth, 'The Plain,' the fifth 'The Catastrophe,' and the others 'The Stunning Trumpet-Blast,' 'The Near Event,' 'The Great Terror,' 'The Trumpet,' 'The Bugle,' and the like, so that all the peoples of the earth may know, of a certainty, and may witness, with outward and inward eyes that He Who is the Lord of Names hath prevailed, and will continue to prevail, under all conditions, over all men.'[1]

Tablet to Napoleon III

Bahá'u'lláh's first Tablet to Napoleon III, sent while He was in Adrianople, had been received by the monarch with discourtesy and disrespect.* He is reported to have flung down the Tablet saying 'If this man is God, I am two gods!' The second Tablet to Napoleon III was revealed (in Arabic)

* see vol. 2, p. 368.

and sent to him in 1869, after Bahá'u'lláh had received a communication from one of the Emperor's ministers informing Him that up till then there had been no reply forthcoming. This Tablet, unlike the previous one which was written in a mild tone, is revealed in majestic language, has the tone of supreme authority and declares unmistakably that its Author is none other than the King of Kings. Its opening paragraph alone is sufficient to convey to the reader a glimpse of the majesty of Bahá'u'lláh's utterance:

> O King of Paris! Tell the priest to ring the bells no longer. By God, the True One! The Most Mighty Bell hath appeared in the form of Him Who is the Most Great Name, and the fingers of the will of thy Lord, the Most Exalted, the Most High, toll it out in the heaven of Immortality, in His Name, the All-Glorious . . . Give ear, O King, unto the Voice that calleth from the Fire which burneth in this Verdant Tree, upon this Sinai which hath been raised above the hallowed and snow-white Spot, beyond the Everlasting City: 'Verily, there is none other God but Me, the Ever-Forgiving, the Most Merciful!'[2]

In this Tablet Bahá'u'lláh prophesies Napoleon's downfall, states the reason for it, and declares his doom to be inevitable unless he makes amends and arises to serve His Cause.

These passages gleaned from the Tablet will serve to acquaint the reader with Bahá'u'lláh's compelling utterance rebuking one of the mightiest monarchs of His time:

> O King! We heard the words thou didst utter in answer to the Czar of Russia, concerning the decision made regarding the war (Crimean War). Thy Lord, verily, knoweth, is informed of all. Thou didst say: 'I lay asleep upon my couch, when the cry of the oppressed, who were drowned in the Black Sea, awakened me.' This is what we heard thee say, and, verily, thy Lord is witness unto what I say. We testify that that which wakened thee was not their cry, but

the promptings of thine own passions, for We tested thee, and found thee wanting. Comprehend the meaning of My words, and be thou of the discerning . . . Hadst thou been sincere in thy words, thou wouldst have not cast behind thy back the Book of God, when it was sent unto thee by Him Who is the Almighty, the All-Wise. We have proved thee through it, and found thee other than that which thou didst profess. Arise, and make amends for that which escaped thee. Ere long the world and all that thou possessest will perish, and the kingdom will remain unto God, thy Lord and the Lord of thy fathers of old. It behooveth thee not to conduct thine affairs according to the dictates of thy desires. Fear the sighs of this Wronged One, and shield Him from the darts of such as act unjustly. For what thou hast done, thy kingdom shall be thrown into confusion, and thine empire shall pass from thine hands, as a punishment for that which thou hast wrought. Then wilt thou know how thou hast plainly erred. Commotions shall seize all the people in that land, unless thou arisest to help this Cause, and followest Him Who is the Spirit of God (Jesus) in this, the straight Path. Hath thy pomp made thee proud? By My Life! It shall not endure; nay, it shall soon pass away, unless thou holdest fast by this firm Cord. We see abasement hastening after thee, while thou art of the heedless . . . Abandon thy palaces to the people of the graves, and thine empire to whosoever desireth it, and turn, then, unto the Kingdom. This, verily, is what God hath chosen for thee, wert thou of them that turn unto Him . . . Shouldst thou desire to bear the weight of thy dominion, bear it then to aid the Cause of thy Lord. Glorified be this station which whoever attaineth thereunto hath attained unto all good that proceedeth from Him Who is the All-Knowing, the All-Wise . . . Exultest thou over the treasures thou dost possess, knowing they shall perish? Rejoicest thou in that thou rulest a span of earth, when the whole world, in the estimation of the people of Bahá, is worth as much as the black in the eye of a dead ant? Abandon it unto such as have set their affections upon it, and turn thou unto Him Who is the Desire of the world. Whither are gone the proud and their palaces? Gaze thou into their tombs, that thou mayest profit by this example, inasmuch as We made it a lesson unto every beholder. Were the breezes of Revelation to seize thee, thou wouldst flee the world, and turn unto the Kingdom, and wouldst expend all thou possessest, that thou mayest draw nigh unto this sublime Vision.[3]

It took only a few months for Bahá'u'lláh's prophecies to be fulfilled; the Emperor met his doom in 1870.

Shoghi Effendi has written a brief account of this in *The Promised Day Is Come*:

The significance of the sombre and pregnant words uttered by Bahá'u'lláh in His second Tablet was soon revealed. He who was actuated in provoking the Crimean War by his selfish desires, who was prompted by a personal grudge against the Russian Emperor, who was impatient to tear up the Treaty of 1815 in order to avenge the disaster of Moscow, and who sought to shed military glory over his throne, was soon himself engulfed by a catastrophe that hurled him in the dust, and caused France to sink from her preeminent station among the nations to that of a fourth Power in Europe.

The battle of Sedan in 1870 sealed the fate of the French Emperor. The whole of his army was broken up and surrendered, constituting the greatest capitulation hitherto recorded in modern history. A crushing indemnity was exacted. He himself was taken prisoner. His only son, the Prince Imperial, was killed, a few years later, in the Zulu War. The Empire collapsed, its programme unrealized. The Republic was proclaimed. Paris was subsequently besieged and capitulated. 'The terrible year' marked by civil war, exceeding in its ferocity the Franco-German War, followed. William I, the Prussian king, was proclaimed German Emperor in the very palace which stood as a 'mighty monument and symbol of the power and pride of Louis XIV, a power which had been secured to some extent by the humiliation of Germany.' Deposed by a disaster 'so

> appalling that it resounded throughout the world,' this false and boastful monarch suffered in the end, and till his death, the same exile as that which, in the case of Bahá'u'lláh, he had so heartlessly ignored.[4]

The Tablet of Bahá'u'lláh to Napoleon was taken out of the Prison by a person who hid it in his hat so that it might not be detected by the guards. It was delivered to the French consular agent in 'Akká* who translated it into French and sent it to the Emperor. The reading of the Tablet revealed in such majestic and eloquent language, containing such ominous warnings to the Emperor, deeply affected the son of the French agent who became a believer when he saw to his amazement the fulfilment of Bahá'u'lláh's prophecies within so short a period of time.

For those who have embraced the Cause of Bahá'u'lláh and recognized the divine origin of His Revelation, there can be no comparison between His Words—the Words of God—and the writings of men. Indeed, immeasurable is the difference between the two. Not only are His words creative, not only do they penetrate deep into the hearts of people and revolutionize human society, but from a literary point of view alone, the Writings of Bahá'u'lláh do not always follow the logical pattern which the minds of men have devised. A writer worthy of his name will commonly dwell on one subject at a time and develop his theme step by step in a logical manner. He does not introduce a subject which is not relevant to his theme half-way through. But the revealed Word is not sent down by God in the pattern of man's thinking and logic. It is exalted above human limitations; it is like a limitless ocean beyond the reach of man, an ocean from whose billowing waves only a few drops resembling words fall upon the shores of human understanding. But its outpouring follows no pattern which the mind of man can comprehend.

An example of this non-conformity may be found in the Tablet to Napoleon, where Bahá'u'lláh gives one of His most binding commandments to His followers in these words:

* Louis Catafago, a Christian Arab.

God hath prescribed unto every one the duty of teaching His Cause. Whoever ariseth to discharge this duty, must needs, ere he proclaimeth His Message, adorn himself with the ornament of an upright and praiseworthy character, so that his words may attract the hearts of such as are receptive to his call. Without it, he can never hope to influence his hearers.[5]

And also He counsels His loved ones:

O people of Bahá! Subdue the citadels of men's hearts with the swords of wisdom and of utterance. They that dispute, as prompted by their desires, are indeed wrapped in a palpable veil. Say: The sword of wisdom is hotter than summer heat, and sharper than blades of steel, if ye do but understand. Draw it forth in My name and through the power of My might, and conquer, then, with it the cities of the hearts of them that have secluded themselves in the stronghold of their corrupt desires. Thus biddeth you the Pen of the All-Glorious, whilst seated beneath the swords of the wayward. If ye become aware of a sin committed by another, conceal it, that God may conceal your own sin. He, verily, is the Concealer, the Lord of grace abounding. O ye rich ones on earth! If ye encounter one who is poor, treat him not disdainfully. Reflect upon that whereof ye were created. Every one of you was created of a sorry germ.[6]

Another example is when Bahá'u'lláh chooses to announce, in the middle of His Tablet to Napoleon, that the two greatest Festivals in the Faith are the Festival of Riḍván and the Festival of the Declaration of the Báb, and that these are followed by two other Festivals, His own birthday and that of the Báb. In this Tablet, Bahá'u'lláh also announces the formulation of the law of fasting and stipulates its duration to be nineteen days.*

Such is divine Revelation!

* A great part of the Tablet to Napoleon III is translated into English and published, but some passages such as those referred to above are not translated yet.

Tablet to Pope Pius IX

The Tablet to Pope Pius IX (in Arabic) was revealed by Bahá'u'lláh around the same time as that to Napoleon. In it Bahá'u'lláh identifies Himself as the Lord of Lords and addresses the Pope with the authority and majesty of God, proclaiming to him in unequivocal language the promised return of Christ in the glory of the Father, and summoning him with the commanding voice of the Almighty to leave his palaces and hasten to present himself before the throne of his Lord.

Here are some extracts from this mighty Tablet:

> O Pope! Rend the veils asunder. He Who is the Lord of Lords is come overshadowed with clouds, and the decree hath been fulfilled by God, the Almighty, the Unrestrained . . . He, verily, hath again come down from Heaven even as He came down from it the first time. Beware that thou dispute not with Him even as the Pharisees disputed with Him (Jesus) without a clear token or proof . . .

> Dwellest thou in palaces whilst He Who is the King of Revelation liveth in the most desolate of abodes? Leave them unto such as desire them, and set thy face with joy and delight towards the Kingdom . . . Arise in the name of thy Lord, the God of Mercy, amidst the peoples of the earth, and seize thou the Cup of Life with the hands of confidence, and first drink thou therefrom, and proffer it then to such as turn towards it amongst the peoples of all faiths . . .
>
> Call thou to remembrance Him Who was the Spirit (Jesus), Who when He came, the most learned of His age pronounced judgment against Him in His own country, whilst he who was only a fisherman believed in Him. Take heed, then, ye men of understanding heart! . . .

> O Supreme Pontiff! Incline thine ear unto that which the Fashioner of mouldering bones counselleth thee, as voiced by Him Who is His Most Great Name. Sell all the embellished ornaments thou dost possess, and expend them

in the path of God, Who causeth the night to return upon the day, and the day to return upon the night. Abandon thy kingdom unto the kings, and emerge from thy habitation, with thy face set towards the Kingdom, and, detached from the world, then speak forth the praises of thy Lord betwixt earth and heaven. Thus hath bidden thee He Who is the Possessor of Names, on the part of thy Lord, the Almighty, the All-Knowing.[7]

It is significant that very soon after the revelation of this Tablet, the temporal sovereignty of the Pope, which for centuries had proved to be the most powerful in Christendom but which had been diminishing in its power and influence for some time, was, through the potency of the words of the heavenly Father, dramatically extinguished.

Shoghi Effendi in his evaluation of this event has written:

In 1870, after Bahá'u'lláh had revealed His Epistle to Pius IX, King Victor Emmanuel I went to war with the Papal states, and his troops entered Rome and seized it. On the eve of its seizure, the Pope repaired to the Lateran and, despite his age and with his face bathed in tears, ascended on bended knees the Scala Santa. The following morning, as the cannonade began, he ordered the white flag to be hoisted above the dome of St. Peter. Despoiled, he refused to recognize this 'creation of revolution,' excommunicated the invaders of his states, denounced Victor Emmanuel as the 'robber King' and as 'forgetful of every religious principle, despising every right, trampling upon every law.' Rome, 'the Eternal City, on which rest twenty-five centuries of glory,' and over which the Popes had ruled in unchallengeable right for ten centuries, finally became the seat of the new kingdom, and the scene of that humiliation which Bahá'u'lláh had anticipated and which the Prisoner of the Vatican had imposed upon himself.

'The last years of the old Pope,' writes a commentator on his life, 'were filled with anguish. To his physical infirmities was added the sorrow of beholding, all too often, the Faith outraged in the very heart of Rome, the religious orders despoiled and persecuted, the Bishops and priests debarred from exercising their functions.'

Every effort to retrieve the situation created in 1870 proved fruitless. The Archbishop of Posen went to Versailles to solicit Bismarck's intervention in behalf of the Papacy, but was coldly received. Later a Catholic party was organized in Germany to bring political pressure on the German Chancellor. All, however, was in vain. The mighty process already referred to had to pursue inexorably its course. Even now, after the lapse of above half a century, the so-called restoration of temporal sovereignty has but served to throw into greater relief the helplessness of this erstwhile potent Prince, at whose name kings trembled and to whose dual sovereignty they willingly submitted. This temporal sovereignty, practically confined to the minuscule City of the Vatican, and leaving Rome the undisputed possession of a secular monarchy, has been obtained at the price of unreserved recognition, so long withheld, of the Kingdom of Italy. The Treaty of the Lateran, claiming to have resolved once and for all the Roman Question, has indeed assured to a secular Power, in respect of the Enclaved City, a liberty of action which is fraught with uncertainty and peril. 'The two souls of the Eternal City,' a Catholic writer has observed, 'have been separated from each other, only to collide more severely than ever before.'

Well might the Sovereign Pontiff recall the reign of the most powerful among his predecessors, Innocent III who, during the eighteen years of his pontificate, raised and deposed the kings and the emperors, whose interdicts deprived nations of the exercise of Christian worship, at the feet of whose legate the King of England surrendered his crown, and at whose voice the fourth and the fifth crusades were both undertaken.[8]

Tablet to Czar Alexander II

Another Tablet revealed in 'Akká was a Tablet to the Czar of Russia, Alexander II. It was revealed in Arabic. In it Bahá'u'lláh proclaims His station, identifies Himself as the

Heavenly Father and calls on him to arise in His Name, proclaim His Mission and summon the nations to His Cause. These are some of the words of Bahá'u'lláh addressed to the Czar:

> O Czar of Russia! Incline thine ear unto the voice of God, the King, the Holy, and turn thou unto Paradise, the Spot wherein abideth He Who, among the Concourse on high, beareth the most excellent titles, and Who, in the kingdom of creation, is called by the name of God, the Effulgent, the All-Glorious. Beware lest thy desire deter thee from turning towards the face of thy Lord, the Compassionate, the Most Merciful . . . Beware lest thy sovereignty withhold thee from Him Who is the Supreme Sovereign. He, verily, is come with His Kingdom, and all the atoms cry aloud: 'Lo! The Lord is come in His great majesty!' He Who is the Father is come and the Son (Jesus), in the holy vale, crieth out: 'Here am I, here am I, O Lord, My God!', whilst Sinai circleth round the House, and the Burning Bush calleth aloud: 'The All-Bounteous is come mounted upon the clouds! Blessed is he that draweth nigh unto Him, and woe betide them that are far away.'
>
> Arise thou amongst men in the name of this all-compelling Cause, and summon, then, the nations unto God, the Exalted, the Great.[9]

Describing the pre-eminent nature of His Revelation, Bahá'u'lláh writes:

> Say: This is an Announcement whereat the hearts of the Prophets and Messengers have rejoiced. This is the One Whom the heart of the world remembereth and is promised in the Books of God, the Mighty, the All-Wise. The hands of the Messengers were, in their desire to meet Me, upraised towards God, the Mighty, the Glorified . . . Some lamented in their separation from Me, others endured hardships in My path, and still others laid down their lives for the sake of My Beauty, could ye but know it. Say: I, verily, have not sought to extol Mine Own Self, but rather God Himself

were ye to judge fairly. Naught can be seen in Me except God and His Cause, could ye but perceive it. I am the One Whom the tongue of Isaiah hath extolled, the One with Whose name both the Torah and the Evangel were adorned . . .[10]

The exhortations of Bahá'u'lláh fell on deaf ears. Unmoved by the proclamation of so mighty a message, Alexander II ruled over his country until 1881 when he was assassinated, and with the rise of Bolshevism in 1917 his dynasty was extinguished.

There is a passage in this Tablet in which Bahá'u'lláh refers to the Czar's supplication to God but does not reveal its details. He writes:

We, verily, have heard the thing for which thou didst supplicate thy Lord, whilst secretly communing with Him. Wherefore, the breeze of My loving-kindness wafted forth, and the sea of My Mercy surged, and We answered thee in truth. Thy Lord, verily, is the All-Knowing, the All-Wise.[11]

A certain believer Áqá Muḥammad-Raḥím, a native of Iṣfahán, was confronted with a question from a Russian Consul in Esterábád concerning the above passage. This is his story as recorded in the memoirs of Ustád 'Alí-Akbar-i-Banná* of Yazd.

Áqá Muḥammad-Raḥím became a believer at a time of persecutions and sufferings. But he did not become inhibited by opposition. He taught the Faith openly and as a result some people embraced the Faith while others rose up in opposition, intent upon harming him, especially his father who was bitterly against him. Eventually he had to

* Ustád 'Alí-Akbar was an outstanding follower of Bahá'u'lláh who was martyred in Yazd in 1903. He lived for some years in 'Ishqábád and rendered notable services to the Faith. His memoirs deal mainly with the history of the Cause and the believers in 'Ishqábád. The Tablet of Tajallíyát was revealed in his honour. We shall refer to him in more detail in the next volume.

forgo wealth and prosperity at home, and, detached from all earthly things, he migrated to Sabzivár (Province of Khurásán) where he worked for some time in the copper mines. Later, as a result of persecutions against the believers in Sabzivár he left for 'Ishqábád where he resided till the end of his life.

Áqá Muḥammad-Raḥím was an accomplished teacher of the Faith as well as a writer. He visited 'Akká twice during the lifetime of Bahá'u'lláh and attained His presence. He told us the following story:

'Before I went on my first pilgrimage to attain the Holy Presence of Bahá'u'lláh, a Russian Consul in Esterábád had intimated to an Armenian merchant that he would like to meet a Bahá'í from Sabzivár who could bring some Bahá'í books for him. He had also offered to pay the expenses involved. The Armenian merchant gave this message to Ḥájí Muḥammad-Káẓim, a merchant of Iṣfahán (a Bahá'í). The Ḥájí and other believers consulted together and decided that I should go.

The Armenian merchant wrote a letter of introduction to the Consul which I took with me along with some Bahá'í books. I travelled to Esterábád and two days later I went to the Consul and handed him the letter. He invited me to stay at his home, which I did. We used to talk together in the evenings. He talked about some parts of the history of the Faith that he knew, and I enlightened him on subjects that he was not familiar with. One night he said to me: 'The main purpose in calling you here is to ask you the meaning of the following passage which appears in Bahá'u'lláh's Tablet to the Czar: "We, verily have heard the thing for which thou didst supplicate thy Lord, whilst secretly communing with Him. Wherefore, the breeze of My loving-kindness wafted forth, and the sea of My mercy surged, and We answered thee in truth. Thy Lord, verily, is the All-Knowing, the All-Wise." '

What did the Czar ask in his prayer which was granted to him? I did not know what to answer, so I said, 'God knows that.' 'That is obvious,' he said, 'but how do you interpret this passage?' I meditated for a little while on the subject and came to the conclusion that kings don't ask anything from God except victory in their conquests and defeat for their enemies . . . To reverse the situation after Russia's defeat in the Crimean War, the Czar had prayed to God to make him victorious in his fight against the Ottomans and to enable him to conquer their cities. I conveyed all these thoughts to the Consul and suggested that he ought to write a letter to the Czar and inform him that his prayers would be answered and that he should carry out his plans and intentions.

After a few days he paid my travelling expenses and I returned home. But in my heart I was apprehensive lest my interpretation of the Tablet might have been incorrect. I was worried about this subject. Fear and hope dwelt together in my heart until I travelled to 'Akká and arrived at the Caravanserai. It did not take very long before Mírzá Áqá Ján [Bahá'u'lláh's amanuensis] came to see me. Among other things he asked me: 'What things did you say to the Russian Consul?' I remained silent and became apprehensive. An hour later Ghuṣn-i-Akbar [Mírzá Muḥammad-'Alí, the son of Bahá'u'lláh who later became the Arch-Breaker of the Covenant of Bahá'u'lláh] came to visit me. He also asked the same question. That added to my anxiety.

The following morning, the Most Great Branch ['Abdu'l-Bahá] came. I felt obliged to tell Him the whole story exactly as it had happened and I confessed to the mistake I had made in my statement. 'Abdu'l-Bahá said to me, 'Be happy and relieved, for the statement you have made was the truth, because on a certain day the Blessed Beauty intimated that at that very moment someone was reading the Tablet of the Czar. Then Bahá'u'lláh mentioned you. He said, "The Russian Consul asked one of Our servants: 'What was the prayer of the King?' The answer he received was a correct one." Then He revealed your name, saying, "That person was Áqá Muḥammad-Raḥím-i-Isfahání."'* I thanked God for this and was very happy to hear it.'[12]

* These are not the exact words of Bahá'u'lláh or 'Abdu'l-Bahá. They are the recollections of Áqá Muḥammad-Raḥím.

These thoughts of Áqá Muḥammad-Raḥím, conveyed to the Russian Consul, refer to the war of 1877–8 between Russia and Turkey. The Czar went to war apparently to avenge the defeat of his father in the Crimean War. At first his armies made considerable progress and were moving toward Constantinople. Then their progress was halted by the Turks and many Russian soldiers were killed in the battles which followed. The Czar saw the prospect of defeat again, and Áqá Muḥammad-Raḥím thought this must have been the time that the Czar had turned to God in prayer beseeching His help. Bahá'u'lláh states in His Tablet that the Czar's prayers were answered.

It should be noted here that in the *Súriy-i-Ra'ís*, revealed a few years before when He was on His way to 'Akká, Bahá'u'lláh had foretold the calamities which were to befall the Turkish Government and people as a punishment from God for the cruelties they had inflicted on Him and His disciples. And later, in the *Kitáb-i-Aqdas* (The Most Holy Book), He made a further denunciation of the tyrannical regime in Turkey and prophesied its downfall.*

The murder of Sulṭán 'Abdu'l-'Azíz in 1876 was the initial punishment, followed by the war of 1877–8 which brought victory to the Russians and set in motion the process of the disintegration of the Ottoman Empire. Adrianople was occupied by the Russians and no less than eleven million people were freed from the cruelties of that tyrannical regime.

Tablet to Queen Victoria

A Tablet in Arabic replete with counsels and exhortations was addressed by Bahá'u'lláh to Queen Victoria. In it He proclaims the coming of the Lord in His great glory and summons her to His Cause:

O Queen in London! Incline thine ear unto the voice of thy

* see below, pp. 151–2.

Lord, the Lord of all mankind, calling from the Divine Lote-Tree; Verily, no God is there but Me, the Almighty, the All-Wise! Cast away all that is on earth, and attire the head of thy kingdom with the crown of the remembrance of thy Lord, the All-Glorious. He, in truth, hath come unto the world in His most great glory, and all that hath been mentioned in the Gospel hath been fulfilled . . . Lay aside thy desire, and set then thine heart towards thy Lord, the Ancient of Days. We make mention of thee for the sake of God, and desire that thy name may be exalted through thy remembrance of God, the Creator of earth and heaven. He, verily, is witness unto that which I say.[13]

Bahá'u'lláh commends the Queen in this Tablet for having 'forbidden the trading in slaves' and for having 'entrusted the reins of counsel into the hands of the representatives of the people'. It should be noted here that Bahá'u'lláh in the *Kitáb-i-Aqdas*, the Book of Laws, forbids the trading of slaves. He approves the system of government in which representatives of the people take part. In His Tablet to the Queen, Bahá'u'lláh exhorts the members of the British Parliament in these words:

It behoveth them [the members of the Parliament] however, to be trustworthy among His servants, and to regard themselves as the representatives of all that dwell on earth. This is what counselleth them, in this Tablet, He Who is the Ruler, the All-Wise . . . Blessed is he that entereth the assembly for the sake of God, and judgeth between men with pure justice. He, indeed is of the blissful . . . [14]

What a great contrast between these sublime teachings, which constitute the distinguishing character of the future institutions of the Bahá'í Commonwealth,* and the present political systems in which everyone fights for himself and his country to the exclusion of others!

The fundamental teaching of the oneness of mankind, which

* For a study of the Bahá'í World Commonwealth see *The World Order of Bahá'u'lláh*, pp. 161–206, and other writings of Shoghi Effendi.

is deeply rooted in the Faith of Bahá'u'lláh and the attainment of which, on a spiritual level, is promised by Him to take place in the fullness of time in the Golden Age of His Faith, plays a significant part in the attitudes and conduct of His followers in their daily lives. Such a universal outlook that all humanity is one, created by the same God through His love, transcends all other standards for a Bahá'í.

Bahá'u'lláh, in His Tablet to the Queen, has established this basic principle for the members of a Parliament. The exhortation that they ought to 'regard themselves as the representatives of all that dwell on earth' may be acceptable to some on moral grounds, but cannot be carried out in practice in a world so divided against itself, and its implementation may be looked upon as an impossibility by those who have not as yet recognized the divine origin of the Cause of Bahá'u'lláh. But those who have embraced His Faith and who are already witnessing the spirit of universal love practised in their local, national and international councils, entertain no doubt that as these embryonic institutions grow and develop to a point where they will be adopted as systems of government, the members of these councils the world over will have acquired such a universal outlook as to fully conform with Bahá'u'lláh's exhortation revealed in the above Tablet. It is then that the Most Great Peace referred to by Bahá'u'lláh will be established.

On World Unity

In the Tablet to the Queen Bahá'u'lláh counsels the rulers of the world to establish peace on earth. Then He makes this important statement:

> Now that ye have refused the Most Great Peace, hold ye fast unto this, the Lesser Peace, that haply ye may in some degree better your own condition and that of your dependants.[15]

Any unbiased observer who is willing to study the Writings of Bahá'u'lláh will come to the conclusion that each one of His teachings or counsels, revealed over a hundred years ago, has become part of the spirit of the age, especially those which deal with social aspects of the life of man on this planet. Unaware of the source of these teachings, humanity is increasingly being driven by forces beyond its control to uphold and enforce them.

One such teaching is the creation of the Lesser Peace which is a form of political peace. Its terms are to be concluded between the nations of the world and its aim to abolish global wars. Bahá'ís believe that since Bahá'u'lláh has advocated it, similar to the rest of His Teachings, the Lesser Peace will inevitably be established. The creative words of God uttered by Him will exert their influence in such a way that man will have no choice but to establish the Lesser Peace. Already man has built up such an arsenal of destructive weapons that he could wipe out the entire human race with them. Probably the Lesser Peace will come into being as a last resort and as a desperate measure to save humanity from total destruction.

The Lesser Peace, a political system, although vastly inferior to the Most Great Peace and far removed from the bounties and perfections inherent in the latter, is nevertheless an important milestone in the emergence of that glorious destiny of mankind prophesied by Bahá'u'lláh. Concerning the Most Great Peace, which may be regarded as synonymous with both the establishment of the Kingdom of God on Earth prophesied by Christ, and the Bahá'í World Commonwealth, Shoghi Effendi writes:

> The Most Great Peace, on the other hand, as conceived by Bahá'u'lláh—a peace that must inevitably follow as the practical consequence of the spiritualization of the world and the fusion of all its races, creeds, classes and nations—can rest on no other basis, and can be preserved through no other agency, except the divinely appointed ordinances that are implicit in the World Order that stands associated with His Holy Name.[16]

With the establishment of the Most Great Peace and the spiritualization of the peoples of the world, man will become a noble being adorned with divine virtues and perfections. This is one of the fruits of the Revelation of Bahá'u'lláh, promised by Him. The nobility of man and his spiritual development will lead him in the future to such a position that no individual could enjoy eating his food or resting at home while knowing that there was one person somewhere in the world without food or shelter. It is Bahá'u'lláh's mission to create such a new race of men.*

In His Tablet to the Queen, Bahá'u'lláh further counsels the elected representatives of the people throughout the world in these words:

> O ye the elected representatives of the people in every land! Take ye counsel together, and let your concern be only for that which profiteth mankind, and bettereth the condition thereof, if ye be of them that scan heedfully. Regard the world as the human body which, though at its creation whole and perfect, hath been afflicted, through various causes, with grave disorders and maladies. Not for one day did it gain ease, nay its sickness waxed more severe, as it fell under the treatment of ignorant physicians, who gave full rein to their personal desires, and have erred grievously. And if, at one time, through the care of an able physician, a member of that body was healed, the rest remained afflicted as before. Thus informeth you the All-Knowing, the All-Wise.
>
> We behold it, in this day, at the mercy of rulers so drunk with pride that they cannot discern clearly their own best advantage, much less recognize a Revelation so bewildering and challenging as this. And whenever any one of them hath striven to improve its condition, his motive hath been his own gain, whether confessedly so or not; and the unworthiness of this motive hath limited his power to heal or cure.[17]

* see vol. 2, pp. 142–3.

Over one hundred years have now passed since these words were uttered by the Supreme Manifestation of God, the True Physician come to heal the ills of mankind. The world situation has dangerously deteriorated since these prophetic words were issued by Bahá'u'lláh. Only when mankind as a whole has recognized Bahá'u'lláh as the Divine Physician and has embraced His Faith will these words of His, addressed to Queen Victoria, be universally fulfilled:

> That which the Lord hath ordained as the sovereign remedy and mightiest instrument for the healing of all the world is the union of all its peoples in one universal Cause, one common Faith. This can in no wise be achieved except through the power of a skilled, an all-powerful and inspired Physician. This, verily, is the truth, and all else naught but error.[18]

The followers of Bahá'u'lláh, therefore, do not subscribe to the view, commonly held by the peoples of the world everywhere, that the grave problems besetting mankind may be resolved by administering the usual remedies which the minds of men are devising. They conscientiously believe that the appalling world conditions will not be totally improved by any scientific, economic or political measures, and that none of the expedient methods used during the past century, nor those that are currently being pursued, can succeed in healing the diseased body of mankind. A discerning unbiased person can also come to the same conclusion. For it is very clear that in spite of all the efforts being made by the generality of mankind, its rulers and its wise men, to improve the world situation, and in spite of all their knowledge and accomplishments, the plight of humanity is worsening day by day.

Shoghi Effendi, as far back as 1931, wrote:

> Humanity, whether viewed in the light of man's individual conduct or in the existing relationships between organized communities and nations, has, alas, strayed too far and

suffered too great a decline to be redeemed through the unaided efforts of the best among its recognized rulers and statesmen—however disinterested their motives, however concerted their action, however unsparing in their zeal and devotion to its cause. No scheme which the calculations of the highest statesmanship may yet devise; no doctrine which the most distinguished exponents of economic theory may hope to advance; no principle which the most ardent of moralists may strive to inculcate, can provide, in the last resort, adequate foundations upon which the future of a distracted world can be built.

No appeal for mutual tolerance which the worldly-wise might raise, however compelling and insistent, can calm its passions or help restore its vigour. Nor would any general scheme of mere organized international coöperation, in whatever sphere of human activity, however ingenious in conception, or extensive in scope, succeed in removing the root cause of the evil that has so rudely upset the equilibrium of present-day society. Not even, I venture to assert, would the very act of devising the machinery required for the political and economic unification of the world—a principle that has been increasingly advocated in recent times—provide in itself the antidote against the poison that is steadily undermining the vigour of organized peoples and nations.

What else, might we not confidently affirm, but the unreserved acceptance of the Divine Programme enunciated, with such simplicity and force as far back as sixty years ago, by Bahá'u'lláh, embodying in its essentials God's divinely appointed scheme for the unification of mankind in this age, coupled with an indomitable conviction in the unfailing efficacy of each and all of its provisions, is eventually capable of withstanding the forces of internal disintegration which, if unchecked, must needs continue to eat into the vitals of a despairing society. It is towards this goal—the goal of a new World Order, Divine in origin, all-embracing in scope, equitable in principle, challenging in its features—that a harassed humanity must strive.

> To claim to have grasped all the implications of Bahá'u'lláh's prodigious scheme for world-wide human solidarity, or to have fathomed its import, would be presumptuous on the part of even the declared supporters of His Faith. To attempt to visualize it in all its possibilities, to estimate its future benefits, to picture its glory, would be premature at even so advanced a stage in the evolution of mankind.[19]

World unity as envisaged by Bahá'u'lláh does not consist merely of a system in which humanity enjoys political unity and the sharing of the resources of the world equitably among its peoples and nations. It goes much further than that. The unity described by Bahá'u'lláh in His Writings is the unity of hearts, and this can only be realized when mankind recognizes the Manifestation of God for this age and turns to Him as a focal point, believing in His words that everyone has been created by the same God, and obeying His commandment to love all human beings.

The following statement by Bahá'u'lláh is the key to world unity:

> We fain would hope that the people of Bahá may be guided by the blessed words: 'Say: All things are of God.' This exalted utterance is like unto water for quenching the fire of hate and enmity which smouldereth within the hearts and breasts of men. By this single utterance contending peoples and kindreds will attain the light of true unity. Verily He speaketh the truth and leadeth the way. He is the All-Powerful, the Exalted, the Gracious.[20]

History has shown that the words and teachings of the Manifestations of God are creative. They are endowed with such potency that they penetrate into the hearts and move the people to obey them. Indeed, the greatest mission of every Manifestation of God during His own Dispensation has been to release such spiritual forces into the world as to revitalize all those who turn to Him. But the words of men, no matter how exalted they may be, are incapable of influencing the hearts of people and making them united.

The coming of a Manifestation of God is very similar to the appearance of springtime in nature. The rays of the sun and the vernal showers of that season give new life to the physical world. The fruits appear in the summer as a result of the life-giving forces of the spring. Then winter follows, and nature becomes dormant and cold. When the next spring arrives, the same process is repeated again.

The coming of the Manifestations of God follows the same pattern. Each time they appear they give spiritual life to the body of mankind. But each one has a Dispensation, a specific period during which His teachings revive humanity and impart to it the impulses which cause its progress. Then comes decline, leading to the end, when the teachings of that particular religion lose their influence altogether. It is after such a stage that God sends a new messenger to mankind to release fresh spiritual forces for its regeneration. And the teachings are designed in accordance with the conditions of the new age.

The teachings of God in this day, revealed by Bahá'u'lláh, revolve around unity, and it is to this goal that a disconsolate humanity is striving. But with all his resources and capabilities, man is helpless to establish a lasting peace among the warring nations and peoples of the world. This in spite of the fact that humanity has advanced enormously in many fields of knowledge and has within its ranks brilliant men and women who have produced great achievements in almost every aspect of life on this planet. But one thing they have proved themselves to be incapable of—namely to unite the hearts of men who are each other's enemy, and make them love one another.

Referring to the unity established among the warring tribes of Arabia, the *Qur'án* states:

> It is he [God] who hath strengthened thee with his help, and

with that of the faithful: and hath united their hearts. If thou hadst expended whatever riches are in the earth, thou couldst not have united their hearts, but God united them; for he is mighty and wise.[21]

A cursory study of the nature and composition of the world-wide Bahá'í Community can demonstrate the supernatural influence of the words of Bahá'u'lláh in bringing unity to the hearts of millions of people of diverse origins, people who come from every conceivable background, in all parts of the world. The unity which binds the members of this multi-racial, world-encircling community is inspired not by a desire for friendship or other expedient reasons. It is generated through the knowledge of the advent of a universal Manifestation of God* in this age, and submission to His commandments. When the individual recognizes Bahá'u'lláh as the Mouthpiece of God in this age, he can then easily accept and carry out His teachings, relinquish all kinds of age-long prejudices which have divided mankind, and replace them with an all-embracing love for every human being. This is similar to the transforming influence of the words of Christ which inspired the Christians to turn the other cheek in the early days of Christianity.

* see vol. 1, p. 309.

7

Súriy-i-Haykal

One of the most momentous of the Writings of Bahá'u'lláh is the *Súriy-i-Haykal* or *Súratu'l-Haykal* (Súrih of the Temple). Bahá'u'lláh ordered the Súrih and the Tablets to the Kings to be copied in the form of a pentacle symbolizing the human temple. The Tablets were copied in the following order: the *Súriy-i-Haykal* itself, then the Tablet to Pope Pius IX, the Tablet to Napoleon III, the Tablet to Czar Alexander II, the Tablet to Queen Victoria and the Tablet to Náṣiri'd-Dín Sháh. Associating this with the prophecy of Zechariah in the Old Testament, Bahá'u'lláh concludes the *Súriy-i-Haykal* with these words:

> Thus have We built the Temple with the hands of power and might, could ye but know it. This is the Temple promised unto you in the Book. Draw ye nigh unto it. This is that which profiteth you, could ye but comprehend it. Be fair, O peoples of the earth! Which is preferable, this, or a temple which is built of clay? Set your faces towards it. Thus have ye been commanded by God, the Help in Peril, the Self-Subsisting. Follow ye His bidding, and praise ye God, your Lord, for that which He hath bestowed upon you. He, verily, is the Truth. No God is there but He. He revealeth what He pleaseth, through His Words 'Be and it is.'[1]

Throughout the Tablet, the Pen of the Most High addresses the Haykal (Temple) and reveals the glory and majesty with which it is invested. In answer to a question, Bahá'u'lláh has stated[2] that the Haykal which is addressed in this Súrih is the Person of Bahá'u'lláh, and so is the voice which addresses the

Haykal. It is fascinating to know that the One Who speaks with the voice of God in this Tablet is identical with the One spoken to.

In this Súrih it is stated that the Haykal has been made a mirror to reflect the sovereignty of God and to manifest His Beauty and Grandeur to all mankind. It has been given the power to do whatsoever It desires. Oceans of knowledge and utterance have been placed within Its heart, and It has been made the Manifestation of God's own Self for all who are in heaven and on earth.

Speaking in this Súrih of the transcendent glory with which the Haykal is invested, Bahá'u'lláh states:

> Naught is seen in My temple but the Temple of God and in My beauty but His Beauty, and in My being but His Being, and in My self but His Self, and in My movement but His Movement and in My acquiescence but His Acquiescence, and in My pen but His Pen, the Mighty, the All-Praised. There hath not been in My soul but the Truth, and in Myself naught could be seen but God.[3]

To fully appreciate the majesty and power of this outstanding work of Bahá'u'lláh in the absence of a translation is impossible. Suffice it to say that every time He addresses the Haykal He unveils a new facet of God's Revelation, as if opening a new door leading to some mystery enshrined in His Writings, a mystery hitherto hidden from the eyes of men. If the pure in heart is enabled to have just a glimpse of this infinite realm of divine Revelation which is beyond his comprehension, such a glimpse can endow his soul with an insight which no human agency can ever hope to confer upon it.

In one of His Tablets referring to the vastness and richness of His Revelation, Bahá'u'lláh states:

> . . . immerse yourselves in this Ocean in whose depths lay hidden the pearls of wisdom and of utterance . . .[4]

These words of Bahá'u'lláh become a reality when the

believer, in a state of detachment from this world, meditates upon the verses of the *Súriy-i-Haykal*. For he will find many such pearls hidden within its verses. The concept of the Haykal (Temple), in the form of the human temple and representing the Person of Bahá'u'lláh, in itself invokes many thoughts and opens many doors to a deeper understanding of His Revelation. Whereas the human temple is made of flesh and bone, the Haykal is constituted of the Word of God. It is portrayed vividly by Bahá'u'lláh in this celebrated Súrih, and He adds more mystery and realism to it when He addresses some limbs and organs of that Temple as well as the letters (H, Y, K, and L) which constitute the word.

Every word and letter uttered by the Manifestation of God assumes meaning and significance beyond the understanding of man. For example, there are lengthy Tablets revealed by the Báb and Bahá'u'lláh explaining the meaning of only one letter mentioned in the Holy Books of older religions. We have already given examples of this in a previous volume.* In the *Súriy-i-Haykal*, Bahá'u'lláh reveals the significance of the letters which form the word 'Haykal', and the potentialities with which each one has been invested by God. It is difficult to convey these without having access to the words of Bahá'u'lláh. Bahá'u'lláh states that the Haykal is the source of the creation of the new race of men, that through each one of its letters, God will raise up wonderful beings whose numbers are known to none except Him and whose faces will shine with the radiance of their Lord. These souls will circle around the Cause of God as a shadow moves around the sun. They will protect the Faith from the onslaught of the deniers and will offer up their lives willingly for the promotion of His Cause among men. This Tablet is replete with glad-tidings of the appearance of a band of devoted believers whom Bahá'u'lláh refers to as the new race of men. These words are revealed in the *Súriy-i-Haykal*:

* see vol. 1, p. 126.

> The day is approaching when God will have, by an act of His Will, raised up a race of men the nature of which is inscrutable to all save God, the All-Powerful, The Self-Subsisting.[5]

Bahá'u'lláh exhorts the eye of the Haykal not to gaze upon the world of creation but to focus only upon the beauty of His Lord. He promises the advent of a day when He will have created, through this eye, people of penetrating insight who will see the signs and tokens of His Revelation with a vision bestowed upon them through His bounty and favour.

To the ear of the Haykal, Bahá'u'lláh gives counsel to become deaf to the voices of the ungodly and to listen to the melodies of His Revelation. Again, He states that through this ear He will create a race of men with ears purified and worthy to hear the Word of God as revealed by Him in this day.

The tongue of the Haykal is also addressed in the same vein—it has been created to mention the name of God and celebrate His praise. He gives the joyous tidings that through the creation of this tongue, God will raise up souls who will conquer the hearts of men through the power of their utterance and the sway of their word.

Bahá'u'lláh calls on the Haykal to stretch out its hands upon all the dwellers of earth and heaven, and to hold within its grasp the reins of the Cause of God. He prophesies that through these hands, He will soon create hands of power and might through whom God will reveal His omnipotence and ascendancy to all the peoples of the world. Concerning these hands Bahá'u'lláh reveals in the Súrih:

> He will, ere long, out of the Bosom of Power draw forth the Hands of Ascendancy and Might — Hands who will arise to win victory for this Youth and who will purge mankind from the defilement of the outcast and the ungodly. These Hands will gird up their loins to champion the Faith of God, and will, in My name the self-subsistent, the mighty, subdue the peoples and kindreds of the earth.[6]

The heart of the Haykal, Bahá'u'lláh states, is the source of all knowledge. Of this knowledge He declares:

> Within the treasury of Our Wisdom there lies unrevealed a knowledge, one word of which, if we chose to divulge it to mankind, would cause every human being to recognize the Manifestation of God and to acknowledge His omniscience, would enable every one to discover the secrets of all the sciences, and to attain so high a station as to find himself wholly independent of all past and future learning. Other knowledges We do as well possess, not a single letter of which We can disclose, nor do We find humanity able to hear even the barest reference to their meaning. Thus have We informed you of the Knowledge of God, the All-Knowing, the All-Wise.[7]

Bahá'u'lláh affirms that through the outpouring of knowledge from the heart of the Haykal, He will soon raise up scientists of great calibre who will bring about such marvellous technological achievements that no one can as yet imagine them. This prophecy of Bahá'u'lláh has already been fulfilled—and this is only the beginning. We have previously stated* that the Revelation of the Báb ushered in a new era in the fields of science and technology, especially in communications, to prepare the way for the coming of Bahá'u'lláh. His Message being for all mankind, it is only logical that the same God who has revealed it would also create the means for its universal propagation, so that the news of the coming of Bahá'u'lláh might reach every part of the world.

The technological developments which have taken place in the field of communications since the advent of the Báb bear ample testimony to this. As the Faith of Bahá'u'lláh grew, the means of communication kept pace with it. During the early days of Bahá'u'lláh's ministry, His disciples had to travel mainly on foot or by donkey and mule to teach the Faith, but it did not take very long until some began to travel by steamship.

* see vol. 1, pp. 216–18.

They took His Message to India and other countries in this way.

Soon after the passing of Bahá'u'lláh, the time had come for the expansion of the Faith throughout the world, especially the West, but the pace was still slow. When 'Abdu'l-Bahá journeyed to the West, He travelled by steamship, railway and automobile. The Bahá'í communities in those days were, for the most part, isolated from each other and movement was slow. But today the Bahá'í community is engaged in enormous teaching activity covering the whole world. Wherever there is freedom of religion they are bringing the message of Bahá'u'lláh to the notice of their countrymen and consequently more people embrace the Faith. Hundreds of national and international teaching projects, and administrative functions involving peoples of all nations and races, are carried out in the five continents of the globe. All these activities are made possible by using the fast and marvellous system of communications which has become available in recent times. The Bahá'ís believe that this is no coincidence: that God, having called the peoples of the world to unity through the message of Bahá'u'lláh, has also provided the means by which that unity may be established. In the meantime, humanity benefits without realizing why these marvellous inventions have come about.

Those who are unfamiliar with the Faith or have not recognized the station of Bahá'u'lláh will no doubt view with scepticism the argument that the advent of the modern communications system is primarily due to the appearance of a universal religion in the world. It seems far-fetched and unacceptable. But in surveying the progress of their Faith, the followers of Bahá'u'lláh have seen that whenever the propagation of the Faith or the building of its Administrative Order* needed some new material means, they were miraculously provided in time. Some of the new inventions

* see the writings of Shoghi Effendi for an appreciation of the Administrative Order of Bahá'u'lláh.

which have played a vital part in the development of the Faith have come about just in time to serve a particular need. To cite one example of many: Bahá'u'lláh revealed many Tablets, Epistles and Books which, if compiled, would produce about one hundred volumes. 'Abdu'l-Bahá's writings are no less in range. The Writings of Bahá'u'lláh and 'Abdu'l-Bahá contain, among other things, teachings both spiritual and social, laws, exhortations and explanations about many subjects including man, the purpose of his life and his relationship to God. Added to these are the voluminous writings of Shoghi Effendi, the Guardian of the Faith. In addition to his famous works, he has written no less than twenty-six thousand letters, some of them so lengthy that they warranted being printed in the form of a book. His writings contain invaluable guidance which, as the authorized Interpreter of the Words of Bahá'u'lláh, he has given to the Bahá'í world. It can be seen therefore that the Bahá'í Holy Writings are enormous in range and contain matters of vital interest for all humanity.

When the Universal House of Justice, the supreme governing body of the Bahá'í community, came into being in 1963, one of the most essential needs was the collating of all the Writings of the Central Figures of the Faith and the making of a comprehensive index of all the subjects they contained. This was a vital necessity for the supreme institution of the Faith which had to have access to each and every subject recorded in these Writings, so that it could guide the Bahá'í community in accordance with the teachings of Bahá'u'lláh, and also legislate whenever feasible on matters which are not explicitly mentioned in these Writings.

Up until the formation of the Universal House of Justice, it was impossible even to attempt to make this comprehensive index. Such a colossal undertaking, involving the provision of a detailed list of every subject within such a vast range of writings, would not have been a practical proposition given the small size of the Bahá'í community because of the non-existence of technological aids at that time. The invention of these aids, such as photocopiers and electronic processors, and their commercial use, were almost synchronized with the birth of the Supreme Body of the Faith of Bahá'u'lláh. And soon this vital task was undertaken. Had it not been for this timely development, insignificant as it may seem today, it is difficult to imagine how the Universal House of Justice could have discharged its sacred functions in the Bahá'í world effectively, bearing in mind that prior to taking every major decision, the Supreme Body has to refer to the Writings of Bahá'u'lláh, 'Abdu'l-Bahá and Shoghi Effendi and take into consideration their words which have a bearing on the subject.

Indeed, as the believers play their part in the propagation and consolidation of the Cause of Bahá'u'lláh, God provides the means for its progress and eventual establishment as a world religion for all mankind. Both the constructive and destructive forces in the world assist in its promotion. The process of the breaking up of the old order is in itself a positive step, paving the way for the spreading of the new.

On the other hand, through the transforming power of the Revelation of Bahá'u'lláh, God is creating a new race of men who arise to champion His Cause. Through the sacrificial outpourings of their substance and resources, they attract the spiritual forces which together with all the material aids sent down by Providence, propel the Cause of God forward.

Bahá'u'lláh in the *Súriy-i-Haykal* rebukes the people of the Bayán* for their blindness to His Revelation in spite of the fact that the Báb had nurtured and prepared them for His Coming. He identifies Himself with the Báb in the *Súriy-i-Haykal* when He addresses the Bábís:

> Had the Primal Point (The Báb) been someone else beside Me as ye claim, and had attained My presence, verily He

* The followers of the Báb. However, the term 'people of the Bayán' here applies to followers of the Báb who did not embrace the Cause of Bahá'u'lláh.

> would have never allowed Himself to be separated from Me, but rather We would have had mutual delights with each other in My Days.[8]

Bahá'u'lláh in the Súrih expatiates on His sufferings at the hands of the breakers of the Covenant of the Báb, those who denied His trust and turned away from His Cause. He describes how he had chosen one of his brothers, Mírzá Yaḥyá, showered upon him a sprinkling from the Ocean of His Knowledge, clothed him with the ornament of a name, and exalted him to such a station that all the believers turned to him in devotion and protected him from every tribulation.* Yet when Mírzá Yaḥyá witnessed the ascendancy of the Bearer of the Message of God for this age, he rose up against Him, attempted to take His life and repudiated His Cause. In a challenging tone Bahá'u'lláh declares that if the followers of Mírzá Yaḥyá did not turn to Him [Bahá'u'lláh] and lend their support, God would assist Him with His supreme Hosts, both visible and invisible, and would assuredly raise up a new race of men who would champion His Cause and make Him victorious in the end.

Bahá'u'lláh in the *Súriy-i-Haykal* reveals that the power of God is beyond the comprehension of man. Through this power all created things have come into being. If it be His will, He can in one instant take life from everything and in another bestow a new life upon it. These are His Own Words:

> It is in Our power, should We wish it, to enable a speck of floating dust to generate, in less than the twinkling of an eye, suns of infinite, of unimaginable splendour, to cause a dewdrop to develop into vast and numberless oceans, to infuse into every letter such a force as to empower it to unfold all the knowledge of past and future ages.[9]

* see vols. 1 and 2. The title 'Subḥ-i-Azal' (The Morn of Eternity) was conferred upon Mírzá Yaḥyá. He was nominated by the Báb as head of the Bábí community.

He further explains that created things may be likened to the leaves of a tree which derive their sustenance and life from the root but outwardly seem to be flourishing independently of it.

It is in the *Súriy-i-Haykal* that, while admonishing the people for their perversity and blindness to His revelation, Bahá'u'lláh refers to the Manifestation of God who will come after Him.* These are His words:

> By those words which I have revealed, Myself is not intended, but rather He Who will come after Me. To it is witness God, the All-Knowing . . . Deal not with Him as ye have dealt with Me.[10]

There is no doubt that this passage refers to the Manifestation of God who comes after Bahá'u'lláh, since Shoghi Effendi has confirmed this in His writings.† There is a similar passage revealed in another Tablet concerning the next Manifestation of God:

> I am not apprehensive for My own self, My fears are for Him Who will be sent down unto you after Me—Him Who will be invested with great sovereignty and mighty dominion.[11]

However, the following passage from the Writings of Bahá'u'lláh, which sounds similar to the passages quoted above, relates to the person of 'Abdu'l-Bahá:

> By God, O people! Mine eye weepeth, and the eye of 'Alí (the Báb) weepeth amongst the Concourse on high, and Mine heart crieth out, and the heart of Muḥammad crieth out within the Most Glorious Tabernacle, and My soul shouteth and the souls of the Prophets shout before them that are endued with understanding . . . My sorrow is not for myself, but for Him Who shall come after Me, in the shadow

* According to the text of the *Kitáb-i-Aqdas* (Bahá'u'lláh's Most Holy Book) the next Manifestation of God will not appear before the lapse of at least a thousand years.

† see *Dispensation*, p.117.

> of My Cause, with manifest and undoubted sovereignty, inasmuch as they will not welcome His appearance, will repudiate His signs, will dispute His sovereignty, will contend with Him, and will betray His Cause . . .[12]

In the Writings of Bahá'u'lláh there are references to the symbolic appearance of the Maid of Heaven to Him.* In the *Súriy-i-Haykal* He describes in a fascinating manner the proclamation of His mission by the Maiden symbolizing the 'Most Great Spirit' which animated Him throughout His Ministry. This is how He reveals the descent of this mysterious Spirit upon Himself:

> While engulfed in tribulations I heard a most wondrous, a most sweet voice, calling above My head. Turning My face, I beheld a Maiden—the embodiment of the remembrance of the name of My Lord—suspended in the air before Me. So rejoiced was she in her very soul that her countenance shone with the ornament of the good-pleasure of God, and her cheeks glowed with the brightness of the All-Merciful. Betwixt earth and heaven she was raising a call which captivated the hearts and minds of men. She was imparting to both My inward and outer being tidings which rejoiced My soul, and the souls of God's honoured servants. Pointing with her finger unto My head, she addressed all who are in heaven and all who are on earth, saying: 'By God! This is the Best-Beloved of the worlds, and yet ye comprehend not. This is the Beauty of God amongst you, and the power of His sovereignty within you, could ye but understand. This is the Mystery of God and His Treasure, the Cause of God and His glory unto all who are in the kingdoms of Revelation and of creation, if ye be of them that perceive.'[13]

It is impossible for man to understand the nature of the Manifestations of God and the spirit which motivates them. Just as it is impossible for a creature in the animal kingdom to

* see vol. 1.

appreciate the nature of man, so it is beyond the capacity of a human being to grasp the inner reality of God's Messengers, for they abide in a spiritual realm far above the reach of men. In former Dispensations the Holy Spirit manifested itself to the Founders of the great world religions and enabled them to reveal the teachings of God to humanity. But a human being can never understand nor experience this. In order to convey to his followers that He was animated by the power of God, each Manifestation of God has spoken in symbolic language concerning the appearance of the Holy Spirit to Him. In the Holy Writings of former religions we read how Moses heard the voice of God through the Burning Bush or how the Dove descended upon Christ or how Muḥammad received His Revelation through the Angel Gabriel. All these are different symbols of the same entity, the Holy Spirit, which acts as an intermediary between God and His Manifestations. This link is similar to the rays of the sun by which energy is transmitted to the planets. Bahá'u'lláh, being the Supreme Manifestation of God,* whose advent has been hailed in the Heavenly Books as the advent of the Day of God Himself, † has stated in some of His Tablets that the Holy Spirit was created through one word of His. And in the *Súriy-i-Haykal* He declares:

> The Holy Spirit Itself hath been generated through the agency of a single letter revealed by this Most Great Spirit, if ye be of them that comprehend.[14]

In His Writings, Bahá'u'lláh has indicated that whereas in past Dispensations the Prophets and Messengers of God received their Revelation through an intermediary, in this Dispensation the voice of God may be heard directly from the Person of Bahá'u'lláh. Affirming this in one of His Tablets,[15] Bahá'u'lláh states that the same voice which Moses heard through the Burning Bush may be heard directly from Bahá'u'lláh in this Day.

* see vol. 1, pp. 295–6.

† see vol. 1, pp. 64, 236–8.

In reading such statements, however, one may be erroneously led to think that Bahá'u'lláh is identifying Himself with the Godhead. Such a conclusion is due to our lack of understanding of the infinite Realms of God. Our minds are limited, while the world of the Manifestations of God is beyond our capacity to appreciate. Bahá'u'lláh has clearly stated that God in His essence is unknowable and inaccessible to all, including His Manifestations. In one of His prayers Bahá'u'lláh describes His relationship with God in these words:

> When I contemplate, O my God, the relationship that bindeth me to Thee, I am moved to proclaim to all created things 'verily I am God!'; and when I consider my own self, lo, I find it coarser than clay![16]

The station of Bahá'u'lláh is that of the Supreme Manifestation of God. Only by reading His own words and meditating on them in a prayerful attitude may we be enabled to acquire a limited understanding of His divine powers and attributes, Whom Shoghi Effendi describes as 'transcendental in His majesty, serene, awe-inspiring, unapproachably glorious'.[17]

The *Súriy-i-Haykal* contains many challenging themes. Every line is charged with enormous power and every subject is indicative of the greatness of the Cause of Bahá'u'lláh, such greatness that sometimes it staggers the imagination.

Although extensive parts of the Tablets which are added to the Súrih have been translated into English by Shoghi Effendi and published, only a few passages from the Súrih itself have been translated. We have already included most of them in this account, and quote the following in conclusion:

> The onrushing winds of the grace of God have passed over all things. Every creature hath been endowed with all the potentialities it can carry. And yet the peoples of the world have denied this grace! Every tree hath been endowed with

the choicest fruits, every ocean enriched with the most luminous gems. Man, himself, hath been invested with the gifts of understanding and knowledge. The whole creation hath been made the recipient of the revelation of the All-Merciful, and the earth the repository of things inscrutable to all except God, the Truth, the Knower of things unseen. The time is approaching when every created thing will have cast its burden. Glorified be God Who hath vouchsafed this grace that encompasseth all things, whether seen or unseen![18]

8

Kings and Ecclesiastics

The proclamation of the message of Bahá'u'lláh to the kings and rulers of the world had been initiated in Constantinople when He issued His first Tablet to Sulṭán 'Abdu'l-Azíz of Turkey. It reached its climax in Adrianople with the revelation of the *Súriy-i-Mulúk* (Súrih of the Kings), a lengthy Epistle addressed to the kings collectively. It continued with the Tablets which form part of the *Súriy-i-Haykal*, and it was completed by the revelation of the *Kitáb-i-Aqdas* in the course of the first few years of Bahá'u'lláh's imprisonment in 'Akká.

Kings Addressed in the *Kitáb-i-Aqdas*

The *Kitáb-i-Aqdas*, designated by Bahá'u'lláh as the 'unerring Balance', is the Mother Book of His Dispensation. It is more fully discussed in Chapters 13–17 of this volume. But it is significant that in this Book also Bahá'u'lláh addressed the kings, rulers and ecclesiastical leaders collectively, and some individually.

These are some passages gleaned from the *Kitáb-i-Aqdas* in which Bahá'u'lláh's majestic utterances are directed to the rulers of the world, summoning them to His Cause.

> O kings of the earth! He Who is the sovereign Lord of all is come. The Kingdom is God's, the omnipotent Protector, the Self-Subsisting. Worship none but God, and, with radiant hearts, lift up your faces unto your Lord, the Lord of all names. This is a Revelation to which whatever ye possess can never be compared, could ye but know it.
>
> We see you rejoicing in that which ye have amassed for

others and shutting out yourselves from the worlds which naught except My guarded Tablet can reckon. The treasures ye have laid up have drawn you far away from your ultimate objective. This ill beseemeth you, could ye but understand it. Wash from your hearts all earthly defilements, and hasten to enter the Kingdom of your Lord, the Creator of earth and heaven, Who caused the world to tremble and all its peoples to wail, except them that have renounced all things and clung to that which the Hidden Tablet hath ordained . . . O kings of the earth! The Most Great Law hath been revealed in this Spot, this scene of transcendent splendour. Every hidden thing hath been brought to light, by virtue of the Will of the Supreme Ordainer, He Who hath ushered in the Last Hour, through Whom the Moon hath been cleft, and every irrevocable decree expounded.

Ye are but vassals, O kings of the earth! He Who is the King of Kings hath appeared, arrayed in His most wondrous glory, and is summoning you unto Himself, the Help in Peril, the Self-Subsisting. Take heed lest pride deter you from recognizing the Source of Revelation, lest the things of this world shut you out as by a veil from Him Who is the Creator of heaven. Arise, and serve Him Who is the Desire of all nations, Who hath created you through a word from Him, and ordained you to be, for all time, the emblems of His sovereignty.

By the righteousness of God! It is not Our wish to lay hands on your kingdoms. Our mission is to seize and possess the hearts of men. Upon them the eyes of Bahá are fastened. To this testifieth the Kingdom of Names, could ye but comprehend it. Whoso followeth his Lord, will renounce the world and all that is therein; how much greater, then, must be the detachment of Him Who holdeth so august a station! Forsake your palaces, and haste ye to gain admittance into His Kingdom. This, indeed, will profit you both in this world and in the next. To this testifieth the Lord of the realm on high, did ye but know it.[1]

To Kaiser William I, Emperor of Germany, Bahá'u'lláh addressed these words in the *Kitáb-i-Aqdas*:

Say: O King of Berlin! Give ear unto the Voice calling from this manifest Temple: Verily, there is none other God but Me, the Everlasting, the Peerless, the Ancient of Days. Take heed lest pride debar thee from recognizing the Dayspring of Divine Revelation, lest earthly desires shut thee out, as by a veil, from the Lord of the Throne above and of the earth below. Thus counselleth thee the Pen of the Most High. He, verily, is the Most Gracious, the All-Bountiful. Do thou remember the one whose power transcended thy power, and whose station excelled thy station. Where is he? Whither are gone the things he possessed? Take warning, and be not of them that are fast asleep. He it was who cast the Tablet of God behind him, when We made known unto him what the hosts of tyranny had caused Us to suffer. Wherefore, disgrace assailed him from all sides, and he went down to dust in great loss. Think deeply, O King, concerning him, and concerning them who, like unto thee, have conquered cities and ruled over men. The All-Merciful brought them down from their palaces to their graves. Be warned, be of them who reflect.

We have asked nothing from you. For the sake of God We, verily, exhort you, and will be patient as We have been patient in that which hath befallen Us at your hands, O concourse of kings![2]

In the above passages, Bahá'u'lláh refers to Napoleon III as the 'one whose power transcended thy power', and summons the Emperor to heed His call. But it was a call which remained unheeded.

The decline in the fortunes of William I and of his grandson William II was then set in motion, culminating in the dissolution of his Empire and the establishment of the Republic. In another passage in the same Book, Bahá'u'lláh reveals this remarkable prophecy which now after two World Wars is clearly seen to be fulfilled:

O banks of the Rhine! We have seen you covered with gore, inasmuch as the swords of retribution were drawn against you; and you shall have another turn. And We hear the lamentations of Berlin, though she be today in conspicuous glory.[3]

Another King addressed in a tone of rebuke in the *Kitáb-i-Aqdas* was the Hapsburg monarch, Francis Joseph, Emperor of Austria and King of Hungary. He visited Jerusalem when Bahá'u'lláh was in 'Akká. With these words Bahá'u'lláh admonishes the Emperor:

> O Emperor of Austria! He Who is the Dayspring of God's Light dwelt in the prison of 'Akká, at the time when thou didst set forth to visit the Aqṣá Mosque.* Thou passed Him by, and inquired not about Him, by Whom every house is exalted, and every lofty gate unlocked. We, verily, made it* a place whereunto the world should turn, that they might remember Me, and yet thou hast rejected Him Who is the Object of this remembrance, when He appeared with the Kingdom of God, thy Lord and the Lord of the worlds. We have been with thee at all times, and found thee clinging unto the Branch and heedless of the Root. Thy Lord, verily, is a witness unto what I say. We grieved to see thee circle round Our Name, whilst unaware of Us, though We were before thy face. Open thine eyes, that thou mayest behold this glorious Vision, and recognize Him Whom thou invokest in the daytime and in the night season, and gaze on the Light that shineth above this luminous Horizon.[4]

Soon after the revelation of these words, repeated tragedies and disasters involving the members of the royal family brought much gloom to the Emperor's reign. These were only precursors to the final dissolution of a dynasty which had lasted for almost five hundred years, and the dismemberment of a mighty empire.

Another Kingdom which Bahá'u'lláh repeatedly condemned was that of Turkey. As has already been stated† He had warned

* Jerusalem.
† vol. 2, p. 58.

and severely condemned its rulers since His days in Constantinople.

These are some of the prophetic words of Bahá'u'lláh revealed in the *Súriy-i-Ra'ís*:

> Hearken, O Chief . . . to the Voice of God, the Sovereign, the Help in Peril, the Self-Subsisting . . . Thou hast, O Chief, committed that which hath made Muḥammad, the Apostle of God, groan in the Most Exalted Paradise. The world hath made thee proud so much so that thou hast turned away from the Face through Whose brightness the Concourse on high hath been illumined. Soon thou shalt find thyself in evident loss . . . The day is approaching when the Land of Mystery (Adrianople) and what is beside it shall be changed, and shall pass out of the hands of the King, and commotions shall appear, and the voice of lamentation shall be raised, and the evidences of mischief shall be revealed on all sides, and confusion shall spread by reason of that which hath befallen these captives at the hands of the hosts of oppression. The course of things shall be altered, and conditions shall wax so grievous, that the very sands on the desolate hills will moan, and the trees on the mountain will weep, and blood will flow out of all things. Then wilt thou behold the people in sore distress.[5]

Now, in the *Kitáb-i-Aqdas*, after the revelation of the *Lawḥ-i-Fu'ád* in which He clearly prophesied the Sulṭán's extinction,* Bahá'u'lláh reveals these prophetic words:

> O Spot † that are situate on the shores of the two seas! The throne of tyranny hath, verily, been established upon thee, and the flame of hatred hath been kindled within thy bosom, in such wise that the Concourse on high and they who circle around the Exalted Throne have wailed and lamented. We behold in thee the foolish ruling over the wise, and darkness vaunting itself against the light. Thou art indeed filled with manifest pride. Hath thine outward splendour made thee

* see above, p. 87.
† Constantinople.

> vainglorious? By Him Who is the Lord of mankind! It shall soon perish, and thy daughters and thy widows and all the kindreds that dwell within thee shall lament. Thus informeth thee the All-Knowing, the All-Wise.[6]

The downfall of Sulṭán 'Abdu'l-'Azíz, the end of his shameful reign and that of his successors, the extinction of a dynasty which had lasted for six and a half centuries, the dismemberment of an empire which had once stretched as far as Hungary in Europe to the Caspian Sea in Asia and to Oran in Africa, and above all the collapse of the Caliphate, the most powerful institution in Islám—all these took place in that short period of time after the 'Prisoner of 'Akká' had issued His clear warnings of the dire retributive calamities which were to descend upon the despotic rulers of the Land of Turkey.

Shoghi Effendi makes some significant remarks about the extinction of the Ottoman dynasty and the Caliphate:

> Though Bahá'u'lláh had been banished from His Native land, the tide of calamity which had swept with such fury over Him and over the followers of the Báb, was by no means receding. Under the jurisdiction of the Sulṭán of Turkey, the arch-enemy of His Cause, a new chapter in the history of His ever-recurring trials had opened. The overthrow of the Sultanate and the Caliphate, the twin pillars of Sunní Islám, can be regarded in no other light except as the inevitable consequence of the fierce, the sustained and deliberate persecution which the monarchs of the tottering House of 'U<u>th</u>mán, the recognized successors of the Prophet Muḥammad, had launched against it. From the city of Constantinople, the traditional seat of both the Sultanate and the Caliphate, the rulers of Turkey had, for a period covering almost three quarters of a century, striven, with unabated zeal, to stem the tide of a Faith they feared and abhorred. From the time Bahá'u'lláh set foot on Turkish soil and was made a virtual prisoner of the most powerful potentate of Islám to the year of the Holy Land's liberation from Turkish yoke, successive Caliphs, and in particular the

Sulṭáns ‘Abdu’l-‘Azíz and ‘Abdu’l-Ḥamíd, had, in the full exercise of the spiritual and temporal authority which their exalted office had conferred upon them, afflicted both the Founder of our Faith and the Centre of His Covenant with such pain and tribulation as no mind can fathom nor pen or tongue describe. They alone could have measured or borne them . . .

The orders which these foes issued, the banishments they decreed, the indignities they inflicted, the plans they devised, the investigations they conducted, the threats they pronounced, the atrocities they were prepared to commit, the intrigues and baseness to which they, their ministers, their governors, and military chieftains had stooped, constitute a record which can hardly find a parallel in the history of any revealed religion. The mere recital of the most salient features of that sinister theme would suffice to fill a volume. They knew full well that the spiritual and administrative Centre of the Cause they had striven to eradicate had now shifted to their dominion, that its leaders were Turkish citizens, and that whatever resources these could command were at their mercy. That for a period of almost three score years and ten, while still in the plenitude of its unquestioned authority, while reinforced by the endless machinations of the civil and ecclesiastical authorities of a neighbouring nation, and assured of the support of those of Bahá’u’lláh’s kindred who had rebelled against, and seceded from, His Cause, this despotism should have failed in the end to extirpate a mere handful of its condemned subjects must, to every unbelieving observer, remain one of the most intriguing and mysterious episodes of contemporary history.

The Cause of which Bahá’u’lláh was still the visible leader had, despite the calculations of a short-sighted enemy, undeniably triumphed. No unbiased mind, penetrating the surface of conditions surrounding the Prisoner of ‘Akká, could any longer mistake or deny it. Though the tension which had been relaxed was, for a time, heightened after Bahá’u’lláh’s ascension and the perils of a still unsettled situation were revived, it was becoming increasingly evident that the insidious forces of decay, which for many a long year were eating into the vitals of a diseased nation, were now moving towards a climax. A series of internal convulsions, each more devastating than the previous one, had already been unchained, destined to bring in their wake one of the most catastrophic occurrences of modern times. The murder of that arrogant despot in the year 1876; the Russo-Turkish conflict that soon followed in its wake; the wars of liberation which succeeded it; the rise of the Young Turk movement; the Turkish Revolution of 1909 that precipitated the downfall of 'Abdu'l-Ḥamíd; the Balkan wars with their calamitous consequences; the liberation of Palestine enshrining within its bosom the cities of 'Akká and Haifa, the world centre of an emancipated Faith; the further dismemberment decreed by the Treaty of Versailles; the abolition of the Sultanate and the downfall of the House of 'U<u>th</u>mán; the extinction of the Caliphate; the disestablishment of the State Religion; the annulment of the <u>Sh</u>arí'ah Law and the promulgation of a universal Civil Code; the suppression of various orders, beliefs, traditions and ceremonials believed to be inextricably interwoven with the fabric of the Muslim Faith—these followed with an ease and swiftness that no man had dared envisage. In these devastating blows, administered by friend and foe alike, by Christian nations and professing Muslims, every follower of the persecuted Faith of Bahá'u'lláh recognized evidences of the directing Hand of the departed Founder of his religion, Who, from the invisible Realm, was unloosing a flood of well-deserved calamities upon a rebellious religion and nation.

Compare the evidences of Divine visitation which befell the persecutors of Jesus Christ with these historic retributions which, in the latter part of the first century of the Bahá'í Era, have hurled to dust the chief adversary of the religion of Bahá'u'lláh. Had not the Roman Emperor, in the second half of the first century of the Christian Era, after a distressful siege of Jerusalem, laid waste the Holy City, destroyed the Temple, desecrated and robbed the Holy of Holies of its treasures, and transported them to Rome, reared a pagan colony on the mount of Zion, massacred the Jews, and exiled and dispersed the survivors?

Compare, moreover, these words which the persecuted Christ, as witnessed by the Gospel, addressed to Jerusalem, with Bahá'u'lláh's apostrophe to Constantinople, revealed while He lay in His far-off Prison, and recorded in His Most Holy Book: 'O Jerusalem, Jerusalem, thou that killest the Prophets and stonest them which are sent unto thee, how often would I have gathered thy children together, even as a hen gathereth her chickens under her wings!' And again, as He wept over the city: 'If thou hadst known, even thou, at least in this thy day, the things which belong unto thy peace! but now they are hid from thine eyes. For the days shall come upon thee, that thine enemies shall cast a trench about thee, and compass thee round, and keep thee in on every side, and shall lay thee even with the ground, and thy children within thee; and they shall not leave in thee one stone upon another; because thou knewest not the time of thy visitation.'[7]

To the Presidents of the Republics of America, Bahá'u'lláh has addressed these words recorded in the *Kitáb-i-Aqdas*:

Hearken ye, O Rulers of America and the Presidents of the Republics therein, unto that which the Dove is warbling on the Branch of Eternity: There is none other God but Me, the Ever-Abiding, the Forgiving, the All-Bountiful. Adorn ye the temple of dominion with the ornament of justice and of the fear of God, and its head with the crown of the remembrance of your Lord, the Creator of the heavens. Thus counselleth you He Who is the Dayspring of Names, as bidden by Him Who is the All-Knowing, the All-Wise. The Promised One hath appeared in this glorified Station, whereat all beings, both seen and unseen, have rejoiced. Take ye advantage of the Day of God. Verily, to meet Him is better for you than all that whereon the sun shineth, could ye but know it. O concourse of rulers! Give ear unto that which hath been raised from the Dayspring of Grandeur:

> Verily, there is none other God but Me, the Lord of Utterance, the All-Knowing. Bind ye the broken with the hands of justice, and crush the oppressor who flourisheth with the rod of the commandments of your Lord, the Ordainer, the All-Wise.[8]

In all these Writings, one message in particular was conveyed in an unequivocal language, expressed with vigour, eloquence and majesty, and that was that God had manifested Himself and that His Vicegerent on earth was summoning the Kings to Himself. The warnings in all these messages were unmistakably clear and explicit and might be summed up by the following passage revealed in the *Súriy-i-Mulúk* (Súrih of the Kings):

> If ye pay no heed unto the counsels which, in peerless and unequivocal language, We have revealed in this Tablet, Divine chastisement shall assail you from every direction, and the sentence of His justice shall be pronounced against you. On that day ye shall have no power to resist Him, and shall recognize your own impotence. Have mercy on yourselves and on those beneath you.[9]

The forces of 'Divine chastisement' released by the creative power of the Words of Bahá'u'lláh have been exerting pressure upon the kings and the institution of kingship since those historic summons were issued and not heeded. How remarkable has been the fulfilment of the prophecy of Bahá'u'lláh foreshadowing the decline in the fortunes of royalty who had wielded absolute power throughout the ages! 'From two ranks amongst men', is Bahá'u'lláh's clear pronouncement, 'power has been seized: kings and ecclesiastics.'[10] So swift was the downfall of the kings that within the span of a few decades after Bahá'u'lláh's warnings, many powerful monarchies toppled to the ground, and most remaining ones lost their influence altogether. Revolutions, often combined with violence, took place in different parts of the world and dramatically changed the whole system of political and governmental institutions.

On Monarchy

In the Tablet of Salmán already referred to in Chapter 1, Bahá'u'lláh makes this significant remark concerning the institution of kingship. He writes:

> One of the signs of the maturity of the world is that no one will accept to bear the weight of kingship. Kingship will remain with none willing to bear alone its weight. That day will be the day whereon wisdom will be manifested among mankind. Only in order to proclaim the Cause of God and spread abroad His Faith will anyone be willing to bear this grievous weight. Well is it with him who, for love of God and His Cause, and for the sake of God and for the purpose of proclaiming His Faith, will expose himself unto this great danger, and will accept this toil and trouble.[11]

In His Writings, Bahá'u'lláh has given three signs for the maturity of mankind. One is the above statement concerning the decline in the fortunes of kings. Another, to which we have made a reference in the previous volume,* is the transmuting of elements, the achievement of alchemy. The third, mentioned in the *Kitáb-i-Aqdas*, is the adoption of an international auxiliary language.

From all that has been said it must not be inferred, however, that the Bahá'í teachings condemn the institution of kingship. On the contrary, in one of His Tablets, Bahá'u'lláh has declared:

> Although a republican form of government profiteth all the peoples of the world, yet the majesty of kingship is one of the signs of God. We do not wish that the countries of the world should remain deprived thereof . . .[12]

* vol. 2, p. 268.

The Bahá'í teachings envisage the re-establishment in the future of properly functioning constitutional monarchies in various countries of the world.

In another Tablet, Bahá'u'lláh prophesies the future of this institution in these words:

> Ere long will God make manifest on earth kings who will recline on the couches of justice, and will rule amongst men even as they rule their own selves. They, indeed, are among the choicest of My creatures in the entire creation.[13]

Shoghi Effendi has written the following explanation of the Bahá'í teachings on the institution of monarchy:

> Let none, however, mistake or unwittingly misrepresent the purpose of Bahá'u'lláh. Severe as has been His condemnation pronounced against those sovereigns who persecuted Him, and however strict the censure expressed collectively against those who failed signally in their clear duty to investigate the truth of His Faith and to restrain the hand of the wrong-doer, His teachings embody no principle that can, in any way, be construed as a repudiation, or even a disparagement, however veiled, of the institution of kingship. The catastrophic fall, and the extinction of the dynasties and empires of those monarchs whose disastrous end He particularly prophesied, and the declining fortunes of the sovereigns of His Own generation, whom He generally reproved—both constituting a passing phase of the evolution of the Faith,—should, in no wise, be confounded with the future position of that institution. Indeed, if we delve into the writings of the Author of the Bahá'í Faith, we cannot fail to discover unnumbered passages in which, in terms that none can misrepresent, the principle of kingship is eulogized, the rank and conduct of just and fair-minded kings is extolled, the rise of monarchs, ruling with justice and even professing His Faith, is envisaged, and the solemn duty to arise and insure the triumph of Bahá'í sovereigns is inculcated. To conclude from the above quoted words, addressed by Bahá'u'lláh to the monarchs of the earth, to infer from the recital of the

woeful disasters that have overtaken so many of them, that His followers either advocate or anticipate the definite extinction of the institution of kingship, would indeed be tantamount to a distortion of His teaching.[14]

In the *Kitáb-i-Aqdas* Bahá'u'lláh prophesies a time when the kings and rulers of the world will embrace His Cause, and He showers His blessings upon such a ruler. These are His words:

> How great the blessedness that awaiteth the king who will arise to aid My Cause in My Kingdom, who will detach himself from all else but Me! Such a king is numbered with the companions of the Crimson Ark — the Ark which God hath prepared for the people of Bahá. All must glorify his name, must reverence his station, and aid him to unlock the cities with the keys of My Name, the omnipotent Protector of all that inhabit the visible and invisible kingdoms. Such a king is the very eye of mankind, the luminous ornament on the brow of creation, the fountain-head of blessings unto the whole world. Offer up, O people of Bahá, your substance, nay your very lives, for his assistance.[15]

Speaking of future monarchs who will embrace the Cause, it is appropriate at this juncture to recount the story of Ḥájí Sháh Khalílu'lláh-i-Fárání, a believer of wide repute who, in company with his illustrious father, Áqá Mír Muḥammad Big, attained the presence of Bahá'u'lláh in 'Akká in the year AH 1306 (AD 1889). He was a native of Fárán* in the Province of Khurásán. In his memoirs he describes their arrival in 'Akká and how they attained the presence of Bahá'u'lláh:

> At last we arrived in the City of 'Akká and were taken to the Bahá'í Pilgrim House situated in the Khán † where pilgrims and some resident Bahá'ís were staying. We enjoyed the company of these devoted and sincere believers immensely. In the afternoon of our arrival, 'Abdu'l-Bahá came to visit

* see p. 62.
† Khán-i-'Avámíd. (A.T.)

us. He illumined our eyes by the effulgent rays of His countenance. He showered upon us His loving kindness, asked about our journey and the state of the friends in various towns, and breathed into our hearts the spirit of joy and gladness.

The following day we were summoned to the presence of the Blessed Beauty. God is my witness as to our state and condition at that time. A flood of tears was flowing from our eyes as we beheld His countenance. Through His all-bountiful favours, the Tongue of Grandeur* spoke to us and said 'Did you see how the Hand of Power took you and brought you here? Otherwise, Fárán is situated on one side of the world and 'Akká on the other . . . '† He spoke to us words of such loving kindness and showered upon us so many bounties that my pen is unable to record them . . . Each day we attained His presence and were fed from the living waters of His grace. The eyes of His bountiful favours were often directed toward us . . . One day we were summoned at the time of revelation‡ and heard the melodies of holiness. Gracious God! at such a time not only was the soul exhilarated, but it seemed as if even the door, the walls, the trees and the fruits were made to vibrate with excitement. The Blessed Beauty was seated upon the throne of utterance, the verses of God were pouring out as a copious rain and the shrill voice of the Pen of the Most High could be heard. Each day we received our portion of bounties from His presence and were in the utmost joy . . . One day we were told at the Pilgrim House that His Blessed Person was going to the Mansion of Bahjí§ . . . we were summoned to His presence in the Mansion . . . and some accommodation was assigned to us in that neighbourhood.[16]

In a spoken chronicle to some friends, Ḥájí Sháh Khalílu'lláh has recounted a story of Bahá'u'lláh who one day visited them in their residence:

* Bahá'u'lláh. (A.T.)

† These are not to be taken as the exact words of Bahá'u'lláh. (A.T.)

‡ On the revelation of the Word of God see vol. 1, pp. 18–44.

§ Bahá'u'lláh had moved to the Mansion a long time before this but at times He visited 'Akká and stayed there for some time. (A.T.)

One day Bahá'u'lláh informed my father that He would be visiting us in the afternoon. That day He arrived with a few of his disciples. We were both highly honoured by His presence and immersed in the ocean of His grace and bounties. After some time He arose to depart. We accompanied Him to the door and as He went out, He signalled to us not to accompany Him further. I watched from behind His graceful stature and the majesty of His walk, until He disappeared from my sight. I was so carried away, and in that state I said to myself: What a pity! If only the kings of the world could recognize Him and arise to serve Him, both the Cause and the believers would be exalted in this day.

The following day when we attained His presence, He turned His face to me and addressed the following words to me with infinite charm and loving kindness. He said: 'If the kings and rulers of the world had embraced the Faith in this day, you people could never have found an entry into this exalted Court. You could never have had the opportunity to attain Our presence, nor could you ever have acquired the privilege of hearing the words of the Lord of Mankind. Of course the time will come when the kings and rulers of the world will become believers, and the Cause of God will be glorified outwardly. But this will happen after the meek and the lowly ones of the earth have won this inestimable bounty.'*[17]

Ḥájí Sháh Khalíl'u'lláh grew up in a Bahá'í atmosphere. His father was an outstanding believer, very influential among the people and endowed with a deep understanding and knowledge of God. His home was a centre of Bahá'í activities in Fárán. Ḥají Sháh Khalíl'u'lláh followed in the footsteps of his father. He became an eminent Bahá'í whose devotion to and enthusiasm for the Faith endeared him to the believers throughout Persia. In his native town, he was a well-trusted citizen like his father before him, and although he was known

* These are not to be taken as the exact words which Bahá'u'lláh spoke on that occasion. (A.T.)

to be a Bahá'í he was respected by a great many non-Bahá'ís who often turned to him for help and advice.

Some years after the ascension of Bahá'u'lláh he attained the presence of 'Abdu'l-Bahá and basked in the sunshine of His love for some time in 'Akká. During Shoghi Effendi's ministry too he was twice given the privilege of visiting the Holy Land, where he had the honour of going into the presence of Shoghi Effendi almost every day during his pilgrimage.

Ḥájí Sháh Khalíl'u'lláh was a great teacher of the Faith. Through his loving disposition he attracted many people to the Cause of God. His spiritual qualities, coupled with the burning love he cherished for Bahá'u'lláh and His Faith, made him an outstanding Bahá'í who warmed the hearts of the believers wherever he went.

Religious Leaders Addressed in the *Kitáb-i-Aqdas*

Another category of people who wielded enormous power was the clergy. Throughout the whole period of recorded history these men held the reins of power in their hands, and guided the masses in their ways. This was perhaps necessary as in former days most people were illiterate and needed to be led by someone. The authority with which religious leaders acted within the community, both in the East and the West, was so deeply rooted in the hearts of people that even kings were bound to obey them. To cite one example: the kings of the Qájár dynasty in Persia ruled as powerful dictators of a totalitarian regime. At one stage, one of the leading divines of Persia had forbidden people to smoke. Although this order did not last very long, everyone had to obey it until it was rescinded. Even the Qájár King in his palace did not dare to smoke. Such was the sway of the word of the clergy when Bahá'u'lláh appeared! With a stroke of His mighty Pen, He abolished the institution of priesthood and announced that He had seized their power, a power they had wielded from time immemorial.

ḤÁJÍ SHÁH KHALÍLU'LLÁH-I-FÁRÁNÍ

An eminent Bahá'í who attained the presence of Bahá'u'lláh in 'Akká

MÍRZÁ 'AZÍZU'LLÁH-I-JADHDHÁB

A Bahá'í of Jewish origin who was directed by Bahá'u'lláh to proclaim the Faith to Baron Rothschild

To Shaykh Báqir, a Muslim Persian Mujtahid whom Bahá'u'lláh stigmatized as 'Wolf' because of his orders to execute two illustrious Bahá'ís, Bahá'u'lláh has addressed these words:

> O heedless one! Rely not on thy glory and thy power. Thou art even as the last trace of sunlight upon the mountain-top. Soon will it fade away, as decreed by God, the All-Possessing, the Most High. Thy glory, and the glory of such as are like thee, have been taken away, and this, verily, is what hath been ordained by the One with Whom is the Mother Tablet . . . [18]

In the *Kitáb-i-Aqdas* Bahá'u'lláh addresses the divines of all religions collectively; these are some extracts from His words:

> Say: O leaders of religion! Weigh not the Book of God with such standards and sciences as are current amongst you, for the Book itself is the unerring balance established amongst men. In this most perfect balance whatsoever the peoples and kindreds of the earth possess must be weighed, while the measure of its weight should be tested according to its own standard, did ye but know it.
>
> The eye of My loving-kindness weepeth sore over you, inasmuch as ye have failed to recognize the One upon Whom ye have been calling in the daytime and in the night season, at even and at morn. Advance, O people, with snow-white faces and radiant hearts, unto the blest and crimson Spot, wherein the Sadratu'l-Muntahá is calling: 'Verily, there is none other God beside Me, the Omnipotent Protector, the Self-Subsisting!'
>
> O ye leaders of religion! Who is the man amongst you that can rival Me in vision or insight? Where is he to be found that dareth to claim to be My equal in utterance or wisdom? No, by My Lord, the All-Merciful! All on the earth shall pass away; and this is the face of your Lord, the Almighty, the Well-Beloved.
>
> We have decreed, O people, that the highest and last end of all learning be the recognition of Him Who is the Object

of all knowledge; and yet, behold how ye have allowed your learning to shut you out, as by a veil, from Him Who is the Dayspring of this Light, through Whom every hidden thing hath been revealed. Could ye but discover the source whence the splendour of this utterance is diffused, ye would cast away the peoples of the world and all that they possess, and would draw nigh unto this most blessed Seat of glory.

Say: This, verily, is the heaven in which the Mother Book is treasured, could ye but comprehend it. He it is Who hath caused the Rock to shout, and the Burning Bush to lift up its voice, upon the Mount rising above the Holy Land, and proclaim: 'The Kingdom is God's, the sovereign Lord of all, the All-Powerful, and Loving!'

We have not entered any school, nor read any of your dissertations. Incline your ears to the words of this unlettered One, wherewith He summoneth you unto God, the Ever-Abiding. Better is this for you than all the treasures of the earth, could ye but comprehend it.[19]

And again:

O concourse of divines! When My verses were sent down, and My clear tokens were revealed, We found you behind the veils. This, verily, is a strange thing . . . We have rent the veils asunder. Beware lest ye shut out the people by yet another veil. Pluck asunder the chains of vain imaginings, in the name of the Lord of all men, and be not of the deceitful. Should ye turn unto God, and embrace His Cause, spread not disorder within it, and measure not the Book of God with your selfish desires. This, verily, is the counsel of God aforetime and hereafter . . . Had ye believed in God, when He revealed Himself, the people would not have turned aside from Him, nor would the things ye witness today have befallen Us. Fear God, and be not of the heedless . . . This is the Cause that hath caused all your superstitions and idols to tremble . . .

O concourse of divines! Beware lest ye be the cause of strife in the land, even as ye were the cause of the repudiation of the Faith in its early days. Gather the people around this

Word that hath made the pebbles to cry out: 'The Kingdom is God's, the Dawning-Place of all signs!' . . . Tear the veils asunder in such wise that the inmates of the Kingdom will hear them being rent. This is the command of God, in days gone by, and for those to come. Blessed the man that observeth that whereunto he was bidden, and woe betide the negligent.[20]

In many of His Tablets Bahá'u'lláh has made references to the divines. The following are just a few:

When We observed carefully, We discovered that Our enemies are, for the most part, the divines.

Among the people are those who said: 'He hath repudiated the divines.' Say: 'Yea, by My Lord! I, in very truth, was the One Who abolished the idols!'

We, verily, have sounded the Trumpet, which is Our Most Sublime Pen, and lo, the divines and the learned, and the doctors and the rulers, swooned away except such as God preserved, as a token of His grace, and He, verily, is the All-Bounteous, the Ancient of Days.

O concourse of divines! Fling away idle fancies and imaginings, and turn, then, towards the Horizon of Certitude. I swear by God! All that ye possess will profit you not, neither all the treasures of the earth, nor the leadership ye have usurped. Fear God, and be not of the lost ones.

Say: O concourse of divines! Lay aside all your veils and coverings. Give ear unto that whereunto calleth you the Most Sublime Pen, in this wondrous Day.

The world is laden with dust, by reason of your vain imaginings, and the hearts of such as enjoy near access to God are troubled because of your cruelty. Fear God, and be of them that judge equitably.[21]

Shoghi Effendi has written in some detail on this topic in his *The Promised Day Is Come*. These are some of his remarks:

> ... The decline in the fortunes of the crowned wielders of temporal power has been paralleled by a no less startling deterioration in the influence exercised by the world's spiritual leaders. The colossal events that have heralded the dissolution of so many kingdoms and empires have almost synchronized with the crumbling of the seemingly inviolable strongholds of religious orthodoxy. That same process which, swiftly and tragically, sealed the doom of kings and emperors, and extinguished their dynasties, has operated in the case of the ecclesiastical leaders of both Christianity and Islám, damaging their prestige, and, in some cases, overthrowing their highest institutions. 'Power hath been seized' indeed, from both 'kings and ecclesiastics.' The glory of the former has been eclipsed, the power of the latter irretrievably lost.
>
> Those leaders who exercised guidance and control over the ecclesiastical hierarchies of their respective religions have, likewise, been appealed to, warned, and reproved by Bahá'u'lláh, in terms no less uncertain than those in which the sovereigns who presided over the destinies of their subjects have been addressed. They, too, and more particularly the heads of Muslim ecclesiastical orders, have, in conjunction with despots and potentates, launched their assaults and thundered their anathemas against the Founders of the Faith of God, its followers, its principles, and its institutions. Were not the divines of Persia the first who hoisted the standard of revolt, who inflamed the ignorant and subservient masses against it, and who instigated the civil authorities, through their outcry, their threats, their lies, their calumnies, and denunciations, to decree the banishments, to enact the laws, to launch the punitive campaigns, and to carry out the executions and massacres that fill the pages of its history? So abominable and savage was the butchery committed in a single day, instigated by these divines, and so typical of the 'callousness of the brute and the ingenuity of the fiend' that Renan, in his 'Les

Apôtres,' characterized that day as 'perhaps unparalleled in the history of the world.'

It was these divines, who, by these very acts, sowed the seeds of the disintegration of their own institutions, institutions that were so potent, so famous, and appeared so invulnerable when the Faith was born. It was they who, by assuming so lightly and foolishly, such awful responsibilities, were primarily answerable for the release of those violent and disruptive influences that have unchained disasters as catastrophic as those which overwhelmed kings, dynasties, and empires, and which constitute the most noteworthy landmarks in the history of the first century of the Bahá'í era.

This process of deterioration, however startling in its initial manifestations, is still operating with undiminished force, and will, as the opposition to the Faith of God, from various sources and in distant fields, gathers momentum, be further accelerated and reveal still more remarkable evidences of its devastating power.[22]

Bahá'u'lláh proclaimed His Message to the leaders of the world collectively and to a few monarchs individually. But this proclamation was not meant only for the kings or religious leaders alone. The peoples of the world had to hear it also through their leaders as there was no other form of communication. The mass media of today was non-existent in the days of Bahá'u'lláh. It was God's purpose that leaders of the world hear the advent of His Manifestation, respond positively to His summons, embrace His Cause and communicate His Message to their peoples. But no one responded. Yet God had fulfilled His role in His Covenant with man by vouchsafing His Revelation to mankind and proclaiming it to him. It now rested with man to respond of his own volition to the call of His Creator.

Proclamation to the Jewish Leadership

A survey of Bahá'u'lláh's letters to the leaders of the world indicates that all the nations and major religions of the world were given the opportunity to hear of His coming. Probably one exception was the Jewish people as they did not belong to a particular state at the time. One year before His passing, Bahá'u'lláh had made a remark concerning His proclamation to the rulers of the world. He is reported to have said that by then He had fully proclaimed His Mission to the crowned heads of the world, but He desired to convey the Message of God to Baron Rothschild* who could be considered as the leader of the Jewish people at the time. This remark was addressed to a believer of Jewish descent, Mírzá 'Azízu'lláh-i-Jadhdháb who had gone to 'Akká to attain the presence of Bahá'u'lláh for the third time in the year AH 1308 (AD 1891). Bahá'u'lláh directed him to write to Baron Rothschild and proclaim the Faith to him and if possible pay him a visit.

The story of the life of Mírzá 'Azízu'lláh and his services to the Cause of God are interesting and inspiring indeed. He was of Jewish descent. His father, living in the city of Mashhad, was a learned man and well versed in the Old Testament and other religious books. He used to teach the Old Testament to the Jewish youth. Pure-hearted and with great insight into religious matters, he recognized the truth of the Faith of Islám and secretly declared his conversion to the Muslim authorities. With the exception of his wife, no other members of the Jewish community, not even his own children, were aware of his conversion to Islám. This was about sixteen years before the birth of the Bábí Faith. In particular, he advised his family to watch for the coming of the Lord of Hosts, as he had discovered according to the Holy Books that His advent was at hand.

A few years later, in 1838, some tragic incident resulted in the massacre of about thirty-five Jews in the city of Mashhad by

* Probably Baron Nathaniel Mayer, Lord Rothschild of London (1840–1915), then considered the lay head of world Jewry; or else Baron Edmond de Rothschild of Paris (1845–1934), the great benefactor of thousands of Jews then settling in Palestine.

the Muslims. All the surviving Jews took refuge in the homes of Muslim clergy and in order to save their lives, agreed to accept the Faith of Islám. They were officially converted by the clergy, but, of course, in secret they practised the Jewish Faith. Although their lives had been saved, the Jews newly converted to Islám continued to live in a separate quarter of the city and were not fully integrated with the Muslim community. They were referred to as the 'newcomers' and were still persecuted by the Muslims.

Mírzá 'Azízu'lláh lived in this community. He went to a Muslim school as a child, but soon left it. Instead, he learnt the Old Testament, became fully acquainted with the Jewish Faith, and practised it in secret. Although his education was elementary, he became a successful merchant and emerged as a man of ability and enterprise.

The first time he heard the word 'Bahá'u'lláh' was when one of his brothers, who had become a Bahá'í, mentioned the story of the martyrdom of Badí' to him. But Mírzá 'Azízu'lláh, being very staunch in the Jewish Faith, did not show any interest, and the brother did not pursue the matter any further.

Some time passed and the two brothers had to undertake a series of journeys together on business. In the course of these journeys Mírzá 'Azízu'lláh decided to polish up his elementary knowledge of reading and writing Persian. Being a talented man, it did not take him very long to become proficient as a reader.

One day when his brother was out he took a Bahá'í book and began to read it. He was moved by what he read, but discounted the whole idea of a new Faith. Then one night he had a dream, of which he has written this account in his memoirs:

> In my dream, I heard the announcement that the Lord of Hosts, the Promised One of all ages, had appeared, and that He was inspecting the company of the Prophets and all their followers. I went along immediately to the appointed place.

I saw a vast place on which multitudes of people were assembled in lines. Each prophet along with his followers was seated facing the Qiblih.* I was surprised by the extraordinary light and vision which was given to my eyes, as I could easily see all the people lined up in that vast area.

Opposite the multitudes and facing them, a venerable figure was seated upon a chair uttering some words. I was standing at the end of a line. His blessed Person was over fifty years of age, had a long black beard and was wearing a green Táj† sewn with green silk thread. With His blessed hand He signalled me to go to Him. With my hands I gesticulated to say, how can I come with all these crowds in front of me? He waved His hands to the multitudes and they all prostrated themselves on the ground. He then beckoned me to go forward. I was not sure at this point whether it was to me or someone else that He was signalling. He then repeated His command. This time I went forward immediately, stepping on the backs of people who lay prostrate in front of me, until I reached Him. I prostrated myself at His feet and kissed them. He then helped me up to my feet with His hand and recited the verse of the Qur'án: 'Blessed be God, the most excellent Creator.'[23]

Although this dream made a great impression on Mírzá 'Azízu'lláh, he still remained steadfast in his Jewish faith until some time later when he was converted to the Faith of Bahá'u'lláh by Ḥájí 'Abdu'l-Majíd, the father of Badí'. Soon after embracing the Faith, Mírzá 'Azízu'lláh and his brother journeyed to 'Akká to attain the presence of Bahá'u'lláh. This was in the year 1876, his first pilgrimage to the Holy Land. When the appointed time arrived, Mírzá 'Azízu'lláh was ushered into the room of Bahá'u'lláh in 'Akká. As soon as his eyes saw the person of Bahá'u'lláh he was awestruck to find

* literally: point of adoration. A point to which the faithful turn at the time of prayer.
† head-dress similar to the one that Bahá'u'lláh used to wear.

himself in the presence of the One whom he had seen some years before in that memorable dream, wearing the same clothes and the same green head-dress. With all the devotion and love in his heart Mírzá 'Azízu'lláh promptly prostrated himself at the feet of his Lord. Bahá'u'lláh bent down, helped him up to his feet and recited the verse of the *Qur'án*: 'Blessed be God, the most excellent Creator!'

During his stay in 'Akká, Mírzá 'Azízu'lláh attained the presence of Bahá'u'lláh and 'Abdu'l-Bahá many times. As a result, he became endowed with a new spirit of faith and assurance. The first time that he attained the presence of Bahá'u'lláh, he witnessed the revelation of Bahá'u'lláh's Tablets and heard His voice as He revealed them. This experience left an abiding impression upon him. The only regret he had was that he could not read Arabic and hence was unable to fully appreciate the Holy Writings. This was because he had left school so young and had missed the opportunity to learn Arabic. He felt remorseful over this. Someone in 'Akká volunteered to teach him Arabic, but he declined the offer as he had no time or patience to learn a language so vast in vocabulary and so complex in grammar.

The next day when he attained the presence of Bahá'u'lláh, he approached Him by way of the heart and begged that through His bountiful favours, He might enable him to understand Arabic without going through the usual method of learning the language. His wish was granted, and Mírzá 'Azízu'lláh one day became very excited when he found himself reading and understanding the *Qur'án* and the Tablets of Bahá'u'lláh in Arabic.

Many early believers were uneducated but they were endowed by Bahá'u'lláh with a knowledge which men of learning but devoid of faith did not possess. Earlier on* we have described this form of knowledge, a knowledge which wells out of the heart and is not dependent on learning.

Concerning the special mission given him during his last

* pp. 94–5.

pilgrimage to 'Akká, to proclaim the Faith to Baron Rothschild, Mírzá 'Azízu'lláh has recorded the following in his memoirs:

> After leaving the Holy Land,* I arrived in Istanbul. There I knew a certain broker who had the knowledge of the French language. I asked him if he would teach me a little French every day, so that on my journey to meet Rothschild I would be able to converse a little in that language. In the meantime, I composed a letter to Rothschild which was rendered into French. In this communication I informed him of the coming of Bahá'u'lláh and of the fulfilment of the prophecies of the Old Testament concerning the advent of the Lord of Hosts who had revealed Himself on Mount Carmel at this time. I explained that the followers of Bahá'u'lláh were inviting us to embrace His Cause, adducing proofs and demonstrating that prophecies have been fulfilled. I reminded him that he was considered as the head of the Jewish People. Therefore, I asked him to refer this matter to the Jewish divines in Jerusalem so that they might respond to this question. I explained further that either one had to nullify the proofs and the prophecies of the Old Testament or to accept this blessed Cause. After sending this communication I began to learn French. In those days, Áqá Siyyid Aḥmad-i-Afnán† was in Istanbul. He was very curious to find out the reason for my learning French at this time in my life, and for what purpose I was thinking of going to Paris and London. But since the visit to Rothschild was a confidential matter I did not disclose it . . .[24]

Unfortunately the memoirs of Mírzá 'Azízu'lláh are not conclusive in that there is no mention of whether he succeeded in meeting the Baron or not.

Another interesting mission which Mírzá 'Azízu'lláh undertook during 'Abdu'l-Bahá's ministry was to visit Leo

* This was in 1891. (A.T.)

† A member of the Afnán family who ran a business in Istanbul.

Tolstoy, the famous Russian philosopher and writer. Tolstoy was already informed of the Revelations of the Báb and Bahá'u'lláh, and had praised Their teachings. Mírzá 'Azízu'lláh succeeded in meeting him in September 1902 and in the course of an interview spoke to him at length on the history and the teachings of the Faith and explained the station of Bahá'u'lláh as the Promised One of all ages. The detailed discussions, questions and answers in this interview and the favourable response of Tolstoy, who believed that the Cause of Bahá'u'lláh would spread throughout the world are all recorded in his memoirs.

9

The Pride of Martyrs

Dispatch of the *Lawḥ-i-Sulṭán*

A Tablet of great significance, described by Bahá'u'lláh as the 'rumbling' of His proclamation to the kings and rulers of the world, was revealed in Adrianople and addressed to Náṣiri'd-Dín Sháh of Persia. But it was sent to him from 'Akká. An account of the *Lawḥ-i-Sulṭán* has been given in the previous volume. Its dispatch required a personal messenger as it would have been impossible for the Sháh to receive the Tablet through any other channel.

Clergy and government in Persia were hand-in-hand in ruthlessly persecuting the defenceless followers of the new Faith during the reign of Náṣiri'd-Dín Sháh. Anybody or anything remotely connected with the name Bábí or Bahá'í could become a target for assault and destruction. There could be dangerous consequences for a person found to be in possession of a letter which had some connection with the Faith. When travellers entered a city they would be questioned about their identity and could be searched by officials who lived by bribery and extortion; often through harassment, imprisonment and torture, these men extracted from people as much money as they could. Whenever they came across a Bahá'í, they would thoroughly search him for Bahá'í materials such as letters, books and Tablets, and if they found any, not only would these be confiscated but also the Bahá'í's life would be in great danger. Because of these difficulties all the Writings of Bahá'u'lláh were taken to Persia by individual believers, very often by Shaykh Salmán. He exercised such tact

BÁDÍ', THE PRIDE OF MARTYRS

In front of him may be seen the branding irons in the brazier of fire

ÁQÁ RIḌÁY-I-SA'ÁDATÍ

who attained the presence of Bahá'u'lláh in 'Akká (see p. 302)

and wisdom in his journeys that none of the Tablets he was carrying ever fell into the hands of the enemy.*

To send a Tablet to the Sháh of Persia, however, was a different matter. Not only was a great deal of wisdom needed to protect the Tablet, but the messenger had to be willing to lay down his life as well. When Bahá'u'lláh revealed the Tablet He had commented that the person who was to take it to Náṣiri'd-Dín Sháh had not yet been created. This person had to be endowed with supreme faith and manifest such courage and forbearance in the face of suffering and torture as to astonish the world. Bahá'u'lláh wrote a few lines about the delivery of the Tablet on its cover:

He is God, exalted is He.

We ask God to send one of His servants, and to detach him from Contingent Being, and to adorn his heart with the decoration of strength and composure, that he may help his Lord amidst the concourse of creatures, and, when he becometh aware of what hath been revealed for His Majesty the King, that he may arise and take the Letter, by the permission of his Lord, the Mighty, the Bounteous, and go with speed to the abode of the King. And when he shall arrive at the place of his throne, let him alight in the inn, and let him hold converse with none till he goeth forth one day and standeth where he [i.e. the King] shall pass by. And when the Royal harbingers shall appear, let him raise up the Letter with the utmost humility and courtesy, and say, 'It hath been sent on the part of the Prisoner.' And it is incumbent upon him to be in such a mood that, should the King decree his death, he shall not be troubled within himself, and shall hasten to the place of sacrifice saying, 'O Lord, praise be to Thee because that Thou hast made me a helper to Thy religion, and hast decreed unto me

* Honoured by Bahá'u'lláh by the appellation 'Messenger of the Merciful', Shaykh Salmán carried His Tablets to the believers and brought back their letters to Him. He performed this service for several decades. For his life story see vol. 1, pp. 109–13, vol. 2, *passim*.

martyrdom in Thy way! By Thy Glory, I would not exchange this cup for [all] the cups in the worlds, for Thou hast not ordained any equivalent to this, neither do Kawthar and Salsabíl* rival it!' But if he [i.e. the King] letteth him [i.e. the messenger] go, and interfereth not with him, let him say, 'To Thee be praise, O Lord of the worlds! Verily I am content with Thy good pleasure and what Thou hast predestined unto me in Thy way, even though I did desire that the earth might be dyed with my blood for Thy love. But what Thou willest is best for me: verily Thou knowest what is in my soul, while I know not what is in Thy soul; and Thou art the All-Knowing, the Informed.'[1]

The Story of Badí'

The person who was created anew and performed this sacred mission was a youth of seventeen by the name of Áqá Buzurg, entitled Badí'. The father of Badí', Ḥájí 'Abdu'l-Majíd-i-Ní<u>sh</u>ápúrí known as Abá Badí' (father of Badí') was one of the outstanding believers of the Bábí Faith and later became a devoted follower of Bahá'u'lláh. An account of his life and martyrdom at an old age is given in a previous volume.† Although Badí' grew up in the home of a very devoted believer, he was not touched sufficiently by the spirit of the Faith as to make him believe in the Cause and he remained cold and aloof in relation to it.

Towards the end of His sojourn in Adrianople, Bahá'u'lláh sent Nabíl-i-A'ẓam to Persia to strengthen the faith of the believers, especially because of Mírzá Yaḥyá's opposition to the Cause of God. In the course of his journeys, Nabíl went to the city of Ní<u>sh</u>ápúr where he was entertained by Abá Badí', 'the father of Badí'', who expressed to Nabíl great disappointment in his son. Nabíl, in his unpublished history, has recorded that in Ní<u>sh</u>ápúr, Abá Badí' invited him to his home and himself began to entertain him. Nabíl asked him,

* The names of two rivers in Paradise.
† see vol. 2, pp. 128–36.

'Do you not have a grown-up son?' He replied that he had one but that he was not obedient to him.* Nabíl called for the son and he came in. He was a simple-hearted tall youth, and Nabíl requested that he act as his host.

Gradually, he became attracted to matters pertaining to God and spiritual things and wept throughout the night. In the morning he prepared the tea and went to town; after he had gone Abá Badí' came to talk to Nabíl. He said, 'I have never heard him weep before . . . I am prepared to serve him if he remains steadfast in the Cause.' Áqá Buzurg insisted that he would like to accompany Nabíl to Mashhad but his father wanted him first to finish his studies, then study the *Kitáb-i-Íqán* and make a copy of it † before going on such a journey.

After Nabíl left Khurásán and arrived in Ṭihrán, Shaykh-i-Fání, ‡ a devoted believer, went to Níshápúr. He disclosed his plans to travel to Baghdád and then to Adrianople, and stated that he had permission from Bahá'u'lláh to take one person with him. Abá Badí' provided his son with funds and a beast of burden for transport to accompany the Shaykh to Baghdád where they could join Nabíl and from there all of them proceed together to the presence of Bahá'u'lláh. Badí' accompanied the Shaykh as far as Yazd. There he parted company with him, gave him all his possessions and alone travelled on foot to Baghdád. The spirit of devotion to the Faith had so touched Badí' that he was longing to gaze upon the countenance of Bahá'u'lláh and partake of His glory in person.

* The reason behind the question was that Nabíl must have been surprised that Abá Badí' was entertaining him personally. Because in those days the young generally paid great respect to their parents, and in a case such as this, a young son would not allow his father to serve the guest personally, bearing in mind that it was against the custom of the time for the female members of the family to entertain guests of the opposite sex.

† In the early days of the Faith, the Holy Writings were not published. Handwritten copies were made by individual believers.

‡ Shaykh Aḥmad-i-Níshápúrí, not to be confused with Shaykh Muḥammad-i-Ḥiṣárí, also entitled Shaykh-i-Fání.

While Badí' was in Baghdád, the enemies of the Cause fatally wounded Áqá 'Abdu'r-Rasúl-i-Qumí* an ardent follower of Bahá'u'lláh who had taken upon himself the arduous task of carrying water† to the House of Bahá'u'lláh in that city. The supply of water to that House was essential as some believers were living there. When Badí' learned of the tragic story of the martyrdom of Áqá 'Abdu'r-Rasúl, he volunteered for the job and began to carry skins of water from the river to the House of Bahá'u'lláh and the believers; consequently, he too became a target of assaults by the enemy. He was attacked several times as he was carrying water and each time stabbed with knives or daggers. Undeterred by the malice of the fanatic mob, this youth, whose destiny was to become a new creation of God in this Day and a spiritual giant of this Dispensation, continued in this work. God vouchsafed His protection to him during those turbulent days.

We have already recounted the fate of the believers living in Baghdád. They were eighty-eight in all who were exiled to Mosul.‡ But Badí' was not among them. He had gone to Mosul before the exiles arrived, and was able to serve them in the same capacity of water carrier. After some time the news reached the believers that Bahá'u'lláh had been exiled to 'Akká. Badí' could wait no longer. He departed from Mosul and walked all the way to 'Akká.

He arrived there early in 1869. This was some time after Ḥájí Sháh-Muḥammad-i-Amínu'l-Bayán and Ḥájí Abu'l-Ḥasan-i-Amín (the two Trustees of Bahá'u'lláh§) had arrived in the city. Badí' seems to have entered the city without much difficulty. The watchful eyes of Siyyid Muḥammad-i-Iṣfahání and his accomplice Áqá Ján, who were housed above the gate

* see vol. 2, p. 333.

† In those days in the Middle East, there was no running water in houses. Water had to be carried from springs or rivers; there were water carriers in every town. The most common method was to carry large leather skins filled with water on one's back.

‡ see vol. 2, p. 334.

§ see above, ch. 4.

of the city so that they might report to the authorities the arrival of any person they suspected of being a Bahá'í, failed to recognize the youth carrying his water skins and wearing a long cloak of coarse cotton of the type worn among the Arabs.

Badí' wandered in the city for some time not knowing the residence of his Lord or how to enter it. He went to a mosque and there he sighted a few Persians and he knew that the one standing in front of them was none other than 'Abdu'l-Bahá. He waited till the prayer was finished and then approached the Master with great reverence and handed him a note containing two lines of a poem he had hurriedly composed on the spot. In it he had, without introducing himself, declared his loyalty to the Master and his faith in Bahá'u'lláh in moving and tender language. 'Abdu'l-Bahá warmly welcomed Badí' and managed to take him to the barracks.*

In one of the Tablets[2] written by Mírzá Áqá Ján, it is stated that Badí' was ushered into the Presence of Bahá'u'lláh alone on two occasions. No one knew what was happening in these audiences except that Bahá'u'lláh had said that God was about to create a new creation and Badí' himself was unaware of it. In another Tablet,[3] Bahá'u'lláh states that He created him anew with the hands of power and might and sent him out as a ball of fire. It was in the course of these two meetings that Bahá'u'lláh gave him the name Badí'—Wonderful.

In yet another Tablet[4] Bahá'u'lláh has testified that He took a handful of dust, mixed it with the waters of might and power and breathed into it a new spirit from His presence, adorned it with the ornament of a name (Badí') in the Kingdom of Creation and sent it out to the King with a Book revealed by God.

In a Tablet[5] to the father of Badí', Bahá'u'lláh recounts in moving language the exciting events which took place when

* 'Azízu'lláh-i-Ja<u>dh</u><u>dh</u>áb (see p. 168), a devoted believer, has recorded in his memoirs that 'Abdu'l-Aḥad (see p. 54) took Badí' with his water-carrying skin inside the barracks. It is possible that 'Abdu'l-Bahá had instructed 'Abdu'l-Aḥad to accompany him to the prison.

his son had attained His presence. He indicates that when He desired to create a new creation He summoned Badí' to come to His room and uttered 'one word' to him, a word which caused his whole being to tremble. He affirms that had it not been for the divine protection vouchsafed to him at that moment, Badí' would have swooned away. Then the Hand of Omnipotence, according to Bahá'u'lláh's description, began to create him anew and breathed into him the spirit of might and power. So great was the infusion of this might, as attested by Bahá'u'lláh, that single and alone he could have conquered the world through the power of God, had he been ordered to do so.

Bahá'u'lláh states that when this new creation came into being he smiled in His presence and manifested such steadfastness that the Concourse on High* were deeply moved and exhilarated and the voice of God was heard calling aloud: 'Hallowed and glorified be Bahá for having fashioned a new and wonderful creation.' Bahá'u'lláh testifies that He disclosed to his eyes the 'Kingdom of Revelation', and as a result his whole being was filled with an ecstasy that rid him of all attachments to this world and made him arise to assist his Lord and bring victory to His Cause.

There are many references in the Writings to the Kingdom of Revelation of which Bahá'u'lláh speaks in the above Tablet. This Kingdom, sometimes translated as the 'Kingdom of the Cause', is far above the understanding of man. We have written briefly about this in the previous volume.† This is the Kingdom through which all Revelations have been sent down. The kingdom of creation, of which man is a part, has also come into being through the instrumentality of the Kingdom of Revelation. The two kingdoms are often referred to together in the Writings. Man dwelling within the kingdom of creation has the duty to serve the Kingdom of Revelation, because a

* The company of the souls of the Prophets and Holy Ones in the next world.

† see vol. 2, pp. 184–5.

lower kingdom always serves a higher one. The Cause of Bahá'u'lláh has been vouchsafed to humanity through the instrumentality of the Kingdom of Revelation, therefore the true function of a believer is to serve the Cause of Bahá'u'lláh, and many thousands have even sacrificed their lives to this end.

That Bahá'u'lláh had enabled Badí', while in His presence, to see the Kingdom of Revelation is a unique bounty of which we can have no understanding. The only thing we can deduce from observing this illustrious youth is that whatever had happened to him in the presence of Bahá'u'lláh, he was entirely a different person when he left. Before, he was only 'a handful of dust', but after his two audiences with Bahá'u'lláh he became a new creation into which 'the spirit of might and power' had been breathed. And it is for no light reason that this youth of seventeen is named as one of the nineteen Apostles of Bahá'u'lláh. We are not attempting to compare the station of these Apostles because it is beyond any man to judge the station that God has destined for His chosen ones in the spiritual worlds of God; nevertheless, we observe that he is placed second on the list, the first being Mírzá Músá, Áqáy-i-Kalím,* the most faithful brother of Bahá'u'lláh.

That Badí' had been carried away into a world of joy and eternal ecstasy as a result of meeting Bahá'u'lláh is not in itself a unique experience. Every one of His followers with a pure heart was deeply moved and exhilarated when they came in contact with Him, like a piece of iron which becomes magnetized when in contact with a magnet. But the case of Badí was a special one. Ḥájí Mírzá Ḥaydar-'Alí, the account of whose life and services have been given in previous volumes* and who is often remembered as the 'Angel of Mount Carmel'—a designation by which 'Abdu'l-Bahá had called him—has explained some of his experiences in the presence of Bahá'u'lláh in 'Akká and made a comment about Badí'. Ḥájí Mírzá Ḥaydar-'Alí describes the effect of being in the presence of Bahá'u'lláh when He chanted a Tablet He had revealed for

* see vols. 1 and 2.

him. This is the translation of some of his words:

> This Tablet . . . was chanted by the Beauty of the All-Bountiful.* What an effect it had on me! To what a world did I ascend! To what a paradise did I enter! What did I see! In what way did I hear that voice and that melody! . . . These I cannot tell. I entered that Paradise which no eye had seen, and no ear had heard, nor any heart had felt. I saw the Kingdom of grandeur and majesty, and felt the might, the transcendent power, the glory, and the sovereignty of the ever-living, the ever-abiding, the incomparable God. But to speak of it, write about it, give an image or likeness of it, exalt and sanctify it, allude to it, extol and praise it, or describe and narrate it, all these are impossible for this humble servant or anyone else in the world. We have only access to words and terms, whereas that experience and condition are exalted above all things. They cannot be put into words or described by talks. No one can interpret the inner feelings of one's conscience . . . But this condition remains only for a single moment. It is a fleeting experience. Its manifestation within the human being is due to a special bounty of God. Its duration, varying from the twinkling of an eye to a longer period, depends upon one's capacity to become the recipient of this bounty. The deeds and actions of the person demonstrate its existence. But it has never been heard that this condition lasted for three or four months in a person except in Badí' . . . [6]

When Badí' learnt that Bahá'u'lláh was looking for someone to deliver a special Tablet to Náṣiri'd-Dín Sháh, he begged to be allowed to carry out this service, knowing full well that he would have to lay down his life. Bahá'u'lláh accepted him for this important mission, instructed him to proceed to Haifa where he would be given the Tablet and instructed him also not to associate with any believer, either on the way or in Ṭihrán. The Tablet to the Sháh of Persia was not handed to Badí' in 'Akká. Bahá'u'lláh entrusted Ḥájí Sháh-Muḥammad-

* Bahá'u'lláh. [A.T.]

i-Amín* with a small case and a Tablet to be delivered into the hands of Badí'.

The following is the story as recounted by Ḥájí Sháh-Muḥammad to Ḥájí Mírzá Ḥaydar-'Alí and recorded by the latter.

> . . . I was given a small case . . . and was instructed to hand it to Badí' at Haifa together with a small sum of money. I did not know anything about the contents of the case. I met him at Haifa and gave him the glad-tidings that he had been honoured with a trust . . . We left the town and walked up Mount Carmel where I handed him the case. He took it into his hands, kissed it and knelt with his forehead to the ground. I also delivered to him a sealed envelope [a Tablet of Bahá'u'lláh for Badí' himself]. He took twenty or thirty paces, sat down facing the most Holy Court ['Akká], read the Tablet and again prostrated himself to the ground. His face was illumined with the radiance of ecstasy and the tidings of joy. I asked him if I could read the Tablet also. He replied: 'There is no time.' I knew it was all a confidential matter. But what it was, I had no idea. I could not imagine such a mission.
>
> I mentioned that we had better go to the town [Haifa] in order that, as instructed [by Bahá'u'lláh] I might give him some money. He said, 'I will not come to the town; you go and bring it here.' I went; when I returned I could not find him, in spite of much searching. He had gone . . . We had no news of him until we heard of his martyrdom in Ṭihrán. Then I knew that the case had contained the Tablet of Bahá'u'lláh to the Sháh and the sealed envelope contained a Tablet which imparted the glad-tidings of the martyrdom of the one who was the essence of steadfastness and strength.[7]

The same chronicler has written the following account given by a certain believer, Ḥájí 'Alí, who met Badí' on his way to Persia and travelled with him for some distance:

> He was a very happy person, smiling, patient, thankful,

* The first Trustee of Bahá'u'lláh; see p. 73.

gentle and humble. All that we knew about him was that he had attained the presence of Bahá'u'lláh and was now returning to his home in Khurásán. Many a time he could be seen walking about a hundred feet from the road in either direction, turning his face towards 'Akká, prostrating himself to the ground saying: 'O God! do not take back through Thy justice what thou hast vouchsafed unto me through Thy bounty and grant me strength for its protection.'[8]

The Tablet[9] that Bahá'u'lláh sent to Badí' himself when he was in Haifa is very moving and beautiful. In it He calls him by his new name Badí', exhorts him to put on the new and wonderful robe of the remembrance of God and crown himself with the crown of His Love. He reminds him that earthly life will eventually come to an end, and urges him to sacrifice his mortal frame in the path of the Beloved, so that he may attain to everlasting life and eternal glory.

Badí' travelled on foot all the way to Ṭihrán. On arrival in the summer of 1869, he discovered that the King was on a camping expedition. He made his way to the area and sat on top of a rock far away, but opposite the royal pavilion. There he sat for three days and three nights in a state of fasting and prayer, awaiting the passing of the royal escort. What thoughts must have passed through his mind as he communed with his Lord, and what feelings of emotion must have filled his being as he sat so close to fulfilling the sacred mission with which he was entrusted, no one can say. One thing we can be sure of, that he possessed a supreme power and a supreme joy and was confident of victory.

On the fourth day, the Sháh looking through his binoculars spotted a man dressed in a white garb sitting motionless and in a most respectful attitude on a rock opposite. He guessed that he had some demand to make for justice or was seeking help for his difficulties. He sent his men to find out who he was and what he wanted. Badí' told them that he had a letter from a very important personage for the Sháh and must hand it to him personally. The officers searched him and then brought him to the King. It seems very surprising that these officials, drunk with pride, ruthless and cruel in every way, did not grab the letter from him and walk away. The only explanation is that they must have felt the extraordinary power with which Bahá'u'lláh had invested His messenger. Otherwise, it was very unusual to allow an ordinary citizen to come and meet the sovereign face to face.

Only those well versed in the history of Persia in the nineteenth century can appreciate the immense dangers which faced an ordinary person like Badí' wishing to meet a palace official, let alone the King. A despot such as Náṣiri'd-Dín Sháh ruled his country with a rod of iron. The government officials showed their authority through tyranny. They were accustomed to deal ruthlessly with anyone who dared to utter a word, or raise a finger against them or the established regime. The mere sighting of a soldier wearing the military uniform, or of a low-ranking government officer, was sufficient to frighten people away. As these men passed through the streets most people showed their respect for them; sometimes they had to bribe them and the timid often ran away.

To meet the King was far more frightful! When the forward section of the royal escort arrived in the street, the cry of the herald who announced to the public the approach of the King's entourage would strike terror into the hearts of the citizens. It was a familiar term to all when he shouted: 'Everyone die', 'Everyone go blind.' The significance of these instructions was that as the King and his men passed by, everyone must stand still as a dead corpse and all eyes must be cast down as if blind.

Knowing the circumstances which prevailed at the time, we can appreciate the courage and steadfastness of Badí' and the spirit of ascendancy and superhuman audacity which this youth of seventeen manifested as he stood assured and confident, straight as an arrow, face to face with the King. Calmly and courteously he handed him the Tablet and in a loud voice movingly called out the celebrated verse from the

Qur'án: 'O King, I have come unto thee from Sheba with a weighty message.'*

Badí' was arrested. The Sháh, who must have remembered the attempt on his life by two Bábís about two decades earlier, was taken aback by the courage and fearlessness of Bahá'u'lláh's messenger. Sending the message to Mullá 'Alíy-i-Kání, a well-known Muslim divine, to provide an answer, he ordered his men to get from Badí', first through persuasion and promises, and then by torture if he refused to cooperate, the names of other Bahá'ís. The officer in charge was Káẓim Khán-i-Qarachih-Dághí. When he failed to persuade Badí' to reveal names of other Bahá'ís to him, he ordered that he be stripped of his clothes and branded several times with hot bars of iron. Badí' endured these tortures for three successive days with a fortitude that astonished the officials who were watching him. They saw him utterly joyous while being tortured. It seemed to them that he was not feeling the pain; he often seemed to be laughing. This in spite of the fact that at times the smoke and smell created by the burning flesh was so intense that some officials could not stand it and had to leave the tent. The Sháh, who was usually eager to see the photographs of prisoners, ordered a photograph to be taken of Badí', especially when he had heard the stories of his fortitude under torture. This photograph shows the brazier of fire containing the rods of iron in the foreground and is the best testimony to the spirit of steadfastness and resignation, of calm and assurance which Badí''s face portrays.

As the three successive days of torture by branding yielded no information about the identity of other believers, the Chief Officer, Káẓim Khán, threatened Badí' with death unless he cooperated. Badí' smiled at this threat and, as he did not reveal any name, his head was beaten to a pulp with a butt of a rifle.

* *Qur'án* xxvii, 22. This verse differs slightly from what Badí' uttered in the presence of the Sháh. The verse refers to words which were addressed to Solomon by his messenger, Hoopoe, a mystical bird, when it brought for him tidings from Sheba.

His body was thrown into a pit and earth and stones heaped upon it. This was in July 1869.

In 1913 when 'Abdu'l-Bahá visited Paris, a high-ranking Persian officer by the name of Muḥammad-Valí Khán, a Field Marshal (Sipah-Salár-i-A'ẓam), was staying in Paris for medical treatment. Mme. Dreyfus-Barney, a devoted American believer, met this man. Mme. Barney had in earlier years attained the presence of 'Abdu'l-Bahá in the Holy Land and had asked many questions of Him. 'Abdu'l-Bahá's answers were written down and later compiled by her and published under the title *Some Answered Questions.*

In Paris Mme. Dreyfus-Barney, having met the above-named Persian officer, presented him with a copy of that book. When Muḥammad-Valí Khán read the account given by 'Abdu'l-Bahá of Bahá'u'lláh's Tablets to the kings including Náṣiri'd-Dín Sháh, he took up his pen and wrote in the margin some first-hand information he had personally heard from the fore-mentioned Káẓim Khán, the officer in charge who tortured and eventually martyred Badí'. This is a translation of his notes:

> 6 Rabí'u'l-Avval 1331
> 26 February AD 1913
> Paris, Hôtel d'Albe, Avenue Champs Elysée
>
> That year, when this letter [Bahá'u'lláh's Tablet] was sent, the messenger came to the Sháh in the summer resort of Lár, and this is the full account of what happened.
>
> The late Náṣiri'd-Dín Sháh was very fond of the summer resorts of Lár, Núr* and Kujúr. He ordered my father, Sá'idu'd-Dawlih the Sardár [Sirdar], and myself (then a youth with the rank of Sarhang [Colonel]) to go to Kujúr and find provisions and victuals for the royal camp.† 'I am

* Bahá'u'lláh's ancestral home is in the district of Núr (Núr means light). (A.T.)

† When Náṣiri'd-Dín Sháh went on a hunting expedition or touring in the summer he took a large entourage with him. They included his ministers, thousands of troops with their officers, servants and executioners. (A.T.)

coming', he said, 'to the summer resort of Lár and from there to the resort of Baladih of Núr and thence to Kujúr.' These resorts adjoin each other and are contiguous. My father and I were in the environs of Manjíl-i-Kujúr when news reached us that the Sháh had arrived at Lár, and that there he had put someone to death, by having him strangled. Then it was reported that this man [who was put to death] was a messenger of the Bábís. At that time the word 'Bahá'í' was not known and we had never heard it. All the people rejoiced over the slaying of that messenger. Then the Sháh came to Baladih of Núr. My father and I went forth to greet him. Near the village of Baladih, where a large river flows, they had set up the Sháh's pavilion, but the Sháh had not yet arrived. Káẓim Khán-i-Turk, the Farrásh-Báshí of the Sháh, had brought the advance equipage.* We wanted to pass by. My father, who had the rank of Mír-Panj [General] and had not yet received the title of Sá'idu'd-Dawlih, was acquainted with this Káẓim Khán. He told me, 'Let us go and visit this Farrásh-Báshí.' We rode up to the pavilion and dismounted. Káẓim Khán was seated with much pomp in his tent. We entered the tent. He received my father respectfully and showed me great kindness. We sat down and tea was served. The talk was about the journey. Then my father said, 'Your Honour the Farrásh-Báshí, who was this Bábí and how was he put to death?' He replied, 'O Mír-Panj! let me tell you a tale. This man was a strange creature. At Safíd-Áb-i-Lár, the Sháh mounted to go hunting. As it happened I had not mounted. Suddenly I saw two cavalrymen galloping towards me. The Sháh had sent for me. I immediately mounted, and when I reached the Sháh, he told me that a Bábí had brought a letter. "I ordered his arrest," the Sháh said, "and he is now in the custody of Kishikchí-Báshí [Head of the Sentries]. Go and take him to the Farrásh-Khánih. Deal with him gently at first, but if not

* He is the same Káẓim Khán-i-Qarachih-Dághí whose father, Ismá'íl Khán, was a son-in-law of Fatḥ-'Alí Sháh and was present at the conference in Ṭabríz when the Báb formally proclaimed his prophetic mission to the company of divines and Náṣiri'd-Dín Mírzá, heir to the throne. (A.T.)

successful use every manner of force to make him confess and reveal who his friends are and where they are to be found—until I return from the hunt." I went, took him from the Kishikchí-Báshí and brought him away, hands and arms tied. But let me tell you something of the sagacity and the alertness of the Sháh. This man was unmounted in that plain and as soon as he raised his paper to say that he had a letter to deliver, the Sháh sensed that he must be a Bábí and ordered his arrest and the removal of any letter he had. He was then detained but had not given his letter to anyone and had it in his pocket. I took this messenger home. At first I spoke to him kindly and gently; "Give me a full account of all this. Who gave you this letter? From where have you brought it? How long ago was it? Who are your comrades?" He said, "This letter was given to me in 'Akká by Ḥaḍrat-i-Bahá'u'lláh.* He told me: 'You will have to go to Írán, all alone, and somehow deliver this letter to the Sháh of Írán. But your life may be endangered. If you accept that, go; otherwise I will send another messenger.' I accepted the task. It is now three months since I left. I have been looking for an opportunity to give this letter into the hands of the Sháh and bring it to his notice. And thanks be to God that today I rendered my service. If you want Bahá'ís, they are numerous in Írán, and if you want my comrades, I was all alone and have none." I pressed him to tell me the names of his comrades and the names of the Bahá'ís of Írán, particularly those of Ṭihrán. And he persisted with his denial: "I have no comrade and I do not know the Bahá'ís of Írán." I swore to him: "If you tell me these names I will obtain your release from the Sháh and save you from death." His reply to me was: "I am longing to be put to death. Do you think that you frighten me?" Then I sent for the bastinado,† and *farráshes* (six at a time) started to beat him. No matter how much he was beaten he never cried out, nor did he implore. When I saw how it was I had him released from the bastinado and brought him to sit beside

* His Holiness Bahá'u'lláh. (H.M.B.)

† The victim is made to lie on his back while his feet, inserted in a loop, are raised and the soles beaten with a cane or a whip. (A.T.)

me and told him once again: "Give me the names of your comrades." He did not answer me at all and began to laugh. It seemed as if all that beating had not harmed him in any way. This made me angry. I ordered a branding-iron to be brought and a lighted brazier.* While they were preparing the brazier I said: "Come and speak the truth, else I will have you branded"; and at that I noticed that his laughter increased. Then I had him bastinadoed again. Beating him that much tired out the *farráshes*. I myself was also tired out. So I had him untied and taken to the back of another tent, and told the *farráshes* that by dint of branding they ought to get a confession from him. They applied red-hot iron several times to his back and chest. I could hear the sizzling noise of the burning flesh and smell it too. But no matter how hard we tried we could get nothing out of him. It was about sunset that the Sháh returned from hunting and summoned me. I went to him and related all that had happened. The Sháh insisted that I should make him confess and then put him to death. So I went back and had him branded once again. He laughed under the impact of the red-hot iron and never implored. I even consented that this fellow should say that what he had brought was a petition and make no mention of a letter. Even to that he did not consent. Then I lost my temper and ordered a plank to be brought. A *farrásh*, who wielded a pounder used for ramming in iron pegs, put this man's head on the plank, and stood over him with the raised pounder. I told him: "If you divulge the names of your comrades you will be released, otherwise I will order them to bring that pounder down on your head." He began to laugh and give thanks for having gained his object. I consented that he should say it was a petition he had brought, not a letter. He even would not say that. And all those red-hot rods applied to his flesh caused him no anguish. So, in the end, I gave a sign to the *farrásh*, and he brought down the pounder on this fellow's head. His

* Branding a person was a common form of torture in those days in Persia. Rods of iron were placed in a brazier full of burning coal. When the rods became red hot they were placed on the naked body of a person and kept in that position until they got cold. (A.T.)

skull was smashed and his brain oozed through his nostrils. Then I went myself and reported it all to the Sháh.'

This Káẓim Khán-i-Farrásh-Báshí was astounded by that man's behaviour and endurance, astonished that all the beatings and application of red-hot metal to his body had no effect on him, causing him no distress . . . That same letter the Sháh sent to Ṭihrán for Mullá 'Alíy-i-Kaní and other mullás to read and to answer. But they said that there was nothing to answer; and Ḥájí Mullá 'Alí wrote to Mustawfíyu'l-Mamálik (who was the Premier at the time) to tell the Sháh that, 'If, God forbid, you should have any doubts regarding Islám and your belief is not firm enough, I ought to take action to dispel your doubts. Otherwise such letters have no answer. The answer was exactly what you did to his messenger. Now you must write to the Ottoman Sulṭán to be very strict with him and prevent all communications.' Sulṭán 'Abdu'l-'Azíz was living then. It was during his reign.

27 Rabí'u'l-Avval 1331, 2 March AD 1913
Written at the Hôtel d'Albe in Paris.

Tonight I could not sleep. Mme. Dreyfus had sent me this book and I had not yet read it. It is early morning. I opened the book and read on till I reached the theme of Letters to the Kings, and to Náṣiri'd-Dín Sháh. Because I had been there on that journey and had heard this account personally from Káẓim Khán-i-Farrásh-Báshí, I wrote it down.

A year and a half later, on the journey to Karbilá, this Káẓim Khán went mad. The Sháh had him chained and he died miserably. The year I went to Tabríz, as the Governor-General of Ádharbáyján, I found a grandson of his, begging. 'Take heed, O people of insight and understanding.'

Muḥammad-Valí, Sipahdár-i-A'ẓam.[10]

The Sháh is reported to have been immensely displeased with the attitude of the divines in refusing to meet the challenge and write an answer to Bahá'u'lláh, but he could do nothing to change their decision.

The Fortitude of the Martyrs

That Badí' endured such unbearable tortures with joy and seemed not to feel the pain during those sessions of torture is no unique event in the history of the Faith. Numerous were other martyrs during the Dispensations of the Báb and Bahá'u'lláh who gave their lives willingly and demonstrated to the public in no uncertain terms that they were longing to attain the crown of martyrdom in the path of their Lord. They demonstrated a heroism and a self-sacrifice unprecedented in the annals of mankind. There are many who endured agonizing tortures and did not appear to feel the pain. A notable example is Mullá Muḥammad-Riḍáy-i-Muḥammad-Ábádí otherwise known as Shaykh Riḍáy-i-Yazdí.

The story of Mullá Riḍá in prison is recounted in a previous volume.* The gaoler and his men flogged his bare back most brutally for a considerable time. And yet he raised not the faintest cry and showed not the slightest expression of agony on his face. At the end of the ordeal he confided to his fellow Bahá'í prisoner that he had never felt the slightest pain and that during the beating he was in the presence of Bahá'u'lláh, communing with Him.

Mullá Riḍá and Badí' were not the only ones who showed this extraordinary fortitude. The history of the Faith is replete with similar stories. The power of faith is such that, as Christ affirmed, it can move mountains. In the Writings of Bahá'u'lláh we can find similar statements affirming that when man acquires faith, he can accomplish great tasks consistent with the measure of his faith.

Let us try to discover, through the study of the Writings as well as the history of the Cause, the reason for this extraordinary fortitude shown by many martyrs of the Faith. History confirms that any time a believer has been conducted to the scene of his martyrdom by his would-be executioners or

* see vol. 1, p. 88. For a similar story, when Mullá Riḍá was bastinadoed, see vol. 1, pp. 85–6.

has been savagely tortured prior to his death, he has been faced with making a choice between giving his life in the path of God, or recanting his faith as a result of which he would be set free.

If at that moment of decision he is unable to sever himself from the things of the world, from its delights and pleasures, or from the joys and contentment of life at home where he could continue to live among his loved ones, then such a person remains fully attached to this world and consequently severs his connection with Bahá'u'lláh. It is at this point under the threat of death that the individual becomes deprived of the sustaining power of Bahá'u'lláh, and as a result becomes filled with such fear that he will recant his faith in order to save his own life. Although counted as one of the believers before he was confronted with these severe tests and trials; yet because he has not been able to detach himself from worldly affections, he succumbs under the pressure of tests, and like a man who has been standing on the summit of a lofty mountain, falls into the abyss.

We have already discussed in great detail the idea that the only barrier which separates man from the Manifestation of God is attachment to this world. It is this barrier that stops the flow of divine power to the human soul and denudes the individual of the mantle of courage and faith.

On the other hand, if the believer at the hour of his gravest test decides not to barter the precious gift of his faith for this transitory life, such a person reaches the pinnacle of detachment. This is the absolute limit, for there can be no greater detachment than to give one's life. The moment that this decision is made, by virtue of becoming completely detached from this world, he becomes filled with such powers from on high as to become a spiritual giant. The confirmations of Bahá'u'lláh will instantly descend on him and will surround and strengthen him.

Although he still tarries among men, in reality he is transported into another world. Fear will completely disappear from his being. Instead his face will radiate such joy and strength that it bewilders the onlookers as they see him give his life.

Bahá'u'lláh confirms in many of His Tablets that great powers will descend upon a soul who becomes detached from the things of this world. To cite an example, in one of His Tablets[11] He states that if a believer becomes detached from all save God, He will be enabled to influence the realities of all created things, and to do anything he desires. Such a person will not observe anything but the face of his Beloved and will be afraid of no one even if all the peoples of the world arise against him.

Those few such as Badí' or Mullá Riḍá who have ascended the pinnacle of faith, were possessed of extraordinary powers including superhuman fortitude. They were so drawn to Bahá'u'lláh that physical separation from Him did not sever the link of the true communion with Him. That they considered themselves in the presence of Bahá'u'lláh was not a mere expression of words or an illusion. It must have been a real experience for them. Badí', for example, at the time of his martyrdom or during those many hours of torture, was so closely linked with Bahá'u'lláh and saw himself so truly in the presence of his Beloved that he was not affected by any affliction whatsoever.

To appreciate such a state of being is not possible for anyone who has not reached to the loftiest summit of faith. But thousands of men and women who went to the field of martyrdom and joyously laid down their lives in the path of God must have experienced the presence of Bahá'u'lláh so vividly and with such real feeling that the giving of life became a joy instead of torture. To cite an example, the following is a story which Ḥájí Muḥammad-Ṭáhir-i-Málmírí[12] has recounted about Mírzá Áqáy-i-Ḥalabí Sáz who was a devoted believer and had had the privilege of attaining the presence of Bahá'u'lláh. He was a tinsmith and had a shop in one of the bazaars of Yazd. In 1891, seven Bahá'ís were put to death by the order of Maḥmúd Mírzá, the Jalálu'd-Dawlih, the Governor of Yazd. They are known as the first seven martyrs of Yazd, the story of whose martyrdom Bahá'u'lláh wrote to *The Times* of London.* The seven were chained together and conducted towards the bazaar amid scenes of jubilation, and at each major crossroads one of them was executed in a most barbaric fashion. The other believers who were shopkeepers or merchants were ordered to stay at their premises and were forced to join others in decorating their shops to celebrate the event.

Ḥájí Mírzá was sitting in his shop, his heart filled with grief owing to the tragic turn of events. Then came the tense moment when the few remaining of the seven, chained together, passed in front of his shop. The next junction where one of them was to be beheaded was not far away and could be easily sighted. Ḥájí Muḥammad-Ṭáhir-i-Málmírí has recounted that Ḥájí Mírzá used to tell the believers in Yazd of his unusual experience on that occasion. He saw to his great surprise that Bahá'u'lláh Himself passed in front of his shop only a few hundred paces behind the martyrs-to-be and was walking quickly in order to reach them. Ḥájí Mírzá immediately stepped out of his shop to follow Bahá'u'lláh, who signalled him with the movement of His hand that he should return to the shop. From there, Ḥájí Mírzá looked out and saw that Bahá'u'lláh reached the party at the junction and at that very moment the executioner removed the chain from one man and executed him.

Of course, Ḥájí Mírzá knew that Bahá'u'lláh was in 'Akká and not in Yazd, but he had no doubt that it was Bahá'u'lláh whom he saw in the bazaar. From this amazing vision he realized that the martyrs were not alone at the time of martyrdom, that their unparalleled courage and heroism was not entirely due to themselves, that Bahá'u'lláh strengthened them with His unfailing power and that those who had reached the pinnacle of faith and assurance were bound to feel the

* An account of this will appear in the next volume.

presence of Bahá'u'lláh at their side. It is interesting to note that some years later, Ḥájí Mírzá himself was martyred in Yazd.*

What Ḥájí Mírzá witnessed in the bazaar, although there is no way of proving it, was not mere imagination. The Revelation of Bahá'u'lláh is not a man-made, man-inspired cult. Any cult which the minds of men have created can only be expressed within the bounds of man's experience by virtue of its limitations. On the contrary, the Revelation of Bahá'u'lláh has originated from God, it has released unimaginable potentialities, both material and spiritual, within human society and like other religions it has brought forth mysteries which human beings can in no wise fathom. The history of the Faith shows episodes similar to that experienced by Ḥájí Mírzá.

To cite one example: when the Báb was imprisoned in the castle of Máh-Kú, the warden of the Castle was a man named 'Alí-Khán, who discharged his functions with the utmost severity and refused to allow any of the followers of the Báb to gain admittance into His presence. Shaykh Ḥasan-i-Zunúzí, one of the ardent disciples of the Báb, came to Máh-Kú, but was refused admission. Nabíl-i-A'ẓam has recounted the following story as related by Siyyid Ḥusayn-i-Yazdí, the amanuensis of the Báb:

> 'For the first two weeks,' Siyyid Ḥusayn further related, 'no one was permitted to visit the Báb. My brother and I alone were admitted to His presence. Siyyid Ḥasan would, every day, accompanied by one of the guards, descend to the town and purchase our daily necessities. Shaykh Ḥasan-i-Zunúzí, who had arrived at Máh-Kú, spent the nights in a masjid outside the gate of the town. He acted as an intermediary between those of the followers of the Báb who occasionally visited Máh-Kú and Siyyid Ḥasan, my brother, who would in turn submit the petitions of the believers to their Master and would acquaint Shaykh Hasan with His reply.

* For a story of his life see vol. 2, pp. 358–68.

'One day the Báb charged my brother to inform Shaykh Ḥasan that He would Himself request 'Alí Khán to alter his attitude towards the believers who visited Máh-Kú and to abandon his severity. "Tell him," He added, "I will tomorrow instruct the warden to conduct him to this place." I was greatly surprised at such a message. How could the domineering and self-willed 'Alí Khán, I thought to myself, be induced to relax the severity of his discipline? Early the next day, the gate of the castle being still closed, we were surprised by a sudden knock at the door, knowing full well that orders had been given that no one was to be admitted before the hour of sunrise. We recognised the voice of 'Alí Khán, who seemed to be expostulating with the guards, one of whom presently came in and informed me that the warden of the castle insisted on being allowed admittance into the presence of the Báb. I conveyed his message and was commanded to usher him at once into His presence. As I was stepping out of the door of His antechamber, I found 'Alí Khán standing at the threshold in an attitude of complete submission, his face betraying an expression of unusual humility and wonder. His self-assertiveness and pride seemed to have entirely vanished. Humbly and with extreme courtesy, he returned my salute and begged me to allow him to enter the presence of the Báb. I conducted him to the room which my Master occupied. His limbs trembled as he followed me. An inner agitation which he could not conceal brooded over his face. The Báb arose from His seat and welcomed him. Bowing reverently, 'Alí Khán approached and flung himself at His feet. "Deliver me," he pleaded, "from my perplexity. I adjure You, by the Prophet of God, Your illustrious Ancestor, to dissipate my doubts, for their weight has well-nigh crushed my heart. I was riding through the wilderness and was approaching the gate of the town, when, it being the hour of dawn, my eyes suddenly beheld You standing by the side of the river engaged in offering Your prayer. With outstretched arms and upraised eyes, You were invoking the name of God. I stood still and watched You. I was waiting for You to terminate Your devotions that I might approach and rebuke You for having ventured to leave the castle without my leave. In Your communion with God, You seemed so wrapt in worship that You were utterly forgetful of Yourself. I quietly approached You; in Your state of rapture, You remained wholly unaware of my presence. I was suddenly seized with great fear and recoiled at the thought of awakening You from Your ecstasy. I decided to leave You, to proceed to the guards and to reprove them for their negligent conduct. I soon found out, to my amazement, that both the outer and inner gates were closed. They were opened at my request, I was ushered into your presence, and now find You, to my wonder, seated before me. I am utterly confounded. I know not whether my reason has deserted me." The Báb answered and said: "What you have witnessed is true and undeniable. You belittled this Revelation and have contemptuously disdained its Author. God, the All-Merciful, desiring not to afflict you with His punishment, has willed to reveal to your eyes the Truth. By His Divine interposition, He has instilled into your heart the love of His chosen One, and caused you to recognize the unconquerable power of His Faith."'

This marvellous experience completely changed the heart of 'Alí Khán. Those words had calmed his agitation and subdued the fierceness of his animosity. By every means in his power, he determined to atone for his past behaviour. 'A poor man, a shaykh,' he hastily informed the Báb, 'is yearning to attain Your presence. He lives in a masjid outside the gate of Máh-Kú. I pray You that I myself be allowed to bring him to this place that he may meet You. By this act I hope that my evil deeds may be forgiven, that I may be enabled to wash away the stains of my cruel behaviour toward Your friends.' His request was granted, whereupon he went straightway to Shaykh Ḥasan-i-Zunúzí and conducted him into the presence of his Master.[13]

The Station of Badí'

Returning to the story of Badí': after his martyrdom, the Pen of Bahá'u'lláh lamented his sufferings, extolled his act of self-sacrifice and heroism and referred to him as the 'Pride of Martyrs' (Fakhru'sh-Shuhadá). In almost every Tablet revealed in a space of three years, He referred to Badí' in glowing terms, recalling his martyrdom and his indomitable faith. And these Tablets He designated as the 'Salt of My Tablets'.

In these Tablets, Bahá'u'lláh not only glorifies the station of Badí', but also attaches great importance to the proclamation of His message to the Sháh of Persia. In one of these Tablets[14] He states in referring to Badí' that He had offered up the life of one of His servants after having created him anew with the hands of might and power, and sent him straight into the mouth of a serpent, so that the peoples of the world might become assured that the Almighty God stands transcendent and supreme over His creation. Bahá'u'lláh further states that He sent Badí' with a Book in which He had proclaimed His Cause and declared conclusively His proofs to all humanity: He affirms that He had removed from the person of Badí' every trace of fear, adorned him with the ornament of faith and power, fired his soul with the utterance of a Word and sent him out as a ball of fire to proclaim His Cause.

Statements such as these may be found in numerous Tablets which flowed from the Pen of Bahá'u'lláh during these three years.

The proclamation of the Cause of Bahá'u'lláh to the Sháh of Persia had a special significance. This momentous Tablet,* handed to the person of the sovereign himself, was meant to introduce the Faith of Bahá'u'lláh in its true perspective to the inhabitants of Persia. The people in that country knew a good deal about the Bábí Faith and the majority were antagonistic to it. For over two decades the people of Persia had witnessed memorable acts of heroism performed by that small band of God-intoxicated heroes whose devotion and self-sacrifice had

* The main topics of the *Lawḥ-i-Sulṭán* (Tablet to the Sháh) are briefly described in vol. 2, pp. 337–57.

lit a great conflagration throughout the country.

The Message of the Báb, the accounts of His martyrdom and the transforming power of His Cause had already reached every corner of that land and from there its reverberations had echoed to the western world. But the people of Persia did not differentiate between the Revelation of Bahá'u'lláh and that of the Báb. Most people considered the Bahá'í Faith to be the same as the Bábí Faith and did not appreciate the vast differences in the teachings of the two.

As attested by Bahá'u'lláh in a Tablet,[15] not until this momentous epistle was delivered to the King had the nature of the Cause of God, or the claims of its Founder, or its principles and teachings, been clearly enunciated to those who held the reins of power in their hands. He mentions in the same Tablet that before Badí' had delivered that weighty epistle to the King, God's testimony had not been fulfilled and the conclusive proofs of His Faith had not been declared. But after the proclamation of His Message, there was no remaining excuse for anyone to arise against His Cause. And, since the people of Persia did not respond to the Call of God, which was clearly raised in that Message, sufferings and tribulations which had already been prophesied by the Pen of Bahá'u'lláh descended upon them as a punishment from God.

Divine Chastisement

In one instance this took the form of a famine which soon after the martyrdom of Badí' claimed the lives of a great many people in that land. The effect of the famine was so devastating that Ḥájí Mullá 'Alí-Akbar-i-Shahmírzádí, known as Ḥájí Ákhund,* wrote a letter to Bahá'u'lláh, begged forgiveness for the people of Persia and asked for relief in their sufferings. In a Tablet to him,[16] Bahá'u'lláh affirms that the famine was God's punishment for the martyrdom of Badí', declares that prior to

* One of the four Hands of the Cause whom Bahá'u'lláh appointed a few years before the end of His life. We shall write about this in the next volume.

that He had prophesied in His Tablets impending afflictions and tribulations, and states that were it not for the sake of the believers, the whole nation would have been struck down by God. He then responds favourably to Ḥají Á<u>kh</u>und's intercession and assures him that soon the situation would change and God would grant them relief.

In one of the forementioned Tablets,[17] Bahá'u'lláh states that after the proclamation of His Message to the <u>Sh</u>áh of Persia, and through Him to the public, there was no excuse left for anyone. He then makes an interesting comment about the inevitability of God's punishment and states that the believers ought to meditate as to why the wrath of God, which afflicted the people so promptly, had allowed the <u>Sh</u>áh himself a period of respite.

This is a point which had puzzled many believers in relation to Náṣiri'd-Dín <u>Sh</u>áh, stigmatized by Bahá'u'lláh as the 'Prince of Oppressors', one who had inflicted so much persecution on the followers of the Báb and Bahá'u'lláh. Yet in spite of all his cruel acts he reigned for fifty years, whereas Napoleon's downfall was precipitated so soon after Bahá'u'lláh's warning was issued.

Bahá'u'lláh has explained this point in different ways. In one of His Tablets[18] He describes the perversity of the divines in Persia and their continual attacks on the Cause of God from the pulpits and states that if it were not for the mercy of God which pervades all created things, the entire company of the enemies of the Cause of God would have perished. There were two reasons why they were being spared. One was God's forgiveness, and the other, the misdeeds of some who confessed allegiance to His Faith.

In order to appreciate the second reason, let us look at the relationship of the believers and Bahá'u'lláh. The Author of the Faith regards the believers as the 'loved ones' of God. To the non-Bahá'í public too, the believers, individually as well as collectively, are so closely linked with Bahá'u'lláh that their behaviour, whether good or bad, is attributed to Him.

Therefore, every misdeed of a follower of Bahá'u'lláh could be looked upon by the public as coming from Him. According to Bahá'u'lláh's statement, the application of God's justice is impeded when someone who deserves punishment has been grievously wronged by those who profess allegiance to His Cause and are associated with His Name. For how can God punish a person for rising up against His Faith, when some of His 'loved ones' have ill-treated him?

Ḥájí Mírzá Ḥabíb'u'lláh-i-Afnán, who, in company with his illustrious father, Mírzá Áqá, entitled Núr'u'd-Dín (light of faith),* attained the presence of Bahá'u'lláh in Haifa and 'Akká in 1891, has recorded the following in his memoirs:

> The late Ḥájí Abu'l-Ḥasan-i-Shírází . . . was present. He submitted to Bahá'u'lláh that the reign of Yazíd† came to an end three years after the martyrdom of Imám Ḥusayn, whereas it is almost fifty years since the Martyrdom of the Báb, and Náṣiri'd-Dín Sháh is still reigning with undiminished power. Day and night he is trying his best to oppose the Cause, and yet God has not seized him, instead he had been given such a long period of respite. Bahá'u'lláh's reply was that this delay was due to an attack by some ignorant believers who in the early days of the Faith made an attempt on his life. Bahá'u'lláh assured him that his turn would also come.[19]

In the forementioned Tablet[20] to Ḥájí 'Abdu'l-Majíd, the father of Badí', Bahá'u'lláh states that the Temple of the Cause of God was adorned by Badí' and that his station was so exalted that no pen could describe it. Through him, Bahá'u'lláh affirms, the pillars of tyranny were shaken and the countenance of victory unveiled itself. He had attained to such

* He was one of the distinguished members of the family of the Báb. He was the only son of the sister of the wife of the Báb, a devoted follower of Bahá'u'lláh and one whose services to the Cause were valued by Him. We shall give a brief account of his life in the next volume.

† Yazíd I, one of the Umayyad Caliphs of Islám, responsible for the martyrdom of Imám Ḥusayn.

heights in the worlds above that no mention could be made of it.

In this Tablet Bahá'u'lláh reiterates one of the basic teachings of God. He states that he has prescribed unto every son* to serve his father and that this is a commandment in the Book of God. He calls upon Ḥájí 'Abdu'l-Majíd not only to forgive his son for his failure to serve him during his life, but to be pleased with him.

Ḥájí 'Abdu'l-Majíd became one of the proudest fathers when he heard the news of Badí' and the story of his martyrdom. In 1876 he travelled to 'Akká where he attained the presence of Bahá'u'lláh. Here are his own words:

> One day I had the honour to be in the presence of the Blessed Beauty when He was talking about Badí' who had attained His presence, carried His Blessed Tablet to Ṭihrán [for Náṣiri'd-Dín Sháh] and won the crown of martyrdom. As He was speaking, my tears were flowing profusely and my beard became wet. Bahá'u'lláh turned to me and said 'Abá Badí'! A person who has already spent three-quarters of his life should offer up the remainder in the path of God . . .' I asked 'Is it possible that my beard which is now soaked in my tears may one day be dyed crimson with my blood?' The Blessed Beauty replied 'God willing . . .'[21] †

And so it happened: the father of Badí' too became a martyr. His story is told in a previous volume.‡

* This obviously applies to a daughter as well.

† The words attributed to Bahá'u'lláh are not necessarily His exact words.

‡ vol. 2, pp. 129–36.

10

The Death of The Purest Branch

A little under two years had passed since Bahá'u'lláh's confinement in the barracks, when suddenly a most tragic event occurred. It was the untimely death of Mírzá Mihdí, entitled the Purest Branch, the younger brother of 'Abdu'l-Bahá, who was fatally wounded when he fell from the roof of the barracks.

In 1848, at a time when the followers of the Báb were engulfed by sufferings and persecutions, a son had been born in Ṭihrán to Bahá'u'lláh and His illustrious wife Ásíyih Khánum, entitled Navváb.* He was four years younger than 'Abdu'l-Bahá and was given the name 'Mihdí', after a brother of Bahá'u'lláh who was dear to Him and had died a year before. Later the Pen of the Most High bestowed upon this son the title 'Ghuṣnu'lláhu'l-Aṭhar' (The Purest Branch).

Unlike 'Abdu'l-Bahá, Mírzá Mihdí could not remember much of a life of luxury in Ṭihrán, for when he was just over four years of age His father had been imprisoned in the Síyah-Chál, and all His possessions plundered and seized by the enemies of the Cause. During the four months that Bahá'u'lláh lay in that horrible dungeon, the Holy Family spent their days in anguish and fear, not knowing what would happen to Him. Often frightened and anxious, this child, tender in age and delicate by nature, found his only shelter and refuge within the arms of a loving and devoted mother. But Providence deprived him of this also. As the journey to Baghdád, undertaken in the severe cold of the winter, was laden with hardships and dangers unbearable for a child as delicate as Mírzá Mihdí, he

* See vol. 1, p. 15.

MÍRZÁ MIHDÍ, THE PUREST BRANCH

Bahá'u'lláh's cherished son whose death in the barracks of 'Akká released enormous forces for the unity of the human race

THE PUREST BRANCH WITH 'ABDU'L-BAHÁ

A photograph taken in Adrianople

had to be left behind in Ṭihrán in the care of relatives. For about seven years he tasted the agony and heartbreak of separation from his beloved parents. It seems that at this early age, his soul was being prepared by the Almighty through pain and suffering to play a major part in the arena of sacrifice and to shed an imperishable lustre upon the Cause of his heavenly Father.

Mírzá Mihdí was taken to Ba<u>gh</u>dád to join the Family in the year AH 1276 (*circa* AD 1860). It was in that city that this pure and holy youth, noted for his meekness, came in touch with the Divine Spirit and was magnetized by the energizing forces of Bahá'u'lláh's Revelation. From that time on, he devoted every moment of his life to the service of his heavenly Father. He was Bahá'u'lláh's companion in Ba<u>gh</u>dád, Adrianople and 'Akká, and served Him as an amanuensis* towards the end of his life, leaving to posterity some Tablets in his handwriting. The last ten years of his life were filled with the hardship and suffering inflicted on Bahá'u'lláh and His companions in the course of the three successive banishments from Ba<u>gh</u>dád to 'Akká.

The Purest Branch resembled 'Abdu'l-Bahá, and throughout his short and eventful life he displayed the same spiritual qualities which distinguished his illustrious Brother. The believers loved and venerated him as they did 'Abdu'l-Bahá.

In 'Akká, the Purest Branch lived in the barracks near his Father. Often he attained the presence of Bahá'u'lláh late in the afternoon to act as His amanuensis. On 22 June 1870, early in the evening, Bahá'u'lláh informed His son that he was not needed that day to write and that instead he could go up on the roof for prayer and meditation as was his custom. It was a normal practice of the prisoners to go on the roof for fresh air in the evening of a hot summer day. The Purest Branch had

* It must be noted that although Mírzá Áqá Ján was Bahá'u'lláh's amanuensis, there were also others who were engaged in this task from time to time.

often paced up and down that roof chanting prayers and meditating. But on that fateful evening as he chanted the verses of the *Qaṣídiy-i-Varqá'íyyih*, one of Bahá'u'lláh's most moving poems revealed in Kurdistán,* he was carried away in a state of utter detachment and joy. As he paced along that familiar space wrapped in his customary meditations with his eyes closed, he fell through an open skylight on to an open crate lying on the floor below. He was badly wounded, and bled profusely. He was so terribly injured that they had to remove his clothes by tearing them from him. The following is a summary of an account given by Ḥusayn-i-Áshchí, the cook in Bahá'u'lláh's household, and a devoted believer. In this he describes the tragic circumstances of the fall and death of the Purest Branch:

> It is not possible for anyone to visualize the measure of humility and self-effacement and the intensity of devotion and meekness which the Purest Branch evinced in his life. He was a few years younger than the Master, but slightly taller than him. He used to act as Bahá'u'lláh's amanuensis and was engaged in transcribing the Writings . . . When he had finished writing he was in the habit of going on to the roof of the barracks for prayers. There was a skylight, an opening in the middle of the roof near where the kitchen was situated. As he was pacing in a state of prayer, attracted to the Kingdom of Abhá, with his head turned upwards, he fell through the skylight down on some hard objects. The terrific loud sound of the impact made us all run to the scene of the tragedy where we beheld in astonishment what had happened as decreed by God, and were so shocked as to beat upon our heads. Then the Ancient Beauty came out of his room and asked what he had done which caused his fall. The Purest Branch said that he knew the whereabouts of the skylight and in the past had been careful not to come near it, but this time it was his fate to forget about it.
>
> We carried his precious person to his room and called a doctor who was an Italian, but he could not help . . . In spite

* see vol. 1, pp. 62–4.

> of much pain and agony, and being weak, he warmly greeted those who came to his bedside, showered an abundance of love and favours upon them and apologized to everyone, saying he was ashamed that while they were all sitting, he had to lie down in their presence . . .[1]

Members of the Holy Family and some of the companions gathered around him and all were so distressed and grief-stricken that 'Abdu'l-Bahá with tearful eyes entered the presence of Bahá'u'lláh, prostrated Himself at His feet and begged for healing. Bahá'u'lláh is reported to have said 'O my Greatest Branch,* leave him in the hands of his God.' He then proceeded to the bedside of his injured son, dismissed everyone from His presence and stayed beside him for some time. Although no one knows what took place in that precious hour between the lover and the Beloved, we can be sure that this son of Bahá'u'lláh, whose devotion and love for the Cause of His Father knew no bounds, must have been exhilarated by the outpouring of bounties and love from his Lord.

It must be remembered that the relationship of Bahá'u'lláh and the members of His family who remained faithful to the Cause was not identical to the relationship which exists between members of other families. Normally, a father and a son at home have a very intimate and informal attitude towards each other. But in the case of Bahá'u'lláh and His faithful children, it was very different indeed, although that intimate relationship of father and son did indeed exist. However, the station of Bahá'u'lláh as a Manifestation of God completely overshadowed His position as a physical father. 'Abdu'l-Bahá, the Greatest Holy Leaf and the Purest Branch looked upon Bahá'u'lláh not merely as their father, but as their Lord. And because they had truly recognized His station, they acted at all times as most humble servants at His threshold. 'Abdu'l-Bahá always entered the presence of Bahá'u'lláh with such genuine humbleness and reverence that no one among His followers

* 'Abdu'l-Bahá.

could manifest the spirit of lowliness and utter self-effacement as He did. The humility of 'Abdu'l-Bahá as He bowed before His Father, or prostrated Himself at His feet or dismounted His steed when He approached the Mansion in which Bahá'u'lláh resided, demonstrates this unique relationship which existed between this Father and His faithful sons and daughter.

In the light of all this we can appreciate how the Purest Branch must have felt when his Father went to his bedside. What expressions of devotion, love and thanksgiving must have passed through his lips on that occasion, we cannot imagine. All we know is that Bahá'u'lláh, having the power of life and death in His hands, asked His dying son whether he wished to live. He assured him that if this was his wish God would enable him to recover and grant him good health. But the Purest Branch begged Bahá'u'lláh to accept his life as a ransom for the opening of the gates of the prison to the face of the many believers who were longing to come and enter the presence of their Lord. Bahá'u'lláh accepted his sacrifice and he died on 23 June 1870, twenty-two hours after his fall.

Thus ended the life of one of whom Bahá'u'lláh states that he 'was created of the light of Bahá', whose birth had taken place during some of the darkest hours in the history of the Faith, whose infancy had been spent within the cradle of adversity, whose soul at an early age had been set aglow with the fire of ordeal and separation, whose days of joy had been spent in exile and within the walls of a prison, and whose tragic death had clothed him with the crimson vesture of sacrifice, shedding thereby an imperishable lustre upon the Cause of his glorious Father.

The death of the Purest Branch within the confines of the prison created a bitter commotion among the companions who lamented the loss of one of the most illustrious among the family of Bahá'u'lláh. The following is a summary of Ḥusayn-i-Á<u>sh</u><u>ch</u>í's notes:

When the Purest Branch passed away, Shaykh Maḥmúd* begged the Master to allow him to have the honour of washing the body and not to let anyone † from the city of 'Akká perform this service. The Master gave permission. A tent was pitched in the middle of the barracks. We placed his blessed body upon a table in the middle of the tent and Shaykh Maḥmúd began the task of washing it.‡ The loved ones of God were wailing and lamenting with tearful eyes and, like unto moths, were circling around that candle which the hands of God had lighted. I brought water in and was involved in washing the body. The Master was pacing up and down outside the tent. His face betrayed signs of deep sorrow . . .

The body after being washed and shrouded was placed inside a new casket. At this moment the cry of weeping and mourning and sore lamentation rose up to the heavens. The casket was carried high on the shoulders of men out of the barracks with utmost serenity and majesty. It was laid to rest outside 'Akká in the graveyard of Nabí Ṣáliḥ . . . At the time of returning to the barracks an earth tremor shook the area and we all knew that it was the effect of the interment of that holy being.[2]

Nabíl-i-A'ẓam has said that he, Siyyid Mihdíy-i-Dahají§ and Nabíl-i-Qá'iní∅ were in Nazareth when the earth tremor occurred. It lasted for about three minutes and people were frightened. Later when they heard the news of the death of the Purest Branch they realized that it coincided with the timing of his burial and then they knew the reason for it. Bahá'u'lláh, in one of His Tablets referring to the Purest Branch, confirms the

* see pp. 65–7.

† In Islámic countries the body of the dead is washed before being wrapped in a shroud. There are men in every city whose profession is to wash the dead. (A.T.)

‡ Another person who took part in washing the body was Mírzá Ḥasan-i-Mázindarání, Bahá'u'lláh's cousin. See p. 216.

§ see vol. 2.

∅ see pp. 57–8.

cause of the earth tremor in these words:

> Blessed art thou and blessed he that turneth unto thee, and visiteth thy grave, and draweth nigh, through thee, unto God, the Lord of all that was and shall be . . . I testify that thou didst return in meekness unto thine abode. Great is thy blessedness and the blessedness of them that hold fast unto the hem of thy outspread robe . . . Thou art, verily, the trust of God and His treasure in this land. Erelong will God reveal through thee that which He hath desired. He, verily, is the Truth, the Knower of things unseen. When thou wast laid to rest in the earth, the earth itself trembled in its longing to meet thee. Thus hath it been decreed, and yet the people perceive not . . . Were We to recount the mysteries of thine ascension, they that are asleep would waken, and all beings would be set ablaze with the fire of the remembrance of My Name, the Mighty, the Loving.[3]

After his tragic death the saintly mother of the Purest Branch mourned the passing of her beloved son and wept almost incessantly. When Bahá'u'lláh assured her that God had accepted her son as a ransom, that the believers might attain the presence of their Beloved and that mankind as a whole be quickened, that noble mother was consoled and her weeping ceased.

The blood-stained clothes of the Purest Branch are among the precious relics gathered by the hands of his devoted sister, the Greatest Holy Leaf, and left to posterity as a silent witness to this great sacrifice.

Soon after the martyrdom of the Purest Branch many restrictions in the barracks were relaxed and several believers who were longing to attain the presence of Bahá'u'lláh did so. And about four months after this tragic event, Bahá'u'lláh and His companions left the prison barracks altogether. As we shall see later, Bahá'u'lláh resided in a house in 'Akká, and soon many pilgrims from Persia came and attained His presence.

In December 1939 Shoghi Effendi, the Guardian of the Faith, in the face of great dangers and difficulties and in the company of a few friends, with great care and with his own hands, removed the remains of the Purest Branch, together with those of his illustrious mother, from two different cemeteries in 'Akká, and at a profoundly moving ceremony on Christmas Day in the presence of a few believers, carried the caskets on his own shoulders and buried those sacred remains on the slope of Mount Carmel, adjacent to the resting place of the Greatest Holy Leaf and in the vicinity of the Shrine of the Báb.*

The death of the Purest Branch must be viewed as Bahá'u'lláh's own sacrifice, a sacrifice on the same level as the crucifixion of Christ and the martyrdom of the Báb. Shoghi Effendi, the Guardian of the Faith, states that Bahá'u'lláh has exalted the death of the Purest Branch to the 'rank of those great acts of atonement associated with Abraham's intended sacrifice of His son, with the crucifixion of Jesus Christ and the martyrdom of the Imám Ḥusayn . . .'[4] In another instance, Shoghi Effendi states[5] that in the Bábí Dispensation, it was the Báb himself who sacrificed His life for the redemption and purification of mankind. In the Dispensation of Bahá'u'lláh, it was the Purest Branch who gave his life releasing thereby all the forces necessary for bringing about the unity of mankind.

Although we will not be able to fully understand the mystery of sacrifice in this world, we can find through the Writings that there is a tremendous power released when man sacrifices something in the path of God. We have already discussed this theme in volume 2. In one of His Tablets, 'Abdu'l-Bahá explains that not until a seed completely disintegrates under the soil can it produce a tree. It is then that an object as insignificant as a seed, by sacrificing itself completely, will be transformed into a mighty tree with branches, fruits and flowers. It is the same when man sacrifices something of his own.

A human being has two opposite forces working within

* see Appendix III.

him, the animal and the spiritual. The animal nature inclines man to the material world. The Manifestations of God have exhorted their followers to detach themselves from material inclinations so that their spiritual side may dominate over the physical. As we have already stated in this and previous volumes,* by detachment is not meant renunciation of the world, mendicancy or asceticism. In a nutshell, detachment is to submit one's will to the will of God and to seek His good pleasure above one's own. Therefore, the challenge to every believer in this life is detachment from all else save God. To become detached from something of this world is often a painful process and this is where sacrifice becomes necessary, because man is attracted to the material world and to his own self by nature. When the believer sacrifices something of this world, an act which entails pain and suffering or deprivation of material benefits, he will attain to a higher spiritual status, depending on the measure of sacrifice.

And when he gives up something dear to him for the sake of the Cause of God, as testified by Bahá'u'lláh in His writings, mysterious forces will be released which will enable the Faith to grow. To offer up one's time, to labour for the establishment of the Faith in a locality, to give up the comforts of home and to go as a Bahá'í pioneer to foreign lands, to offer up one's substance for the promotion of the Cause, to be persecuted for one's faith, all these sacrifices are meritorious in the sight of God and will undoubtedly bring victory to the Cause of Bahá'u'lláh, provided one's motives are pure and sincere. But to lay down one's life in the path of God when circumstances demand it is the ultimate in the realm of sacrifice. It is like a seed which sacrifices its all to the soil. Thousands of martyrs in Persia, faced with the challenge of either relinquishing their Faith or dying, have released enormous spiritual forces for the promotion and consolidation of the Cause of Bahá'u'lláh by their sacrifice. For two things are primarily responsible for the spreading of the Faith and its

* For more discussion on this important subject see vols. 1 and 2.

penetration into the hearts of men. One is the outpouring of the world-vivifying, soul-stirring energies of the Revelation of Bahá'u'lláh which like the rays of the sun in spring give new life to all created things, the other is the blood of the martyr which waters the tree of His Cause. In one of his letters[6] to the believers of the East, Shoghi Effendi has attributed all the great victories of the Cause in the western world, including the conversion to the Faith of Queen Marie of Rumania,* to the mysterious forces released by the blood of countless martyrs in Persia. However, in this Dispensation Bahá'u'lláh has exhorted His followers not to seek martyrdom. He has instead decreed that the believers should live to teach the Faith, and has exalted the reward of teaching to that of martyrdom.†

Being the sacrifice of Bahá'u'lláh Himself, the Purest Branch by offering his life as a ransom for the opening of the gates of the prison, released incalculable spiritual energies within human society, energies which in the fullness of time, according to Bahá'u'lláh, will bring about the unity of the human race. In a prayer revealed by Bahá'u'lláh on the day that the Purest Branch died, Bahá'u'lláh has made the following statement which Shoghi Effendi described as 'astounding'.

> Glorified art Thou, O Lord, my God! Thou seest me in the hands of Mine enemies, and My son bloodstained before Thy face, O Thou in Whose hands is the kingdom of all names. I have, O my Lord, offered up that which Thou hast given Me, that Thy servants may be quickened and all that dwell on earth be united.[7]

Without these utterances by Bahá'u'lláh, revealing the tremendous potentialities of this sacrifice, probably no one among His followers could have visualized the significance of the death of this noble son. Quoting the above passages, Shoghi Effendi in a letter addressed to the believers in the East[8]

* For further information see *God Passes By*, pp. 389–95.
† see vol. 2, p. 94.

on the occasion of the transfer of the remains of the Purest Branch and his illustrious mother to their glorious resting places on Mount Carmel, has made it clear that the quickening of the peoples of the world, the unity of the nations on this planet, and the oneness of mankind—which are the primary objectives of this Revelation—will be all realized through the mysterious forces released by the sacrifice of the Purest Branch.

How befitting, therefore, that the buildings intended to house the international administrative institutions of the Faith—the vehicle through which the world-redeeming, world-embracing Order of Bahá'u'lláh is to be established on the surface of this planet, thereby achieving the unity of the human race—are to be situated on the slopes of Mount Carmel around an arc in whose very centre lie not only the remains of the illustrious daughter of Bahá'u'lláh, the Greatest Holy Leaf, and of her mother, but also those of a noble son sacrificed by his Almighty Father so that we, his servants, 'may be quickened and all that dwell on earth may be united'.

Elaborating on the future unfoldment of the World Centre of the Faith, and its spiritual links with these three members of Bahá'u'lláh's family, Shoghi Effendi, as far back as 1939, wrote these highly illuminating words:

> For it must be clearly understood, nor can it be sufficiently emphasized, that the conjunction of the resting-place of the Greatest Holy Leaf with those of her brother and mother incalculably reinforces the spiritual potencies of that consecrated Spot which, under the wings of the Báb's overshadowing Sepulchre, and in the vicinity of the future Mashriqu'l-Adhkár,* which will be reared on its flank, is destined to evolve into the focal centre of those world-shaking, world-embracing, world-directing administrative institutions, ordained by Bahá'u'lláh and anticipated by 'Abdu'l-Bahá, and which are to function in consonance with

* Literally 'the dawning-place of the mention of God', a Bahá'í House of Worship. See below, pp. 345–8. (A.T.)

the principles that govern the twin institutions of the Guardianship and the Universal House of Justice. Then, and then only, will this momentous prophecy which illuminates the concluding passages of the Tablet of Carmel* be fulfilled: 'Ere long will God sail His Ark upon thee (Carmel), and will manifest the people of Bahá who have been mentioned in the Book of Names.'

To attempt to visualize, even in its barest outline, the glory that must envelop these institutions, to essay even a tentative and partial description of their character or the manner of their operation, or to trace however inadequately the course of events leading to their rise and eventual establishment is far beyond my own capacity and power. Suffice it to say that at this troubled stage in world history the association of these three incomparably precious souls who, next to the three Central Figures of our Faith, tower in rank above the vast multitude of the heroes, Letters, martyrs, hands, teachers and administrators of the Cause of Bahá'u'lláh, in such a potentially powerful spiritual and administrative Centre, is in itself an event which will release forces that are bound to hasten the emergence in a land which, geographically, spiritually and administratively, constitutes the heart of the entire planet, of some of the brightest gems of that World Order now shaping in the womb of this travailing age.[9]

The Pen of the Most High did not stop revealing the words of God because of that mournful event, the death of the Purest Branch. The Manifestation of God is never preoccupied with one matter at a time and nothing of this world can thwart Him from His all-encompassing vision. He is not limited, as human beings are, in His dealings with things. We have already discussed this aspect of the Manifestation of God in previous volumes.† On the same day when the spirit of the Purest

* The Tablet of Carmel revealed by Bahá'u'lláh may be considered as the Charter for building the World Centre of the Faith. We shall refer to this Tablet in the next volume. (A.T.)

† see vol. 1, pp. 262–3; vol. 2, pp. 416–17.

Branch ascended to the Realms above, Bahá'u'lláh revealed a Tablet in honour of one of the believers in Qazvín. In it He pays glowing tribute to His son and bestows upon him His benedictions. This is part of the Tablet:

> At this very moment My son is being washed before My face, after Our having sacrificed him in the Most Great Prison. Thereat have the dwellers of the Abhá Tabernacle wept with a great weeping, and such as have suffered imprisonment with this Youth in the path of God, the Lord of the promised Day, lamented. Under such conditions My Pen hath not been prevented from remembering its Lord, the Lord of all nations. It summoneth the people unto God, the Almighty, the All-Bountiful. This is the day whereon he that was created by the light of Bahá has suffered martyrdom, at a time when he lay imprisoned at the hands of his enemies.
>
> Upon thee, O Branch of God! be the remembrance of God and His praise, and the praise of all that dwell in the Realm of Immortality, and of all the denizens of the Kingdom of Names. Happy art thou in that thou hast been faithful to the Covenant of God and His Testament, until Thou didst sacrifice thyself before the face of thy Lord, the Almighty, the Unconstrained. Thou, in truth, hast been wronged, and to this testifieth the Beauty of Him, the Self-Subsisting. Thou didst, in the first days of thy life, bear that which hath caused all things to groan; and made every pillar to tremble. Happy is the one that remembereth thee, and draweth nigh, through thee, unto God, the Creator of the Morn.[10]

Lawḥ-i-Pisar-'Amm (Tablet to the Cousin)

This Tablet was revealed in the barracks of 'Akká in honour of Mírzá Ḥasan-i-Mázindarání, a cousin of Bahá'u'lláh. We have already stated that Mírzá Ḥasan managed to enter the barracks and remained there for some time. He was present when the Purest Branch passed away and assisted Shaykh Maḥmud in washing his body. This Tablet was revealed when Bahá'u'lláh directed Mírzá Ḥasan to return home. This kinsman of Bahá'u'lláh was very dear to Him. It was Bahá'u'lláh Himself who, in the early days of the ministry of the Báb, had converted his father Mullá Zaynu'l-'Ábidín (a paternal uncle of Bahá'u'lláh) to the Faith. His son Mírzá Ḥasan was devoted to the Cause and had dedicated himself to the service of its Author.

In the opening passages of this Tablet, Bahá'u'lláh urges Mírzá Ḥasan to offer thanks to God for having enabled him to enter the presence of His Lord, being the first among Bahá'u'lláh's relatives to do so in the Holy Land. Also, to treasure His gracious favours through which the ties of kinship were not severed. He affirms that the bounty of retaining this family tie was so precious that nothing in this world could equal it.

As already stated in previous volumes,* a number of Bahá'u'lláh's relatives including uncles and cousins, as well as brothers and sisters, fully recognized the station of Bahá'u'lláh and became his devoted followers. In His sight they were distinguished from the rest, for they had strengthened their physical relationship with spiritual ties of faith. Since the primary mission of the Manifestation of God is to confer spiritual life upon the souls, those who become deprived of this are therefore reckoned as dead in His estimation. In the Writings of Bahá'u'lláh and in the Holy Books of other religions, the word 'dead' is often used to refer to those devoid of faith and spiritual life. In the light of this, it becomes clear that those among Bahá'u'lláh's relatives who were not illumined with the light of faith had, indeed, severed their relationship with Him.

In this Tablet Bahá'u'lláh exhorts Mírzá Ḥasan to make mention of his Lord and to conduct himself in such wise that people might inhale from him the fragrances of the Beloved, and witness the purity and excellence of his deeds, deeds which

* see vol. 1, pp. 8, 12–16, 49–51, 122–3; vol. 2, p. 205n.

were praiseworthy in the sight of God. He counsels him to detach himself from the world and its transitory vanities. Instead he should endeavour to adorn himself with the glory of His Name which is imperishable and everlasting.

The rest of the Tablet consists of exhortations to other people. First, there is a long message which appears to be addressed to Bahá'u'lláh's half-brother Mírzá Riḍá-Qulí. He does not mention his name in this Tablet, but from the tone and contents of Bahá'u'lláh's words, one may deduce that it is probably for him. In a previous volume* we have referred to this brother briefly. Although his wife Maryam,† a cousin of Bahá'u'lláh, was a devoted believer, Mírzá Riḍá-Qulí himself was not touched sufficiently by the light of the Faith to enter into the fold. He remained distant from Bahá'u'lláh and there is a suggestion in this Tablet that at one stage he had requested Bahá'u'lláh not to write to him. It must be noted that from time to time Bahá'u'lláh had maintained communication with this brother and urged him to open his inner eyes so that he might behold his Lord and embrace His Faith. In this Tablet Bahá'u'lláh expresses His grief and deep sorrow for a brother who remained aloof from the Cause of God, and with loving-kindness exhorts him to arise and make amends.

Mírzá Riḍá-Qulí was held in high esteem in Ṭihrán. The following account by Ḥájí Mírzá Ḥaydar-'Alí throws some light on his attitude towards Bahá'u'lláh. The story relates to Mírzá Ḥusayn-Khán-i-Mushíru'd-Dawlih‡ who was the Persian Ambassador in Turkey for ten years. He was recalled to Ṭihrán and in 1871 was made Prime Minister:

> And when he [the Mushíru'd-Dawlih] went to Ṭihrán, the Ministers, leaders and dignitaries came to visit him. Among them was the late Ḥájí Mírzá Riḍá-Qulí, a half-brother of the Ancient Beauty. He was introduced as a brother of

* see vol. 1, p. 12.
† see vol. 1, pp. 12–13.
‡ see vol. 2, *passim*.

Bahá'u'lláh. Due to embarrassment and fear he said, 'I have a father, why can't you introduce me through him?' On hearing this the Mushíru'd-Dawlih exclaimed in a rebuking tone: 'You ought to pride yourself on and glory in being a brother of Bahá'u'lláh. It is a very great honour and a source of pride for Persia and the people of Persia that Bahá'u'lláh is a native of this country. Every Prince, minister or ruler who went from Persia to Istanbul at any time, became, in various ways, the cause of disgrace and humiliation for the government and the people of Persia . . . Although exiled by the government, Bahá'u'lláh conducted Himself with such firmness and dignity and manifested such an ascendancy and glory that He truly revived Persia and her peoples . . .[11]

That such a glowing tribute should be paid by Mírzá Ḥusayn-Khán, the Mushíru'd-Dawlih,* who in earlier years as Persian Ambassador in Turkey had assiduously worked against Bahá'u'lláh, but who later changed his attitude, is a proof that nothing can be as effective as pure and holy deeds in convincing people of the truth of the Cause of God. We find in the Writings of Bahá'u'lláh numerous exhortations concerning this. In the *Ishráqat* (Splendours) Bahá'u'lláh states:

> In this Revelation the hosts that can render it victorious are the hosts of praiseworthy deeds and upright character.[12]

In another Tablet He declares:

> Man is like unto a tree. If he be adorned with fruit, he hath been and will ever be worthy of praise and commendation. Otherwise a fruitless tree is but fit for fire. The fruits of the human tree are exquisite, highly desired and dearly cherished. Among them are upright character, virtuous deeds and a goodly utterance. The springtime for earthly trees occurreth once every year, while the one for human trees appeareth in the Days of God—exalted be His glory.

* For further information about him and the change that took place in his attitude towards Bahá'u'lláh see vol. 2, pp. 399–401.

> Were the trees of men's lives to be adorned in this divine Springtime with the fruits that have been mentioned, the effulgence of the light of Justice, would, of a certainty, illumine all the dwellers of the earth and everyone would abide in tranquillity and contentment beneath the sheltering shadow of Him Who is the Object of all mankind.[13]

And in the *Lawḥ-i-Dunyá* (Tablet of the World) Bahá'u'lláh declares:

> This Wronged One hath forbidden the people of God to engage in contention or conflict and hath exhorted them to righteous deeds and praiseworthy character. In this day the hosts that can ensure the victory of the Cause are those of goodly conduct and saintly character. Blessed are they who firmly adhere unto them and woe betide such as turn away therefrom.[14]

11

The Wronged One of the World

The Prison Gates Open

About four months had passed since the death of the Purest Branch when, as he had wished on his death-bed, the gates of the prison of 'Akká were opened. Bahá'u'lláh, His family and companions left the barracks after being confined there for a period of two years, two months and five days. This transfer, which took place in the autumn of 1870, became necessary as the barracks were needed to accommodate Turkish troops. Bahá'u'lláh and His family were confined in a house while some of His companions took residence in other houses and the rest were consigned to the caravanserai, named the Khán-i-'Avámíd.

Bahá'u'lláh resided in a number of houses, staying a few months in each. First He moved to the house of Malik, and later the nearby house of Manṣúr Khavvám was added to it. From there He moved to the house of Rábi'ih. Eventually His residence was transferred to the house of 'Údí Khammár. This house was attached to the house of 'Abbúd; the partition between the two houses was later removed, and the two houses became one, the whole becoming known as the house of 'Abbúd. The eastern section was the house of Khammár and the western, facing the sea, was that of 'Abbúd. 'Údí Khammár was a Christian, so was 'Abbúd, and they were close relatives. The house of 'Údí Khammár was very inadequate for the needs of Bahá'u'lláh and His household. Bahá'u'lláh occupied the small upstairs room in the eastern side of the house. The other room upstairs was overcrowded—at one time thirteen people of both sexes had to sleep in that room in rows. It is a well-known story that one night the person who used to sleep on a shelf in that room fell down on the top of others while asleep!

As for the Khán-i-'Avámíd (Inn of the Pillars), it was a caravanserai unfit for a dwelling-place. Most of the companions of Bahá'u'lláh were consigned to this place, occupying rooms on the upper floor mostly in the western and southern wings of the building. 'Abdu'l-Bahá occupied one room Himself and for some time this was the room in which He entertained guests. The pilgrims arriving from Persia were first received by 'Abdu'l-Bahá in this room. He saw to it that they were ready to attain the presence of Bahá'u'lláh. Not only did the pilgrims learn from Him, through His courtesy and utter selflessness, lessons of humility before Bahá'u'lláh, but also they were helped to improve their outward appearance—for example by putting on new clothes when they were to attain His presence.

The rooms in the Khán-i-'Avámíd were damp and filthy. 'Abdu'l-Bahá sold a certain gift which had been given to Him in Baghdád and with the proceeds began to repair the rooms for the companions of Bahá'u'lláh. He left the repair of His own room to the last. The money ran out and as a result His room remained unrepaired and in very bad condition. Not only were its walls damp but the roof leaked and the floor was covered with dust. He sat and slept on a mat in that room. His bed cover was a sheepskin. The room was infested with fleas and when He slept under the sheepskin, fleas gathered and began biting. 'Abdu'l-Bahá had worked out a tactic of defeating the fleas by turning over his sheepskin at intervals. He would sleep for a while before the fleas found their way again to the inner side. He would then turn the sheepskin over again. Every night He had to resort to this tactic eight to ten times.

These companions of Bahá'u'lláh had to live in an austerity similar to that when they were in the barracks. Food was scarce and rations far from adequate for each person. Yet they spent their time in the utmost joy. Their greatest longing was to be called to the presence of their Lord. Their attachment to Bahá'u'lláh was the source of their strength. It enabled them to live in the utmost happiness in spite of all the hardships which were heaped upon them in those gloomy surroundings. As time went on, however, the situation changed, the companions of Bahá'u'lláh were able to find other accommodation in town and managed to engage in some humble professions. The Khán-i-'Avámíd then became the first Bahá'í Pilgrim House in the Holy Land. Some individuals remained there and had the task of serving the pilgrims, who stayed for months—and some for years. Notable among those who lived there for a long time were Zaynu'l-Muqarribín and Mishkín-Qalam to whom reference has been made in volume 1.

Lawḥ-i-Ru'yá (Tablet of Vision)

The *Lawḥ-i-Ru'yá* in Arabic, similar in style to the *Lawḥ-i-Ḥúríyyih,** was revealed in 1873 in the house of 'Údí Khammár on the eve of the anniversary of the birth of the Báb which in that year fell on 1 March.† Bahá'u'lláh revealed this Tablet for one of the believers in order to show him a glimpse of the world of the spirit in this dark world, stating that if it were His will, He could make manifest from an atom the lights of the sun, and from a drop the waves of an ocean. This Tablet, remarkable for its allusive language, portrays a spiritual vision beautiful in its concept and descriptive in its style of imagery. Its perusal uplifts the heart and fascinates the mind.

Bahá'u'lláh portrays His vision of the appearance of the Maid of Heaven before Him, a vision which is beyond the comprehension of mortals and cannot be understood in its reality. The 'Maiden' has sometimes been described symbolically as the personification of the 'Most Great Spirit',

* see vol. 1, p. 125.

† The birth of the Báb and Bahá'u'lláh are celebrated in the East according to the lunar calendar.

which descended upon Bahá'u'lláh. The descent of the Holy Spirit in other Dispensations upon the Manifestations of God has been described figuratively in the form of the Burning Bush, the Sacred Fire, the Dove or the Angel Gabriel.

In the *Lawḥ-i-Ru'yá* Bahá'u'lláh describes His vision of a Maiden dressed in white and illumined with the light of God. She entered the room in which Bahá'u'lláh was seated upon His throne of Lordship. She displayed an indescribable enthusiasm and devotion, circled around Him, was enraptured by the inebriation of His Presence, was thunderstruck at His Glory. And when she recovered, she remained in a state of bewilderment. She longed to offer up her life for her Beloved and finding Him captive in the hands of the unfaithful, she bade Him leave 'Akká to its inhabitants and repair to His other dominions 'whereon the eyes of the people of names have never fallen', words which found their fulfilment nineteen years later with the ascension of Bahá'u'lláh. In the absence of a translation it is not possible to convey the beauty of the verses and the mystery of the subject revealed in the *Lawḥ-i-Ru'yá*. The theme of this Tablet is as enchanting as it is unfathomable and mysterious.

Soon after Bahá'u'lláh moved to the house of 'Údí Khammár, a serious crisis which had been growing within the community suddenly erupted into a major catastrophe which engulfed Bahá'u'lláh, 'Abdu'l-Bahá and other companions. This was the murder by seven believers of Siyyid Muḥammad-i-Iṣfahání,* Áqá Ján-i-Kaj-Kuláh † and Mírzá Riḍá-Qulíy-i-Tafrishí, all of whom claimed to be followers of Mírzá Yaḥyá. This heinous act, contrary to all the principles and to the spirit of the teachings of Bahá'u'lláh, brought the greatest sorrow to His heart and tarnished the good name of the Faith for a considerable time.

It will be remembered that soon after their arrival in the

* see p. 56; also vols. 1 and 2.
† see p. 56; also vol. 2, pp. 326, 402.

barracks, Siyyid Muḥammad and Áqá Ján had been transferred to quarters overlooking the city gate where they could spy on all Bahá'ís trying to enter 'Akká. In this way many of the pilgrims had been expelled from the city. Siyyid Muḥammad had adopted the name 'Quddús Effendi' (Holy One) and Áqá Ján began to use the name 'Sayfu'l-Ḥaqq' (The Sword of Truth), a title bestowed on him by Mírzá Yaḥyá. They then began to do everything in their power to misrepresent Bahá'u'lláh. One of their comrades was the above-named Mírzá Riḍá-Qulí who had been used to associate freely with the companions of Bahá'u'lláh. But he lived a life contrary to the teachings of the Faith, and committed some shameful deeds in the company of some Christians in the city. Through his reprehensible conduct, he brought public disgrace upon the Faith and Bahá'u'lláh finally expelled him from the community.

Having been disgracefully dismissed, Mírzá Riḍá-Qulí and his sister Badrí Ján,* an estranged wife of Mírzá Yaḥyá, joined hands with Siyyid Muḥammad and Áqá Ján in a campaign of calumnies against Bahá'u'lláh designed to discredit Him in the eyes of the people, who had been beginning to unbend towards the company of exiles. The effect of this campaign of lies and misrepresentations was that the mind of the public was poisoned against Bahá'u'lláh and His faithful companions. The fire of sedition and strife which these four ignited in the hearts of the people of 'Akká began to engulf the community of the Most Great Name. People began to show open enmity and malice towards the believers. It was at this time that Bahá'u'lláh decided to close the door of His house to the faces of friends and foes alike. He did not allow anyone to attain His presence. 'Abdu'l-Bahá also left the Khán-i-'Avámíd and stayed close to His Father in the house of 'Údí Khammár. The seclusion of Bahá'u'lláh in His house, reminiscent of the time

* She had left Mírzá Yaḥyá in the Adrianople days and taken refuge in the house of Áqáy-i-Kalím, the faithful brother of Bahá'u'lláh. She and her brother had journeyed with the companions to 'Akká.

when He had retired to the house of Riḍá Big in Adrianople, isolated Him from everyone, and brought grief to the hearts of His companions.

Lawḥ-i-Qad Iḥtaraqa'l-Mukhliṣún (The Fire Tablet)

Towards the end of 1871 Bahá'u'lláh received a letter from one of His devoted followers in Persia, Ḥájí Siyyid 'Alí-Akbar-i-Dahají, a nephew of Siyyid Mihdí, the Ismu'lláh.* In answer to his letter, Bahá'u'lláh revealed the *Lawḥ-i-Qad Iḥtaraqa'l-Mukhliṣún*, or the *Lawḥ-i-Iḥtiráq*, translated into English and known in the west as the Fire Tablet. In the previous volume reference has been made to Ḥají Siyyid 'Alí-Akbar, the recipient of this Tablet, and a brief account of his life and services to the Cause is given there.† He was so much loved by Bahá'u'lláh that when he passed away Bahá'u'lláh gave his uncle the name 'Alí-Akbar, in memory of that devoted believer.

The *Lawḥ-i-Qad Iḥtaraqa'l-Mukhliṣún* is one of Bahá'u'lláh's most celebrated Tablets; it is possessed of great powers, and the believers often recite it at times of difficulties and suffering. Of this Tablet Bahá'u'lláh states: 'Should all the servants read and ponder this, there shall be kindled in their veins a fire that shall set aflame the worlds.'[1] The Fire Tablet is in Arabic rhyming verse; it moves the heart when chanted in the original language. It was revealed at a time when great afflictions and sorrows had surrounded Bahá'u'lláh as a result of the hostility, betrayal and acts of infamy perpetrated by those few individuals who had once claimed to be the helpers of the Cause of God. Bahá'u'lláh pours out His heart in this Tablet and expatiates on His afflictions. For nothing brings more sorrow to the heart of the Manifestation of God than unfaithfulness and treachery from within the community. Imprisonment and all manner of persecution by the outside

* see vol. 2, pp. 118–19, 272–4, 290.

† vol. 2, pp. 274–5.

enemy can do no harm to the Cause. What harms it are the actions of those who bear His name and yet commit deeds contrary to His good-pleasure. These few breakers of the Covenant of the Báb, who followed Mírzá Yaḥyá and rose up against Bahá'u'lláh from within, created such havoc in the community and among the inhabitants of 'Akká that the Pen of Bahá'u'lláh lamented in this Tablet in a manner unprecedented in all His Writings.

When this Tablet was revealed the followers of Bahá'u'lláh became aware of the immensity of His sufferings at the hands of the wicked and ungodly. He addresses Ḥájí Siyyid 'Alí-Akbar, its recipient, in these words: 'O 'Alí-Akbar, thank thy Lord for this Tablet whence thou canst breathe the fragrance of My meekness, and know what hath beset Us in the path of God, the Adored of all the worlds.'[2]

In a passage (untranslated) addressed to the aforementioned Siyyid Mihdíy-i-Dahají, Bahá'u'lláh states that He revealed the Fire Tablet for the Siyyid's nephew so that it might create in him feelings of joy as well as igniting in his heart the fire of the love of God.

In order that the mind of man, limited and finite as it is, may be able to reflect and meditate on the sufferings heaped upon the Manifestation, and at the same time see a glimpse of His All-Glorious Being, Bahá'u'lláh has revealed this Tablet in a special way. It seems as if it is His human Person, as distinct from the Manifestation of God, that recounts His afflictions and dwells on the iniquities perpetrated by His enemies. Then comes the voice of God and Bahá'u'lláh's response to it. But in reality, Bahá'u'lláh, the Supreme Manifestation of God, cannot be divided into two. His human nature and divine spirit are so mingled together that at no time can He be regarded as a man devoid of the Most Great Spirit which always animated Him. It cannot be assumed that at times a Manifestation of God ceases to be a Manifestation and becomes purely a man. On the contrary, He is always a Manifestation of God, although He often hides His glory* and appears to be like an ordinary human being. To appreciate this indivisibility, let us consider man with his two natures. We observe that whereas man combines within himself the animal and the spiritual natures, yet he is always a man and at no time can he be considered to be a pure animal devoid of the human spirit or temporarily become robbed of his powers as a man. Similarly, the Manifestation of God can never be divided into separate parts.

Probably the basic reason that Bahá'u'lláh in the Fire Tablet has spoken with the voice of man is to enable the believers to appreciate how grievous were the attacks launched against Him, and how much His companions suffered when they were unable to attain His presence. In the opening passages, Bahá'u'lláh refers to this separation between Him and His loved ones and invokes the Almighty to succour and comfort them.

> Indeed the hearts of the sincere are consumed in the fire of separation:
> Where is the gleaming of the light of Thy Countenance, O Beloved of the worlds?
> Those who are near unto Thee have been abandoned in the darkness of desolation:
> Where is the shining of the morn of Thy reunion, O Desire of the worlds?
> The bodies of Thy chosen ones lie quivering on distant sands:
> Where is the ocean of Thy presence, O Enchanter of the worlds?

In other passages Bahá'u'lláh alludes to His withdrawal from everyone, such as when he refers to Himself being 'veiled by evil suggestions', or when He states that the 'sea of grace is stilled', and 'the door leading to the Divine Presence is locked'.

In this Tablet one comes across statements clearly referring to the evil doings of Siyyid Muḥammad and his henchmen. He

* see p. 2.

refers to them as the 'infidels' who 'have arisen in tyranny', describes their activities as the 'barking of dogs', the 'whisperings of Satan', states that through their deeds 'the lamps of truth and purity, of loyalty and honour, have been put out', and affirms that through their evil spirit 'the leaves are yellowed by the poisoning winds of sedition'.

Bahá'u'lláh expatiates on His sufferings in this Tablet. He makes mention of 'abasement' and 'sorrows' which have afflicted Him, states that His 'Face is hidden in the dust of slander' and that His 'robe of sanctity is sullied by the people of deceit'. These heart-rending passages are clear references to the effects of the vast campaign of misrepresentation and slander carried out by Siyyid Muḥammad against Bahá'u'lláh in public, and bear ample testimony to the harrowing afflictions which had been heaped upon Him.

Having dwelt on His sufferings, Bahá'u'lláh then, as the 'Tongue of Grandeur', replies to Himself. These are among His utterances:

> We have made abasement the garment of glory,
> And affliction the adornment of Thy temple, O Pride of the worlds.
> Thou seest the hearts are filled with hate,
> And to overlook is Thine, O Thou Concealer of the sins of the worlds.
> When the swords flash, go forward!
> When the shafts fly, press onward! O Thou Sacrifice of the worlds.

In this Tablet Bahá'u'lláh invokes the wrath of God for His enemies, when He asks, 'Where is the lion of the forest of Thy might?' 'Where is the meteor of Thy fire?' or 'Where are the signs of Thy avenging wrath?' God is loving and forgiving, but occasionally He appears in His wrath. One of these occasions is when some individual opposes His Manifestation while knowing who He is and the station He occupies. Whereas the Manifestation of God can invoke the wrath of God upon such people, man has no right to do so. In this Dispensation Bahá'u'lláh has forbidden His followers to condemn other men.

In one of His Tablets[3] revealed in 'Akká, Bahá'u'lláh refers to this subject. He quotes the following passage from the Fire Tablet: 'The necks of men are stretched out in malice; Where are the swords of Thy vengeance . . .', and states that although outwardly these words seem to contradict the teaching of God for this age and invoke His wrath and vengeance, they are not meant to advocate contention and strife. Rather, such statements were made in order to convey the enormity of the sufferings caused by a few wicked people. Their transgressions reached such proportions that the Pen of the Most High was made to lament in the way it did.

Having clarified the reasons for invoking the wrath of God, Bahá'u'lláh in this Tablet warns the believers against using such terms as a pretext for creating strife and sedition. He exhorts them to unity, love and compassion toward all the peoples of the world, states that the hosts which can render the Cause of God victorious are praiseworthy deeds and an upright character and asserts that the commander of these hosts is the fear of God.*

As we survey the Writings of Bahá'u'lláh and those of the other Central Figures of the Faith, we observe that the greatest portion of these consists of exhortations and commandments on living a life based on the spiritual teachings of God. In most of His Tablets, Bahá'u'lláh exhorts His followers to goodly character, pure deeds, and praiseworthy conduct. He calls on them to foster the spirit of fellowship and unity among the peoples of the world and become the embodiments of loving kindness to all who dwell on earth.

Exhorting Badí'u'lláh, one of His sons, to live the life of servitude, Bahá'u'lláh has revealed the following passage. His counsels in this Tablet may be said to epitomize His teachings on the question of individual conduct in this life.

* see vol. 2, pp. 94–6.

Be generous in prosperity, and thankful in adversity. Be worthy of the trust of thy neighbour, and look upon him with a bright and friendly face. Be a treasure to the poor, an admonisher to the rich, an answerer of the cry of the needy, a preserver of the sanctity of thy pledge. Be fair in thy judgment, and guarded in thy speech. Be unjust to no man, and show all meekness to all men. Be as a lamp unto them that walk in darkness, a joy to the sorrowful, a sea for the thirsty, a haven for the distressed, an upholder and defender of the victim of oppression. Let integrity and uprightness distinguish all thine acts. Be a home for the stranger, a balm to the suffering, a tower of strength for the fugitive. Be eyes to the blind, and a guiding light unto the feet of the erring. Be an ornament to the countenance of truth, a crown to the brow of fidelity, a pillar of the temple of righteousness, a breath of life to the body of mankind, an ensign of the hosts of justice, a luminary above the horizon of virtue, a dew to the soil of the human heart, an ark on the ocean of knowledge, a sun in the heaven of bounty, a gem on the diadem of wisdom, a shining light in the firmament of thy generation, a fruit upon the tree of humility.[4]

Submission of the Manifestation of God to Trials

In the Fire Tablet we observe two different features of Bahá'u'lláh. The first is the station of sovereignty and lordship, a station exalted above the world of man. In this station He is not affected by the tumult and conflicts of this life, because He is animated by the Most Great Spirit which makes Him independent of all things except God. The other station is that of meekness and submission to God. This is a station in which Bahá'u'lláh is referred to in many of His Tablets as the 'Wronged One of the World'. In this station He submits Himself to His enemies, welcomes sufferings and accepts bondage and imprisonment so that mankind in this Dispensation may become freed from the fetters of tyranny and oppression and attain the light of unity.

In the *Lawḥ-i-Sulṭán* (Tablet to Náṣiri'd-Dín Sháh) Bahá'u'lláh makes these thought-provoking remarks:

> By God, Though weariness lay Me low, and hunger consume me and the bare rock be My bed, and My fellows the beasts of the field, I will not complain, but will endure patiently as those endued with constancy and firmness have endured patiently, through the power of God, the eternal King and Creator of the nations, and will render thanks unto God under all conditions. We pray that, out of His bounty—exalted be He—He may release, through this imprisonment, the necks of men from chains and fetters, and cause them to turn, with sincere faces, towards His Face, Who is the Mighty, the Bounteous.[5]

In another Tablet, Bahá'u'lláh makes it clear that He has accepted suffering for the sake of the redemption of human kind. These are His exalted words:

> The whole earth is now in a state of pregnancy. The day is approaching when it will have yielded its noblest fruits, when from it will have sprung forth the loftiest trees, the most enchanting blossoms, the most heavenly blessings. Immeasurably exalted is the breeze that wafteth from the garment of thy Lord, the Glorified! For lo, it hath breathed its fragrance and made all things new! Well it is with them that comprehend. It is indubitably clear and evident that in these things He Who is the Lord of Revelation hath sought nothing for Himself. Though aware that they would lead to tribulations, and be the cause of troubles and afflictive trials, He, solely as a token of His loving-kindness and favour, and for the purpose of quickening the dead and of redeeming all who are on earth, hath closed His eyes to His own well-being and borne that which no other person hath borne or will bear.[6]

Here and in many other Tablets Bahá'u'lláh has stated that no one on earth has been, or will be, subjected to so much suffering as He. It may be difficult for those who are not fully familiar with the Faith of Bahá'u'lláh to accept such a statement. They may argue that there have been many people who were afflicted with unbearable tortures and life-long sufferings. In order to appreciate the words of Bahá'u'lláh let us suppose that there was a community somewhere in the world whose people were savage, barbarous and brutally cruel. Those born and brought up within such a community, who had lived there all their lives and had never been in touch with civilization would find life to be normal. Although to the outsider the standard would seem to be very cruel, yet for the members of that community every event that took place in their midst would be a natural happening and accepted as such. As in every other community, there must be moments of joy and comfort as well as sadness and suffering for the people who belonged to this society. However, should a noble person who had lived in a highly civilized society be forced to join this uncivilized community, it is only natural that he would suffer much more than the rest. Because he had been used to a far superior standard in his life, it could be said of him that he had undergone such cruelties and hardships, both mental and physical, that no one else in that community had experienced.

It is the same with a Manifestation of God who is sent to live among men. There is a vast contrast between the world of man and the world of the Manifestation of God. The former is limited and full of imperfections while the latter is the realm of perfections far exalted above the comprehension of human beings. Coming from such a realm, possessing all the Divine virtues and embodying God's attributes, these exalted Beings descend into this world and become prisoners among human beings. Man's ignorance, his cruelty, his ungodliness, his selfishness, his insincerity and all his sins and shortcomings act as tools of torture inflicting painful wounds upon the soul of the Manifestation of God who has no alternative but to bear them in silence with resignation and submissiveness. One act of unfaithfulness—even a glance betraying the insincerity of the individual or an unworthy thought emanating from his mind—is as painful torture to Him. But He seldom reveals the shortcomings of men, or dwells on His own pain and suffering. Like a teacher who has to descend to the level of a child and act as if he does not know, the Manifestation of God comes as a man appearing to be the same as others.* He has the sin-covering eye to such an extent that some may think that He does not know.

Throughout the forty years of His ministry, Bahá'u'lláh treated people in this way. He submitted Himself to His enemies and bore life-long hardships and persecutions with resignation; He always closed His eyes to the shortcomings of the believers unless someone was harming the Faith or bringing disgrace upon it. He poured upon His followers loving encouragement for whatever service they rendered. Even in the case of proud and conceited followers such as Jamál-i-Burújirdí or Siyyid Mihdíy-i-Dahají † who were actively engaged in teaching the Faith, He always showered his bounties and favours upon them, at the same time counselling them to rectitude of conduct and purity of motive. His sin-covering eye was so all-encompassing that these and many other people believed that Bahá'u'lláh did not know what was hidden in their hearts!

Murder of Three Azalís

Now, when Bahá'u'lláh retired to the house of 'Údí Khammár and allowed no one to attain His presence, Siyyid Muḥammad and his associates took advantage of this. On the one hand, they began to mix with some of the faithful followers of Bahá'u'lláh, and on the other, they intensified their campaign to misrepresent the Author of the Faith. Mírzá Riḍá-Qulí had some Tablets of Bahá'u'lláh in his possession. He and Siyyid

* see pp. 2–3.

† These two men, who ranked foremost among teachers of the Faith, were only cast out of the community when they became Covenant-breakers. For further details see vol. 2.

Muḥammad interpolated these Writings with passages designed to arouse the animosity of the populace, and distributed the falsified texts widely. Mírzá Riḍá-Qulí and his sister Badrí Ján, who had been cast out of the community by Bahá'u'lláh, publicly claimed that they had left the Bahá'ís voluntarily and were now Muslims. Siyyid Muḥammad and Áqá Ján did likewise.

Not long after the revelation of the Fire Tablet Bahá'u'lláh revealed another significant Tablet[7] in which He clearly prophesied the appearance of a great affliction. He described it as the ocean of tribulation surging and its billowing waves surrounding the Ark of the Cause of God. It took only one day for Bahá'u'lláh's prophecies to be fulfilled. For in the afternoon troops surrounded His house, summoned Him to the office of the Governor (Mutaṣarrif) and kept Him in custody there. The reason was that Siyyid Muḥammad, Áqá Ján and Riḍá-Qulí had been slain by seven of Bahá'u'lláh's followers. This frightful act, so contrary to Bahá'u'lláh's admonitions, unleashed the anger and hatred of the inhabitants of 'Akká against the community and its leader.

It was Badrí Ján, the sister of the murdered Mírzá Riḍá-Qulí, who went to Government House and shamelessly accused Bahá'u'lláh of ordering the death of these men. This she did in spite of the fact that she knew well that Bahá'u'lláh always exhorted His followers to avoid any act which might inflict the slightest hurt upon a fellow human being, how much more such an odious act. She knew that Bahá'u'lláh had expressly forbidden those of his followers who had asked permission to deal with the offenders themselves, from taking any action in the matter. She also knew that He Himself had cut off His association with the believers.

Indeed, Siyyid Muḥammad himself had written several letters to the friends in Persia telling them that Bahá'u'lláh had completely dissociated Himself from all His companions.

The seven believers who, against the advice of Bahá'u'lláh and without His knowledge, perpetrated such a ghastly crime, knew well that their action would invoke the wrath of Bahá'u'lláh. They knew that He who had expelled Mírzá Riḍá-Qulí from the community merely on the grounds of misbehaviour in public, would disown them and drive them out of His presence for ever, if they carried out their intention which was far more reprehensible than the misdeeds of Mírzá Riḍá-Qulí. Indeed, some of them had concluded that by committing such a crime and dishonouring the good name of the Faith, they would never be forgiven by God and their souls would be damned in all the worlds of God. But they could not bear to see Bahá'u'lláh and His loved ones being so mercilessly attacked with slanders and false accusations. They decided that they would rather sacrifice their spiritual existence by committing this reprehensible crime than allow their Lord to suffer in this way.

Bahá'u'lláh Himself has described the details of His imprisonment in a Tablet revealed in the words of Mírzá Áqá Ján, His amanuensis. Shoghi Effendi, writing about this tragic episode, has based part of his narrative on this Tablet. These are his words:

> Their* strict confinement had hardly been mitigated, and the guards who had kept watch over them been dismissed, when an internal crisis, which had been brewing in the midst of the community, was brought to a sudden and catastrophic climax. Such had been the conduct of two of the exiles,† who had been included in the party that accompanied Bahá'u'lláh to 'Akká, that He was eventually forced to expel them, an act of which Siyyid Muḥammad did not hesitate to take the fullest advantage. Reinforced by these recruits, he, together with his old associates, acting as spies, embarked on a campaign of abuse, calumny and intrigue, even more pernicious than that which had been launched by him in Constantinople, calculated to arouse an already prejudiced and suspicious populace to a new pitch

* Bahá'u'lláh and His fellow-exiles. (A.T.)
† Mírzá Riḍá-Qulí and his sister Badrí Ján. (A.T.)

THE HOUSE OF ‘ABBÚD IN ‘AKKÁ, *c.* 1920

The balcony surrounds the room Bahá’u’lláh was later to occupy. The house of ‘Údí Khammár may be seen at the back; this was His residence at first

THE K͟HÁN-I-‘AVÁMÍD

The caravanserai in ‘Akká where many of Bahá’u’lláh’s followers were

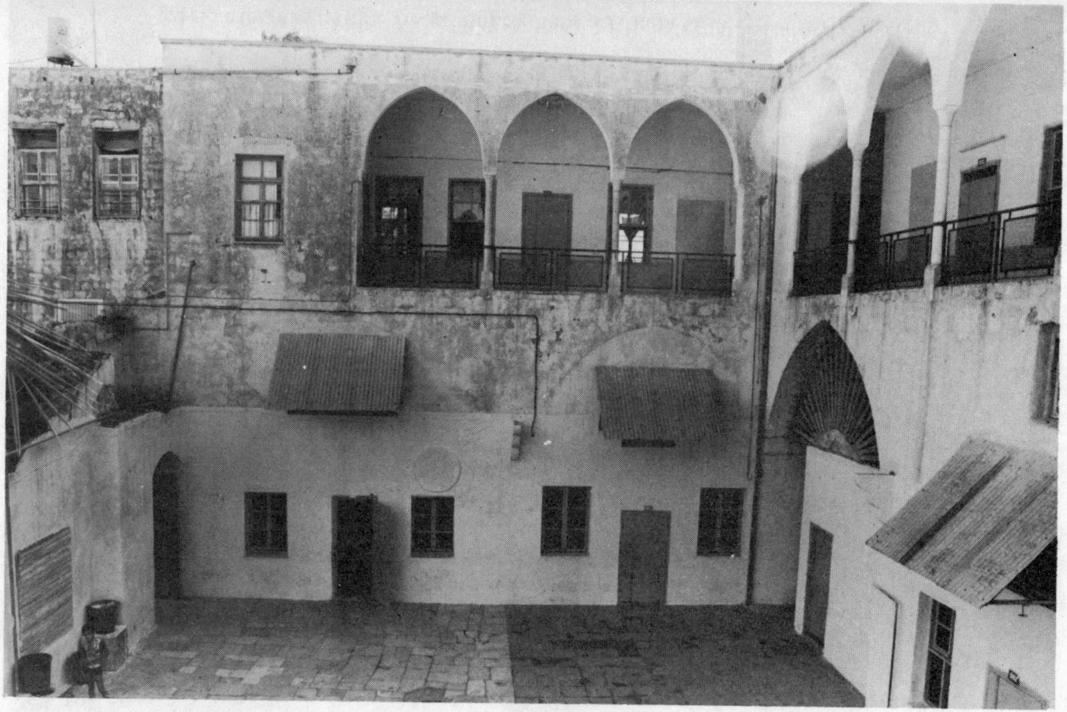

THE GOVERNORATE

A modern view looking across to the room where Bahá'u'lláh was interrogated. The building is now used as a school

THE <u>KH</u>ÁN-I-<u>SH</u>ÁVIRDÍ

A caravanserai in 'Akká where Bahá'u'lláh was kept in custody for one night

of animosity and excitement. A fresh danger now clearly threatened the life of Bahá'u'lláh. Though He Himself had stringently forbidden His followers, on several occasions, both verbally and in writing, any retaliatory acts against their tormentors, and had even sent back to Beirut an irresponsible Arab convert, who had meditated avenging the wrongs suffered by his beloved Leader, seven of the companions clandestinely sought out and slew three of their persecutors, among whom were Siyyid Muḥammad and Áqá Ján.

The consternation that seized an already oppressed community was indescribable. Bahá'u'lláh's indignation knew no bounds. 'Were We,' He thus voices His emotions, in a Tablet revealed shortly after this act had been committed, 'to make mention of what befell Us, the heavens would be rent asunder and the mountains would crumble.' 'My captivity,' he wrote on another occasion, 'cannot harm Me. That which can harm Me is the conduct of those who love Me, who claim to be related to Me, and yet perpetrate what causeth my heart and My pen to groan.' And again: 'My captivity can bring on Me no shame. Nay, by My life, it conferreth on Me glory. That which can make Me ashamed is the conduct of such of My followers as profess to love Me, yet in fact follow the Evil One.'

He was dictating His Tablets to His amanuensis when the governor, at the head of his troops, with drawn swords, surrounded His house. The entire populace, as well as the military authorities, were in a state of great agitation. The shouts and clamour of the people could be heard on all sides. Bahá'u'lláh was peremptorily summoned to the Governorate, interrogated, kept in custody the first night, with one of His sons, in a chamber in the Khán-i-Shávirdí, transferred for the following two nights to better quarters in that neighbourhood, and allowed only after the lapse of seventy hours to regain His home. 'Abdu'l-Bahá was thrown into prison and chained during the first night, after which He was permitted to join His Father. Twenty-five of the companions were cast into another prison and shackled, all of whom, except those responsible for that odious deed, whose imprisonment lasted several years, were, after six days, moved to the Khán-i-Shávirdí, and there placed, for six months, under confinement.

'Is it proper,' the Commandant of the city, turning to Bahá'u'lláh, after He had arrived at the Governorate, boldly inquired, 'that some of your followers should act in such a manner?' 'If one of your soldiers,' was the swift rejoinder, 'were to commit a reprehensible act, would you be held responsible, and be punished in his place?' When interrogated, He was asked to state His name and that of the country from which He came. 'It is more manifest than the sun,' He answered. The same question was put to Him again, to which He gave the following reply: 'I deem it not proper to mention it. Refer to the farmán of the government which is in your possession.' Once again they, with marked deference, reiterated their request, whereupon Bahá'u'lláh spoke with majesty and power these words. 'My name is Bahá'u'lláh (Light of God), and My country is Núr (Light). Be ye apprized of it.' Turning then, to the Muftí, he addressed him words of veiled rebuke, after which He spoke to the entire gathering, in such vehement and exalted language that none made bold to answer Him. Having quoted verses from the Súriy-i-Múlúk, He, afterwards, arose and left the gathering. The Governor, soon after, sent word that He was at liberty to return to His home, and apologized for what had occurred.

A population, already ill-disposed towards the exiles, was, after such an incident, fired with uncontrollable animosity for all those who bore the name of the Faith which those exiles professed. The charges of impiety, atheism, terrorism and heresy were openly and without restraint flung into their faces. 'Abbúd, who lived next door to Bahá'u'lláh, reinforced the partition that separated his house from the dwelling of his now much-feared and suspected Neighbour. Even the children of the imprisoned exiles, whenever they ventured to show themselves in the streets during those days, would be pursued, vilified and pelted with stones.[8]

The perpetrators of the crime were sentenced to long imprisonment by the authorities. Others were kept in confinement for six months and were released as it gradually became apparent that they had not been involved. As time went on it became clear to everyone that Bahá'u'lláh Himself could never have had anything to do with such an odious act, let alone being the motivating force behind it.

Problems of Historical Evaluation

One of the tragic aspects of the life of Bahá'u'lláh is that the majority of people who came into contact with the Faith failed utterly to appreciate Him and His claims. The above incident provides some examples of this. Of course, it is to be expected that those who were His avowed enemies should misrepresent Him. Similarly some non-Bahá'í historians, orientalists and missionaries—those who were biased or prejudiced—gave false impressions of Him also. Yet even those who were unbiased or friendly could never succeed in making the right judgement, because they did not know the true nature of Bahá'u'lláh's claims or His station.

Bahá'u'lláh had strictly forbidden His followers to teach His Faith within the Ottoman Empire. This is why even some important personalities who were His well-wishers and admirers regarded Him as merely a religious leader or the head of a sect, One who was very great, whose majesty and authority overwhelmed them, but whose station they did not fully understand. For this reason we find that most non-Bahá'í contemporary historians and writers have left to posterity accounts which are either totally false and full of prejudice, or which contain a great deal of misinformation.

There is no way by which a scholar, however unbiased and objective he is, can write a true version of the history of the life of Bahá'u'lláh, or submit an authentic appreciation of His mission, unless he be a believer in His Faith. Just as a layman can never evaluate the work of a scientist except in a superficial way—he has to be a scientist himself to understand the true significance of a scientific discovery—so he who writes the history of a religion has to relate historical events to the truth of God's Revelation which is enshrined in that religion. This is not possible for the sceptic. The art of writing any history lies not merely in describing events, but in relating them to each other and putting them into their proper context. And in religious history the Revelation itself is obviously central—it cannot be left out. The Founders of religions receive their teachings through divine revelation, an experience which man can never have. This makes it beyond scientific enquiry.

The only work of history that can portray, to a limited degree, the true image of Bahá'u'lláh and His Revelation is one written by a believer devoted to Him and well-versed in His writings—one who understands His claims and can interpret His actions and utterances in the light of His teachings. But even such a person can never hope to evaluate fully the events associated with the life of the Manifestation of God, for the simple reason that it is beyond man to fully understand Him. In the *Kitáb-i-Aqdas* (The Most Holy Book) Bahá'u'lláh states:

> Say: O leaders of religion! Weigh not the Book of God with such standards and sciences as are current amongst you, for the Book itself is the unerring balance established amongst men. In this most perfect balance whatsoever the peoples and kindreds of the earth possess must be weighed, while the measure of its weight should be tested according to its own standard, did ye but know it.[9]

Several disciples of Bahá'u'lláh have written their accounts of Him, and each one in accordance with his spiritual capacity has recorded some aspects of the history of the Faith. Nabíl-i-A'ẓam has written a detailed narrative, a part of which is edited and published as *The Dawn-Breakers*. His narratives are considered by the Bahá'ís to be among the most authentic histories of the ministries of the Báb and Bahá'u'lláh.

No account of the history of the Faith would be complete without mentioning *God Passes By* by Shoghi Effendi, the Guardian of the Faith. This book deals with the historical events associated with the ministries of the Báb, Bahá'u'lláh and 'Abdu'l-Bahá, as well as the birth and development of the Administrative Order. It is a masterpiece of history—concise yet filled with vivid detail of the most significant events of the first Bahá'í century. Shoghi Effendi in his masterly style has condensed volumes of material within the compass of a few hundred pages. Almost every line of this book is laden with much information, superbly gleaned, without appearing to be, from numerous narratives and historical documents as well as profuse quotations from the vast reservoir of the writings of the Central Figures of the Faith.

Being the Guardian of the Faith, Shoghi Effendi was more qualified than anyone else to write such a book on Bahá'í history. As the unerring interpreter of Bahá'u'lláh's Writings, he was, next to 'Abdu'l-Bahá, endowed with a unique capacity to understand and appreciate the Revelation of Bahá'u'lláh to an extent that no other human being can ever hope to achieve. He elucidates every major event in the light of the Revelation of Bahá'u'lláh and injects into every subject a measure of the truth of the Faith. In the course of writing the accounts of the lives of the Central Figures of the Cause and their disciples, he explains the true motive behind their actions, calculates the effects of these actions, puts into the right perspective the heroism and self-sacrifice of the Bábí and Bahá'í martyrs, enumerates the victories and crises that the Faith has encountered, recounts the downfall of its enemies, demonstrates the unfoldment of its world-embracing institutions and foreshadows its future destiny.

In contrast to the writings of Shoghi Effendi, one who had truly understood the station of Bahá'u'lláh and was in a position to explain His actions, we come across the writings of those who had very little knowledge of the Faith and have left behind much erroneous information. How can a man who is either full of prejudice or, if unbiased, is blind to the reality of the Manifestation of God, write a correct account of His life and be able to interpret His words and actions? How could the unbelieving contemporaries of Jesus, including the Jews in His days, be expected to render a true appreciation of His life and teachings? They could not do this because they were veiled from His glory. The same is true in Bahá'u'lláh's day.

One example is the incident of the slaying of the three men in 'Akká. Many people, both high and low in the city, in the early stages considered Bahá'u'lláh as the instigator of this odious deed. But as time went on most of them realized their mistake and began to see the loftiness of His virtues and the purity of His deeds. Some Western writers heard biased stories and distorted versions of His interrogation, and wrote these down in their dispatches and memoirs. What these men did not realize was that those who heard Bahá'u'lláh speaking to the officials at the time of enquiry were not familiar with His claims, nor did they understand the terminology He used in His utterances.

For instance, while in the seat of honour and in the presence of officials and dignitaries of the city including the Muftí of 'Akká, Bahá'u'lláh recited, in a vibrant voice, some passages from the *Súriy-i-Mulúk* (Súrih of the Kings) and some other Tablets. Those who are familiar with these Writings know that unless one is well versed in Bahá'u'lláh's teachings and utterances, one will not be able to appreciate the significance of the various allusions He has made in these Tablets, allusions which were clear to the believers, but almost incomprehensible to others. The outcome of all this is gross misunderstanding by those non-Bahá'í authors who have written an account of Bahá'u'lláh's interrogation.

To cite one example: Laurence Oliphant, a traveller of note, in his book *Haifa, or Life in the Holy Land*, alleged that Bahá'u'lláh after being interrogated was set free as He had 'with an enormous bribe . . . purchased an exemption for all further attendance at Court'.[10] Had Oliphant been interested to learn a little more about Bahá'u'lláh, who had for almost thirty years submitted Himself unconditionally to His enemies, he could not have made such a gross misrepresentation. If Bahá'u'lláh had been interested in freeing Himself from imprisonment in the manner alleged, He could easily have freed Himself from the Síyah-Chál of Ṭihrán, twenty years before, or from the sufferings of Adrianople or the barracks of 'Akká. If the writer of this account had been able to investigate, however summarily, the teachings of this Faith and the Divine perfections and virtues with which its Author was invested, he could have discerned that the story reported to him was a lie aimed at damaging the integrity of Bahá'u'lláh. Moreover, had he known about the life of austerity which Bahá'u'lláh and His family had lived and were living at the time, he would have written a different account altogether.

It is not the aim of this book to engage in refuting the misrepresentations of various non-Bahá'í writers. However, in this case it is interesting to look further into Oliphant's report which contains other untrue allegations. For instance, it is alleged that when Bahá'u'lláh was asked by the interrogating officer about His profession, He replied, '. . . I am not a camel driver . . . nor am I the Son of a carpenter'—allusions to the Prophet Muḥammad and Jesus Christ respectively. Here again the person who had made this malicious statement to Oliphant intended to introduce Bahá'u'lláh as a proud man and a heretic who had no regard for other Prophets.

Those who are familiar with Bahá'u'lláh and His teachings know that nothing could be further from the truth. In innumerable Tablets Bahá'u'lláh has paid glowing tributes to Muḥammad and Christ. None of the followers of these two religions have ever written about their respective founders in a way which could match the sincerity, the power, the beauty, the profundity and eloquence of Bahá'u'lláh's utterances when He extols and glorifies the station of these two Manifestations of God and pays homage to them. To cite one example: in the course of a Tablet revealed in answer to some questions by a certain Christian Bishop residing in Constantinople, Bahá'u'lláh pays the following tribute to Jesus Christ.

> Know thou that when the Son of Man yielded up His breath to God, the whole creation wept with a great weeping. By sacrificing Himself, however, a fresh capacity was infused into all created things. Its evidences, as witnessed in all the peoples of the earth, are now manifest before thee. The deepest wisdom which the sages have uttered, the profoundest learning which any mind hath unfolded, the arts which the ablest hands have produced, the influence exerted by the most potent of rulers, are but manifestations of the quickening power released by His transcendent, His all-pervasive, and resplendent Spirit.
>
> We testify that when He came into the world, He shed the splendour of His glory upon all created things. Through Him the leper recovered from the leprosy of perversity and ignorance. Through Him, the unchaste and wayward were healed. Through His power, born of Almighty God, the eyes of the blind were opened, and the soul of the sinner sanctified.
>
> Leprosy may be interpreted as any veil that interveneth between man and the recognition of the Lord, his God. Whoso alloweth himself to be shut out from Him is indeed a leper, who shall not be remembered in the Kingdom of God, the Mighty, the All-Praised. We bear witness that through the power of the Word of God every leper was cleansed, every sickness was healed, every human infirmity was banished. He it is Who purified the world. Blessed is the man who, with a face beaming with light, hath turned towards Him.[11]

There are also many Tablets in which Bahá'u'lláh has paid exalted tribute to the Prophet of Islám. Moreover, there are numerous laudatory passages in His writings concerning the Manifestations of God in general. The perusal of the *Kitáb-i-Íqán*, for example, will enable the reader to observe the profoundly respectful language with which He refers to God's Chosen Ones on earth and extols their station. All these bear ample testimony to Bahá'u'lláh's noble vision of the Prophets of the past, and how He held them in high esteem and honour. Indeed, He would not tolerate it if anyone in His presence belittled their station or spoke of them in a discourteous manner.

The following story demonstrates this point. It concerns Mírzá Taqí Khán-i-Amír Niẓám, who for many years was Persia's Prime Minister during the reign of Náṣiri'd-Dín Sháh. It was he who ordered the execution of the Báb, and committed great atrocities against the Bábí community.

'Abdu'l-Bahá recounts[12] that one day Mírza Taqí Khán attended a gathering (presumably in Ṭihrán) at which Bahá'u'lláh was present. He was referring to some verses of the *Qur'án* in a disrespectful manner and mockingly questioned the truth of the following verse:

> He knoweth that which is on the dry land and in the sea; there falleth no leaf, but he knoweth it; neither is there a single grain in the dark parts of the earth, neither a green thing, nor a dry thing, but it is written in the perspicuous book [*Qur'án*].[13]

Bahá'u'lláh's immediate response was to disapprove the attitude of Mírzá Taqí Khán and to affirm that the above verse was undoubtedly true. When he asked for further explanation, Bahá'u'lláh told him that it meant that the *Qur'án* was the repository of the Word of God; it contained various subjects such as history, commentaries, prophecies and so on. Within its pages were enshrined verities of great significance and indeed one might discover that everything was mentioned in this Book.

'Am I mentioned in it?' asked Mírzá Taqí Khán arrogantly.

'Yes, you are,' was Bahá'u'lláh's prompt response.

'Am I alluded to or referred to clearly by name?' he asked.

'Clearly by name,' Bahá'u'lláh stated.

'It is strange', Mírzá Taqí Khán retorted with some degree of sarcasm, 'that I have not yet found a reference to myself in the *Qur'án*!'

'The reference to your name', Bahá'u'lláh said, 'is in this verse: "She said, I fly for refuge unto the merciful from thee if thou art Taqí."'*[14]

On hearing such a disparaging reference attributed to him by Bahá'u'lláh, Mírzá Taqí Khán became extremely angry, but did not reveal his anger. Instead he made a further attempt to ridicule the verse of the *Qur'án* in question and discredit Bahá'u'lláh. He asked, 'What about my father, Qurbán, is there a reference to him in the *Qur'an* also?'

'Yes, there is,' Bahá'u'lláh affirmed.

'Is he alluded to or referred to by name?' he asked.

'He is referred to by name in this verse,' responded Bahá'u'-llah, '". . . come unto us with the Qurbán† consumed by fire."'[15]

Another story which demonstrates that Bahá'u'lláh always defended the Prophets of the past is the following recounted by Mírzá Abu'l-Faḍl.‡ It relates to the time when Bahá'u'lláh was a youth in Ṭihrán, before the birth of the Bábí Faith:

> Although He [Bahá'u'lláh] had not entered any of the schools§ in Persia and had not acquired knowledge in any institutions of learning, nevertheless from His early youth signs of greatness and majesty, of good judgement and keen intelligence were strikingly apparent in His countenance. When He was in their gatherings, great men of learning were unable to speak because of His vigorous and awe-inspiring utterances which have always been the early signs

* Naturally, those who rendered the *Qur'án* into English have translated the word 'Táqí', which means 'fearful'.

† Translated as 'sacrifice'.

‡ see p. 91.

§ Bahá'u'lláh received the modest education customary for the people of His class. He did not attend the schools of higher learning which were set aside for theologians and divines. See vol. 1, pp. 18–20.

of the truth of the Manifestations of God.

A leading figure of the Muslim community recounted the following story. 'One day I was present at a meeting in which a number of state dignitaries and high-ranking government personalities were gathered in the presence of the celebrated religious philosopher, Mírzá Naẓar-'Alíy-i-Ḥakím-i-Qazvíní. He was a leader and a spiritual guide to Muḥammad-Sháh of the Qájár dynasty, and one to whom all the sages and devout mystics of the time turned for guidance.

'This famous philosopher, talking in terms of knowledge current at the time, was expounding the subject of man's attainment to the highest level of spiritual perfection. He talked in this vein until the dormant passion of egotism and sensuality was aroused in him, and it then took over the reins of speech. He diverted from his topic and turned his attention to his own accomplishments. Speaking of his own attainments and perfections, he said: "For example, if at this moment my servant arrived and informed me that Jesus Christ was standing outside the door and was asking for permission to attain my presence, I would find myself in no need of Him and would not deign to meet Him."

'A few of those present remained silent and the majority, as is customary among flatterers, agreed with him. Bahá'u'lláh was present at that meeting. Such a disparaging remark about Christ . . . prompted Him to voice his objection. He could not bear to hear the Manifestation of God treated with insolence. His face showing signs of emotion, Bahá'u'lláh asked the learned philosopher whether he would be willing to answer a question. When he agreed, Bahá'u'lláh said, "In spite of the fact that the King is an ardent admirer of yours, suppose that right now the chief executioner arrived here with ten soldiers to arrest you and take you to the King. Would you, in these circumstances, be frightened and disturbed or would you respond to his orders calmly and without fear?" After a little pause the learned man replied, "To be honest, I should be very frightened, would not be able to remain calm and even my tongue would be powerless to move." Bahá'u'lláh said, "A person who is in such a weak position ought not to utter such a claim!" Those present were awestruck at the firmness of His speech and amazed by the strength of His argument.'[16]

The Majesty of Bahá'u'lláh

Some of the disciples of Bahá'u'lláh who attained His presence have referred to the transcendental majesty of His person. This was such a striking feature of Bahá'u'lláh that people who came face to face with Him were awed by His presence and often became speechless. Ḥájí Mírzá Ḥaydar-'Alí in the course of recounting the stories of his own pilgrimage to 'Akká has commented on this in these words:

> Outwardly He was a Prisoner, condemned and wronged, but in reality He was the Sun of Glory, the Manifestation of grandeur and majesty, the King of the Kingdom of poise and dignity. Although he showed much compassion and loving-kindness, and approached anyone who came to His presence with tender care and humbleness, and often used to make humorous remarks to put them at ease, yet in spite of these, no one, whether faithful or disbelieving, learned or unlettered, wise or foolish, was able to utter ten words in His presence in the usual everyday manner. Indeed, many would find themselves to be tremulous with an impediment in their speech.
>
> Some people asked permission to attain His presence for the sole purpose of conducting arguments and engaging in controversies. As a favour on His part, and in order to fulfil the testimony and to declare conclusively the proofs, He gave these permission to enter the court of His majesty and glory. As they entered the room, heard His voice welcoming them in, and gazed at His countenance beaming with the light of grandeur, they could

not help but prostrate themselves at His door. They would then enter and sit down. When He showed them where to sit, they would find themselves unable to utter a word or put forward their questions. When they left they would bow to Him involuntarily. Some would be transformed through the influence of meeting Him and would leave with the utmost sincerity and devotion, some would depart as admirers, while others would leave His presence, ignorant and heedless, attributing their experience to pure sorcery.

When a believer describes what he has experienced in the presence of Bahá'u'lláh, his impressions may be interpreted as being formed through his attitude of self-effacement and a feeling of utter nothingness in relation to Him. But to what can it be attributed when one enters into His presence as an antagonist and leaves as a believer, or comes in as an enemy but goes out as a friend, or comes to raise controversial arguments, but departs without saying anything and, due to wilful blindness, attributing this to magic? To be brief, the bounties which were vouchsafed to a person as a result of attaining His presence were indescribable and unknowable. The proof of the sun is the sun itself.[17]

To cite one example: although in 'Akká Bahá'u'lláh occasionally allowed certain non-Bahá'ís to attain His presence, this was the exception rather than the rule and as the years went by He was less inclined to give audiences to people. There was a time when one of the Governors of the City of 'Akká wanted to attain the presence of Bahá'u'lláh and for years He would not give him permission to do so. Instead, he was to see 'Abdu'l-Bahá. Some years passed, and in spite of repeated requests permission was not granted, until the Central Government in Syria required the Governor to visit Bahá'u'lláh. This being so, he, in the company of a European General, was admitted into His presence. No sooner had they entered the room than they were both struck by His majestic presence. So much were they awed by His person that they knelt at the door. Although Bahá'u'lláh had indicated seats for them, they did not change their position. It was unbearably difficult for the General to sit in that posture, especially as he was a stout man. Since Bahá'u'lláh had nothing to say to them and they remained silent throughout the audience, after about ten minutes they asked permission to leave.

As has already been stated in a previous volume,* Bahá'u'lláh used to associate freely with the public when in Baghdád and to a lesser extent in Adrianople. Now in 'Akká He almost completely dissociated Himself from the people of the city and left it to 'Abdu'l-Bahá to keep in touch with the public. The contrast between His days in Baghdád and those in 'Akká was great indeed. When in Baghdád, Bahá'u'lláh had not yet declared His mission. Officially, He and His companions were regarded by the public as the followers of the Báb. He had freedom and so He moved among the people. At one time in Baghdád, His typical engagements during the day were as follows:

After having breakfast in the inner section† of His house, He went to the outer apartment set aside for the reception of visitors. The friends used to gather in that room where they attained His presence for about a half to one hour. During this time He used to either sit or pace up and down the room. He then proceeded to an oriental inn (coffee house) in the old part of the city, accompanied by at least two believers. The inn was owned by a certain Siyyid Ḥabíb, an Arab, who was not a Bábí, but a great admirer of Bahá'u'lláh and one who showed extraordinary reverence towards Him. Many people, both high and low, attained His presence in this inn. Bahá'u'lláh often used to speak to them about the Faith of the Báb and expound some verities of the Cause of God. After the meeting in the inn, which usually lasted over an hour, He used to return

* see vol. 2, p. 63.

† Houses in the Middle East had inner and outer sections. The outer apartments were always set aside for visitors and guests. The inner apartment was private.

to His house, where in the afternoon the believers were able to attain His presence again. He then went back to the inn and returned home about the time of sunset. Then, some evenings, the believers used to come to His house and attain His presence there. Also at times, some eminent personalities, civil and religious dignitaries, Persian princes, and others, came to His presence to seek guidance and sit at His feet, but Bahá'u'lláh never went to their houses although sometimes He visited the homes of the believers.

In Adrianople Bahá'u'lláh did not appear in public as much as He had done in Baghdád. Occasionally He visited mosques and sometimes received important guests such as the Governor of the city. But as we have already stated, as the years went by in 'Akká, He seldom received anybody outside the circle of the believers. Of course, there were always exceptional cases. For instance, a short time after the slaying of the three Azalís, the Governor, Ṣálih Pashá, who was ill-disposed towards Bahá'u'lláh, was dismissed and replaced by Aḥmad Big Tawfíq, who was much more sagacious than his predecessor. Soon after he was installed as Governor, Badrí Ján, the sister of the murdered Mírzá Riḍá-Qulí, went to see him intent upon discrediting Bahá'u'lláh. In an attempt to completely poison the mind of the Governor, she brought false and slanderous accusations against Bahá'u'lláh, representing Him as One who was aspiring to rule over all men, the kings included. To prove her allegations she left him a copy of the *Súriy-i-Mulúk* (Súrih of the Kings) and some other Tablets.

The reading of this Epistle had the opposite effect on the Governor. According to Bahá'u'lláh's own testimony in a Tablet[18] revealed in the words of His amanuensis, Mírzá Áqá Ján, the Governor himself took the Súrih and other Tablets to 'Abdu'l-Bahá and told Him that as a result of reading those, he had been convinced of the truth of the Cause, and he begged to be allowed to meet Bahá'u'lláh. After some time, 'Abbúd came to Bahá'u'lláh and requested that permission be given for the

Governor to attain His presence, a request to which Bahá'u'lláh gave His consent. It was in the course of that meeting that the heart of the Governor was touched with love for Bahá'u'lláh and was deeply impressed with His spiritual powers. He begged to be allowed to perform a service for Him. Bahá'u'lláh declined the offer of a personal service, and instead suggested the restoration of a disused aqueduct for the benefit of the inhabitants of the city, a suggestion to which the Governor responded positively.*

It was this same Governor who had recognized the distinguishing qualities of 'Abdu'l-Bahá and had become His ardent admirer. He often came to the Master for guidance on difficult matters which he faced in the course of his duties. And it was he who raised no objection to the inflow of pilgrims from Persia, although he knew he was acting contrary to the provisions of the edict of the Sulṭán in this regard.

Although in 'Akká Bahá'u'lláh did not associate with the public generally, the outpourings of His grace and bounty upon the people did not cease. For 'Abdu'l-Bahá, on behalf of His Father, spread His wings of loving-kindness and protection over the inhabitants of 'Akká and its neighbouring lands. To him came for advice and help both high and low. The governors, religious leaders, business men, tourists, the ordinary people of 'Akká and its poor came to either seek His help or to sit at His feet and receive enlightenment from His person. During the lifetime of Bahá'u'lláh, the modest room in which 'Abdu'l-Bahá received people was always open till the early hours of the morning. He attended to the peoples' needs with such genuine love and care that He earned the title 'Father of the Poor' and some referred to Him as the 'Master of 'Akká'. His all-embracing love and powers emanated from Bahá'u'lláh who had conferred upon His Son all the energies latent within His Revelation.

* For further details of this episode see pp. 24–5.

12

First Converts Outside the Muslim Community

It was mainly through 'Abdu'l-Bahá's labours and the influence of His magnetic personality that the animosity of the people of 'Akká towards Bahá'u'lláh and the company of exiles began to change gradually into understanding and, eventually, respect. The door of Bahá'u'lláh's house which had been closed to the faces of friends and foes alike was now opened, and some believers travelled from Persia and were able to attain His presence in the house of 'Údí Khammár.

The Story of Ismu'lláhu'l-Aṣdaq

Notable among the visitors was Mullá Ṣádiq-i-Khurásání.* 'Ṣádiq' meaning 'truthful', Bahá'u'lláh entitled him Ismu'lláhu'l-Aṣdaq (the Name of God, the Most Truthful). As we shall see, he was instrumental in confirming the first Jewish convert to the Faith of Bahá'u'lláh.

It was Bahá'u'lláh who, unasked, had sent a Tablet to Ismu'lláhu'l-Aṣdaq in Khurásán and invited him to travel to 'Akká for the purpose of attaining His presence. He was one of the most outstanding and devoted believers in this Dispensation. He was a man of learning. Prior to his conversion to the Faith of the Báb he had been a Muslim divine esteemed for his uprightness and dignity, and renowned throughout the province of Khurásán for his piety and truthfulness. A Shaykhí, he had had the unique privilege of

* see also vol. 1, pp. 92–3; vol. 2, pp. 110, 293n, 388.

meeting the Báb several times in the city of Karbilá prior to His declaration. He had been deeply impressed by the radiance and gentleness mingled with majesty which the youthful Báb evinced as He prayed most tearfully at the Shrine of Imám Ḥusayn. Ismu'lláhu'l-Aṣdaq is reported to have exclaimed when his eyes first fell on Him, 'Glorified be our Lord, the Most High!' He had become a devoted admirer of that Youth while in Karbilá, in spite of the fact that the Ismu'lláh was a learned divine, one who was held in high esteem by the people, while the Báb was a youth with little education. He had also witnessed the extraordinary reverence shown to that Youth by Siyyid Káẓim-i-Rashtí,* the celebrated leader of the Shaykhí community, who knew that He was none other than the Qá'im Himself, the Promised One of Islám.

Soon after the Declaration of the Báb in 1844, when Mullá Ḥusayn was on his way to Ṭihrán, he met Ismu'lláhu'l-Aṣdaq in the city of Iṣfáhán, informed him of the advent of the Báb and gave him some of His Writings to read. Upon reading a few pages he became an ardent believer. But Mullá Ḥusayn, as bidden by the Báb, was not allowed to reveal the identity of the Báb as yet.

In his narratives, Nabíl-i-A'ẓam records the circumstances in which the Ismu'lláh became an ardent believer:

> Mullá Ṣádiq-Khurásání, formerly known as Muqaddas, and surnamed by Bahá'u'lláh, Ismu'lláhu'l-Aṣdaq, who according to the instructions of Siyyid Káẓim, had during the last five years been residing in Iṣfáhán and had been preparing the way for the advent of the new Revelation, was also among the first believers who identified themselves with the Message proclaimed by the Báb. As soon as he learned of the arrival of Mullá Ḥusayn in Iṣfáhán, he hastened to meet him. He gives the following account of his first interview, which took place at night in the home of Mírzá Muḥammad-'Alíy-i-Nahrí: 'I asked Mullá Ḥusayn to divulge the name of Him who claimed to be the promised

* see Nabíl-i-A'ẓam, *The Dawn-Breakers*, for further information.

Manifestation. He replied, "To enquire about that name and to divulge it are alike forbidden." "Would it, then, be possible," I asked, "for me, even as the Letters of the Living, to seek independently the grace of the All-Merciful and, through prayer, to discover His identity?" "The door of His grace," he replied, "is never closed before the face of him who seeks to find Him." I immediately retired from his presence, and requested his host to allow me the privacy of a room in his house where, alone and undisturbed, I could commune with God. In the midst of my contemplation, I suddenly remembered the face of a Youth whom I had often observed while in Karbilá, standing in an attitude of prayer, with His face bathed in tears at the entrance of the shrine of Imám Ḥusayn. That same countenance now reappeared before my eyes. In my vision I seemed to behold that same face, those same features, expressive of such joy as I could never describe. He smiled as He gazed at me. I went towards Him, ready to throw myself at His feet. I was bending towards the ground, when, lo! that radiant figure vanished from before me. Overpowered with joy and gladness, I ran out to meet Mullá Ḥusayn, who with transport received me and assured me that I had, at last, attained the object of my desire. He bade me, however, repress my feelings. "Declare not your vision to anyone," he urged me; "the time for it has not yet arrived. You have reaped the fruit of your patient waiting in Iṣfáhán. You should now proceed to Kirmán, and there acquaint Ḥájí Mírzá Karím Khán* with this Message. From that place you should travel to Shíráz and endeavour to rouse the people of that city from their heedlessness. I hope to join you in Shíráz and share with you the blessings of a joyous reunion with our Beloved." '[1]

Soon after he embraced the Faith of the Báb, persecutions and sufferings descended upon the Ismu'lláh and he bore them with exemplary patience and joy. He was one of the three believers who were severely tortured for the first time in the history of the Faith in Persia. The other two were Quddús†

* see vol. 1, Appendix IV.

† The last but the greatest of the company of the Báb's disciples. See *The Dawn-Breakers*.

and Mullá 'Alí-Akbar-i-Ardistání. The scene of these harrowing persecutions was the city of Shíráz. Nabíl recounts the following story concerning Ismu'lláhu'l-Aṣdaq, whom he refers to as Mullá Ṣádíq:

> An eye-witness of this revolting episode, an unbeliever residing in Shíráz, related to me the following: 'I was present when Mullá Ṣádíq was being scourged. I watched his persecutors each in turn apply the lash to his bleeding shoulders, and continue the strokes until he became exhausted. No one believed that Mullá Ṣádíq, so advanced in age and so frail in body, could possibly survive fifty such savage strokes. We marvelled at his fortitude when we found that, although the number of the strokes of the scourge he had received had already exceeded nine hundred, his face still retained its original serenity and calm. A smile was upon his face, as he held his hand before his mouth. He seemed utterly indifferent to the blows that were being showered upon him. When he was being expelled from the city, I succeeded in approaching him, and asked him why he held his hand before his mouth. I expressed surprise at the smile upon his countenance. He emphatically replied: "The first seven strokes were severely painful; to the rest I seemed to have grown indifferent. I was wondering whether the strokes that followed were being actually applied to my own body. A feeling of joyous exultation had invaded my soul. I was trying to repress my feelings and to restrain my laughter. I can now realise how the almighty Deliverer is able, in the twinkling of an eye, to turn pain into ease, and sorrow into gladness. Immensely exalted is His power above and beyond the idle fancy of His mortal creatures." ' Mullá Ṣádíq, whom I met years after, confirmed every detail of this moving episode.[2]

This episode may be considered only as a prelude to many more agonizing persecutions that this man of God went through till the end of his life. Many times in the course of his travels throughout the length and breadth of Persia where he was engaged in teaching the Faith, he was surrounded by the enemies who inflicted all kinds of tortures and afflictions upon him and were intent on taking his life. He was one of the companions of Quddús and Mullá Ḥusayn in the Fortress of Shaykh Ṭabarsí.* After going through harrowing experiences of pain and suffering in that fortress, his life was providentially spared so as to manifest, at a later time, yet greater heroism and self-sacrifice in the path of the One who was the object of the adoration of the Báb and His disciples.

Ismu'lláhu'l-Aṣdaq recognized the station of Bahá'u'lláh as readily as he had the Báb's. He attained the presence of Bahá'u'lláh in Baghdád and became fully convinced of His exalted station as 'Him Whom God shall make manifest' long before Bahá'u'lláh made His Declaration in the Garden of Riḍván. For about fourteen months he basked in the sunshine of Bahá'u'lláh's loving-kindness in that city, and then, as bidden by Him, returned to Persia, ablaze with the love of his new-found Master. He stood out as a tower of strength among the believers and became an instrument for guiding countless souls into the Cause of God. Among them were many people who became renowned in the Faith, such as Aḥmad-i-Yazdí, the recipient of the celebrated *Tablet of Aḥmad*, and Ḥájí Mírzá Ḥasan-Álí, the youngest uncle of the Báb.

The journey to 'Akká, the scene of his second pilgrimage, was undertaken at an advanced age. The sufferings and hardships of well-nigh thirty years had taken their toll and left him frail, laden with infirmities and weakness. When Bahá'u'lláh summoned him to 'Akká, He instructed him to leave his son† at home and travel in the company of a believer who could take care of him throughout the journey. He arrived in 'Akká probably in the early part of 1874, because Shaykh Káẓim-i-Samandar‡ states that when he, together with two of his companions, Ḥájí Naṣír-i-Qazvíní§ and Manṣúr-i-

* see *The Dawn-Breakers*.

† He was 'Alí-Muḥammad, known as Ibn-i-Aṣdaq, later appointed by Bahá'u'lláh as a Hand of the Cause of God.

‡ see pp. 88–91.

§ see vol. 2, pp. 245–7.

Uskú'í, arrived in 'Akká, Ismu'lláhu'l-Ạsdaq was present there. Shaykh Káẓim arrived in 'Akká on 1 March 1874. This pilgrimage to the presence of his Lord was the crowning glory of the life of Ismu'lláhu'l-Aṣdaq. After staying several months in 'Akká, during which he was ushered into the presence of Bahá'u'lláh many times, he was bidden, in a Tablet revealed for him in 'Akká, to return home.

In this Tablet[3] Bahá'u'lláh showers His blessings upon him and affirms that in both this visit and his previous one to Baghdád, he had drunk deep of the waters of everlasting life from the hands of his Lord. He then commands him to convey His counsels to the friends so that they may be enabled to adorn themselves with the ornament of goodly character and live a saintly life. He states that the most meritorious of all deeds in this day is to remain steadfast in the Cause of God in such wise that the vain imaginings of the people may be powerless to influence them.

Lawḥ-i-Aḥbáb (Tablet of the Friends)

Bahá'u'lláh has revealed many Tablets in honour of Ismu'lláhu'l-Aṣdaq. Among them is the *Lawḥ-i-Aḥbáb*. This is one of Bahá'u'lláh's well-known Tablets revealed in Arabic and contains many passages of loving encouragement addressed to various individuals. This Tablet appears to have been revealed when Bahá'u'lláh was still in the barracks of 'Akká or soon after He had left it. For in it He mentions that He had written Tablets to some of the kings and also pays glowing tribute to Badí'. It is one of those Writings referred to as the 'Salt of His Tablets'.

In the *Lawḥ-i-Aḥbáb*, Bahá'u'lláh showers praises upon Ismu'lláhu'l-Aṣdaq in such profusion that it is not possible to describe them all. He refers to him as the one who recognized the Promised One as soon as he heard His call—a reference to his meeting Mullá Ḥusayn and reading some passages from the Writings of the Báb. It is clear from the utterances of

Bahá'u'lláh in this and other Tablets that Bahá'u'lláh regarded him as one of His most devoted followers and a true believer in every sense of the word, one who would be worthy of emulation by all.

Most of the *Lawḥ-i-Aḥbáb* contains passages addressed to the friends. Bahá'u'lláh's counsels in this Tablet are many and cannot be summarized. They are revealed in such terms that no pen can describe them. The power and beauty of the words of the Manifestation of God can be felt only in their own utterances, and not through man's explanation of them. Nevertheless, here is an attempt, however inadequate, to refer to a few of His teachings in this Tablet.

Bahá'u'lláh exhorts the believers to steadfastness in His Cause and to detachment from everything beside God, and to unity among themselves. He reminds them that He has accepted sufferings and tribulations so that mankind might become united. He warns them never, therefore, to allow differences to enter their midst. He gives them a commandment: first to live their lives in accordance with His teachings and then to conquer the hearts of men in His Name by holy deeds and exalted character. He enjoins on them to teach the Cause with wisdom, counsels them to arise for the triumph of His Faith in such wise that no earthly power can deter them from executing their purpose, assures them that the glances of His loving-kindness are directed towards them, and prophesies the advent of a day when the banners of victory will be planted in every city, when the peoples of the world will glory in the believers' names and lament over all the sufferings they have borne in the path of their Lord.

The following words of 'Abdu'l-Bahá paying tribute to this noble and outstanding believer, Ismu'lláhu'l-Aṣdaq, upon whom He conferred posthumously the rank of Hand of the Cause of God, stand out as a eulogy to his cherished memory:

> He was like a surging sea, a falcon that soared high. His visage shone, his tongue was eloquent, his strength and

steadfastness astounding. When he opened his lips to teach, the proofs would stream out; when he chanted or prayed, his eyes shed tears like a spring cloud. His face was luminous, his life spiritual, his knowledge both acquired and innate; and celestial was his ardour, his detachment from the world, his righteousness, his piety and fear of God.[4]

No story of Ismu'lláhu'l-Aṣdaq would be complete without referring to his imprisonment in the Síyáh-Chál of Ṭihrán where he succeeded in confirming the faith of the first believer of Jewish background. Soon after this historic conversion, a great many of the Jewish people in Persia recognized Bahá'u'lláh as the promised Lord and became ardent and active believers. To appreciate the story, it is essential to understand the circumstances prevailing at the time in Persia concerning the religious minorities and their attitude to the new-born Faith.

Religious Minorities in Persia

At the time of the coming of the Báb, there were three religious minorities in Persia—the Zoroastrians, the Jews and the Christians. The great majority of the nation consisted of Shí'ah Muslims. Of the three minorities, the Jews and, to a lesser extent, the Zoroastrians were treated with contempt and at times were persecuted by the fanatic mob, often at the instigation of the Muslim clergy. The Christians, mostly of Armenian and Assyrian background, enjoyed greater freedom and respect. This was mainly due to their religious ties with European governments which exercised great influence in Persia at the time.

The Zoroastrians, and more especially the Jews, were the underprivileged people. They lived in ghettos and always went in fear of persecution. In their relationship to Muslims, they had to observe certain rules, such as showing respect to a Muslim in the street, and never having an argument with him.

If accompanying him, never to walk alongside him but to be one or two steps behind. Not to touch his garments as otherwise they would become defiled. The money which a Jew or a Zoroastrian handed to a devout Muslim would have to be washed before he could put it in his pocket.

Ḥájí Muḥammad-Ṭáhir-i-Málmírí has recorded some of the incidents that used to occur daily in a certain area of Yazd and which often sparked off disturbances involving the large Zoroastrian community there. The following is a summary of his notes:

> The Muslim clergy wielded great power and the government was weak. Every day, they would find a pretext and invent a story against the Zoroastrians. For instance, they would inform the public that a cerain Zoroastrian was seen to be riding his donkey in the presence of Muslims.* It was understood that such an act was an offence, because it was not considered courteous to ride if a Muslim was walking. This accusation would result in the corporal punishment of the victim. Or, they would claim that the colour of the head-dress of a certain Zoroastrian merchant was dark and somewhat resembled the colour of the head-dress of the Siyyids.† The colour ought to have been bright yellow. The mass hysteria created as a result of such an incident was so powerful that almost instantly it could bring about an upheaval in the city.
>
> On another day, they would accuse a certain Zoroastrian that he had passed a Muslim in the street but failed to salute him. Or that a certain Muslim had reason to beat up a Zoroastrian, but in the course of being beaten up, the poor Zoroastrian had mustered such audacity as to raise his hand as if intending to defend himself. Such a person would then be punished by the authorities. It was an established ruling

* A great part of the Zoroastrian community in Persia lived in Yazd and surrounding villages. Those in the villages often had to ride on donkeys to come to the city, but once in the bazaars they had to dismount as a sign of respect to the Muslims.

† The descendants of the Prophet Muḥammad. Theirs was the exclusive right to wear green turbans.

that every Zoroastrian who came out of his house had to carry a piece of cloth with him. This was needed if he had to sit somewhere, for he would not be allowed to sit* unless he spread the cloth and sat on it, as otherwise he would have defiled the earth.[5]

Being ill-treated during centuries of Islámic rule, the Jews and Zoroastrians immensely disliked the Muslims and had developed some defensive tactics. The most effective one was to keep their distance from Islámic peoples and institutions. They despised the culture, the Arabic language and anything to do with Islám.

The Báb and Bahá'u'lláh appeared within such a society. Both were from Islámic background. The Báb was a descendant of the Prophet Muḥammad. Like Jesus Christ, who was from Jewish background and practised that Faith, the Báb and Bahá'u'lláh before the birth of the New Faith were practising Muslims. And when they revealed themselves as the Manifestations of God, their words and teachings, especially those of the Báb, had such strong links with the religion of Islám that in the early days the new Faith appeared to the minority religions in Persia to be a sect of Islám. For this reason it was very natural for Jews and Zoroastrians to avoid the Bábís and Bahá'ís at all costs. Another disadvantage was that a great part of the Writings of the Báb and Bahá'u'lláh were revealed in Arabic which was not only incomprehensible to them, but despised and hated because it was the language of Islám.

It will be readily seen that the conversion of Jews and Zoroastrians to the Faith of Bahá'u'lláh which to all outward appearances was the extension of Islám, whose literature was in the Arabic language and whose followers were exclusively from Muslim background, was one of the miracles of the time. It also demonstrates the creative power of the Revelation of

* In those days people did not use chairs in shops, business premises and homes, and it was common to sit on the floor.

Bahá'u'lláh which, in spite of so many barriers, exerted a tremendous influence upon these people, vivified their souls, granted them a new vision, enrolled them under the banner of His Cause and enabled them to render meritorious services in spreading His message, first among their own communities and later the whole nation.

There can be no greater proof of the universality of the message of Bahá'u'lláh and the authenticity of His claim to be the Promised One of all ages, than the Jews and Zoroastrians of Persia embracing His Faith in the nineteenth century. Their conversion was not superficial, nor was it an expedient measure to free themselves from the yoke of suppression and tyranny. Rather, when these people joined the ranks of the Bahá'ís, their sufferings were multiplied. Not only would they become fresh targets for attack by the Muslims who abhorred their conversion to the Faith of Bahá'u'lláh, but also their own communities often persecuted them, and in some instances they were martyred by their own people. For instance, in Yazd the Zoroastrian priests rose up against a number of people in that community who had become Bahá'ís. The fierce persecutions which started within the Zoroastrian enclave by the Zoroastrian people and often in alliance with the Muslim clergy and fanatics against the newly converted followers of Bahá'u'lláh are reminiscent of the cruelties perpetrated by the Muslims, the chief adversaries of the Faith in Persia. Thus, in the villages surrounding Yazd, a couple of Bahá'ís of Zoroastrian background were martyred. In the city an outstanding personality within the community was done to death because of his genuine interest and sympathy towards the newly emerging Faith.

The fate of the Jews who had embraced the Cause of Bahá'u'lláh was no brighter. They too were subjected to harassment and persecution from within their ghettos as well as from outside. The conversion of Jews and Zoroastrians to the Cause of Bahá'u'lláh was a genuine act of faith. They fully recognized Him as the Promised One of their own Holy

Books, One who is described by Shoghi Effendi in these words:

> He Who in such dramatic circumstances was made to sustain the overpowering weight of so glorious a Mission was none other than the One Whom posterity will acclaim, and Whom innumerable followers already recognize, as the Judge, the Lawgiver and Redeemer of all mankind, as the Organizer of the entire planet, as the Unifier of the children of men, as the Inaugurator of the long-awaited millennium, as the Originator of a new 'Universal Cycle', as the Establisher of the Most Great Peace, as the Fountain of the Most Great Justice, as the Proclaimer of the coming of age of the entire human race, as the Creator of a new World Order, and as the Inspirer and Founder of a world civilization.
>
> To Israel He was neither more nor less than the incarnation of the 'Everlasting Father,' the 'Lord of Hosts' come down 'with ten thousands of saints'; to Christendom Christ returned 'in the glory of the Father,' to Shí'ah Islám the return of the Imám Ḥusayn; to Sunní Islám the descent of the 'Spirit of God' (Jesus Christ); to the Zoroastrians the promised Sháh-Bahrám; to the Hindus the reincarnation of Krishna; to the Buddhists the fifth Buddha.[6]

The entry into the Faith by members of these two religious minorities in Persia during its early days demonstrated to the people of that country that the Cause of Bahá'u'lláh was an independent religion. It silenced and discomfited the enemies who, in order to undermine the new Faith, had dismissed it as the outcome of an irresponsible adventure by its Founders who were of Muslim extraction, and had falsely introduced it to the public as a sect of Islám.

It also demonstrated the power of Bahá'u'lláh's creative Word in that once they accepted Bahá'u'lláh, the followers of these two religions also acknowledged the authenticity and the divine origin of the Messages of all the Prophets, the Founders of the world's major religions, including Christ and

Muḥammad. A great many Muslims in the early days of the Faith were amazed to hear words of praise and glorification of the Prophet Muḥammad and proofs of the truth of His Mission coming from the Bahá'ís who had once belonged to the Jewish or Zoroastrian communities. This angered the fanatic Muslims very much. For they knew that for over one thousand years very few, if any, Muslims had succeeded in making the Jews or Zoroastrians acknowledge the truth of Islám, and now, through the words of Bahá'u'lláh, thousands had been converted. But there were others among the Muslims who were pure-hearted and were deeply moved when they heard these people had accepted the truth of Islám; consequently some were led to investigate the Faith of Bahá'u'lláh and eventually become Bahá'ís.

The Bahá'í community in Persia consisted from the early days of believers who had come from the three major religious backgrounds. The majority were from the Islámic and the rest from the Jewish and Zoroastrian Faiths. But the Faith did not make much headway among the Christians in Persia. The majority of the Christians who entered the Faith came from countries of the Western world. This process started during the early years of 'Abdu'l-Bahá's ministry.

The Story of Ḥakím Masíḥ, the First Jewish Believer

The first of the Jewish community to recognize the truth of the Mission of Bahá'u'lláh in Persia was a notable physician named Masíḥ (Messiah) referred to as Ḥakím Masíḥ.* Being highly skilled in his profession, he was appointed as a physician to the court of Muḥammad Sháh, and when the Sháh made a journey to 'Iráq, Ḥakím Masíḥ accompanied him. When in Baghdád, he learnt that Ṭáhirih was staying in the home of one of the early believers, and was holding discussions with the divines in the city. He went there to see what was being said. No sooner

* The title of Ḥakím was given to people who were skilled physicians and were endowed with wisdom and divine knowledge.

had he heard the utterances of Ṭáhirih addressed to the company of divines, and witnessed their helplessness to refute her proofs in support of her newly found Faith, than he was captivated by her powerful arguments and sheer personality. Although he was not allowed to enter into any discussions, Ḥakím Masíḥ was very curious to find out how Ṭáhirih had acquired such eloquence and powers which bordered on the supernatural.

Shaykh Káẓim-i-Samandar* has recorded the following in his memoirs:

> I met Ḥakím Masíḥ who was of Jewish descent. He was the first among the Jews to enter the community of the friends (i.e. Bahá'ís). It surprised me when I discovered that he was friendly, faithful, full of enthusiasm and love; and so said to him, 'There is a large gap between the Faith of Moses and this great Cause, how did you make this long and glorious journey and arrive at this abode?' He said, 'My visit to Baghdád coincided with the time that Ṭáhirih was in that city. Through some circumstances I was present at some of the meetings where she conversed with the divines. I was astonished and awestruck by the way she talked, by the manner in which she conducted her conversations, and by the power of her utterances. I became attracted and began to meditate and decided to investigate this Cause and deepen my knowledge of it. I made some enquiries in Baghdád and later in other places, until I attained my heart's desire.[7]

Some years after meeting Ṭáhirih in Baghdád, Ḥakím Masíḥ met Ismu'lláhu'l-Aṣdaq, a meeting brought about by Providence. The Ismu'lláh had been arrested because of his allegiance to the Faith, put in chains and brought to Ṭihrán under escort. This cruel act was carried out by order of the Governor of Khurásán who was enforcing an edict issued by no less than eighteen divines of Islám in that province. The Ismu'lláh was forced to take with him his youngest son, Ibn-i-Aṣdaq, who was a mere child at the time. Two other believers

* see pp. 88, 257.

were also chained and taken to Ṭihrán with him.

The intention was to execute them in the capital city. Instead, the Government ordered that they be imprisoned in the Síyah-Chál. Father and child were chained together and kept in that terrible dungeon for about two years and four months.

The hardships of prison life took their toll and the young child became seriously ill. The chief gaoler, a certain Mashhadí 'Alí, was a kind person and he sent for a physician. But no physician could be found who would be willing to treat a patient who was a Bábí. In desperation he called on Ḥakím Masíḥ who was Jewish. He accepted and immediately went to the prison.

For a period of two months he regularly attended the child until he recovered from his illness. At the same time, having been so deeply impressed by Ṭáhirih, this gave him the opportunity to learn about the Faith from an illustrious believer. Even after his patient had fully recovered he used to spend hours in the prison, sitting at the Ismu'lláh's feet and learning about the Faith. Soon after, he became a believer fully aware that the Promised One of the Old Testament, the 'Everlasting Father', the Lord of Hosts, had manifested Himself. When Bahá'u'lláh was informed of His conversion, He revealed an exalted Tablet in his honour. He has revealed other Tablets for him too, but unfortunately most of these were destroyed. This is because in those days the believers used to protect their Bahá'í materials by hiding them underground or inside the walls, so that they might not fall into the hands of the enemy. Sadly, when unearthed, the Tablets of Ḥakím Masíḥ were found to have been destroyed by moisture.

In one of these Tablets,[8] Bahá'u'lláh urges Ḥakím Masíḥ to be steadfast in the Cause of God so that he may not be shaken by the winds of opposition which were blowing from the direction of the enemies. He states that the people were following the dictates of their passions and corrupt desires, and directs him to counsel such people to abandon their evil ways and turn to their God. Bahá'u'lláh, in this Tablet, showers His favours upon Ḥakím Masíḥ and affirms that He has bestowed upon him a great station. Ḥakím Masíḥ taught the Faith to his family who became ardent believers. Notable among his descendants was Dr Luṭfu'lláh Ḥakím, his youngest grandson, who served the Master and Shoghi Effendi with exemplary devotion and was elected to the Universal House of Justice in 1963 when that Supreme Body of the Faith came into being for the first time.

The light of the new Faith of God which shone forth in the heart of Ḥakím Masíḥ illumined many more among his co-religionists in Persia. At first, a few embraced the Cause of Bahá'u'lláh in Hamadán and Ká<u>sh</u>án and soon great numbers from the Jewish community joined the Faith and swelled the ranks of the believers in Persia. There are many Tablets revealed by Bahá'u'lláh in honour of the believers of Jewish background.

Zoroastrians Enter the Faith

The introduction and growth of the Cause among the followers of Zoroaster was no less spectacular and far-reaching. The following story is related by 'Abdu'l-Bahá:

> . . . they relate that the possessions of a certain Babi in Kashan were plundered, and his household scattered and dispersed. They stripped him naked and scourged him, defiled his beard, mounted him face backwards on an ass, and paraded him through the streets and bazaars with the utmost cruelty, to the sound of drums, trumpets, guitars and tambourines. A certain guebre* who knew absolutely naught of the world or its denizens chanced to be seated apart in a corner of a caravansaray. When the clamour of the people rose high he hastened into the street, and, becoming

* Zoroastrian. (A.T.)

ḤAKÍM MASÍḤ

The first believer converted to the Faith from the Jewish community of Persia

KAY-<u>KH</u>USRAW-I-<u>KH</u>UDÁDÁD

Believed to be the first to embrace the Faith of Bahá'u'lláh from the Zoroastrian community

cognizant of the offence and the offender, and the cause of his public disgrace and punishment in full detail, he fell to making search, and that very day entered the society of the Bábís, saying, 'This very ill-usage and public humiliation is a proof of truth and the very best of arguments. Had it not been thus it might have been that a thousand years would have passed ere one like me became informed.'[9]

Ḥájí Mu'ínu's-Salṭanih, a historian from Tabríz, has stated that the believer who was persecuted in the above account was a certain Ḥájí Muḥammad-Riḍá, a merchant of Káshán, and that the Zoroastrian who acknowledged the truth of the Faith of the Báb was Suhráb-i-Púr-Kávús. Unfortunately, there is not much information available about him.

The first to believe among the Zoroastrians during the ministry of Bahá'u'lláh is reputed to be Kay-Khusraw-i-Khudádád and the story of his becoming aware of the truth of the Faith is similar to that of Suhráb-i-Púr-Kávús. Kay-Khusraw, a native of Yazd, was also living in Káshán as a merchant. He saw one of the believers tortured and put to death. This harrowing scene evoked in him an urge to investigate the Cause and as a result he became a follower. Some early believers among the Zoroastrians who came in contact with him in Káshán owe their allegiance to the Cause through his teaching work.

Kay-Khusraw-i-Khudádád was well-known in the Zoroastrian community. He was a member of a special 'Council of Zoroastrians' set up by Mánikchí Ṣáḥib. The latter went from India to Persia with a view to helping his co-religionists in that country and obtaining more freedom for them He met Náṣiri'd-Dín Sháh and succeeded in securing a royal decree absolving the Zoroastrians from payment of a certain religious tax which for years had been imposed upon religious minorities in Persia. He also invited a number of prominent Zoroastrians to serve on the above Council which was recognized by the Sháh.

Lawḥ-i-Mánikchí Ṣáḥib

Mánikchí passed through Baghdád on his way to Persia when Bahá'u'lláh was in that city. He attained His presence there and became His admirer. In later years he maintained friendly contact with Bahá'u'lláh through correspondence. He was assisted in this by Mírzá Abu'l-Faḍl, who after embracing the Faith worked as a secretary for Mánikchí for some years. In answer to a letter, Bahá'u'lláh revealed a Tablet for him known as the *Lawḥ-i-Mánikchí Ṣáḥib*.[10] This is mainly revealed in pure Persian,* for the latter was keen to promote the Persian language in its original form. Although Mánikchí did not become a Bahá'í, he remained a sympathetic friend.

From the literary point of view, the Tablet of Bahá'u'lláh to Mánikchí Ṣáḥib is a masterpiece of the pure Persian language. In its lucidity and eloquence, its richness and beauty, it is no less outstanding than other celebrated Tablets revealed either in Arabic or Persian. This Tablet contains some of the choicest utterances of Bahá'u'lláh. The celebrated passage, 'Ye are the fruits of one tree and the leaves of one branch', was revealed in this Tablet.† Bahá'u'lláh here invites the peoples of the world to enter the portals to freedom which have been opened wide through His Revelation, and to drink deep from the springs of knowledge which have welled forth from His utterances. He uses the analogy of an eyelid, a small shutter, which can obstruct the vision, to illustrate that the veil of covetousness can likewise obscure the light of the soul. He likens harsh

* When Islám became the main religion of Persia, Arabic words were introduced into the Persian language. The present Persian language incorporates many Arabic words, which have become part of the Persian vocabulary. As against this, there is the 'pure Persian' which is not commonly spoken, but is occasionally written. Some scholars have excelled themselves in this field: Mírzá Abu'l-Faḍl was one. But pure Persian is not in general use. In most of Bahá'u'lláh's Writings in Persian, Arabic and Persian words are used together. Only a small number of Bahá'u'lláh's Writings, those addressed to Zoroastrian believers, are mainly revealed in pure Persian.

† This famous passage is to be found also in the *Ishráqát*.

words to a deadly sword, and a kindly tongue to refreshing food, states that God, the Creator, approves of any process through which the individual may be enabled to shed some of his ignorance and increase his knowledge and understanding, affirms that man will experience peace and tranquillity when he becomes the well-wisher of all that dwell on earth and exhorts the peoples to leave the darkness of enmity and enter the light of unity.

The following is a small portion of the Tablet to Mánikchí which has been translated into English by Shoghi Effendi:

> The All-Knowing Physician hath His finger on the pulse of mankind. He perceiveth the disease, and prescribeth, in His unerring wisdom, the remedy. Every age hath its own problem, and every soul its particular aspiration. The remedy the world needeth in its present-day afflictions can never be the same as that which a subsequent age may require. Be anxiously concerned with the needs of the age ye live in, and centre your deliberations in its exigencies and requirements.
>
> We can well perceive how the whole human race is encompassed with great, with incalculable afflictions. We see it languishing on its bed of sickness, sore-tried and disillusioned. They that are intoxicated by self-conceit have interposed themselves between it and the Divine and infallible Physician. Witness how they have entangled all men, themselves included, in the mesh of their devices. They can neither discover the cause of the disease, nor have they any knowledge of the remedy. They have conceived the straight to be crooked, and have imagined their friend an enemy.
>
> Incline your ears to the sweet melody of this Prisoner. Arise, and lift up your voices, that haply they that are fast asleep may be awakened. Say: O ye who are as dead! The Hand of Divine bounty proffereth unto you the Water of Life. Hasten and drink your fill. Whoso hath been re-born in this Day, shall never die; whoso remaineth dead, shall never live.[11]

Lawḥ-i-Haft Pursi<u>sh</u> (Tablet of Seven Questions)

The Council of Zoroastrians which was set up by Mánik<u>ch</u>í Ṣáḥib consisted of the most prominent Zoroastrians of Yazd. At one time there were nineteen councillors, six of whom became Bahá'ís. As we have already mentioned, Kay-<u>Kh</u>usraw-i-<u>Kh</u>udádád, the first believer, was among them. Others who joined the Faith were men of learning or people held in high esteem by the community. Notable among them was the renowned Ustád Javán-Mard, the Secretary of the Council. He was a teacher by profession and became a devoted believer. He wrote a letter to Bahá'u'lláh and asked some questions. The *Lawḥ-i-Haft Pursi<u>sh</u>*, in pure Persian, was revealed in his honour. Bahá'u'lláh in this Tablet calls him by a new name, <u>Sh</u>ír-Mard (Lion of a man). The following is a short extract from the *Lawḥ-i-Haft Pursi<u>sh</u>*, translated by Shoghi Effendi:

> O high priests! Ears have been given you that they may hearken unto the mystery of Him Who is the Self-Dependent, and eyes that they may behold Him. Wherefore flee ye? The Incomparable Friend is manifest. He speaketh that wherein lieth salvation. Were ye, O high priests, to discover the perfume of the rose-garden of understanding, ye would seek none other but Him, and would recognize, in His new vesture, the All-Wise and Peerless One, and would turn your eyes from the world and all who seek it, and would arise to help Him . . . Whatsoever hath been announced in the Books hath been revealed and made clear. From every direction the signs have been manifested. The Omnipotent One is calling, in this Day, and announcing the appearance of the Supreme Heaven.[12]

<u>Sh</u>ír-Mard was the first Zoroastrian Bahá'í to be buried instead of having his body disposed of in the Da<u>kh</u>mih* as was

* An open tower, usually built outside the city in which the dead bodies of Zoroastrians are placed and exposed to nature. After the flesh has been devoured by vultures, the bones are thrown into a deep well.

the custom among his people. Other Bahá'ís from the Zoroastrian background followed his example and built a special Bahá'í Cemetery. This action provoked fierce opposition from the community. The Bahá'í Cemetery was attacked and some of the graves were desecrated.

This opposition was not over the issue of burials only. The mere act of conversion to a new Faith, something which had never happened to Zoroastrians since the early days of Islám, provoked the wrath of the high priests against the newly converted Bahá'ís who openly proclaimed to the community that the Sháh-Bahrám, the Promised One of the Zoroastrians, had been manifested in the person of Bahá'u'lláh. Soon persecutions began, sometimes with the tacit approval of the Muslim clergy. A certain Master Khudábakhsh, a distinguished member of the Council of Zoroastrians and a school teacher of wide repute, although not officially a Bahá'í, was shot dead because of his sympathy and generous support for the Bahá'ís. Others were persecuted in different ways. But soon the number of converts to the Faith of Bahá'u'lláh grew, and to the astonishment of both Muslims and Zoroastrians, a great many families acknowledged the station of Bahá'u'lláh and swelled the ranks of the believers especially in Yazd and its surrounding villages.

The conversion of Muslims, Jews and Zoroastrians to the Faith of Bahá'u'lláh in Persia in the early days of the ministries of the Báb and Bahá'u'lláh was followed by the conversion of adherents of other Faiths in other parts of the world. Within a short period of time, the followers of all religions, creeds and ideologies as well as pagans, agnostics and atheists, representing peoples of all colours, races and tribes, embraced the Faith, and began to build unitedly the foundations of the Bahá'í world community. So dynamic has been the process of entry into the Faith by the peoples of the world that within less than a hundred years since Bahá'u'lláh's Declaration in the Garden of Riḍván, an army of pioneers and travelling teachers from every conceivable background has arisen to circle the globe for the spreading of the Cause of Bahá'u'lláh and the diffusion of the light of His Faith to the world's multitudes. This process which began in the early days of the Faith is now gathering momentum and will continue to forge ahead until the goals of the unification of the entire human race and universal allegiance to the Cause of Bahá'u'lláh are totally fulfilled.

THE HOUSE OF 'ÚDÍ KHAMMÁR IN 'AKKÁ

The room where the *Kitáb-i-Aqdas* was revealed is at the upper left

THE ROOM WHERE THE *KITÁB-I-AQDAS* WAS REVEALED

The room of Bahá'u'lláh in the house of 'Údí Khammár. The furnishings were added later

13

Kitáb-i-Aqdas. 1. The Law of God

In the early part of 1873, almost five years after His arrival in 'Akká, Bahá'u'lláh, then confined in the house of 'Údí Khammár, revealed the *Kitáb-i-Aqdas*, the Most Holy Book, regarded as the Mother Book of this Dispensation, a Book unique and incomparable among the world's sacred scriptures, designated by Himself as the 'Source of true felicity', the 'unerring Balance', the 'Straight path', the 'quickener of mankind', the 'river of mercy', the 'Ark of His laws'. To it the Prophets of the past have alluded as the 'new heaven', the 'new earth', the 'Tabernacle of God', the 'Holy City', the 'Bride' and the 'New Jerusalem coming down from God'. Shoghi Effendi has acclaimed it as the charter of Bahá'u'lláh's new world order and of future world civilization.

This book, written in Arabic, the brightest emanation from the Pen of the Most High, stands out from among all Bahá'u'lláh's writings as the 'Mother Book' of His Dispensation. Next to it in rank is the *Kitáb-i-Íqán* (Book of Certitude).* Of the *Kitáb-i-Aqdas*, Bahá'u'lláh states, 'this Book is a heaven which We have adorned with the stars of Our commandments and prohibitions', and again, 'verily, it is My weightiest testimony unto all people, and the proof of the All-Merciful unto all who are in heaven and all who are on earth'.[1]

As well as being the mightiest and most exalted of Bahá'u'lláh's writings, the *Kitáb-i-Aqdas* is from the literary point of view one of the most beautiful. It is matchless in its eloquence, unsurpassed in its lucidity, enchanting in its style, superb in its composition and varied in its theme. Every

* see vol. 1, ch. 10.

sentence is simple and easily intelligible to the reader: it is impossible to suggest a better or more eloquent construction. It is the masterpiece of Bahá'u'lláh's utterances. Though basically a book of laws and ordinances, it is so revealed that its laws are interwoven with passages of spiritual counsel and exhortation, of weighty pronouncements and divine guidance. The manner in which this is done is unique and original. It fascinates the reader with its beauty and enchantment. Of it Bahá'u'lláh speaks, 'By My life! It hath been sent down in a manner that amazeth the minds of men.' And in another passage He states:

> By God! such is the majesty of what hath been revealed therein, and so tremendous the revelation of its veiled allusions that the loins of utterance shake when attempting their description.[2]

In revealing the *Kitáb-i-Aqdas*, Bahá'u'lláh may be likened to a celestial bird whose habitation is in the realm of the spirit far above the ken of men, soaring in the spiritual heights of glory. In that station, Bahá'u'lláh speaks about spiritual matters, reveals the verities of His Cause and unveils the glory of His Revelation to mankind. From such a lofty horizon this immortal Bird of the Spirit suddenly and unexpectedly descends upon the world of dust. In this station, Bahá'u'lláh announces and expounds laws. Then the Bird takes its flight back into the spiritual domains. Here the Tongue of Grandeur speaks again with majesty and authority, revealing some of the choicest passages treasured in the *Kitáb-i-Aqdas*. Shoghi Effendi, the Guardian of the Bahá'í Faith, translated a considerable number of these passages into superb English and included most of them in *Gleanings from the Writings of Bahá'u'lláh*.*

This ascent and descent, the revelation of spiritual teachings

* The following passages in *Gleanings* are from the *Kitáb-i-Aqdas*: XXXVII, LVI, LXX, LXXI, LXXII, XCVIII, CV, CLV, CLIX and CLXV.

on the one hand, and the giving of laws on the other, follow one another throughout the Book. There seems to be no visible pattern for the interweaving of the two, nor is there any apparent connection between them. Bahá'u'lláh, after expounding some of His choicest teachings or revealing some of His counsels and exhortations, abruptly changes the subject and gives one or more laws which outwardly seem not to have any relevance to the previous subject.

Every major religion has had laws given by its Founder. These laws have played an important part in governing community affairs and guiding the lives of the individual believers; Judaism and Islám are the best examples. In the Christian Faith, however, there are not many laws given by Christ, and because of this, it may be difficult for people of Christian background to appreciate the significance of religious laws and the vital role they play in the life of the community. Probably the reason why Christ did not reveal many laws for His followers is that His Message was mainly directed towards individual salvation, and left no major guidelines for community affairs. He laid emphasis on the spiritual health of the individual as epitomized in His Sermon on the Mount, but left no laws to govern the activities of communities and nations and to define their relationship to each other.

The laws of every religion are valid and applicable until the next Manifestation of God appears. After that they become out of date and lose their effectiveness; people do not feel the urge to follow them. For instance, the laws of Moses were in accord with the spirit of the age until the appearance of Christ when they became out of date. There are many laws in the Old Testament which were good for the age they were designed for and which were practised for over a thousand years, but they are not applicable any longer. The laws of Islám which were given by the Prophet Muḥammad were valid up to the time of the coming of the Báb. These laws were operative among the Islámic nations for about thirteen hundred lunar years. Ever since the revelation of the *Kitáb-i-Aqdas*, in which the laws of the new age were formulated, most of the laws of Islám have become inoperative. Not only have some of the Islámic governments been forced to abandon the application of Islámic laws in favour of civil laws which they themselves have enacted, but the spirit of the new age, manifesting itself both through constructive and destructive processes, has so radically changed social circumstances that in many instances it has become impossible to implement the laws of Islám.

The laws revealed in the *Bayán* by the Báb were designed to be shortlived. Some of them were incomplete, being either directly or by implication dependent upon the advent of 'Him Whom God shall make Manifest'.* The laws of the Bábí religion were abrogated by the revelation of the *Kitáb-i-Aqdas*. Only a few of the laws given by the Báb were confirmed by Bahá'u'lláh and these were reinstated in that same book. 'Abdu'l-Bahá has declared that those laws of the Báb which were not confirmed in the *Kitáb-i-Aqdas* are to be considered as abrogated.[3] In another Tablet He states that any law revealed elsewhere in the Writings of Bahá'u'lláh, if contrary to the laws of the *Aqdas*, is invalid. But those which are not contrary, or are not mentioned in the *Kitáb-i-Aqdas*, are valid and binding.

Indeed, as we survey the Writings of Bahá'u'lláh, we come across many Tablets which contain some laws or deal with the elucidation and application of laws. Such Tablets are regarded as supplementary to the *Kitáb-i-Aqdas*. It is therefore clear that the *Kitáb-i-Aqdas* on its own does not contain all the laws of Bahá'u'lláh. After its revelation Bahá'u'lláh permitted Zaynu'l-Muqarribín,† one of His devoted companions, who was formerly a *mujtahid* (Doctor of Islámic law) and highly experienced in the application of Islámic law, to ask any questions he might have regarding the application of the laws of Bahá'u'lláh. The answers given by Him are contained in a

* Bahá'u'lláh. See vol. 1, ch. 18.

† see vol. 1, pp. 25–6.

book known as *Questions and Answers* which is to be regarded as an appendix to the *Kitáb-i-Aqdas*.

In a Tablet[4] written by Mírzá Áqá Ján, Bahá'u'lláh's amanuensis, dated 15th of Jamádiyu'l-Avval 1290 (11 July 1873), it is stated that the *Kitáb-i-Aqdas* was revealed around that time. It also refers to the circumstances which led to its revelation. For some years, the believers had been asking questions about the laws of the Faith, but Bahá'u'lláh did not find it timely to respond to them. While in Adrianople He revealed a number of laws in His Persian writings, but did not release them to the believers. Questions continued to come to him while in 'Akká, and when the time was propitious, Bahá'u'lláh revealed the *Kitáb-i-Aqdas*. But from the beginning He stressed to His followers the need to be discreet and wise in the implementation of its laws. He advised them not to practise any of its provisions which might prove to be untimely or could cause agitation or disturbance among the people.

Shortly after the revelation of the *Kitáb-i-Aqdas*, Ḥájí Siyyid Javád-i-Karbilá'í,* a distinguished believer who was held in high esteem by the community, was anxious for the Bahá'ís to implement the laws of that Book. In a Tablet addressed to him, Bahá'u'lláh discloses the pre-eminent position which the *Kitáb-i-Aqdas* occupies, refers to it as the most great magnet through which the hearts of the peoples of the world will be attracted, and prophesies that through it the majesty and sovereignty of God will, ere long, be made manifest. But He counsels Ḥájí Siyyid Javád to exercise caution and wisdom in the implementation of its laws at that time. The following is an extract from the above-mentioned Tablet to Ḥájí Siyyid Javád:

> For a number of years, petitions reached the Most Holy Presence from various lands begging for the laws of God, but We held back the Pen ere the appointed time had come.

* see vol. 1, pp. 221–4.

Thereupon the Day-Star of the laws and ordinances shone forth from above the horizon of the Will of God, as a token of His grace unto the peoples of the world. He, verily, is the Ever-Forgiving, the Most Generous . . . Indeed the laws of God are like unto the ocean and the children of men as fish, did they but know it. However, in observing them one must exercise tact and wisdom . . . Since most people are feeble and far-removed from the purpose of God, therefore one must observe tact and prudence under all conditions, so that nothing might happen that could cause disturbance and dissension or raise clamour among the heedless. Verily, His bounty hath surpassed the whole universe and His bestowals encompassed all that dwell on earth. One must guide mankind to the ocean of true understanding in a spirit of love and tolerance. The *Kitáb-i-Aqdas* itself beareth eloquent testimony to the loving providence of God.[5]

In the same year that the *Kitáb-i-Aqdas* was revealed Bahá'u'lláh allowed Jamál-i-Burújirdí,* who was then in 'Akká, to copy certain parts of it and share it with the friends in Persia. But again He emphasized wisdom and discretion in the application of its laws. It has already been explained in the previous volume that through their mercy and compassion the Manifestations of God do not announce all their new laws to their followers suddenly. Knowing man's strong attachment to old laws and customs, they introduce their new laws gradually over a period of time during which their followers become enlightened and ready to receive them.†

The study of the Writings of Bahá'u'lláh and 'Abdu'l-Bahá makes it clear that most of the laws of the *Kitáb-i-Aqdas*, apart from those which are of a spiritual nature, or in conformity

* It is interesting to note that this proud and egotistical Jamál asked Bahá'u'lláh to make him exempt from obedience to the laws of the *Kitáb-i-Aqdas*. Bahá'u'lláh granted him his wish and conveyed to him that he was free and did not have to obey any of the laws of that Book. For further information on this notorious person who eventually became a Covenant-breaker, see vol. 2.

† For further information on this subject see vol. 2, pp. 353–4.

with the conditions prevailing at the time, are designed for the future when the Bahá'í Faith becomes the religion of the land. It is then that these laws will be fully implemented within the framework of a new civilization which is to emerge later from amidst the chaos and confusion of present-day society.

Shoghi Effendi, the Guardian of the Faith, has described the laws of the *Kitáb-i-Aqdas* as the 'warp and woof' of Bahá'u'lláh's World Order. Without these laws, mankind will not be able to take part in the establishment of the promised Kingdom of God on earth. The World Order of Bahá'u'lláh, however, is still growing in its embryonic form. In the fullness of time it will be born and will usher in an age the glories of which we in this day cannot fully visualize, an age in which the teachings of Bahá'u'lláh will guide and govern the life of man on this planet. Then and only then will the wisdom and significance of all the laws of the *Kitáb-i-Aqdas* become manifest, their relevance to the needs of the age become apparent and their application become a vital necessity.

Within the compass of three pages in *God Passes By* Shoghi Effendi has summarized the *Kitáb-i-Aqdas* in such a masterly fashion that if studied carefully, the reader will know all the basic subjects that are contained in this exalted Book. The following is part of his summary enumerating some of the fundamental laws of this Dispensation:

> In this Book He, moreover, prescribes the obligatory prayers; designates the time and period of fasting; prohibits congregational prayer except for the dead; fixes the Qiblih; institutes the Ḥuqúqu'lláh (Right of God); formulates the law of inheritance; ordains the institution of the Mashriqu'l-Adhkár; establishes the Nineteen Day Feasts, the Bahá'í festivals and the Intercalary Days; abolishes the institution of priesthood; prohibits slavery, asceticism, mendicancy, monasticism, penance, the use of pulpits and the kissing of hands; prescribes monogamy; condemns cruelty to animals, idleness and sloth, backbiting and calumny; censures divorce; interdicts gambling, the use of

opium, wine and other intoxicating drinks; specifies the punishments for murder, arson, adultery and theft; stresses the importance of marriage and lays down its essential conditions; imposes the obligation of engaging in some trade or profession, exalting such occupation to the rank of worship; emphasizes the necessity of providing the means for the education of children; and lays upon every person the duty of writing a testament and of strict obedience to one's government.[6]

There are some laws which Bahá'u'lláh has not formulated in the *Kitáb-i-Aqdas* or other Tablets. He has deliberately left gaps in the structure of His laws and these will have to be filled by the Universal House of Justice, the supreme legislative body of the Faith, authorized by Bahá'u'lláh to enact laws which are not explicitly revealed by Him. The laws enacted by this body can be altered at a later time by the same body when conditions in society will have radically changed and this provision guarantees that laws which are temporary in nature may keep pace with humanity's progress.

The laws that Bahá'u'lláh has formulated, however, are fundamental laws, fixed and unalterable during the entire period of His Dispensation. Only the next Manifestation of God can abrogate them. It should be noted that there are certain laws given by Bahá'u'lláh that are intended for a future condition of society, and these cannot be implemented without the necessary legislation by the Universal House of Justice for their application. Shoghi Effendi writes through his secretary:

> What has not been formulated in the Aqdas, in addition to matters of detail and of secondary importance arising out of the application of the laws already formulated by Bahá'u'lláh, will have to be enacted by the Universal House of Justice. This body can supplement but never invalidate or modify in the least degree what has already been formulated by Bahá'u'lláh. Nor has the Guardian any right whatsoever to lessen the binding effect, much less to abrogate the provisions of so fundamental and sacred a Book.[7]

The *Kitáb-i-Aqdas* has not been translated into any language so far by any Bahá'í authority. The reason for this is that a mere translation without making reference to other Tablets would be very misleading indeed. The Universal House of Justice has explained this point in these words:

> The *Kitáb-i-Aqdas* itself is the kernel of a vast structure of Bahá'í law that will have to come into being in the years and centuries ahead as the unity of mankind is established and develops. Thus to properly understand the contents of that Book one should also read many other Tablets of Bahá'u'lláh relating to them, as well as the interpretations of 'Abdu'l-Bahá and the Guardian, and realize that great areas of detail have been left by Bahá'u'lláh for the Universal House of Justice to fill in and to vary in accordance with the needs of a developing society. In addition, a translation of the *Kitáb-i-Aqdas* made without proper comprehensive footnotes referring to those other Tablets which elucidate His laws as well as to the interpretations of the Master and the Guardian can give a very misleading impression—quite apart from the problem of achieving a beauty of style in the English which can approach that of the original.[8]

In another instance the Universal House of Justice writes:

> The Guardian explained that an essential prelude to the publication of the Most Holy Book was the preparation of a synopsis and codification of its Laws and Ordinances. This would be followed in due time by a complete translation of the Book itself, made by a competent body of experts, and copiously annotated with detailed explanations. Such annotations will undoubtedly have to contain references to the many Tablets of Bahá'u'lláh which supplement the *Aqdas*, to the interpretations penned by 'Abdu'l-Bahá as well as those from the writings of Shoghi Effendi, and will need to elucidate certain passages of the Book or to amplify its religious, cultural and historical references.
>
> It is clear that such a Book, rich in allusion and referring to laws and practices of previous Dispensations, could

easily be misconstrued by anyone unfamiliar with such laws and practices, insufficiently versed in the Teachings of Bahá'u'lláh and not thoroughly informed of His fundamental purposes. In particular, inadequate translations could be seriously misleading. During His own lifetime Bahá'u'lláh commented upon a translation of the *Aqdas* made by one of the believers: 'Although the intention of the translator was good, such an action in these days will lead to differences and is therefore not permissible.'[9]

It is some time now since the Universal House of Justice has accomplished the task of the codification of the laws, and has published the book entitled *Synopsis and Codification of the Laws and Ordinances of the Kitáb-i-Aqdas*. This work entailed a great deal of research into the Writings. Those Tablets of Bahá'u'lláh which supplement the *Kitáb-i-Aqdas*, and the Writings of 'Abdu'l-Bahá and Shoghi Effendi which deal with the interpretation of the laws, have been taken into account in the production of this important work. 'This synopsis and codification', the Universal House of Justice states,

> offers a concise and comprehensive presentation of the laws, ordinances, exhortations and other subjects which appear in both the *Kitáb-i-Aqdas* itself and in the *Questions and Answers* which forms an appendix to that Book. Not all details are included, nor is it possible to give in such a circumscribed form an impression of the loftiness and magnificence of the language of Bahá'u'lláh. In order to provide readers with at least some intimation of this splendour of theme and language, there are included as a prelude to the *Synopsis and Codification*, and in the order in which they appear in the *Kitáb-i-Aqdas*, those passages which have been translated into English by the Guardian of the Faith. It will be the formidable task of future translators to match the beauty and accuracy of Shoghi Effendi's rendition.[10]

Obedience to the Laws of God

Observance of the laws of a religion is of the utmost importance; it is an obligation binding on its followers. The enforcement of some of the laws of the *Kitáb-i-Aqdas* began in the ministry of Shoghi Effendi. Knowing that the believers in the cradle of the Faith had been brought up within a society where the significance of religious laws and their implications were understood, he directed the Spiritual Assemblies in that part of the world to begin the enforcement of some of the laws of the *Kitáb-i-Aqdas* within the Bahá'í community. In the course of His ministry, he elaborated on the application of these laws, elucidated many intricacies and details connected with them, urged the Spiritual Assemblies never to compromise when enforcing the laws and counselled them to uphold the standards of justice and impartiality in all cases. Thus he built up in this particular field a great reservoir of knowledge and experience which will be of great value in the future.

Present-day society in the Western world is not, however, oriented to obedience to religious laws. Not only has it been steadily moving for a long time now towards humanism and materialism, but also the Christian tradition has left the people without a full appreciation of the significance and importance of religious laws within the community. As we have already stated, this is probably because Christ, whose message was primarily directed to the individual, did not give many laws in His Dispensation.

The introduction of the laws of the *Kitáb-i-Aqdas* within such a society and at a time when the Faith is still in its infancy has been slow and gradual. Indeed, from the beginning of the Formative Age of the Faith up to the present time, only a few of the laws of the *Kitáb-i-Aqdas* have been introduced to the Western world. No doubt in the future as the Cause grows and conditions within human society become more favourable, other laws will be introduced.

Concerning the laws of the *Kitáb-i-Aqdas*, Shoghi Effendi has written these words through his secretary:

> He feels it his duty to explain that the Laws revealed by Bahá'u'lláh in the Aqdas are, whenever practicable and not in direct conflict with the Civil Laws of the land, absolutely binding on every believer or Bahá'í institution whether in the East or in the West. Certain laws, such as fasting, obligatory prayers, the consent of parents before marriage, avoidance of alcoholic drinks, monogamy, should be regarded by all believers as universally and vitally applicable at the present time. Others have been formulated in anticipation of a state of society, destined to emerge from the chaotic conditions that prevail today.[11]

The followers of Bahá'u'lláh all over the world strive to develop the characteristics of Bahá'í life in their individual lives and their communities, by trying to put into practice the teachings of Bahá'u'lláh and observing those laws and ordinances which are at present binding on them. A true believer carries out the commandments of Bahá'u'lláh wholeheartedly, for the cornerstone of faith is obedience to the commandments of God as revealed by Bahá'u'lláh in this age.

In order to appreciate this important point, let us study nature. As we have already stated,* God's creation is one entity. The spiritual and physical worlds are closely related to each other; they are not two different creations. In one of His Tablets,[12] Bahá'u'lláh states that every created thing in this physical world has counterparts in all the worlds of God. It follows that the laws and principles which govern this physical life are equally operative in the spiritual worlds of God. But they are applied on a higher level possessing certain new features which are not to be found in the lower kingdom. The same basic laws and principles which operate in nature are also to be found in the world of man and in religion. But again they are applied on a higher level.

* see vol. 1, pp. 1–3.

To cite one example: some of the laws which govern the life of a tree are similar to those in the life of man. A tree thrusts its roots into the soil from which it receives its nourishment and upon which it depends for its existence. But the tree itself, its trunk, branches and leaves grow in the opposite direction. As if it dislikes the soil, the tree moves away from it. This is similar to the state of detachment from material things in the world of man when the soul aspires to spiritual things and away from earthly desires. By moving in the opposite direction the tree receives the rays of the sun and as a result it will blossom and bear fruit. Of course, the growth of a tree is involuntary; it is dictated by nature. But supposing the tree had a choice; what a difference it would have made if, feeling an attachment for the soil, it had inclined its branches and leaves towards the earth and buried itself in the ground! Then it would have rotted away and been deprived of the life-giving rays of the sun.

The same principle is true of man, for he has to live in this material world and is entirely dependent upon this earth for his existence. His soul, however, ought to become detached from the material world and turn instead towards spiritual things. But unlike the plant, which has no control over its growth and development, man has been given the power to determine his own destiny. He has been given free will and can choose the direction in which he wants to move. If he focuses his attention only on material things and becomes attached to this world and its vanities, pomp and glory, his soul will remain in relative darkness. But if like a tree, he does not direct all his affection towards material things, and reaches a state of detachment from this world* and allows his soul to aspire towards heavenly qualities, he could then receive the rays of the Sun of Truth—the Manifestation of God. Then and only then can his soul produce a fruit and give birth to the spirit of faith† which

* Much has been said in these volumes on detachment from the Bahá'í point of view, which is completely opposite to the ideas of renunciation of the world, mendicancy or asceticism.

† see vol. 1, pp. 73–4.

is the ultimate purpose of its creation.

The above example was given merely to demonstrate how the worlds of God, both physical and spiritual, are related by the same laws. It is therefore possible that by studying the laws and principles of the physical world, we may be able to discern a spiritual principle, provided we bear in mind the words and sayings of the Manifestations of God and let their explanations guide us to discover clear parallels between the spiritual and material principles.

The Covenant of God with Man

To understand the importance of obedience to the laws of God, which is a spiritual principle, let us first examine the relationship of God—the Source of life—to His creatures in this physical world, and then from a spiritual point of view we may come to a conclusion. We note that all living things in this world are subject to the laws of nature. The Creator has so arranged life on this planet that the sun pours its energies upon all created things, the earth supplies the food, and the elements make their contribution. And so, God gives life. This is the part He plays.

Living creatures, on the other hand, have to play their part if they are to live. They have to receive the outpourings of energy, but strictly in accordance with the laws that nature has imposed on them. For instance, the fish lives in water, while a bird soars in the air. Both live in accordance with the laws which nature dictates to them. For on this physical level, the reaction of all created things to God's outpourings of energy is involuntary. Each creature is bound by the laws of nature and cannot deviate a hair's breadth from them. But the essential point is that the creatures' response is in harmony with the vivifying forces of life which are released by nature.

It is the same spiritually. The response of man to God's Revelation ought to be that of harmony with His Teachings. But man, although physically an animal, is not spiritually subject to the laws of nature. Instead he is bound by the laws of the Covenant of God with Him. As in every covenant, and as in nature, there are two parties involved here. In the same way that God provides the life-giving energies for the physical world, and the creatures respond to these, the same Creator releases spiritual forces for the development and progress of the soul of man, and the individual must play his part. But unlike the physical world, the response of man to God's bounties is voluntary. Man has free will, whereas other created things are devoid of this faculty.

The mere act of creation brings into being the Covenant of God with man which has two sides. God on his part creates man in His own image which is the act of bestowing upon him His attributes. He provides him with his physical needs in this life and sends His Messengers to throw light upon his path so that he may draw near to Him.

The part that man has to play in this Covenant is to be conscious of these bounties, to recognize His Manifestation and to abide by His teachings and laws. The most natural course, which can alone bring about harmony between the two sides of the Covenant, is for man to obey the precepts laid down by God. To rebel against them is to live in conflict with the laws of creation and to cut oneself away from the good. To believe in God but to think that this Covenant does not exist and that the Creator has not laid down any laws in the spiritual domains of His creation is tantamount to attributing incompetence to Him.

The Covenant of God with man is similar to the terms which a school headmaster lays down for the pupils. The moment a child walks into a school for the first time, he, without knowing it, enters into a covenant with the headmaster. Again, this covenant has two sides. The headmaster provides the child with all his educational needs. He appoints teachers to teach him and draws up the programme. The part that the child has to play is to learn every lesson he is taught and follow every instruction he is given. Only in this way can he acquire knowledge and become mature with wisdom and understanding. When the child is ready to receive a higher level of education, the headmaster delegates a new teacher to teach him more.

The terms of this covenant are drawn up by the headmaster alone, and the child has no say in it. Its author is strong, knowledgeable and wise, but the child, the other party to the covenant, is weak, unlettered and immature. Most arrangements made by the strong for the weak are against the interests of, and are designed to exploit, the latter. But not so in this case, because the motive of the headmaster in drawing up such a contract between himself and the child is pure. His intention is to educate the child and endow him with good qualities and perfections. If the pupil plays his part well and follows the instructions of his master, this covenant becomes the greatest blessing in his life.

Exactly the same is true of God and His Covenant with man. God sends His Messengers to teach humanity from age to age and each one brings a new message suited to the requirements of the time. Similar to the above analogy, this Covenant is also established unilaterally by One Who is the Almighty, the All-Knowing, the All-Wise. It also confers the greatest blessing upon man, for its purpose is to enable him to become a spiritual being and acquire eternal life. To achieve this lofty position, man has to live in accordance with the teachings of the Manifestation of God and obey His commandments.

As the moral and spiritual values in life decline today, a great many people all over the world look upon the word 'obedience' with suspicion and fear. They regard this word to be synonymous with dictatorship, blind acceptance, religious fanaticism and all sorts of fettered beliefs. The majority of those who hold this view are among the honest, open-minded and enlightened peoples of the world. Some may belong to religious groups with a liberal outlook, others may be intellectuals, agnostics or atheists. They are fully aware of the dangers which blind obedience may cause within human society and are weary of any so-called authority, whether religious or secular, which demands obedience to its commands.

Such fears are fully justified and those who campaign against the setting up of such an authority and abhor its reign, are worthy of praise and admiration. For, as we survey the religious field, we come across many a 'false prophet' who, for lust of leadership, appears in the guise of a religious leader, posing as a man of holiness, and for his own personal benefit rules over his followers' minds. There are also millions of people, followers of the worlds' major religions, many of whom are fettered in the cage of outdated religious doctrines and antiquated dogmas. During this century, more and more of these people are becoming awakened to their tragedy, breaking the shackles which had been placed on their minds and freeing themselves from this bondage. They either remain lukewarm, disillusioned followers, or join the rank of agnostics and atheists. The voice of religious leadership, which in older days inspired multitudes, is now heard by these people with various degrees of indifference or hostility. The reason for this change is that God has manifested Himself through Bahá'u'lláh and religious leaders have not recognized Him and in His words they have become as 'fallen stars'.* We have already stated† that every religion has a certain period of validity during which its teachings are operative. That period comes to an end with the birth of a new religion.

As major world religions progressively lose their vitality and effectiveness, religious leaders are losing their grip on the minds of people. Their dictates and edicts, which in older days inspired obedience from their followers, have now become counter-productive. A great many people now rebel against the idea of obedience and they are quite justified in doing so. However, when we study the way of life in human society, we

* see vol. 2, pp. 270–72.

† see vol. 1, pp. 64–6.

note that man wholeheartedly obeys any person or institution that speaks with the voice of truth and has authority to do so. The same person who shuns the word 'obedience' blindly obeys instructions issued from certain authorities in his daily life. For example, a man not knowing the way to a city follows blindly the road signs and never questions their authenticity. The reason for this blind obedience is that he accepts the authority of the body which has placed the signposts. The same is true of a patient who unquestionably obeys his doctor's prescription even to the extent of letting him amputate a limb. Again, this is because he has faith in the physician and accepts his advice without any hesitation.

Obedience is a natural step for man to take provided he finds the truth. Bahá'u'lláh makes this point very clear when He states in the opening paragraph of the *Kitáb-i-Aqdas*:

> The first duty prescribed by God for His servants is the recognition of Him Who is the Dayspring of His Revelation and the Fountain of His laws, Who representeth the Godhead in both the Kingdom of His Cause and the world of creation. Whoso achieveth this duty hath attained unto all good; and whoso is deprived thereof, hath gone astray, though he be the author of every righteous deed. It behoveth every one who reacheth this most sublime station, this summit of transcendent glory, to observe every ordinance of Him Who is the Desire of the world. These twin duties are inseparable. Neither is acceptable without the other. Thus hath it been decreed by Him Who is the Source of Divine inspiration.[13]

This is the part that the individual has to play in the Covenant of God with man, namely to recognize Him as the Source of all good and then follow His commandments. In the light of this, we see that Bahá'u'lláh has attached paramount importance to one of the basic principles of His Faith—the unfettered search after truth by the individual. Every person who becomes a Bahá'í must investigate the truth until he becomes assured in his heart that Bahá'u'lláh is the Manifestation of God for this age. When the individual reaches this stage, he will then want to follow His commandments. And as he deepens his knowledge of the Faith and turns to Bahá'u'lláh to draw from His power, his heart will become the recipient of the knowledge which God can bestow upon a believer. It is then that he can realize the wisdom behind all the laws and teachings which are binding on him. It is then that obedience to the commandments of Bahá'u'lláh becomes coupled with a deep understanding of their purpose, their wisdom, their excellence and their need. It is then that carrying out the teachings of Bahá'u'lláh becomes a source of joy for the individual, and he will find that his thoughts, his aspirations, his words and his deeds are in harmony with the provisions of the Covenant of God with man. It is for such a person that Bahá'u'lláh has revealed the following in the *Kitáb-i-Aqdas*:

> O ye peoples of the world! Know assuredly that My commandments are the lamps of My loving providence among My servants, and the keys of My mercy for My creatures. Thus hath it been sent down from the heaven of the Will of your Lord, the Lord of Revelation. Were any man to taste the sweetness of the words which the lips of the All-Merciful have willed to utter, he would, though the treasures of the earth be in his possession, renounce them one and all, that he might vindicate the truth of even one of His commandments, shining above the Dayspring of His bountiful care and loving-kindness.[14]

Mírzá Abu'l-Faḍl,* the great Bahá'í scholar, states that the laws of God in the Holy Books of past religions and those of the *Kitáb-i-Aqdas* may be divided into three categories. The first category is devotional laws and ordinances which concern man's worship of God. The ordinances of obligatory prayer, fasting and similar devotional acts are among this group of laws.

* see pp. 104ff. and Appendix II.

The second category is laws which benefit the individual only, such as cleanliness and other acts which are aimed at elevating the personal and spiritual condition of the individual.

The third category is the laws which concern society and these constitute the bulk of the laws of the *Kitáb-i-Aqdas*. These laws, together with the principles ordained by Bahá'u'lláh in His Writings, constitute the two pillars which sustain the institutions of His future World Order. Shoghi Effendi, speaking about the laws and distinguishing them from the principles of the Faith, states that both together constitute 'the warp and woof of the institutions upon which the structure of His World Order must ultimately rest'.[15]

In the light of this we can appreciate the preponderating role which the laws of the *Kitáb-i-Aqdas* will play in the future world civilization of which that Book is a charter. Concerning His laws and ordinances, Bahá'u'lláh states in the *Kitáb-i-Aqdas*:

> They whom God hath endued with insight will readily recognize that the precepts laid down by God constitute the highest means for the maintenance of order in the world and the security of its peoples. He that turneth away from them, is accounted among the abject and foolish.[16]

Reward and Punishment

In the *Lawḥ-i-Maqṣúd* Bahá'u'lláh further declares:

> The structure of world stability and order hath been reared upon, and will continue to be sustained by, the twin pillars of reward and punishment.[17]

The application of the laws of Bahá'u'lláh will involve both reward and punishment. He has also conferred upon the Universal House of Justice the right to legislate on the application of His laws, or to specify punishments for the breaking of other laws which He Himself has not formulated.

Law and order are the basis of peace and security in every civilized society and the breaking of these laws must incur some punishment. The same is true of the laws of the *Kitáb-i-Aqdas*. The guarantor for the establishment in the future of a world community in which the oneness of mankind—Bahá'u'lláh's main spiritual principle—is fully realized is justice. The bonds which unite individuals are love, compassion and forbearance, but what binds nations together into a spiritually united world is justice. Bahá'u'lláh has proclaimed this fact in many of His Writings: 'The best beloved of all things in My sight is Justice'[18] is a simple expression by Bahá'u'lláh of this important principle. To uphold the standard of justice, He makes this important statement:

> Justice hath a mighty force at its command. It is none other than reward and punishment for the deeds of men. By the power of this force the tabernacle of order is established throughout the world . . .[19]

In present-day society, punishment is generally meted out to offenders of the law, but the tendency in many parts of the world is to show compassion and reduce sentences as much as possible. This tendency is growing in direct proportion to humanitarianism. Wrongly, it has almost become a common view today that the individual should not be fully blamed for his criminal actions and that most of the blame ought to be directed towards society. It is claimed that the criminal is merely a victim of circumstances over which he has had little control. And so mercy and pardon instead of justice and punishment are the hallmark of modern civilization. Leniency and compassion in the courts of law, supported by modern theories aimed at forgiveness and clemency have increased the reign of violence in the world to alarming proportions.

The teachings of Bahá'u'lláh advocate the opposite attitude to this. Since the laws of the *Kitáb-i-Aqdas* are the laws of God for this age, they must be obeyed without compromise. In this

Book, Bahá'u'lláh categorically states that those who apply the law should not show mercy to a criminal, nor become compassionate when punishing him, for if they do, they will undermine the foundations of justice. Many enlightened people today disagree with what Bahá'u'lláh advocates. They look for mild punishments and plenty of compassion and some advocate education rather than punishment. This is mainly because most people are only concerned with life on this planet and seldom think about life after death, and there are many who do not believe in the latter. The aim of these people is to gain as much, and to lose as little, as they can for as long as they live.

Generally, therefore, there is not much concern about the consequences which the actions of a man will have on the progress of his soul in the next life. Whereas it is a cornerstone of Bahá'í belief that this world is only a transitory stage in the life of man, preparing him for an eternal life. It is like a womb-world in which he has to acquire the spiritual qualities that are essential requirements for his existence in the spiritual worlds of God.* So there is a vast difference between a Bahá'í outlook on life and that of humanists. The former strives to use the opportunitites of this life to reap a rich harvest in the next, while the latter exerts all efforts to prosper while on this earth. It is these contrasting views that constitute the basis for Bahá'u'lláh's emphasis on punishment and the humanist view on leniency and compassion.

From a careful study of the Writings of Bahá'u'lláh one may reach the surprising conclusion that just punishments in general, and those ordained in the *Kitáb-i-Aqdas* in particular, are a mercy of God to man, and a token of His loving-kindness to him. Bahá'u'lláh in one of His Tablets[20] reveals some of the mysteries of this life and the next, describes how everything in this mortal world has counterparts in the spiritual worlds, and explains that the individual's deeds in this life will affect his

* For further information on the soul and its progress in the next world see vol. 1, pp. 72–3.

existence in the next. To illustrate the benefits which will accrue to the soul, if he is punished in this world for his misdeeds, He uses the example of a man who steals a seed of a tree from someone in the spring season. If he returns it to its owner in that same season, he has cleared his debt and does not owe him anything else. But if he fails to give it back in the spring, what does he owe him in the summer? He owes him a tree and its fruits, because to give back the seed in the summer is useless. This analogy explains that if the individual pays for his misdeeds in this life by receiving the punishment which is ordained in the Holy Writings, his burden of sin will be far lighter in the next life. Otherwise, who knows how heavily his soul will have to pay if he somehow avoids punishment in this world.

In the same Tablet Bahá'u'lláh states that pure and holy deeds will be manifested in the spiritual worlds of God and transformed into such exalted and glorious forms that if He were to disclose them, every author of such deeds would discard his human temple and joyously hasten to the realms beyond.

Anyone who has recognized Bahá'u'lláh as the vicegerent of God on earth and has deepened his understanding of the verities of His Cause, will readily acknowledge that the observance of the laws of Bahá'u'lláh is the cause of the salvation of the soul. In the *Kitáb-i-Aqdas* Bahá'u'lláh testifies:

> Think not that We have revealed unto you a mere code of laws. Nay, rather, We have unsealed the choice Wine with the fingers of might and power. To this beareth witness that which the Pen of Revelation hath revealed. Meditate upon this, O men of insight![21]

And again in that same Book He states:

> Consider the mercy of God and His gifts. He enjoineth upon you that which shall profit you, though He Himself

can well dispense with all creatures. Your evil doings can never harm Us, neither can your good works profit Us. We summon you wholly for the sake of God. To this every man of understanding and insight will testify.[22]

Bahá'u'lláh's View of Liberty

Another topic in the *Kitáb-i-Aqdas* which could be misunderstood by some people is that of freedom and liberty. These are the words of Bahá'u'lláh in that Book:

> Consider the pettiness of men's minds. They ask for that which injureth them, and cast away the thing that profiteth them. They are, indeed, of those that are far astray. We find some men desiring liberty, and priding themselves therein. Such men are in the depths of ignorance.
>
> Liberty must, in the end, lead to sedition, whose flames none can quench. Thus warneth you He Who is the Reckoner, the All-Knowing. Know ye that the embodiment of liberty and its symbol is the animal. That which beseemeth man is submission unto such restraints as will protect him from his own ignorance and guard him against the harm of the mischief-maker. Liberty causeth man to overstep the bounds of propriety, and to infringe on the dignity of his station. It debaseth him to the level of extreme depravity and wickedness.
>
> Regard men as a flock of sheep that need a shepherd for their protection. This, verily, is the truth, the certain truth. We approve of liberty in certain circumstances, and refuse to sanction it in others. We, verily, are the All-Knowing.
>
> Say: True liberty consisteth in man's submission unto My commandments, little as ye know it. Were men to observe that which We have sent down unto them from the Heaven of Revelation, they would, of a certainty, attain unto perfect liberty. Happy is the man that hath apprehended the Purpose of God in whatever He hath revealed from the Heaven of His Will, that pervadeth all created things. Say: The liberty that profiteth you is to be found nowhere except in complete servitude unto God, the Eternal Truth. Whoso

hath tasted of its sweetness will refuse to barter it for all the dominion of earth and heaven.[23]

Bahá'u'lláh condemns the idea of absolute liberty for man. Indeed, there is no progressive society or nation in the world in which absolute freedom is allowed. There is the rule of law in every civilized country and people in the exercising of their right to freedom cannot overstep the bounds of constitutional law. There would be anarchy if they were left free to do what they liked. In the words of Bahá'u'lláh, it would 'lead to sedition, whose flame none can quench'. All the freedom-loving nations of the world enjoy their freedom within the limits of the law and other conventions which have come about through tradition and have become accepted as a way of life. It is these laws and traditions, including religion and culture, which give each nation a certain characteristic, and produce an atmosphere in which people live and exercise their lawful rights freely.

Bahá'u'lláh advocates the same, except that man must adopt the teachings of the Manifestation of God for this age to guide and direct him in his life. He will then find ample scope to live in liberty within the framework of His laws and teachings. It is possible that some people who have not accepted the Message of Bahá'u'lláh could argue that although humanity needs to be guided by some laws and principles, nevertheless, the mere act of adopting Bahá'u'lláh's teachings as guide-lines for society would be an infringement on liberty. This view would be correct if Bahá'u'lláh were not the Manifestation of God for this age. But if He is, then His laws and teachings must, and will in the end, be enforced by humanity, and will guide the peoples of the world to exercise their freedom within the framework of the World Order He has come to establish. The essential point, therefore, is to investigate the truth of the claims of Bahá'u'lláh. Once the individual is assured of the authenticity of His Message, he will joyously allow the teachings and commandments of Bahá'u'lláh to govern his life.

It is then that guided by the principles of the Faith he will be able to develop with absolute freedom all that is potential within him and attain to true liberty.

The Infallibility of the Manifestation

In the *Kitáb-i-Aqdas* Bahá'u'lláh declares the doctrine of the Most Great Infallibility of the Manifestations of God, and states that no one else can ever possess it. We have touched upon this subject in the previous volume.* This infallibility is an inherent characteristic of the Manifestations of God, in the same way that light and heat are inherent to the sun. He derives His powers from God and is the knower of all things. His knowledge extends over past, present and future. As we have stated previously,† the reason that His all-encompassing power is hidden behind the veil of His human temple is that if His glory were to be openly revealed to the eyes of men in general, all human beings would instantly recognize Him. And by so doing they would lose their free will and become puppets of God.

However, Bahá'u'lláh always revealed a measure of His hidden glory and omnipotence to those of His loved ones who had recognized His exalted station and were in need of further confirmation of their faith. There are many stories left to posterity by the early believers who had the great privilege of attaining the presence of Bahá'u'lláh, relating how they witnessed the signs of His all-encompassing knowledge which was disclosed to their eyes in accordance with their capacity. The incidents which took place in each case came to them as thunderbolts and dazzled them by the evidences of His glory. Each time He disclosed a measure of His Divine power, the believer concerned reached the highest peaks of assurance and acquired absolute certitude in his faith. When this stage was reached the individual was no longer an ordinary human

* see vol. 2, pp. 261–2.

† see p. 2.

being. He had been transformed into a spiritual giant, a mountain of steadfastness, a new creation possessed of all the powers of this universe, a heroic soul who in spite of the fierce onslaught of the enemy threw himself into the arena of service to the Cause of Bahá'u'lláh and, considering this earthly life as a worthless existence, longed to lay down his life in the path of His Beloved.

Many believers who attained the presence of Bahá'u'lláh have witnessed the signs of His all-encompassing knowledge and left for posterity some of their experiences. To cite some examples we quote the following:

Ḥájí Muḥammad-Ṭáhir-i-Málmírí, who attained the presence of Bahá'u'lláh in 'Akká writes in his memoirs:

> Whenever I came into the presence of the Blessed Beauty, if there were anything I wanted to ask, I would say it by the way of the heart, and He would invariably answer me. This is because, in His presence, the tongue was powerless to utter one word. I always sat in His presence spellbound, oblivious of my own self. One of the questions I wanted to ask concerned the station of the Holy Imáms.* I wanted to know whether they were equal or, as I thought, some of them were exalted above others. For about six months I wanted to ask this question, but every time I attained His presence I forgot to think of it in my heart. One day, as I was going to the Mansion to attain His presence, I kept on continuously reminding myself about this question so that I might remember to communicate it through the heart to Bahá'u'lláh. Even as I was climbing the steps of the Mansion I was thinking of it. Suddenly I heard the voice of Bahá'u'lláh greeting me saying 'Marḥabá' (Welcome). I looked up and saw Him standing at the top of the stairs. I forgot everything! He went to His room, invited me in, and told me to be seated. I sat by the door. He then paced up and

* 'Alí, the son-in-law of Muḥammad, was according to Bahá'í belief the legitimate successor of Muḥammad, and the first Imám. Ten of his descendants succeeded him and are known as the holy Imáms. The Qá'im is believed by Shí'ah Islám to be the return of the twelfth Imám.

> down and revealed a Tablet* in my name. The Tablet was in Persian and halfway through it he said, 'The Imáms all came from God, spoke of God and all returned to Him.'† This answered my question and I realized that their station was equal.[24]

In another instance, Ḥájí Muḥammad-Ṭáhir writes:

> In my heart I often begged the Blessed Beauty to enable me to lay down my life as a martyr in His path. Every time that I turned to Him in my heart with this plea, he would smile at me and reveal to me the signs of His pleasure and bounties . . . until one day when these thoughts entered my mind, he turned to me and said, 'You must live to serve the Cause . . .'[25]

Another believer who attained the presence of Bahá'u'lláh in 'Akká was Áqá Riḍáy-i-Sa'ádatí, a native of Yazd. In his youth Áqá Riḍa was a devout Muslim. He had a passionate love for God and His Prophet Muḥammad. But he was not satisfied with the form of religion. His greatest ambition was to meet Imám Ḥusayn, one of the illustrious successors of the Prophet, face to face. Driven by a mysterious force, Áqá Riḍa went almost out of his mind for some time and his parents were at a loss to discover the cause. Until one day he came in contact with a follower of Bahá'u'lláh who told him that God had manifested Himself, that Bahá'u'lláh was the return of the Imám Ḥusayn‡ and that he could go and attain His presence in 'Akká. Through the help of some of the believers and the reading of the *Kitáb-i-Íqán*, Áqá Riḍá recognized the truth of the Cause. But he could not disclose his Faith to his parents. In his memoirs he writes:

> They (the Bahá'ís) introduced me to a well known Bahá'í,

* This Tablet was not recorded and therefore no copy exists.
† These are not the exact words of Bahá'u'lláh.
‡ Shí'ah Islám expects the appearance of the Qá'im followed by the return of Imám Ḥusayn. Bahá'u'lláh's name was Ḥusayn-'Alí.

> Ustád Káẓim, a builder of wide repute. He used to read the *Kitáb-i-Íqán* for me . . . Through the study of this book, I acquired certitude and assurance and became filled with joy and excitement. Sometimes I used to leave the house with the excuse of going to bring water* . . . I would carry the pitcher with me but instead of going directly to the public cistern which was about four kilometres away, I used to run all the way to the house of Ustád Káẓim, read some passages from the *Kitáb-i-Íqán* and then go to fetch water home.[26]

Áqá Riḍá eventually left Yazd for ʻIshqábád and from there he received permission to go on pilgrimage to ʻAkká where he attained the presence of Bahá'u'lláh. He writes in his memoirs:

> Every time I attained His presence, I would find the portals of His grace and revelation open before my eyes. Each of them was a mighty proof and a precious gift. All those supernatural acts that I witnessed in His blessed presence and the immense joy which flooded my soul as I sat before Him are indescribable and cannot be recorded here . . . In the gatherings of the friends, if the Blessed Beauty turned his face to a person, that individual was unable to gaze upon His countenance and see the effulgent rays of the Sun of Truth. It was therefore Bahá'u'lláh's practice to look to the right side as He spoke, so that the friends might find it easier to look at His face. And if He ever turned His face towards the friends, He would close His eyes and speak . . .
>
> Once I entered into the presence of Bahá'u'lláh at a time that He was reciting the verses of the Tablet of Visitation of Imám Ḥusayn.† At times, He would interrupt and utter some words, or receive the friends as they arrived. Eventually the number reached about forty-five. At this time I began to think of the friends in ʻIshqábád . . . I decided to remember them in His presence and dedicate my pilgrimage to them. I thought of Mírzá Abu'l-Faḍl and five others . . .

* In Yazd people used to carry drinking water from a public cistern to their homes. Each district in the city had a public cistern.

† Bahá'u'lláh revealed a Tablet of Visitation for Imám Ḥusayn which is very moving.

As soon as I remembered them, He promptly turned His face towards me and smiled. He then mentioned the names of Mírzá Abu'l-Faḍl and the other five and said to me: Your remembrance of these people and your pilgrimage on their behalf is accepted by us, accepted by us. He repeated it twice. And so He revealed everything that was in my heart.

I was staggered by this revelation. My sight became blurred and I was close to collapsing. As soon as He saw me in this state, he ordered His servant* to bring in some sweetmeats. He brought a plateful and placed it in front of Bahá'u'lláh who handed one sweet to each person. But to me He gave two. After this we were all dismissed from His presence. But I was so overwhelmed by this experience that when I left I was not in control of my faculties and halfway down the steps I collapsed . . .[27]

Another story recounted by Siyyid Mihdy-i-Gulpáygání, an outstanding believer and a nephew of Mírzá Abu'l-Faḍl, reveals the same truth that Bahá'u'lláh, the Supreme Manifestation of God, was the knower of all things visible and invisible. He used to tell this story to the believers in 'Ishqábád:

An influential person became a Bahá'í in Iṣfahán but he did not live a good life. He went to 'Akká and attained the presence of Bahá'u'lláh and this is his story: 'On the first day of my attaining the presence of the Blessed Beauty, I was among a number of pilgrims who were standing in His presence. He was pacing up and down speaking words of exhortation and encouragement. I was in a state of enchantment as I watched the majesty of His bearing. I said to myself: I know that the Blessed Perfection is the Supreme Manifestation of God and the Promise of all ages. But in some of His writings He describes Himself as the One who has sent all the Messengers of God and the revealer of all heavenly books. I did not understand this. As soon as this thought flashed through my mind, the Blessed Perfection

* Mírzá Áqá Ján, Bahá'u'lláh's amanuensis, acted as His servant. Bahá'u'lláh usually called him 'Abd-i-Háḍir (Servant in Waiting).

came toward me, placed His hand on my shoulder, and in a majestic tone said "Yes, We are the One who has sent the Messengers and revealed all the heavenly Books."* I was awestruck.'[28]

In previous volumes, a great deal has been said concerning the exalted station of Bahá'u'lláh.† There are many passages in the *Kitáb-i-Aqdas* on this theme. He states that the word Prophet‡ or Messenger should not be used to describe His station. He is the Supreme Manifestation of God who has fulfilled the prophecies of the past and ushered in the Day of God. These are the words of Bahá'u'lláh in the *Kitáb-i-Aqdas*:

> This is the Day in which He Who held converse with God hath attained the light of the Ancient of Days, and quaffed the pure waters of reunion from this Cup that hath caused the seas to swell. Say: By the one true God! Sinai is circling round the Dayspring of Revelation, while from the heights of the Kingdom the Voice of the Spirit of God is heard proclaiming: 'Bestir yourselves, ye proud ones of the earth, and haste ye unto Him.' Carmel hath, in this Day, hastened in longing adoration to attain His court, whilst from the heart of Zion there cometh the cry: 'The promise is fulfilled. That which had been announced in the holy Writ of God, the most Exalted, the Almighty, the Best-Beloved, is made manifest.'[29]

'He who held converse with God' and the 'Spirit of God' in the above passage signify Moses and Christ respectively.

There are several passages from the Writings of the Báb which are quoted by Bahá'u'lláh in the *Kitáb-i-Aqdas* as a testimony to the exalted nature of His own Revelation. He points out that

* These are not to be taken as the exact words of Bahá'u'lláh.

† see vol. 1, pp. 303–14; vol. 2, pp. 77–86, 185, 213.

‡ An important mission of the Manifestations of God in the past was to give prophecies of the coming of the Day of God. The last one to do so was the Prophet Muḥammad, known as the 'Seal of the Prophets'. See also vol. 1, p. 66.

some of these passages clearly demonstrate that the Cause of 'Him Whom God shall make manifest'* will become established in the world before that of the Báb Himself. Bahá'u'lláh in this Book also clarifies one of the utterances of the Báb which had caused misunderstanding among the people of the Bayán, those followers of the Báb who had rejected Bahá'u'lláh.

In a Tablet[30] addressed to 'Him Whom God shall make manifest', the Báb states: 'May the glances of Him Whom God shall make manifest illumine this letter at the primary school.'

Some of the Bábís argued that since this Tablet would have to be handed to 'Him Whom God shall make manifest' at the primary school, it followed that He would be a child when He received it. They therefore contended that since Bahá'u'lláh was even older than the Báb, He could not possibly fulfil the promises of the Báb. 'Abdu'l-Bahá in one of His Tablets[31] states that the school referred to is not a physical school. The school of 'Him Whom God shall make manifest' is not the school of the unlettered children. It is a spiritual school which is far beyond the reach of men and it is sanctified from the limitations of this contingent world. Bahá'u'lláh states that He had seen this Epistle, this gift of the Báb, in the School of God which is exalted above the comprehension of men.

Concerning the Tablet of the Báb and the school, Bahá'u'lláh reveals the following in the *Kitáb-i-Aqdas*:

> O Thou Supreme Pen! Move over the Tablet by the leave of Thy Lord, the Creator of the heavens. Call Thou then to mind the day when the Fountainhead of divine unity sought to attend the school which is sanctified of all save God, that perchance the righteous might become acquainted, to the extent of a needle's eye, with that which is concealed behind the veil of the inner mysteries of Thy Lord, the Almighty, the All-Knowing.
>
> Say, We, in truth, entered the school of inner meaning and exposition at a time when the minds of all that dwell on earth were wrapt in heedlessness. We beheld what the

* Bahá'u'lláh. See vol. 1, ch. 18.

Merciful Lord had revealed, accepted the gift He [the Báb] had offered Me of the verses of God, the Help in Peril, the Self-Subsisting, and hearkened to that to which He had attested in the Tablet. We, verily, are the Witness. We responded to His call at Our Own behest, and We are, in truth, the Ordainer.

O people of the Bayán! We entered the School of God when ye were slumbering on your couches, and perused the Tablet when ye were fast asleep. By the righteousness of God, the True One, We had read it before it was revealed, and ye were utterly unaware. Indeed Our knowledge had encompassed the Book when ye were yet unborn.

These utterances are revealed according to your measure, not to God's, and unto this beareth witness that which is enshrined in the knowledge of God, did ye but know. Unto this testifieth He Who is the Mouthpiece of God, could ye but understand. By the righteousness of God! Were We to lift the veil ye would swoon away. Take heed lest ye dispute with Him and His Cause. He hath indeed appeared in such wise as to encompass all things, whether of the past or of the future. Were We to speak forth at this time in the language of the dwellers of the Kingdom, We would say that God raised up this School ere the earth and the heavens were brought into being, and We entered it before the letters 'B' and 'E' were joined and knit together.*[32]

It is interesting to note, however, that when Bahá'u'lláh was resident in 'Iráq, He visited a school and while He was there, 'Abdu'l-Bahá came in and handed Him this Epistle of the Báb. 'Abdu'l-Bahá explains that this was not done by design but happened purely by accident.

* For the significance of the letters 'B' and 'E' see vol. 1, p. 30. (A.T.)

14

Kitáb-i-Aqdas. 2. A New World Order

In the *Kitáb-i-Aqdas*, Bahá'u'lláh refers to a new World Order which may be regarded as one of the fruits of His Revelation. The Báb in the Persian *Bayán* has revealed the following: 'Well is it with him who fixeth his gaze upon the order of Bahá'u'lláh and rendereth thanks unto his Lord! For He will assuredly be made manifest.' And these are the words of Bahá'u'lláh in the *Kitáb-i-Aqdas*:

> The world's equilibrium hath been upset through the vibrating influence of this most great, this new World Order. Mankind's ordered life hath been revolutionized through the agency of this unique, this wondrous System—the like of which mortal eyes have never witnessed.[1]

It was difficult to discern the upheaval in the life of man in 1873 when Bahá'u'lláh revealed these words. But today, a little over a hundred years later, it is evident that 'mankind's ordered life hath been revolutionized'. Describing the decline in the fortunes of humanity, Shoghi Effendi writes:

> Beset on every side by the cumulative evidences of disintegration, of turmoil and of bankruptcy, serious-minded men and women, in almost every walk of life, are beginning to doubt whether society, as it is now organized, can, through its unaided efforts, extricate itself from the slough into which it is steadily sinking. Every system, short of the unification of the human race, has been tried, repeatedly tried, and been found wanting. Wars again and

again have been fought, and conferences without number have met and deliberated. Treaties, pacts and covenants have been painstakingly negotiated, concluded and revised. Systems of government have been patiently tested, have been continually recast and superseded. Economic plans of reconstruction have been carefully devised, and meticulously executed. And yet crisis has succeeded crisis, and the rapidity with which a perilously unstable world is declining has been correspondingly accelerated. A yawning gulf threatens to involve in one common disaster both the satisfied and dissatisfied nations, democracies and dictatorships, capitalists and wage-earners, Europeans and Asiatics, Jew and Gentile, white and coloured. An angry Providence, the cynic might well observe, has abandoned a hapless planet to its fate, and fixed irrevocably its doom. Sore-tried and disillusioned, humanity has no doubt lost its orientation, and would seem to have lost as well its faith and hope. It is hovering, unshepherded and visionless, on the brink of disaster. A sense of fatality seems to pervade it. An ever-deepening gloom is settling on its fortunes as she recedes further and further from the outer fringes of the darkest zone of its agitated life and penetrates its very heart.[2]

The gloom described almost fifty years ago by Shoghi Effendi has deepened even further, and today the world is moving dangerously and at an alarming speed towards the brink of a catastrophe. But, alas, the generality of mankind, its leaders, its intellectuals, its seers and philosophers, have not as yet discovered the real cause for such a revolution in the life of man on this planet. Bahá'u'lláh describes the reason in these words:

A new life is, in this age, stirring within all the peoples of the earth; and yet none hath discovered its cause, or perceived its motive.[3]

To appreciate the reason for the turmoil of this age, the breaking up of the old order and the derangement of the world's equilibrium, we could do no better than to turn to nature and learn from its laws. Because the laws of nature and those of religion, as we have already stated, are closely linked together. Whatever happens in nature is a reflection of something spiritual.

Let us examine, for example, the principle of the conception of a new life and the growth of the embryo. We may study the condition of an egg before and after it is fertilized. Before the conception of the new life, the egg is in its normal state and contains good food. But when the new life begins to grow within it, the condition inside changes radically. The food turns bad and becomes corrupted. Yet the new life lives within this corrupted matter and feeds on it. At first this change is not obvious. But as the new life grows, the condition inside becomes more unstable. And there comes a time when the egg cannot remain whole anymore. Eventually, it breaks open; the young creature is born and the egg is reduced to a broken shell.

Exactly the same is happening in the world of humanity today. For thousands of years mankind's progress was very slow and limited, and few changes took place in the life of nations. One might say that before the coming of Bahá'u'lláh the peoples of the world had lived their lives in peace and tranquillity, compared to what came afterwards.

But over a hundred years ago when Bahá'u'lláh declared His mission, He sowed the seed of a new community in human society. At that moment a new life was conceived and the world has never been the same since—it has been revolutionized. With the coming of Bahá'u'lláh, as the process of growth and development of the embryonic institutions of His Faith was set in motion, so was the process of the extinction of the old order. The new world community is now growing within the womb of the old. The more it grows and becomes lively, the more will human society be plunged into the abyss of darkness and corruption. Its condition will continue to deteriorate until, as prophesied by Bahá'u'lláh over a hundred years ago, it will disintegrate like the egg in the above example. These are the words of Bahá'u'lláh written all those years ago, describing in clear terms the tormenting ordeals which humanity must experience at the time of the breaking up of the old order:

> The world is in travail and its agitation waxeth day by day. Its face is turned towards waywardness and unbelief. Such shall be its plight that to disclose it now would not be meet and seemly. Its perversity will long continue. And when the appointed hour is come, there shall suddenly appear that which shall cause the limbs of mankind to quake. Then and only then will the Divine Standard be unfurled and the Nightingale of Paradise warble its melody.[4]

In another instance, Bahá'u'lláh writes:

> After a time, all the governments on earth will change. Oppression will envelop the world. And following a universal convulsion, the sun of justice will rise from the horizon of the unseen realm.[5]

Shoghi Effendi describes the conception of the institutions of the Faith within the womb of human society in these words:

> Resplendent as has been the Age that has witnessed the inception of the Mission with which Bahá'u'lláh has been entrusted, the interval which must elapse ere that Age yields its choicest fruit must, it is becoming increasingly apparent, be overshadowed by such moral and social gloom as can alone prepare an unrepentant humanity for the prize she is destined to inherit.
>
> Into such a period we are now steadily and irresistibly moving. Amidst the shadows which are increasingly gathering about us we can faintly discern the glimmerings of Bahá'u'lláh's unearthly sovereignty appearing fitfully on the horizon of history . . .
>
> Deep as is the gloom that already encircles the world, the afflictive ordeals which that world is to suffer are still in preparation, nor can their blackness be as yet imagined. We

stand on the threshold of an age whose convulsions proclaim alike the death-pangs of the old order and the birth-pangs of the new. Through the generating influence of the Faith announced by Bahá'u'lláh this New World Order may be said to have been conceived. We can, at the present moment, experience its stirrings in the womb of a travailing age—an age waiting for the appointed hour at which it can cast its burden and yield its fairest fruit.

'The whole earth,' writes Bahá'u'lláh, 'is now in a state of pregnancy. The day is approaching when it will have yielded its noblest fruits, when from it will have sprung forth the loftiest trees, the most enchanting blossoms, the most heavenly blessings. Immeasurably exalted is the breeze that wafteth from the garment of thy Lord, the Glorified! For lo, it hath breathed its fragrance and made all things new! Well is it with them that comprehend . . .'

'The Call of God,' 'Abdu'l-Bahá has written, 'when raised, breathed a new life into the body of mankind, and infused a new spirit into the whole creation. It is for this reason that the world hath been moved to its depths, and the hearts and consciences of men been quickened. Erelong the evidences of this regeneration will be revealed, and the fast asleep will be awakened.'[6]

Although the immediate future is very dark and perilous, the outcome—the emergence of the Community of the Most Great Name—is glorious indeed. At present, the majority of the peoples of the world are either unaware of the existence of the embryonic institutions of the Faith, or cannot fully appreciate the tremendous potentialities which are latent within these institutions. They cannot fully understand their purpose and the role they are destined to play, in the fullness of time, by assuming their full share in the act of government of mankind.

The reason for this ignorance is, that although the Faith of Bahá'u'lláh is being increasingly proclaimed to humanity, the institutions of the Faith have not yet fully evolved to the point of being noticed by the people. In the passage quoted on page

311, Bahá'u'lláh prophesies that the exaltation of His Cause will take place only after dire tribulations and calamities have afflicted humanity. He states:

> And when the appointed hour is come, there shall suddenly appear that which shall cause the limbs of mankind to quake. Then and only then will the Divine Standard be unfurled and the Nightingale of Paradise warble its melody.

This prophecy has not yet been fulfilled. In the terms of the above analogy, the egg has not yet broken to cast its burden. The old order is still lingering on its death bed and the hour of the birth of the new has not yet struck.

The position of the Bahá'í community today is similar to the position of a gardener who claims to have a most beautiful garden full of flowers and trees. But when the enquirer visits the garden he sees no sign of vegetation whatsover. All that the gardener can do is to point to the seeds that he has sown and explain that the plants will emerge in time.

Only when the pangs of the birth of the new order of Bahá'u'lláh have been experienced and the embryonic institutions of His Faith have emerged, will the peoples of the world take notice of them and become aware of their potentialities. This emergence, closely linked with the rolling up of the old order, is only the beginning and must not be confused with that day of days in the distant future when Bahá'u'lláh's World Order will be established throughout the planet. The emergence of the embryonic institutions of the Faith is similar to the birth of a child. A newly born infant cannot use his limbs and organs effectively. A long time must elapse before it can reach the state of maturity and manhood. The emergence of the Bahá'í community from obscurity and the evolution of its institutions are therefore different from the emergence, in the distant future, of the World Order of Bahá'u'lláh.

Indeed, the rolling up of the present-day order and the trembling which, according to Bahá'u'lláh's pronouncement, must seize the limbs of mankind will, on the one hand, pave the way for the establishment of the Lesser Peace,* and on the other, witness the evolution of the Bahá'í national and local institutions of the Faith.

The blessings which the Lesser Peace will confer upon humanity will enable it to produce a new political structure freeing humanity from the curse of war. The social and humanitarian teachings and principles of Bahá'u'lláh which have already become the spirit of the age and which are being pursued by the enlightened peoples of the world will become incorporated in this political structure. Without being conscious of their origin, mankind will increasingly adopt these social teachings in every aspect of its life. These principles include the establishment of a world federated system, a world commonwealth, a world legislature, a world government backed by an international force, a world language, and other institutions as enunciated by Bahá'u'lláh in His teachings. The energies released by the Revelation of Bahá'u'lláh over a hundred years ago will to an increasing degree so penetrate within human society as to leave no other option for humanity but to incorporate such teachings as the equality of the sexes, compulsory education, the abolition of extremes of poverty and wealth and similar ones in all its institutions. This is already evidenced by the application of these Bahá'í principles within many progressive movements in the world.

This new form of government must emerge from amidst the ruins of a doomed and dilapidated present-day order, and govern humanity until such time as the nascent institutions of the Faith of Bahá'u'lláh will have attained their state of maturity. It is then that the Bahá'í World Order will be established in its great glory and this vision of Shoghi Effendi stretching far into the future will be realized.

To the general character, the implications and features of

* see pp. 125ff.

this world commonwealth, destined to emerge, sooner or later, out of the carnage, agony, and havoc of this great world convulsion, I have already referred in my previous communications. Suffice it to say that this consummation will, by its very nature, be a gradual process, and must, as Bahá'u'lláh has Himself anticipated, lead at first to the establishment of that Lesser Peace which the nations of the earth, as yet unconscious of His Revelation and yet unwittingly enforcing the general principles which He has enunciated, will themselves establish. This momentous and historic step, involving the reconstruction of mankind, as the result of the universal recognition of its oneness and wholeness, will bring in its wake the spiritualization of the masses, consequent to the recognition of the character, and the acknowledgement of the claims, of the Faith of Bahá'u'lláh—the essential condition to that ultimate fusion of all races, creeds, classes, and nations which must signalize the emergence of His New World Order.

Then will the coming of age of the entire human race be proclaimed and celebrated by all the peoples and nations of the earth. Then will the banner of the Most Great Peace be hoisted. Then will the world-wide sovereignty of Bahá'u'lláh—the Establisher of the Kingdom of the Father, foretold by the Son, and anticipated by the Prophets of God before Him and after Him—be recognized, acclaimed, and firmly established. Then will a world civilization be born, flourish, and perpetuate itself, a civilization with a fullness of life such as the world has never seen nor can as yet conceive. Then will the Everlasting Covenant be fulfilled in its completeness. Then will the promise enshrined in all the Books of God be redeemed, and all the prophecies uttered by the Prophets of old come to pass, and the vision of seers and poets be realized. Then will the planet, galvanized through the universal belief of its dwellers in one God, and their allegiance to one common Revelation, mirror, within the limitations imposed upon it, the effulgent glories of the sovereignty of Bahá'u'lláh, shining in the plenitude of its splendour in the Abhá Paradise, and be made the footstool of His Throne on high, and acclaimed as the earthly heaven, capable of fulfilling that ineffable destiny fixed for it, from time immemorial, by the love and wisdom of its Creator.[7]

The Bahá'í Administrative Order

The Local and the Universal Houses of Justice, the basic institutions of the Faith, were ordained by Bahá'u'lláh. These are His words in the *Kitáb-i-Aqdas* concerning the institution of the Local House of Justice:

> The Lord hath ordained that in every city a House of Justice be established wherein shall gather counsellors to the number of Bahá,* and should it exceed this number it does not matter . . . It behoveth them to be the trusted ones of the Merciful among men and to regard themselves as the guardians appointed of God for all that dwell on earth. It is incumbent upon them to take counsel together and to have regard for the interests of the servants of God, for His sake, even as they regard their own interests, and to choose that which is meet and seemly. Thus hath the Lord your God commanded you. Beware lest ye put away that which is clearly revealed in His Tablet. Fear God, O ye that perceive.[8]

Local Houses of Justice are already established all over the world in many cities and villages in their embryonic form known as Local Spiritual Assemblies. The growth and development of the Faith and its institutions follow the same pattern as any created thing which has an organic growth. Therefore, in the future, these bodies will be transformed into Houses of Justice as an infant is into an adult, and the passage of time will be needed to bring this about.

Present-day Local Spiritual Assemblies are instituted in localities where there are nine or more adult believers resident. These bodies are elected annually by every adult member of the Bahá'í community, and are charged with the responsibility

* The numerical value of the word 'Bahá' in Arabic is nine. (A.T.)

of directing the affairs of the community in accordance with certain principles laid down in the Writings of the Faith. Bahá'í elections, carried out in a prayerful attitude, are spiritual in nature, and vastly different from any system in existence today.* So is Bahá'í consultation which, as described in a previous chapter,† is designed to take place in an atmosphere of love and unity.

One of the unique features of the Dispensation of Bahá'u'lláh is that He has attached great importance to consultation in every sphere of human activity. Bahá'í communities and institutions, whether local, national or international, function through Bahá'í consultation. These bodies not only consult on community affairs, but are empowered also to deal with personal matters affecting the lives of individual believers. However, Bahá'u'lláh has not limited consultation to the institutions of His Faith. He has stressed the importance of consultation on personal matters with friends and experts. These are some of the words of Bahá'u'lláh gleaned from His Writings on this subject:

> The Great Being saith: The heaven of divine wisdom is illumined with the two luminaries of consultation and compassion. Take ye counsel together in all matters, inasmuch as consultation is the lamp of guidance which leadeth the way, and is the bestower of understanding.[9]

> Consultation bestoweth greater awareness and transmuteth conjecture into certitude. It is a shining light which, in a dark world, leadeth the way and guideth. For everything there is and will continue to be a station of perfection and maturity. The maturity of the gift of understanding is made manifest through consultation.[10]

> In all things it is necessary to consult. This matter should be forcibly stressed by thee, so that consultation may be

* For more information see *Principles of Bahá'í Administration.*

† see pp. 49–51.

> observed by all. The intent of what hath been revealed from the Pen of the Most High is that consultation may be fully carried out among the friends, inasmuch as it is and will always be a cause of awareness and of awakening and a source of good and well-being.[11]

'Abdu'l-Bahá too has written a great deal on this subject. These are only two passages out of many:

> Settle all things, both great and small, by consultation. Without prior consultation, take no important step in your own personal affairs. Concern yourselves with one another. Help along one another's projects and plans. Grieve over one another. Let none in the whole country go in need. Befriend one another until ye become as a single body, one and all . . .[12]

> The purpose of consultation is to show that the views of several individuals are assuredly preferable to one man, even as the power of a number of men is of course greater than the power of one man. Thus consultation is acceptable in the presence of the Almighty, and hath been enjoined upon the believers, so that they may confer upon ordinary and personal matters, as well as on affairs which are general in nature and universal.
>
> For instance, when a man hath a project to accomplish, should he consult with some of his brethren, that which is agreeable will of course be investigated and unveiled to his eyes, and the truth will be disclosed. Likewise on a higher level, should the people of a village consult one another about their affairs, the right solution will certainly be revealed. In like manner, the members of each profession, such as in industry, should consult, and those in commerce should similarly consult on business affairs. In short, consultation is desirable and acceptable in all things and on all issues.[13]

Local Spiritual Assemblies are the bed-rock upon which the National Spiritual Assemblies, designated by 'Abdu'l-Bahá as

'Secondary Houses of Justice', are established. These national bodies are today instituted in most countries of the world and are empowered to 'direct, unify, coordinate and stimulate the activities of the individuals as well as local Assemblies within their jurisdiction'.[14] Their members are also given the responsibility of electing The Universal House of Justice, the Supreme Body of the Faith of Bahá'u'lláh and regarded as the apex of the Bahá'í Administrative Order. This august institution, which was elected for the first time in 1963, is ordained by Bahá'u'lláh with the assurance of divine guidance. He has conferred infallibility upon its decisions and given it the authority to enact laws which are not specifically revealed by Him.

In the *Ishráqát* (Splendours) revealed in the latter part of Bahá'u'lláh's life He declares:

> This passage, now written by the pen of Glory, is accounted as part of the Most Holy Book: The men of God's House of Justice have been charged with the affairs of the people. They, in truth, are the Trustees of God among His servants and the daysprings of authority in His countries.
>
> O people of God! That which traineth the world is Justice, for it is upheld by two pillars, reward and punishment. These two pillars are the sources of life to the world. Inasmuch as for each day there is a new problem and for every problem an expedient solution, such affairs should be referred to the House of Justice that the members thereof may act according to the needs and requirements of the time. They that, for the sake of God, arise to serve His Cause, are the recipients of divine inspiration from the unseen Kingdom. It is incumbent upon all to be obedient unto them. All matters of State should be referred to the House of Justice, but acts of worship must be observed according to that which God hath revealed in His Book.[15]

One of the basic differences between the institutions of the old order and those of the Administrative Order of Bahá'u'lláh is that the latter are animated by the spirit of the Cause of God, whereas the former are as bodies without spirit. The divinely-founded order is alive and growing; the old order is disintegrating and its ability to solve the problems of the world is constantly declining. A man-made institution, to carry out its tasks successfully, must function with vigour and health. Should any of its members fail in the conduct of affairs, the work of the whole system may well become ineffective. It may be likened to a machine which cannot operate unless all its component parts function efficiently, for the failure of one part can paralyse or even wreck the machine as a whole.

In contrast to such a machine, which is lifeless and depends for its proper functioning on perfect coordination between its parts, we may observe that a young and living organism grows healthily without being perfect, and before its faculties are fully matured. A child, for example, can flourish and be active while possessing many imperfections due to immaturity. It has a vigour and a vitality that no lifeless object can rival. Although it makes mistakes, upsets the order of things and creates disturbances around itself, yet no one demands maturity and perfection from it, and no one is unduly concerned about its childish behaviour. For it is normal that as the child grows up it will cease to act immaturely, and in the fullness of time will acquire wisdom and other perfections.

True Bahá'ís understand the nature of their national and local institutions to be organic. They know that these bodies, animated by the spirit of the Cause, are in their infancy. They recognize that these assemblies, the embryos of future National and Local Houses of Justice, may make wrong decisions at times and may on occasion act unjustly, but in spite of these shortcomings they are pulsating with life and growing in strength and vitality day by day. Far from attacking and criticizing them, Bahá'ís rally around them with loving care and pride. For they know that Bahá'u'lláh has vouchsafed His protection to the embryonic institutions of His Faith. And they realize that like any living organism, the local and national institutions of the Faith must have their growing pains until the problems now facing them will gradually disappear.

Though insignificant in the eyes of the outside world and relatively small in numbers, these local and national bodies have already demonstrated their ability to forge ahead, overcome difficult problems, remove apparently insurmountable obstacles, win great victories for the Cause and grow steadily to a point where, in the fullness of time, they will establish the foundations of justice and love for the peoples of the world.

15

Kitáb-i-Aqdas. 3. Divine Education

There are many exhortations in the *Kitáb-i-Aqdas* calling the believers to live a saintly life and to adorn themselves with the ornament of goodly character and divine virtues.

There are many people, not Bahá'ís, who have been brought up to live a good life in their own traditions. They are trained from childhood to be courteous, kind and loving. They evince many good qualities which are inculcated in them until they have become second nature. They perform good deeds habitually. Such people merit the highest praise. But because they are deprived of the spirit of faith borne by God's Messenger to this age, they are like exquisite lamps which have not been lit. To live one's life as a Bahá'í is different in so far as the heart is illumined with the love of Bahá'u'lláh. It is this love which makes the difference and which enables the believer to mirror forth the teachings of Bahá'u'lláh to others. Without this it is impossible for a Bahá'í to achieve all that he could in this life. Indeed, the story of every religion is written in the language of love. Some people recognize Bahá'u'lláh intellectually; this is not sufficient. Not until the individual becomes a true lover can he acquire the spiritual capacity to serve the Cause of God fully in this day.

'Immerse Yourselves in the Ocean of My Words'

But like most things in this life which grow, there is always a beginning to this love for Bahá'u'lláh. When the individual embraces the Cause, the spark of faith appears in his heart. He then begins his journey of love towards Bahá'u'lláh. The candle of his heart is then just lighted. But this love must be allowed to grow, this light must be allowed to become a great fire.

When a person finds a friend he likes, the only way by which he can strengthen the ties of friendship and love is to get to know his friend and become more intimate with him. Should he stay away and remain aloof, the friendship will not endure. The journey of a lover to his beloved may begin with mere acquaintance, but it can develop into a deep love as a result of close association and a selfless devotion.

Similarly, a believer must continue his journey of love to Bahá'u'lláh. The most important step in achieving this is to read the words of Bahá'u'lláh in order to commune with Him and become attracted to His Holy Person. Indeed, this is one of His commandments in the *Kitáb-i-Aqdas*. He enjoins His followers to recite His words* twice a day, in the morning and the evening, and states that those who do not have failed to fulfil their pledge to the Covenant of God. These are His words in that Book:

> Recite ye the verses of God every morning and evening. Whoso reciteth them not hath truly failed to fulfil his pledge to the Covenant of God and His Testament and whoso in this day turneth away therefrom, hath indeed turned away from God since time immemorial. Fear ye God, O concourse of My servants.
>
> Take heed lest excessive reading and too many acts of piety in the daytime and in the night season make you vainglorious. Should a person recite but a single verse from the Holy Writings in a spirit of joy and radiance, this would be better for him than reciting wearily all the Scriptures of God, the Help in Peril, the Self-Subsisting. Recite ye the verses of God in such measure that ye be not overtaken with fatigue or boredom. Burden not your souls so as to cause exhaustion and weigh them down, but rather endeavour to

* The reading of the words of Bahá'u'lláh is not to be confused with saying of prayers which is a different commandment altogether.

> lighten them, that they may soar on the wings of revealed Verses unto the dawning-place of His signs. This is conducive to nearer access unto God, were ye to comprehend.[1]

In another passage in the *Kitáb-i-Aqdas* He states:

> Immerse yourselves in the ocean of My words, that ye may unravel its secrets, and discover all the pearls of wisdom that lie hid in its depths.[2]

The reading of the words of Bahá'u'lláh exerts the same influence upon the soul as food does to the body. It enables the soul to draw nigh to Bahá'u'lláh and become filled with His love. Without regular reading of the Writings twice a day, a Bahá'í cannot grow spiritually and there is no alternative to compensate for this loss.

In the *Kitáb-i-Aqdas*, Bahá'u'lláh states that there is no merit in reading His words when tired. He says that to read a few lines with a spirit of joy and fragrance is better than to read a whole book when depressed and weary. This commandment is very much in tune with the law of nature which advocates that a person eat his food only when he is hungry. Another similarity is that in nature one must eat food regularly every day. To eat once in a lifetime is not sufficient. It is the same with reading the Words of God, which is the food for the spirit. To read the Holy Writings once in a while is not enough. As ordained by Bahá'u'lláh, the individual must, if he is to grow spiritually, read His words which are recorded in His Tablets twice every day. These words with all their vivifying forces must then be allowed to penetrate the heart and to strengthen one's faith.

The reading of the words of Bahá'u'lláh not only enables the faithful to increase his love for Him every day, but also deepens him in the Faith as well.

Deepening in the Faith is often misunderstood. It is taken to imply participation in study classes, courses, and intellectual discussions. Often in these discussions the individual may inject his own ideas, as well as modern theories, into the teachings of Bahá'u'lláh, and make the Faith appear as complicated as a highly involved scientific theory. In fact, the study of the Faith is so simple that any person with common sense, even if he lacks education, can fully understand its truth, provided his heart is pure. If we look at the talks of 'Abdu'l-Bahá in the Western world we notice how in simple language He explained profound subjects.

Real deepening occurs when the believer reads the Writings with the eyes of faith knowing that he is reading the Word of God, not the words of men—a Word which is charged with tremendous potency. Deepening also takes place when the believer associates with someone who is on fire with the love of Bahá'u'lláh. The very company of such a person increases one's faith in God. Bahá'u'lláh states in the *Hidden Words*: '. . . He that seeketh to commune with God, let him betake himself to the companionship of His loved ones; and he that desireth to hearken unto the word of God, let him give ear to the words of His chosen ones.' This is why those who meet a true servant of Bahá'u'lláh often become filled with a new spirit.

In the Heroic Age of the Faith the believers were deepened in faith by meeting together and sharing their knowledge and love of Bahá'u'lláh. One devoted Bahá'í who had been in His presence, whose heart was filled with His love, or who had received Tablets from Him, could impart his fire and faith as well as his knowledge and understanding to others who associated with him. In those days believers did not have access to all the Writings and often did not know much about the teachings of Bahá'u'lláh. But their hearts were so filled with His love that a great many laid down their lives in His path.

There may be a tendency today to become too academic, even mechanical, in the study of the Faith. A purely intellectual approach may so cloud the heart that the rays of the Sun of Truth are unable to shine within it. What the believer needs, in addition to knowledge of the Faith, is to open his heart to the influences of the Revelation of Bahá'u'lláh, to commune with His spirit, rejoice in His Name and seek especially the companionship of His true lovers. Without the infusion of the spirit of faith in his life, without turning with his heart in humbleness to Bahá'u'lláh, he cannot deepen himself in the Cause, because the knowledge of God is first reflected within the heart of man, and then his intellect will grasp it. This is clear in the Writings.

And now let there be a word of warning concerning this vital subject. Reading the writings of Bahá'u'lláh, important as it is, can never be conducive to spiritual progress unless it is combined with service to the Cause. Should a person take food regularly and in abundance, but fail to move about and use his muscles every day, he would soon become an invalid. In the same way, the study of the Writings must be accompanied by deeds, deeds which are enjoined by Bahá'u'lláh in His teachings and laws.

If the individual who has recognized the station of Bahá'u'lláh immerses himself in the ocean of His words, if he opens his heart to the influences of His Revelation, if he associates with devoted Bahá'ís who are on fire with the Faith and eschews fellowship with the ungodly,* and if he arises to serve the Cause, then his love for Bahá'u'lláh will increase day by day, and he will become a deep Bahá'í.

Education of Children

Bahá'u'lláh in the *Kitáb-i-Aqdas* has placed an enormous responsibility upon parents for the proper upbringing and education of their children. These are His words in that book:

Unto every father hath been enjoined the instruction of his

* A person who lives his life contrary to the teachings of God. He may profess belief in God, while many who regard themselves as agnostics or atheists may not be ungodly in reality.

son and daughter in the art of reading and writing and in all that hath been laid down in the Holy Tablet. He that putteth away that which is commanded unto him, the Trustees are then to take from him that which is required for their instruction, if he be wealthy, and if not the matter devolveth upon the House of Justice. Verily, have We made it a shelter for the poor and needy. He that bringeth up his son or the son of another, it is as though he hath brought up a son of Mine; upon him rest My Glory, My loving kindness, My Mercy, that have compassed the world.[3]

'Abdu'l-Bahá in one of His Tablets[4] states that if the parents fail in the proper upbringing of their children, they have committed a sin that God cannot forgive.

Bringing up children, according to Bahá'u'lláh, is not merely teaching them good manners and arranging for their education. It has far-reaching implications. Bahá'í education consists of academic as well as spiritual education. The former can be acquired in all the schools of the world. The latter, which from the Bahá'í point of view is more important, is the acquiring of the knowledge of God and His Manifestations, the understanding of the mysteries of creation, the becoming well versed in the teachings of Bahá'u'lláh, the acquiring of good character, and the becoming equipped for serving the world of humanity.

The following words of Bahá'u'lláh gleaned from His Writings demonstrate the importance which is attached to the upbringing of children:

> Knowledge is as wings to man's life, and a ladder for his ascent. Its acquisition is incumbent upon everyone. The knowledge of such sciences, however, should be acquired as can profit the peoples of the earth, and not those which begin with words and end with words . . . In truth, knowledge is a veritable treasure for man, and a source of glory, of bounty, of joy, of exaltation, of cheer and gladness unto him.[5]

> Schools must first train the children in the principles of religion, so that the Promise and the Threat recorded in the Books of God may prevent them from the things forbidden and adorn them with the mantle of the commandments; but this in such a measure that it may not injure the children by resulting in ignorant fanaticism and bigotry.[6]

> We prescribe unto all men that which will lead to the exaltation of the Word of God amongst His servants, and likewise, to the advancement of the world of being and the uplift of souls. To this end, the greatest means is education of the child. To this must each and all hold fast. We have verily laid this charge upon you in manifold Tablets as well as in My Most Holy Book. Well is it with him who deferreth thereto.
>
> We ask of God that He will assist each and every one to obey this inescapable command that hath appeared and been caused to descend through the Pen of the Ancient of Days.[7]

'Abdu'l-Bahá has also stressed the importance of child education in many of His Tablets. The following are a few examples:

> It is for this reason that, in this new cycle, education and training are recorded in the Book of God as obligatory and not voluntary. That is, it is enjoined upon the father and mother, as a duty, to strive with all effort to train the daughter and the son, to nurse them from the breast of knowledge and to rear them in the bosom of sciences and arts. Should they neglect this matter, they shall be held responsible and worthy of reproach in the presence of the stern Lord.[8]

> . . . from the very beginning, the children must receive divine education and must continually be reminded to remember their God. Let the love of God pervade their inmost being, commingled with their mother's milk.[9]

My wish is that these children should receive a Bahá'í education, so that they may progress both here and in the Kingdom, and rejoice thy heart.

In a time to come, morals will degenerate to an extreme degree. It is essential that children be reared in the Bahá'í way, that they may find happiness both in this world and the next. If not, they shall be beset by sorrows and troubles, for human happiness is founded upon spiritual behaviour.[10]

The Bahá'í teachings on child education attach great importance to the role which a mother plays in bringing up children. These are the words of 'Abdu'l-Bahá concerning this vital role of mothers:

Today it is obligatory for the loved ones of God, and their imperative duty, to educate the children in reading, writing, the various branches of knowledge, and the expansion of consciousness, that on all levels they may go forward day by day.

The mother is the first teacher of the child. For children, at the beginning of life, are fresh and tender as a young twig, and can be trained in any fashion you desire. If you rear the child to be straight, he will grow straight, in perfect symmetry. It is clear that the mother is the first teacher and that it is she who establisheth the character and conduct of the child.

Wherefore, O ye loving mothers, know ye that in God's sight, the best of all ways to worship Him is to educate the children and train them in all the perfections of humankind; and no nobler deed than this can be imagined . . .[11]

One important aspect of the role of the mother in child education and spiritual training is seen in the emphasis which the Bahá'í teachings place on the education of girls. For one day they will become mothers and the first educator of the child is the mother.

These and other basic teachings on child education will enable future educationalists to formulate a programme of

Bahá'í education. As human society inclines itself more and more towards Bahá'í ideals, these teachings will be adopted by mankind. The following was written on behalf of Shoghi Effendi, the Guardian of the Bahá'í Faith, in answer to a question concerning the Bahá'í educational programme:

> You have asked him [Shoghi Effendi] for detailed information concerning the Bahá'í educational programme; there is as yet no such thing as a Bahá'í curriculum, and there are no Bahá'í publications exclusively devoted to this subject, since the teachings of Bahá'u'lláh and 'Abdu'l-Bahá do not present a definite and detailed educational system, but simply offer certain basic principles and set forth a number of teaching ideals that should guide future Bahá'í educationalists in their efforts to formulate an adequate teaching curriculum which would be in full harmony with the spirit of the Bahá'í Teachings, and would thus meet the requirements and needs of the modern age.
>
> These basic principles are available in the sacred writings of the Cause, and should be carefully studied, and gradually incorporated in various college and university programmes. But the task of formulating a system of education which would be officially recognized by the Cause, and enforced as such throughout the Bahá'í world is one which the present-day generation of believers cannot obviously undertake, and which has to be gradually accomplished by Bahá'í scholars and educationalists of the future.[12]

Educating children and youth is of such paramount importance in the Bahá'í teachings that Bahá'u'lláh has praised the work of teachers and educationalists very highly. The teaching profession is held in such high esteem by Him that in the *Kitáb-i-Aqdas* He has ordained, in cases of intestacy, for an inheritance to be divided among seven categories of people,[13] all from within the family except the last which is the teacher or teachers. In His Writings He has showered His favours and bounties in abundance upon those teachers who have recognized His station and are engaged in both spiritual and academic education. We have already cited one example of this.*

'Abdu'l-Bahá likewise has praised the station of teachers who are devoted to their profession. In a Tablet He describes their service as true worship of God, and states that they are the spiritual fathers of the children whom they teach, and therefore their work is highly meritorious in the sight of God.[14]

Teaching the Cause

In many of His Tablets, Bahá'u'lláh has enjoined upon His followers to teach His Faith to the peoples of the world. In the *Kitáb-i-Aqdas* too He exhorts the faithful to arise in the service of His Cause and refers to teaching as the crowning glory of every righteous deed. As stated in the previous volume, the primary purpose of teaching is to bring a soul to its God, and it is therefore regarded by Bahá'u'lláh as the 'most meritorious of all deeds'.†

The prerequisites of teaching are to be found in the Writings of Bahá'u'lláh and 'Abdu'l-Bahá, and Shoghi Effendi has enumerated some of them in his letter entitled *The Advent of Divine Justice*.[15] They may be summarized in a few words: 'Living one's life in accordance with Bahá'í teachings.' Bahá'u'lláh in one of His Tablets states:

> God hath prescribed unto every one the duty of teaching His Cause. Whoever ariseth to discharge this duty, must needs, ere he proclaimeth His Message, adorn himself with the ornament of an upright and praiseworthy character, so that his words may attract the hearts of such as are receptive to his call. Without it, he can never hope to influence his hearers.[16]

This statement leaves no room for doubt, for Bahá'u'lláh says:

* see pp. 90–91.

† see vol. 2, pp. 91–106.

'Without it, he can never hope to influence his hearers.' The word 'never' is very emphatic and rules out any other method. In numerous other Tablets Bahá'u'lláh has revealed similar statements.

'Abdu'l-Bahá in a Tablet writes:

> The aim is this: The intention of the teacher must be pure, his heart independent, his spirit attracted, his thought at peace, his resolution firm, his magnanimity exalted and in the love of God a shining torch. Should he become as such, his sanctified breath will even affect the rock; otherwise there will be no result whatsoever.[17]

The emphasis of the last sentence is clear: 'otherwise there will be no result whatsoever.' There are numerous Tablets of 'Abdu'l-Bahá with similar conclusions.

Shoghi Effendi has also drawn our attention to this truth in many of his letters. To cite one celebrated passage:

> Not by the force of numbers, not by the mere exposition of a set of new and noble principles, not by an organized campaign of teaching—no matter how worldwide and elaborate in its character—not even by the staunchness of our faith or the exaltation of our enthusiasm, can we ultimately hope to vindicate in the eyes of a critical and sceptical age the supreme claim of the Abhá Revelation. One thing and only one thing will unfailingly and alone secure the undoubted triumph of this sacred Cause, namely, the extent to which our own inner life and private character mirror forth in their manifold aspects the splendour of those eternal principles proclaimed by Bahá'u'lláh.[18]

Here Shoghi Effendi leaves no alternative to this vital prerequisite for teaching, for he says (and let us note his double emphasis): 'One thing and only one thing will unfailingly and alone secure the undoubted triumph of this sacred Cause . . .'

Having discussed one of the most important prerequisites for teaching, let us now examine the work of teaching itself.

There are no set methods or procedures, although we have been given certain principles and guide-lines by the Author of the Faith and by 'Abdu'l-Bahá and Shoghi Effendi. These principles and guides are at variance with standards and methods current outside the Faith, where frequently every expedient measure is used to influence people and convert them to various ideologies. The Cause of Bahá'u'lláh is founded on the truth of God's Revelation, and truth cannot be clothed in false standards. It cannot employ the techniques of salesmanship, propaganda, expediency and compromise. The methods used in the commercial world to attract people to new ideas, such as extravagant and sensational publicity based on slogans, extreme statements and similar gimmicks, are all alien to the Cause of God.

In his teaching work a Bahá'í presents the Message of Bahá'u'lláh as one would offer a gift to a king. Since his primary object in teaching is not to increase numbers,* but rather to bring a soul to its God, he ought to approach his fellow men with feelings of love and humility, and above all take to them the transforming power of Bahá'u'lláh and nothing of himself. Indeed, if he tries to project himself, by impressing upon the listener his knowledge and accomplishments, and aims to establish the ascendancy of his arguments while teaching the Faith, then the power of Bahá'u'lláh cannot reach him.

Success in teaching depends on one's ability and readiness to draw from the power of Bahá'u'lláh. There is no alternative. If the believer does not open the way for Bahá'u'lláh through his love for Him, by his life and by teaching His Cause with devotion, His confirmations and assistance cannot reach him, and he will fail in his service to Him. Those who rank foremost among Bahá'í teachers were always conscious of the presence of Bahá'u'lláh at every stage of their teaching activities. It was because of the consciousness of His presence that they were enabled to approach with genuine love and humility those who

* see vol. 2, p. 94.

were seeking the truth, attracting them with the warmth of their faith and the creative power of their words. It was this consciousness which enabled them to radiate the glory of the new-born Faith of God, to demonstrate its truth, to promote its interests, to withstand the onslaught of its enemies and to win imperishable victories for their Lord.

Bahá'u'lláh often counselled His followers how to teach the Faith. For example, He directed Ḥájí Muḥammad-Ṭáhir-i-Málmírí, when he was leaving His presence, to engage in teaching the Cause in his native city of Yazd and gave him some instructions as to how to teach. Foremost among these instructions was to pray for the seeker and urge him also to pray so that the confirmations of God might reach him and open his eyes to the truth of the Cause. Another counsel was to begin teaching with the account of the history of the religions of the past and their Founders, similar to the accounts given in the *Kitáb-i-Íqán*. This would enable the enquirer to get an insight into his own religion that he might recognize the truth and the reality of the Founder of his own Faith. When this stage was reached, the individual would be ready to appreciate and understand the Cause of God for this day.*

To cite another example: there is a Tablet[19] from Bahá'u'lláh in which Fáris† (the Christian Syrian who embraced the Faith in Alexandria) is exhorted to teach with wisdom. He counsels him not to disclose to people everything about the Cause at first, but rather to teach them little by little until they are ready to absorb more. He likens this process to feeding infants who need to be given a little milk at a time until they grow in strength and are able to digest other food. This exhortation of Bahá'u'lláh is the basis of teaching the Cause of God. The principles involved are very similar to those which a school-teacher employs in teaching his pupils little by little and in accordance with their capacity. Before teaching the Cause to any person, it is important to know his background and

* see vol. 1, p. 161.

† see pp. 5–11.

capacity. The most successful teachers are those who after familiarizing themselves with the beliefs and ideas of an individual, reveal the truths of the Faith gradually to him, but what little they impart is the correct remedy and is so potent as to influence and stimulate the soul and enable it to take a step forward and become ready to absorb more.

Ḥájí Mírzá Ḥaydar-'Alí, the celebrated Bahá'í teacher to whose outstanding services we have already referred, has left to posterity the following account of one of his memorable interviews with Bahá'u'lláh in 'Akká, in the course of which He spoke these words about teaching the Cause of God:

> The way to teach is to have a pleasing disposition and to deal with people in a spirit of loving-kindness. One must acknowledge whatever the other person says, even if it is vain imaginings, beliefs which are the result of blind imitation, or absurd talk. One should avoid in engaging in arguments or adducing proofs which bring out stubbornness and contention in the other person. This is because he finds himself defeated, and this will lead to his becoming more veiled from the truth and will add to his waywardness.
>
> The right way is to acknowledge the other person's statements and then present him with the alternative point of view and invite him to examine it to see whether it is true or false. Of course, when it is presented to him with courtesy, affection and loving-kindness, he will hear and will not be thinking in terms of defence, to find answers and look for proofs. He will acknowledge and admit the points. When the person realizes that the purpose behind discussions is not wrangling or the winning of arguments, but rather to convey the truth and to reveal human qualities and divine perfections, he will of course show fairness. His inner eyes and ears and heart will open and, through the grace of God, he will become a new creation and will possess new eyes and new ears.
>
> Bahá'u'lláh spoke a great deal about the evils of controversial argument and aiming to become a winner in

discussion. He then said, 'The Most Great Branch* will listen to any absurd talk with such attentiveness that the person concerned believes that He is deriving enlightenment from him. However, little by little, and in a way that the person cannot realize, He bestows upon him a new vision and a new understanding.'†[20]

The talks of 'Abdu'l-Bahá in the West provide the best example of wisdom in teaching. He addressed audiences who were almost alien to the history and genesis of the Faith and unfamiliar with the claims and the station of its Founder. Yet He disclosed to them with simplicity and brevity only those essential truths which they were capable of understanding and which constituted the first stepping-stones for their eventual recognition of the stupendous Message of Bahá'u'lláh. He clearly avoided at that early stage any elaboration on the many implications of the station of Bahá'u'lláh and His Revelation as well as the unfoldment of His laws and His World Order in the future. Instead, He bestowed upon every one who had the capacity a measure of His all-embracing love, which animated and sustained those few who embraced the Faith in the West.

Perhaps it is a temptation for a Bahá'í teacher, especially if he is a knowledgeable one, to pour out upon a seeker all his knowledge, and bombard him with a series of profound utterances and lengthy discussions with the aim of proving the truth of his own arguments. When this happens it blocks the way for the power of Bahá'u'lláh to reach the heart of the seeker and enlighten him with the light of faith.

In following the footsteps of the Exemplar of the Faith of Bahá'u'lláh we may observe that when someone asked 'Abdu'l-Bahá a question, He often did not give the person all the answers. He gently prepared him to understand the subject. For example, He talked about something which

* 'Abdu'l-Bahá.

† These are not the exact words of Bahá'u'lláh but convey the purport of His talk.

seemed unrelated to the question but in the end led him to discover the truth. One may cite the example of Howard Colby Ives, a Unitarian Minister in the United States who became attracted to 'Abdu'l-Bahá when He visited that country, and eventually became an ardent believer. One gathers from reading his fascinating chronicles *Portals to Freedom* that 'Abdu'l-Bahá led him to the path of truth very gently and slowly. The following story is recorded in that book:

> In all of my many opportunities of meeting, of listening to and talking with 'Abdu'l-Bahá I was impressed, and constantly more deeply impressed, with His method of teaching souls. That is the word. He did not attempt to reach the mind alone. He sought the soul, the reality of everyone He met. Oh, He could be logical, even scientific in His presentation of an argument, as He demonstrated constantly in the many addresses I have heard Him give and the many more I have read. But it was not the logic of the schoolman, not the science of the class room. His lightest word, His slightest association with a soul was shot through with an illuminating radiance which lifted the hearer to a higher plane of consciousness. Our hearts burned within us when He spoke. And He never argued, of course. Nor did He press a point. He left one free. There was never an assumption of authority, rather He was ever the personification of humility. He taught 'as if offering a gift to a king'. He never told me what I should do, beyond suggesting that what I was doing was right. Nor did He ever tell me what I should believe. He made Truth and Love so beautiful and royal that the heart perforce did reverence. He showed me by His voice, manner, bearing, smile, how I should *be*, knowing that out of the pure soil of being the good fruit of deeds and words would surely spring.
>
> There was a strange, awe-inspiring mingling of humility and majesty, relaxation and power in His slightest word or gesture which made me long to understand its source. What made Him so different, so immeasurably superior to any other man I had ever met?[21]

Another story which throws light on the subject is the following by Colby Ives:

> So one cold Spring day, a strong east wind blowing, I made a special journey to ask 'Abdu'l-Bahá about renunciation. I found the house at Ninety-sixth Street almost deserted. It seemed that 'Abdu'l-Bahá was spending a day or two at the home of one of the friends on Seventy-eighth Street and so I walked there and found Him on the point of returning to the home I had just left. But I was too intent on my mission to allow difficulties to interfere. I sought one of the Persian friends and, pointing to the passage in the little volume I carried in my pocket, I asked him if he would request 'Abdu'l-Bahá to speak to me for a few moments on this subject, and I read it to him so that there should be no mistake: 'Prevent me not from turning to the Horizon of renunciation.'
>
> Returning, he handed me the book saying that 'Abdu'l-Bahá requested that I walk with Him back to Ninety-sixth Street and He would talk with me on the way.
>
> I recall that there was quite a little procession of us, a dozen or so, mostly composed of the Persian friends but a few others; Lua Getsinger was one, I remember. The east wind was penetrating. I buttoned my coat closely with a little shiver. But 'Abdu'l-Bahá strode along with his 'abá (cloak) floating in the wind. He looked at me as we walked together at the head of the little group, with a slightly quizzical glance: He said that I seemed cold, a slightly amused glance accompanying the words, and I unaccountably felt a little disturbed. Why should I not feel cold? Could one be expected to live even above the weather? But this slight remark was indicative. Always His slightest word affected me as a summons. 'Come up higher!' He seemed to say.
>
> As we walked a few paces ahead of the others He talked at length about Horizons. Of how the Sun of Reality, like the physical sun, rose at different points, the Sun of Moses at one point, the Sun of Jesus at another, the Sun of Muḥammad, the Sun of Bahá'u'lláh at still others. But

always the same Sun though the rising points varied greatly. Always we must look for the light of the Sun, He said, and not keep our eyes so firmly fixed on its last point of rising that we fail to see its glory when it rises in the new Spiritual Springtime. Once or twice He stopped and, with His stick, drew on the sidewalk an imaginary horizon and indicated the rising points of the sun. A strange sight it must have been to the casual passer-by.

I was greatly disappointed. I had heard Him speak on this subject and had read about it in *Some Answered Questions*. It was not of horizons I wanted to hear, but of renunciation. And I was deeply depressed also because I felt that He should have known my desire for light on this subject, and responded to my longing even if I had not been so explicit in my request; but I *had* been most explicit. As we approached our destination He became silent. My disappointment had long since merged into great content. Was it not enough to be with Him? What, after all, could He tell me about renunciation that was not already in my own heart? Perhaps the way to learn about it was by doing, and I might begin by giving up the longing to have Him talk to me about it. Truly, as the outer silence deepened, my heart burned within me as He talked with me on the way.

We came at last to the steps leading up to the entrance door. 'Abdu'l-Bahá paused with one foot resting on the lower step while the little group slowly passed Him and entered the house. 'Abdu'l-Bahá made as if to follow, but instead He turned and, looking down at me from the little elevation of the step, with that subtle meaning in eyes and voice which seemed to accompany His slightest word, and which to me was always so unfathomable and so alluring: He said that I must always remember that this is a day of great things, very great things.

I was speechless. It was not for me to answer. I did not have the faintest inkling of what lay behind the words, the resonant voice, that penetrating glance. Then He turned and again made as if to ascend but again He paused and turned His now luminous face towards me. My foot was raised to follow but as He turned, I, of course, paused also and hung uncertainly between rest and motion.

He repeated, saying to me *so* impressively, *so* earnestly, that I must never forget this, that *this is a day for very great things.*

What could He mean? What deep significance lay behind these simple words? Why should He speak so to me? Had it anything to do with that still alluring thought of renunciation?

Again 'Abdu'l-Bahá turned to ascend and I made to follow; but for the third time He paused and, turning, as it seemed, the full light of His spirit upon me, He said again, but this time in what seemed like a voice of thunder, with literally flashing eyes and emphatically raised hand: that I should remember His words that This is a Day for *very great things*—VERY GREAT THINGS. These last three words rang out like a trumpet call. The long, deserted city block seemed to echo them. I was overwhelmed. I seemed to dwindle, almost to shrivel, where I stood, as that beautifully dominant figure, that commanding and appealing voice, surrounded me like a sea, and blotted out for the moment, at least, all the petty world and my petty self with it. Who and what was I to be summoned to accomplish great things, very great things? I did not even know what things *were* great in this world awry with misbegotten emphases.

After what seemed a very long moment, in which His burning eyes probed my soul, He gently smiled. The great moment had passed. He was again the courteous, kindly, humble host, the Father whom thought I knew. He touched His fez so that it stood at what I called the humorous angle, and a slightly quizzical smile was around His mouth as He rapidly ascended the steps and entered the open door. I followed closely. We passed through the few steps of the hall to the stairs. I remember the wondering, slightly envious glances that followed me as I followed 'Abdu'l-Bahá up the stairs. The upper hall was empty and 'Abdu'l-Bahá swept through it and up another flight to His room, a large front room on the third floor. And still I followed. I have often marvelled since at my temerity. Had I known more or felt less I never should have dared. It is said that fools rush in where angels fear to tread. Perhaps that is the way that fools are cured of their folly.

We came to the door of 'Abdu'l-Bahá's room. He had not invited me there, nor had He looked once behind Him to see that I was following, and it was with much inward trepidation that I paused at the threshold as He entered the room. Would He be displeased? Had I overstepped the bounds of the respect due 'Abdu'l-Bahá? Had I been lacking in due humility? But my heart was humility itself—He must know that. He swung the door wide and turning beckoned me in.

Again I was alone with 'Abdu'l-Bahá. There was the bed in which He slept, the chair in which He sat. The late afternoon sunlight lay palely across the floor, but I saw nothing. I was conscious only of Him and that I was alone with Him. The room was very still. No sound came from the street nor from the lower rooms. The silence deepened as He regarded me with that loving, all-embracing, all-understanding look which always melted my heart. A deep content and happiness flooded my being. A little flame seemed lit within my breast. And then 'Abdu'l-Bahá spoke: He simply asked me if I were interested in renunciation.

Nothing could have been more unexpected. I had entirely forgotten the question which had so engrossed my thoughts an hour since. Or was it that in that hour during which the word renunciation had not been mentioned, all that I wished or needed to know about it had been vouchsafed me? I had no words to answer His question. Was I interested? I could not say I was and I would not say I was not. I stood before Him silent while His whole Being seemed to reach out to embrace me. Then His arm was around me and He led me to the door. I left His Presence with my soul treading the heights. I felt as though I had been admitted, for the moment at least, into the ranks of the martyrs. And it was a goodly fellowship indeed. During all the long years of renunciation that followed, the memory of that walk with Him; my disappointment that He had not understood; His ringing challenge: This is a Day for *very great things*: my following Him up those long stairs without even knowing whether He wished me to or not, and then the question wrapped in that sublime love: Are you interested in renunciation? has risen before me, a comforting and inspiring challenge. Indeed I *was* interested and my interest has never flagged from that day to this. But I never dreamed that renunciation could be so glorious.[22]

16

Kitáb-i-Aqdas. 4. Worship and Daily Life

The Mashriqu'l-Adhkár

One of the commandments of Bahá'u'lláh in the *Kitáb-i-Aqdas* is the establishment of the institution of the House of Worship, designated by Him 'Mashriqu'l-Adhkár' (Dawning-place of the mention of God). He has ordained that in every locality an edifice be built with the utmost perfection for the exclusive purpose of worshipping God. In it only the word of God may be read or chanted in a way that will exhilarate the ears and uplift the souls. He also counsels parents to teach their children the words of God revealed by Him, so that they may chant them in the Houses of Worship.

These are the words of Bahá'u'lláh revealed in the *Kitáb-i-Aqdas*:

> Blessed is he who directeth his steps towards the Mashriqu'l-Adhkár at the hour of dawn, communing with Him, attuned to His remembrance, imploring His forgiveness. And having entered therein, let him sit in silence to hearken unto the verses of God, the Sovereign, the Almighty, the All-praised. Say, the Mashriqu'l-Adhkár is in truth any House raised in towns or villages, for mention of Me. Thus hath it been named before His Throne; would that ye know it. And those who chant the verses of the Merciful in most melodious tones will attain thereby unto that with which the kingdoms of earth and heaven can never compare. And they will inhale therefrom the fragrance of My realms which none discerneth in this day save those who

> have been granted vision by this sublime Beauty. Say, verily, the verses of the Merciful uplift the stainless hearts unto those realms of the spirit which cannot be described in words or expressed in symbols. Blessed are they that hearken![1]

And again:

> Teach your children that which hath been sent down from the heaven of majesty and power that they may recite the Tablets of the Merciful in the halls of the Mashriqu'l-Adhkárs in most melodious tones. Verily, he who hath been drawn by the magnet of the love of My Name, the Merciful, will recite the verses of God in such wise as to enrapture the hearts of those who are fast asleep. Well is it with him who hath quaffed the choice wine of immortal life from the utterances of his Lord, the Lord of Mercy, through the power of this exalted Name whereby every high and lofty mountain hath been reduced to dust.[2]

We note that Bahá'u'lláh urges His followers to conduct prayer services in the Mashriqu'l-Adhkár at the hour of dawn, a time which is specially conducive to spiritual upliftment. In the earlier days of the Faith when social circumstances were favourable in Persia and people worked very flexible hours, the believers often gathered in the home of a Bahá'í before dawn to pray and to read the Writings of Bahá'u'lláh. No doubt, in the future, when the World Order of Bahá'u'lláh is fully established and in every city a sufficient number of Bahá'í Houses of Worship erected, a new social pattern will emerge which will regulate man's way of life in such spheres as work, rest, leisure and service to the Cause, enabling him to arise before dawn and engage in praise and glorification of God. And this will result in a balance being created between his spiritual and physical needs.

The spiritual activities of future society will mainly circle around the institution of the Mashriqu'l-Adhkár itself, while its humanitarian and administrative activities will be focused upon a cluster of institutions built around it as its dependencies. These, according to 'Abdu'l-Bahá's words, include hospitals, orphanages, schools, universities, hostels and similar institutions. The teachings of Bahá'u'lláh always combine the spiritual and human values together. Like the balance that exists between the soul and the body, the Bahá'í Faith advocates the observance of spiritual and physical laws which can alone guarantee the well-being of man. The Mashriqu'l-Adhkár and its dependencies provide this balance in the community. One is the centre of spiritual forces generated through prayer and thanksgiving to God, the other, the institutions of social service, the focal point of all human endeavour, of love and compassion.

Shoghi Effendi, as far back as 1929, explained some of the salient features of the Mashriqu'l-Adhkár in a letter to the American Bahá'ís who were then engaged in building the first Bahá'í House of Worship in the Western world.

> It should be borne in mind that the central Edifice of the Mashriqu'l-Adhkár, round which in the fullness of time shall cluster such institutions of social service as shall afford relief to the suffering, sustenance to the poor, shelter to the wayfarer, solace to the bereaved, and education to the ignorant, should be regarded apart from these Dependencies, as a House solely designed and entirely dedicated to the worship of God in accordance with the few yet definitely prescribed principles established by Bahá'u'lláh in the *Kitábu'l-Aqdas*. It should not be inferred, however, from this general statement that the interior of the central Edifice itself will be converted into a conglomeration of religious services conducted along lines associated with the traditional procedure obtaining in churches, mosques, synagogues, and other temples of worship. Its various avenues of approach, all converging towards the central Hall beneath its dome, will not serve as admittance to those sectarian adherents of rigid formulae and man-made creeds, each bent, according to his way, to observe his rites, recite his prayers, perform his ablutions, and display the

particular symbols of his faith, within separately defined sections of Bahá'u'lláh's Universal House of Worship. Far from the Mashriqu'l-Adhkár offering such a spectacle of incoherent and confused sectarian observances and rites, a condition wholly incompatible with the provisions of the Aqdás and irreconcilable with the spirit it inculcates, the central House of Bahá'í worship, enshrined within the Mashriqu'l-Adhkár, will gather within its chastened walls, in a serenely spiritual atmosphere, only those who, discarding forever the trapping of elaborate and ostentatious ceremony, are willing worshippers of the one true God, as manifested in this age in the Person of Bahá'u'lláh. To them will the Mashriqu'l-Adhkár symbolize the fundamental verity underlying the Bahá'í Faith, that religious truth is not absolute but relative, that Divine Revelation is not final but progressive. Theirs will be the conviction that an all-loving and ever-watchful Father Who, in the past, and at various stages in the evolution of mankind, has sent forth His Prophets as the Bearers of His Light to mankind, cannot at this critical period of their civilization withhold from His children the Guidance which they sorely need amid the darkness which has beset them, and which neither the light of science nor that of human intellect and wisdom can succeed in dissipating. And thus having recognized in Bahá'u'lláh the source whence this celestial light proceeds, they will irresistibly feel attracted to seek the shelter of His House and congregate therein, unhampered by ceremonials and unfettered by creed, to render homage to the one true God, the Essence and Orb of eternal Truth, and to exalt and magnify the name of His Messengers and Prophets Who, from time immemorial even unto our day, have, under divers circumstances and in varying measure, mirrored forth to a dark and wayward world the light of heavenly Guidance.

But, however inspiring the conception of Bahá'í worship, as witnessed in the central Edifice of this exalted Temple, it cannot be regarded as the sole, nor even the essential, factor in the part which the Mashriqu'l-Adhkár, as designed by Bahá'u'lláh, is destined to play in the organic life of the

Bahá'í community. Divorced from the social, humanitarian, educational and scientific pursuits centring around the Dependencies of the Ma<u>sh</u>riqu'l-A<u>dh</u>kár, Bahá'í worship, however exalted in its conception, however passionate in fervour, can never hope to achieve beyond the meagre and often transitory results produced by the contemplations of the ascetic or the communion of the passive worshipper. It cannot afford lasting satisfaction and benefit to the worshipper himself, much less to humanity in general, unless and until translated and transfused into that dynamic and disinterested service to the cause of humanity which it is the supreme privilege of the Dependencies of the Ma<u>sh</u>riqu'l-A<u>dh</u>kár to facilitate and promote. Nor will the exertions, no matter how disinterested and strenuous, of those who within the precincts of the Ma<u>sh</u>riqu'l-A<u>dh</u>kár will be engaged in administering the affairs of the future Bahá'í Commonwealth, fructify and prosper unless they are brought into close and daily communion with those spiritual agencies centring in and radiating from the central Shrine of the Ma<u>sh</u>riqu'l-A<u>dh</u>kár. Nothing short of direct and constant interaction between the spiritual forces emanating from this House of Worship centring in the heart of the Ma<u>sh</u>riqu'l-A<u>dh</u>kár, and the energies consciously displayed by those who administer its affairs in their service to humanity can possibly provide the necessary agency capable of removing the ills that have so long and so grievously afflicted humanity. For it is assuredly upon the consciousness of the efficacy of the Revelation of Bahá'u'lláh, reinforced on one hand by spiritual communion with His Spirit, and on the other by the intelligent application and the faithful execution of the principles and laws He revealed, that the salvation of a world in travail must ultimately depend. And of all the institutions that stand associated with His Holy Name, surely none save the institution of the Ma<u>sh</u>riqu'l-A<u>dh</u>kár can most adequately provide the essentials of Bahá'í worship and service, both so vital to the regeneration of the world. Therein lies the secret of the loftiness, of the potency, of the unique position of the Ma<u>sh</u>riqu'l-A<u>dh</u>kár as one of the outstanding institutions conceived by Bahá'u'lláh.[3]

The Bahá'í House of Worship is a nine-sided building, symbolic of the number of Bahá.* Bahá'u'lláh has forbidden the display of pictures or statues within its walls and since there are no clergy in the Faith, there are to be no sermons. Another prohibition is the use of musical instruments. Only the human voice may be used in chanting or reading the word of God and glorifying his Name.

The Obligatory Prayer

Bahá'í worship is not limited to a service at the Mashriqu'l-Adhkár. One of the ordinances of Bahá'u'lláh in the *Kitáb-i-Aqdas* is the daily obligatory prayer. It is enjoined upon every believer from the age of fifteen to observe this commandment in the privacy of his own chamber. This is one of the rituals of the Faith of Bahá'u'lláh. But no individual or institution of the Faith has the right to enforce this law. The believer alone is responsible before his God for this act of devotion to Him. In saying the daily obligatory prayer, one must perform all its rites including the turning towards the Qiblih† of the Bahá'í world.

Bahá'u'lláh has revealed three obligatory prayers for the individual and has enjoined on him to recite one of these prayers every day. These are known as the long, the medium and the short obligatory prayers. In the first two Bahá'u'lláh has ordained certain genuflectory actions which are designed to heighten man's devotion and servitude to his Creator.

In order to appreciate the significance of these actions let us recall that the human personality of the Manifestation of God influences the form of the religion He founds. We have

* see p. 316n.

† literally: point of adoration. The Shrine of Bahá'u'lláh is the Qiblih to which Bahá'ís the world over turn when saying their obligatory prayers.

discussed this theme in a previous volume.* To cite one example: we know that the Word of God in its innermost reality is exalted above and independent of any language. It emanates from the Kingdom of Revelation,† and as such it is limitless in its potency and far removed from the material world. However, this spiritual entity is clothed within the mantle of the 'spoken word' which is limited and belongs to the world of man. This is one way in which the personality of the Manifestation of God affects the form of religion. Since Bahá'u'lláh was a native of Persia, the Word of God has been revealed in the Persian and Arabic languages. Had the person of the Manifestation of God been a native of another land, the revealed Word would have assumed a different form altogether.

The effect of the personality of the Manifestation on His religion is not limited to influencing the Word of God. It affects almost every feature of that religion. The genuflectory actions ordained in the obligatory prayers provide an example, for this important religious rite has been formulated and to some extent influenced by the personality of Bahá'u'lláh. These genuflections are intended to convey symbolically man's attitude towards his Lord. The combination of the words uttered with the actions that accompany them will bring about a greater consciousness of the sovereignty of God and of man's impotence and poverty in this life.

The form that these actions take, however, is based in Bahá'u'lláh's own personal background. In the society in which He was brought up, the language was Persian and there were certain expressions which were conveyed by the movements of one's hands or body. Similar to the use of the Persian language in the revelation of the Word of God, Bahá'u'lláh has incorporated these movements, which were known to Him, to express symbolically various feelings such as humility, supplication and servitude to God.

* see vol. 1, pp. 21–2.

† see vol. 2, pp. 184–5.

Every culture has its own language and customs. The person of the Manifestation of God from the human point of view abides within His own environment. He expresses himself like the rest of His countrymen. In the Persian culture it was customary to raise one's hands towards heaven when supplicating the Lord, or to bend one's body when showing humility or to prostrate oneself before one's God when expressing one's utter nothingness before Him. These actions Bahá'u'lláh has incorporated in the obligatory prayers in order to increase the ardour and devotion of the servant when praying to his Lord and to demonstrate both by words and by action, the loftiness, the grandeur and the glory of God, while recognizing his own station of servitude at His threshold.

Bahá'u'lláh has attached utmost importance to the obligatory prayer. 'Abdu'l-Bahá in one of His Tablets[4] describes it as 'the very foundation of the Cause of God' and the 'cause of spiritual life' for the individual. In another Tablet[5] He states that the observance of the ordinance of obligatory prayer is binding on all and no excuse is acceptable, except when a person is mentally deranged or is confronted by extraordinary circumstances.

Apart from the obligatory prayers, which are enjoined on all believers, there are many prayers revealed by the Báb, Bahá'u'lláh and 'Abdu'l-Bahá which are of a different nature and the recital of which do not constitute a religious rite. Their recital is voluntary and can be said whenever the individual is moved to do so, either in private or public.

In Islám it is customary to say the obligatory prayer in congregations. Bahá'u'lláh has forbidden congregational prayers except for the dead. Unlike the obligatory prayer which must be said in private, the special obligatory prayer for the dead is to be recited in congregation. Here we notice the difference between ordinary prayers revealed by the Báb, Bahá'u'lláh and 'Abdu'l-Bahá, which may be recited in public, and the obligatory prayer for the dead which is one of the rites of the Bahá'í Faith and Bahá'u'lláh has permitted its recital in public. The word 'congregational' may cause a misunderstanding in that one may assume that the whole congregation must join in unison to recite the prayer. But this is not so. The prayer for the dead is to be recited by one person in the presence of the congregation. On the other hand, there are Tablets or prayers revealed by Bahá'u'lláh or 'Abdu'l-Bahá which in the original language lend themselves to be chanted in unison. But since these are not part of any rite their recital in this manner is not termed congregational.

Work as Worship

Another form of worship which Bahá'u'lláh has ordained in the *Kitáb-i-Aqdas* is one's work, when carried out in the spirit of service to mankind. This teaching is unique in religious history, and is a source of spiritual and material progress.

> It is enjoined upon every one of you to engage in some form of occupation, such as crafts, trades and the like. We have graciously exalted your engagement in such work to the rank of worship unto God, the True One. Ponder ye in your hearts the grace and the blessings of God and render thanks unto Him at eventide and at dawn. Waste not your time in idleness and sloth. Occupy yourselves with that which profiteth yourselves and others. Thus hath it been decreed in this Tablet from whose horizon the day-star of wisdom and utterance shineth resplendent.
>
> The most despised of men in the sight of God are those who sit idly and beg. Hold ye fast unto the cord of material means, placing your whole trust in God, the Provider of all means. When anyone occupieth himself in a craft or trade, such occupation itself is regarded in the estimation of God as an act of worship; and this is naught but a token of His infinite and all-pervasive bounty.[6]

Although the worship of God is the paramount duty of man and the purpose of his life, yet Bahá'u'lláh states in one of His Tablets[7] that should a person be occupied with the worship of

God throughout his life, but devoid of pure deeds and deprived of those spiritual qualities which help promote the Cause of God, his act of worship is of no benefit to him and will produce no result.

The Nineteen Day Feast

Another institution of vital importance which originated from the Báb and was confirmed and established by Bahá'u'lláh in the *Kitáb-i-Aqdas* is that of the Nineteen Day Feast. Each Bahá'í month,* the members of the Bahá'í community take part in a feast which combines three important features of devotional readings and prayers, of consultation and of fellowship. Bahá'u'lláh states that the main purpose of the Nineteen Day Feast is to create love and unity in the hearts of people.

Abolition of Monasticism and Confession of Sins

In the *Kitáb-i-Aqdas* Bahá'u'lláh categorically condemns mendicancy and asceticism. He strongly disapproves the practice of retiring in solitude, of self-mortification and inflicting hardships upon the body. He affirms that such deeds are not conducive to spiritual gain and have no merit in the sight of God. We have referred to this subject in a previous volume.† In several Tablets Bahá'u'lláh has reiterated this important teaching. In the *Kalimát-i-Firdawsíyyih* (Words of Paradise) revealed in honour of Ḥájí Mírzá Ḥaydar-'Alí, Bahá'u'lláh reveals these words:

> O people of the earth! Living in seclusion or practising asceticism is not acceptable in the presence of God. It behoveth them that are endued with insight and

* In the Bahá'í calendar there are 19 months of 19 days. For more information see vol. 2.

† see vol. 2, pp. 25–7.

> understanding to observe that which will cause joy and radiance. Such practices as are sprung from the loins of idle fancy or are begotten of the womb of superstition ill beseem men of knowledge. In former times and more recently some people have been taking up their abodes in the caves of the mountains while others have repaired to graveyards at night. Say, give ear unto the counsels of this Wronged One. Abandon the things current amongst you and adopt that which the faithful Counsellor biddeth you. Deprive not yourselves of the bounties which have been created for your sake.[8]

In the *Bishárát* (Glad-Tidings) Bahá'u'lláh directs the Christian monks to come out of their cloisters and live a life of service to mankind. These are His words:

> The pious deeds of the monks and priests among the followers of the Spirit*—upon Him be the peace of God—are remembered in His presence. In this Day, however, let them give up the life of seclusion and direct their steps towards the open world and busy themselves with that which will profit themselves and others. We have granted them leave to enter into wedlock that they may bring forth one who will make mention of God, the Lord of the seen and the unseen, the Lord of the Exalted Throne.[9]

Bahá'u'lláh in many of His Writings describes the exalted station of man. He has exhorted him to loftiness of character and whatever will enhance his honour and dignity. In the *Kitáb-i-Aqdas* He has forbidden the practice of the confession of sins which is conducive to humiliation for the individual. Instead He has ordained that the sinner should repent to God and seek forgiveness from Him. In one of His Tablets He states:

> When the sinner findeth himself wholly detached and freed from all save God, he should beg forgiveness and pardon

* Jesus.

from Him. Confession of sins and transgressions before human beings is not permissible, as it hath never been nor will ever be conducive to divine forgiveness. Moreover such confession before people results in one's humiliation and abasement, and God—exalted be His glory—wisheth not the humiliation of His servants. Verily He is the Compassionate, the Merciful. The sinner should, between himself and God, implore mercy from the Ocean of mercy, beg forgiveness from the Heaven of generosity and say:

O God, my God! I implore Thee by the blood of Thy true lovers who were so enraptured by Thy sweet utterance that they hastened unto the Pinnacle of Glory, the site of the most glorious martyrdom, and I beseech Thee by the mysteries which lie enshrined in Thy knowledge and by the pearls that are treasured in the ocean of Thy bounty to grant forgiveness unto me and unto my father and my mother. Of those who show forth mercy, Thou art in truth the Most Merciful. No God is there but Thee, the Ever-Forgiving, the All-Bountiful.

O Lord! Thou seest this essence of sinfulness turning unto the ocean of Thy favour and this feeble one seeking the kingdom of Thy divine power and this poor creature inclining himself towards the day-star of Thy wealth. By Thy mercy and Thy grace, disappoint him not, O Lord, nor debar him from the revelations of Thy bounty in Thy days, nor cast him away from Thy door which Thou has opened wide to all that dwell in Thy heaven and on Thine earth.

Alas! Alas! My sins have prevented me from approaching the Court of Thy holiness and my trespasses have caused me to stray far from the Tabernacle of Thy majesty. I have committed that which Thou didst forbid me to do and have put away what Thou didst ordain me to observe.

I pray Thee by Him Who is the sovereign Lord of Names to write down for me with the Pen of Thy bounty that which will enable me to draw nigh unto thee and will purge me from my trespasses which have intervened between me and Thy forgiveness and Thy pardon.

Verily, Thou art the Potent, the Bountiful. No God is there but Thee, the Mighty, the Gracious.[10]

Another practice denounced by Bahá'u'lláh in the *Kitáb-i-Aqdas* and one that is repugnant to Him is that of using religion and the worship of God for one's own self-advancement. In the past, countless men have used the cloak of religion in order to gain leadership. Some ambitious people posed as holy men in order to win the respect of the community. In this day too there are many who are doing the same. Today the real meanings of piety and holiness have been lost, and instead these words have often become the trademark for the hypocrite disguised in the garb of religion, pretending to be a holy man, while his deeds and private life vastly differ from his words.

For instance, in Persia, the cradle of the Faith of Bahá'u'lláh, many people have been led to believe that one of the signs of spirituality and holiness is for a religious leader to be muttering the words of the *Qur'án* as he walks among the public. Often the clergy are seen in the streets to be moving their lips, pretending to be reciting prayers. Bahá'u'lláh has forbidden this practice in the *Kitáb-i-Aqdas*. Another form of hypocrisy current among many people in Persia in the early days of the Faith was to force a permanent impression of a small prayer tile* on their foreheads in order to advertise their piety to the public. When the ignorant and the fanatic gazed upon one's swollen forehead, they were carried away in adoration of a so-called holy man who had spent so much of his time in prayer prostrating himself so frequently upon the hard prayer tile that a callous had formed on his forehead! Although there must be many religious people who with pure motive live a goodly life, yet the hypocrisy associated with those who pose as pious and holy is widespread.

* The faithful Muslim praying in the mosque performs certain genuflections. One of these is prostration, when the worshipper lies with face to the ground as a token of submission and humility. There is a custom among Shí'ah Muslims when they lie prostrate, to place their foreheads upon a small tile supposed to be made of holy dust gathered from the vicinity of one of their shrines.

In His teachings, Bahá'u'lláh places paramount importance upon purity of motive and sincerity in one's thoughts and actions. In the *Kitáb-i-Aqdas* He enumerates some of the virtues that must adorn a human soul:

> Adorn your heads with the garlands of trustworthiness and fidelity, your hearts with the attire of the Fear of God, your tongues with absolute truthfulness, your bodies with the vesture of courtesy. These are in truth seemly adornings unto the temple of man, if ye be of them that reflect. Cling, O ye people of Bahá, to the cord of servitude unto God, the True One, for thereby your stations shall be made manifest, your names written and preserved, your ranks raised and your memory exalted in the Preserved Tablet. Beware lest the dwellers on earth hinder you from this glorious and exalted station. Thus have We exhorted you in most of our Epistles and now in this, Our Holy Tablet, above which hath beamed the Day-star of the Laws of the Lord, your God, the Powerful, the All-Wise.[11]

In the *Hidden Words*, He rebukes the *'ulamá* in these words:

> O ye that are foolish, yet have a name to be wise! Wherefore do ye wear the guise of shepherds, when inwardly ye have become wolves, intent upon My flock? Ye are even as the star, which riseth ere the dawn, and which, though it seem radiant and luminous, leadeth the wayfarers of My city astray into the paths of perdition.[12]

> O ye seeming fair yet inwardly foul! Ye are like clear but bitter water, which to outward seeming is crystal pure but of which, when tested by the divine Assayer, not a drop is accepted. Yea, the sun beam falls alike upon the dust and the mirror, yet differ they in reflection even as doth the star from the earth: nay, immeasurable is the difference![13]

In another passage He indicates that in this Dispensation nothing but pure deeds will be acceptable to God:

> O my friends! Quench ye the lamp of error, and kindle within your hearts the everlasting torch of divine guidance.

For ere long the assayers of mankind shall, in the holy presence of the Adored, accept naught but purest virtue and deeds of stainless holiness.[14]

Health and Medicine: *Lawḥ-i-Ṭibb* (Tablet of Medicine)

In the *Kitáb-i-Aqdas* Bahá'u'lláh states that God has created the means for the achievement of everything in this life. He urges the people to use them. For instance, He directs His followers to consult a skilled physician when ill. In this example medicine is the means by which an ill person may recover from his illness. Similarly, there are means through which man may overcome his poverty, ignorance, or any other problem.

Of course, prayer plays an important part in the life of man, but prayer without action has little or no effect at all. The two must go hand-in-hand. By adhering to the means for achieving a goal, and by drawing on the power of God through prayer, one's efforts will become crowned wih success. The sick person should follow the advice of a skilled physician by taking the remedy, and at the same time praying for healing.

Bahá'u'lláh has clearly stated that through prayer the sick person may recover from his illness, and has revealed several healing prayers; but He has not made the spiritual approach to healing an alternative to a doctor's prescription. In order to emphasize this point Bahá'u'lláh, in most cases, ordered His companions to seek the advice of a doctor when they were ill, rather than healing them through His divine powers. He also told them to pray for the sick person and when the members of His own family were taken ill, He asked for a doctor to come.

It must also be pointed out that while Bahá'u'lláh emphasizes the importance of prayers for the sick, He does not advocate any other method of spiritual healing such as those practised by faith healers or similar practitioners. In answer to a question by an individual, Shoghi Effendi writes through his secretary:

> There is no such thing as Bahá'í healers or a Bahá'í type of healing. In His Most Holy Book (the Aqdas) Bahá'u'lláh says to consult the best physicians, in other words, doctors who have studied a scientific system of medicine; he never gave us to believe that He himself would heal us through 'healers', but rather through prayer and the assistance of medicine and approved treatments.[15]

Bahá'u'lláh teaches that the science of medicine and the art of healing must be developed. 'Abdu'l-Bahá has stated that the science of medicine will be so perfected in the future that most diseases will be treated with foods, herbs and natural remedies. Although it is not the main mission of Bahá'u'lláh to give guidance on matters dealing with food and health—a role which must be played by science in this age—He has nevertheless given some basic advice about diet and hygiene.

In the Tablet known as the *Lawḥ-i-Ṭibb* (Tablet of Medicine) revealed in honour of Áqá Mírzá Muḥammad-Riḍáy-i-Ṭabíb, a physician from Yazd, Bahá'u'lláh advocates medical treatment when it is necessary, recommends treating the patient first through diet and resorting to medicine if the former proves ineffective. In this Tablet He enumerates some of the basic prescriptions for good health and gives some dietary advice.* He also stresses the importance of contentment under all circumstances for good health, asserts that grief and sorrow will cause man the greatest misery and warns that jealousy will consume the body while anger will burn the liver.

In this Tablet, Bahá'u'lláh exhorts the physician to heal the patient by first turning to God and seeking His assistance, and then prescribing the remedy. He affirms that a physician who has recognized Him and has become filled with His love will exert such an influence that his mere visit will restore health to the patient.

Indeed Áqá Mírzá Muḥammad-Riḍá, for whom this Tablet

* These counsels are not discussed here because they would open up some important medical subjects which are beyond the scope and purpose of this book.

was revealed, lived up to these high ideals. Of him, Ḥájí Muḥammad Ṭáhir-i-Málmírí writes:

> One of the early believers who embraced the Faith when Siyyid Yaḥyáy-i-Dárábí, known as Vaḥíd,* came to Yazd, was Áqá Mírzá Muḥammad-Riḍáy-i-Ṭabíb. He was a skilled and distinguished physician, and an embodiment of grace and steadfastness. The Pen of the Most High revealed the *Lawḥ-i-Ṭibb* in his honour. In that exalted Tablet, Bahá'u'lláh states that the mere visit of a physician who has drunk deep of the wine of His love will cure the patient. Mírzá Muḥammad-Riḍá was truly the fulfilment of these words of Bahá'u'lláh. He used to cure the patient by administering very simple remedies. Truly, he possessed wonderful qualities which made him a very special person in the community of the Most Great Name. Owing to his intense piety he became highly disturbed when Mírzá Yaḥyá broke the Covenant. As a result he was bewildered and stunned; he even became hesitant in the Cause for a short time. Then it was as though Divine Providence sent Mullá Zaynu'l-'Ábidín, a native of Najafábád (he was entitled by Bahá'u'lláh as Zaynu'l-Muqarribín†) to Yazd in order to calm his agitation and dispel his doubts. Zaynu'l-Muqarribín at first stayed in the house of this servant in the district of Malamír, but when he learned of the intense anguish and distress that Mírzá Muḥammad-Riḍá was subjected to, he changed his residence and stayed in his home instead. Consequently, Mírzá Muḥammad-Riḍá became fully aware of the circumstances of the Revelation of Bahá'u'lláh.‡ He later received many Tablets from the Pen of the Most High, and served the Faith of Bahá'u'lláh with devotion and love till the end of his life. He was about eighty years old when he passed away.[16]

* see vol. I, Appendix III.

† see vol. I, pp. 25–6.

‡ In the early days of the Faith, in the absence of proper communication, the Bábís were easily misled by rumours and false propaganda. There was nothing more assuring than meeting those who were truly learned and had first-hand knowledge of the Revelation of Bahá'u'lláh.

In the *Lawḥ-i-Ṭibb* Bahá'u'lláh praises the science of medicine as being the most meritorious of all sciences, and states that it is the means which God has created for the well-being of mankind. And it is at the end of this Tablet that He reveals one of His most celebrated healing prayers:

> Thy Name is my healing, O my God, and remembrance of Thee is my remedy. Nearness to Thee is my hope, and love for Thee is my companion. Thy mercy to me is my healing and my succour in both this world and the world to come. Thou, verily, art the All-Bountiful, the All-Knowing, the All-Wise.

Also in this Tablet Bahá'u'lláh states the importance of courage and steadfastness in His Cause as well as wisdom in teaching it. He categorically affirms that if the believers had faithfully carried out His commandments, the majority of the peoples of the world would have embraced His Faith in His days.

No reference to medicine and its role in healing would be complete without mentioning the power of the Holy Spirit which is exclusive to the Manifestations of God, a power that can heal without any physical means. This is the power that Christ possessed and that Bahá'u'lláh manifested fully in this day. There were many occasions when Bahá'u'lláh or 'Abdu'l-Bahá, upon whom the same powers were conferred, brought miraculous healing to a person when doctors had failed.

Although Bahá'u'lláh has forbidden His followers to attribute miracles to Him, nevertheless there are many accounts left to posterity by His disciples, describing the circumstances in which He either healed incurables or raised the dead. We have described one such case in the previous volume.* But none of these supernatural acts were considered by His followers to be a proof of the truth of His Cause, as otherwise this would amount to the degradation of His exalted station.

* see vol. 1, pp. 290–91.

'Abdu'l-Bahá also possessed this power. Dr Yúnis Khán,* a distinguished and trusted secretary of 'Abdu'l-Bahá and one of the Heralds of the Covenant of Bahá'u'lláh, writes an interesting account in his memoirs. The following is a summary of his reminiscences:

> I heard 'Abdu'l-Bahá many times speaking about the subject of medicine: He used to say that Jináb-i-Kalím (Bahá'u'lláh's faithful brother) was very knowledgeable in herbal medicine and used to practise it. In the early days 'Abdu'l-Bahá also used to prescribe medicine to those who came to him for healing. But later Bahá'u'lláh directed Him not to prescribe for patients, so that the believers might turn to the medical profession and not form the habit of seeking medical advice from unqualified people. This advice was given by Bahá'u'lláh so that His injunction in the *Kitáb-i-Aqdas* to consult a skilled physician might be realized.
>
> Although we all knew that because of this particular commandment in the *Kitáb-i-Aqdas*, 'Abdu'l-Bahá, the healer of spiritual ills, would not consent to prescribe for a physical sickness, yet whenever the doctor's treatment failed to cure, the patient used to turn to the Master and beg for healing from the One who was the Healer of all ills. And since the compassionate nature of 'Abdu'l-Bahá was such that He could not withhold help from an individual who turned to Him, in such cases He would, as a matter of principle, employ some means to cure the patient. This He did by offering some remedy and thus conferring healing on the individual. More surprising is the fact that whereas the believers acted with some restraint, the non-Bahá'í public who were not aware of the real situation used to come to Him for healing more often, and none of them left feeling disappointed.
>
> One of the remedial means which was at 'Abdu'l-Bahá's disposal and which He offered to many a sick person, was a

* For a brief account of his life and service to the Cause see *The Bahá'í World*, vol. XII, pp. 679–81. The title 'Herald of the Covenant' was sometimes given by 'Abdu'l-Bahá and Shoghi Effendi to outstanding promoters of the Covenant.

delicious sauce made from pomegranates. The fruit had been grown in the Garden of Riḍván in 'Akká. To whomsoever 'Abdu'l-Bahá gave this sauce, whether a believer or a non-Bahá'í, He would say that the pomegranates had grown on trees in the Garden of Riḍván, trees which had been blessed by Bahá'u'lláh's eyes. But what were the circumstances which produced healing? Was it an inherent nature of the patient to be cured, was the cure the result of taking the sauce, or was it purely through the will of 'Abdu'l-Bahá? I do not know the answer, but one thing I know that it was proved time and time again that this delicious fruit sauce was the remedy for many an illness! This was one of the topics often discussed among the believers in the Pilgrim House.

Another prescription which 'Abdu'l-Bahá gave to some was that of fasting or cutting down on certain foods. But there was another method which 'Abdu'l-Bahá, the healer of man's spiritual ills, would use. And that was healing without any means . . . Once I was cured by Him without any material means. This is the story:

During the time that Dr. Arasṭú Khán was in 'Akká and staying in the Pilgrim House, I became ill . . . Although this illness lasted for a long time and the pain was intolerable, I did not ask 'Abdu'l-Bahá for a cure. Instead Dr. Arasṭú Khán treated me and used all the tricks he knew. But I was no better . . . One night I experienced an excruciating pain which was beyond endurance. All the pilgrims who heard my groaning became so weary that although it was two hours after midnight, we all agreed to despatch Áqá Muḥammad-Ḥasan, the caretaker of the Pilgrim House, to the house of the Master, and beg for healing. This was done. I do not know whether His blessed Person was asleep or awake at the time. The only thing I know is that when Áqá Muḥammad-Ḥasan had returned, I was in a deep sleep. When I woke up in the afternoon, there was no pain, and in the evening I felt able to walk. For about twenty-five days I had been ill and the last few days confined to bed. During this period I had been deprived of attaining the presence of the Master. So I walked slowly towards His house. I met

Him on the road where I attained His presence. He asked about my health and showered His bounties and grace upon me. I felt it was an opportune moment to beg Him to grant me complete recovery. This I did. He said, 'Very well, but you ought to have a blood-letting operation, either by using a cupping-glass or by phlebotomy.'*

The word cupping-glass frightened me, and like a spoiled child, I pulled up my shoulders and screwed up my face, meaning that I could not bear a knife or a cupping glass! Seeing me in this mode, He said in an amused voice, 'Good gracious, man, I want to send you to face the swords of the enemies and you are afraid of a cupping-glass!'

Being outspoken and known for my blabbing habits, I ventured to say jokingly, 'When that happens, God will show his benevolence to me! But if I wanted to use the cupping-glass as a means of recovery, why would I come to your presence and beg for healing from you?' He smiled . . . and that was the final remedy for me. I was healed without any material means.[17]

One of Bahá'u'lláh's injunctions in the *Kitáb-i-Aqdas* is immaculate cleanliness. He calls on His followers to become the embodiment of purity among the peoples of the world. Although this commandment of Bahá'u'lláh relates to physical cleanliness, and therefore is conducive to man's dignity and distinction, it exerts an appreciable influence on his spiritual state. For outward cleanliness is a sign of spiritual purity and liveliness. In every stage of His life, whether in prison or in freedom, 'Abdu'l-Bahá, the Exemplar of the Teachings of Bahá'u'lláh, lived up to this important teaching. One of His striking features to which friends and foes have paid glowing tribute, was His spotless cleanliness and His outward appearance.

* The cupping-glass is an old method of blood-letting. A cut is made in some part of the body, usually in the back, then bleeding takes place by applying a glass vessel with open mouth to the skin and forming a partial vacuum which helps to suck the blood out. Phlebotomy is another old method of blood-letting by cutting the vein.

In His Writings Bahá'u'lláh has enjoined upon His followers spotless chastity for both men and women. In the *Kitáb-i-Aqdas* He reiterates this important moral issue. At a time when the forces of irreligion are sweeping across the world and standards of morality are declining, the teachings of Bahá'u'lláh on chastity shine as a light in darkness. The exhortations in the following passages gleaned from one of His Tablets demonstrate the highest standard of morality which He inculcates in His followers:

> Say, he is not to be numbered with the people of Bahá who followeth his mundane desires, or fixeth his heart on things of the earth. He is my true follower who, if he come to a valley of pure gold will pass straight through it aloof as a cloud, and will neither turn back, nor pause. Such a man is assuredly of Me. From his garment the Concourse on high can inhale the fragrance of sanctity . . . And if he met the fairest and most comely of women, he would not feel his heart seduced by the least shadow of desire for her beauty. Such an one indeed is the creation of spotless chastity. Thus instructeth you the Pen of the Ancient of Days, as bidden by your Lord, the Almighty, the All-Bountiful.[18]

Having surveyed the Writings of Bahá'u'lláh, Shoghi Effendi, the Guardian of the Bahá'í Faith, has summarized some of Bahá'u'lláh's teachings on this subject. These are his conclusions:

> A chaste and holy life must be made the controlling principle in the behaviour and conduct of all Bahá'ís, both in their social relations with the members of their own community, and in their contact with the world at large. It must adorn and reinforce the ceaseless labours and meritorious exertions of those whose enviable position is to propagate the Message, and to administer the affairs, of the Faith of Bahá'u'lláh. It must be upheld, in all its integrity and implications, in every phase of the life of those who fill the ranks of that Faith, whether in their homes, their travels, their clubs, their societies, their entertainments, their

schools, and their universities. It must be accorded special consideration in the conduct of the social activities of every Bahá'í summer school and any other occasions on which Bahá'í community life is organized and fostered. It must be closely and continually identified with the mission of the Bahá'í Youth, both as an element in the life of the Bahá'í community, and as a factor in the future progress and orientation of the youth of their own country.

Such a chaste and holy life, with its implications of modesty, purity, temperance, decency, and clean-mindedness, involves no less than the exercise of moderation in all that pertains to dress, language, amusements, and all artistic and literary avocations. It demands daily vigilance in the control of one's carnal desires and corrupt inclinations. It calls for the abandonment of a frivolous conduct, with its excessive attachment to trivial and often misdirected pleasures. It requires total abstinence from all alcoholic drinks, from opium, and from similar habit-forming drugs. It condemns the prostitution of art and of literature, the practices of nudism and of companionate marriage, infidelity in marital relationships, and all manner of promiscuity, of easy familiarity, and of sexual vices. It can tolerate no compromise with the theories, the standards, the habits, and the excesses of a decadent age. Nay rather it seeks to demonstrate, through the dynamic force of its example, the pernicious character of such theories, the falsity of such standards, the hollowness of such claims, the perversity of such habits, and the sacrilegious character of such excesses.[19]

Marriage

Bahá'u'lláh has encouraged the people to enter into matrimony and has affirmed it to be a cause of well-being and unity among the children of men. In the *Kitáb-i-Aqdas* He states:

> Enter into wedlock, O people, that ye may bring forth one who will make mention of Me . . .[20]

As indicated in this passage, the main purpose of marriage according to Bahá'í teachings is procreation.

To promote unity and avoid disagreement between families, Bahá'u'lláh has ordained that after the consent of both parties which is an essential element in marriage, the couple must obtain the consent of their natural parents as well. Without the latter a Bahá'í marriage cannot take place. The Bahá'í marriage ceremony is a very simple and moving experience. At present it is conducted under the auspices of Spiritual Assemblies.

Bahá'í teachings emphasize that a true marriage is one that creates a union between man and wife on both the physical and the spiritual levels. Such a marriage becomes an eternal partnership and brings happiness and joy to the hearts.

'Abdu'l-Bahá in one of His Tablets writes:

> Marriage, among the mass of the people, is a physical bond, and this union can only be temporary, since it is foredoomed to a physical separation at the close.
>
> Among the people of Bahá, however, marriage must be a union of the body and of the spirit as well, for here both husband and wife are aglow with the same wine, both are enamoured of the same matchless Face, both live and move through the same spirit, both are illumined by the same glory. This connection between them is a spiritual one, hence it is a bond that will abide forever. Likewise do they enjoy strong and lasting ties in the physical world as well, for if the marriage is based both on the spirit and the body, that union is a true one, hence it will endure. If, however, the bond is physical and nothing more, it is sure to be only temporary, and must inexorably end in separation.
>
> When, therefore, the people of Bahá undertake to marry, the union must be a true relationship, a spiritual coming together as well as a physical one, so that throughout every phase of life, and in all the worlds of God, their union will endure; for this real oneness is a gleaming out of the love of God.[21]

And again:

Bahá'í marriage is the commitment of the two parties one to the other, and their mutual attachment of mind and heart. Each must, however, exercise the utmost care to become thoroughly acquainted with the character of the other, that the binding covenant between them may be a tie that will endure forever. Their purpose must be this: to become loving companions and comrades and at one with each other for time and eternity . . .

The true marriage of Bahá'ís is this, that the husband and wife should be united both physically and spiritually, that they may ever improve the spiritual life of each other, and may enjoy everlasting unity throughout all the worlds of God. This is Bahá'í marriage.[22]

Music: 'Spiritual Food of the Hearts and Souls'

In Islámic communities music had been condemned by the clergy because they considered it to be conducive to pleasure and leading man to lust. In Persia, during the early days of the Faith, musicians were denounced by religious leaders as agents of Satan. The stigma attached to music was so distasteful that musicians had to hide their instruments in public. At weddings, for instance, people had to observe some religious rites in the presence of the clergy. But it was a well-known secret that the musicians were waiting in another room and when the Mullá's performance was finished and he had left, they came out to play their instruments and make merry.

The following story serves to illustrate the severity with which the clergy dealt with anyone who indulged in this art.

In the bazaars in Persia there are shops selling *kebab*. The meat was placed on a wooden board and had to be chopped and then minced with a very large and heavy chopping knife which usually had to be held by its two ends. When the chopping knife hit the meat on the board, it made a loud noise. In a busy shop at least one man would be engaged from morning till night doing this work.

There was a man in the city of Yazd who was working in this

capacity in such a shop, but he was a merry man at heart and loved music, so as he hit the board he cleverly used to produce a rhythm. Though not more than a mere thumping sound, it was attractive to the ear. This, combined with the rhythmic movement of his body, made an interesting spectacle for the passer-by. For some time there was controversy over this man and his way of mincing the meat! Eventually, one of the *mujtahids** of Yazd decided to put an end to this sacrilegious act! The poor man was summoned and warned that he would be severely punished if he continued this practice.

Within such a society, Bahá'u'lláh declares in the *Kitáb-i-Aqdas* that music is a means by which the spirit of man may experience upliftment and joy. These are His words in that Book:

> We have permitted you to listen to music and singing. Beware lest such listening cause you to transgress the bounds of decency and dignity. Rejoice in the joy of My Most Great Name through which the hearts are enchanted and the minds of the well-favoured are attracted.
>
> We have made music a ladder by which souls may ascend to the realm on high. Change it not into wings for self and passion. I seek refuge in God that you be not of the ignorant.[23]

'Abdu'l-Bahá too has praised music and singing, in several Tablets. In one of these He writes:

> This wonderful age has rent asunder the veils of superstition and has condemned the prejudice of the people of the East.
>
> Among some of the nations of the Orient, music and harmony was not approved of, but the Manifested Light, Bahá'u'lláh, in this glorious period has revealed in Holy Tablets that singing and music are the spiritual food of the hearts and souls. In this dispensation, music is one of the arts that is highly approved and is considered to be the cause of the exaltation of sad and desponding hearts.

* Doctor of Islámic law.

Therefore . . . set to music the verses and the divine words so that they may be sung with soul-stirring melody in the Assemblies and gatherings, and that the hearts of the listeners may become tumultuous and rise towards the Kingdom of Abhá in supplication and prayer.[24]

'That No One Should Exalt Himself over the Other'

In the *Kitáb-i-Aqdas* Bahá'u'lláh censures in very strong terms all acts of strife, contention and violence. He absolutely forbids His followers to engage in anything from which the odour of mischief and sedition can be detected. He counsels them never to sow the seeds of dissension or to foment discord among men. Bahá'u'lláh's commandments in this respect are uncompromising. He categorically states that any mischief-maker or stirrer-up of sedition is not of Him and cannot claim allegiance to His Cause.

Bahá'u'lláh enjoins love and unity towards the peoples of the world regardless of their background. In the *Kitáb-i-Aqdas*, He reveals these words:

> Consort with all religions with amity and concord, that they may inhale from you the sweet fragrance of God. Beware lest amidst men the flame of foolish ignorance overpower you. All things proceed from God and unto Him they return. He is the source of all things and in Him all things are ended.[25]

And in the same book Bahá'u'lláh warns His followers not to show pride or haughtiness to anyone, and reminds them that all humanity has come into being from the same substance, and that all shall return to dust. He urges them therefore not to prefer themselves to their neighbours, nor to wish for others what they do not wish for themselves.

One of Bahá'u'lláh's prohibitions in the *Kitáb-i-Aqdas* is slave trading. For thousands of years people took slaves. With the coming of Bahá'u'lláh, however, God released in the world the forces of unity, and proclaimed the equality of human rights. These have now become the spirit of the age and humanity has come a long way during the last hundred years, abandoning the age-long practice of slavery. In forbidding slavery, Bahá'u'lláh in the *Kitáb-i-Aqdas* simply states that it is not proper for a man to buy another man. For all are the servants of the one true God and are equal in His sight.

In the *Hidden Words* Bahá'u'lláh thus admonishes the peoples of the world:

> O Children of Men! Know ye not why We created you all from the same dust? That no one should exalt himself over the other. Ponder at all times in your hearts how ye were created. Since We have created you all from one same substance it is incumbent on you to be even as one soul, to walk with the same feet, eat with the same mouth and dwell in the same land, that from your inmost being, by your deeds and actions, the signs of oneness and the essence of detachment may be made manifest. Such is My counsel to you. O concourse of light! Heed ye this counsel that ye may obtain the fruit of holiness from the tree of wondrous glory.[26]

And again:

> O Brethren! Be forbearing one with another and set not your affection on things below. Pride not yourselves in your glory, and be not ashamed of abasement. By My beauty! I have created all things from dust, and to dust will I return them again.[27]

17

Kitáb-i-Aqdas. 5. The Covenant of Bahá'u'lláh

In several passages in the *Kitáb-i-Aqdas* Bahá'u'lláh prepared His followers for the time when He would depart from this world and, in His own words, ascend to His 'other dominions, whereon the eyes of the people of names have never fallen'.[1] In two of these passages there is a clear indication that after Him, the faithful must turn to the Centre of His Covenant:

> When the Mystic Dove will have winged its flight from its Sanctuary of Praise and sought its far-off goal, its hidden habitation, refer ye whatsoever ye understand not in the Book to Him Who hath branched from this mighty Stock.[2]

And again:

> When the ocean of My presence hath ebbed and the Book of My Revelation is ended, turn your faces toward Him Whom God hath purposed, Who hath branched from this Ancient Root.[3]

Although Bahá'u'lláh did not explicitly identify the Centre of His Covenant in either of these passages in the *Kitáb-i-Aqdas*, there was no doubt in the minds of the believers that Bahá'u'lláh was referring to no other person than 'Abdu'l-Bahá. Bahá'u'lláh made this appointment clear when He quoted the above verse in His Will and Testament known as the Book of His Covenant, and stated that it referred to the Most Great Branch ('Abdu'l-Bahá).*

* The Covenant of Bahá'u'lláh and its Centre, 'Abdu'l-Bahá, will be further discussed in the next volume.

In another passage in the *Kitáb-i-Aqdas* concerning his ascension,* Bahá'u'lláh assures His loved ones of His unfailing support and confirmation in these words:

> Let not your hearts be perturbed, O people, when the glory of My Presence is withdrawn, and the ocean of My utterance is stilled. In My presence amongst you there is a wisdom, and in My absence there is yet another, inscrutable to all but God, the Incomparable, the All-Knowing. Verily, We behold you from Our realm of glory, and shall aid whosoever will arise for the triumph of Our Cause with the hosts of the Concourse on high and a company of Our favoured angels.[4]

Not only did Bahá'u'lláh allude in the *Kitáb-i-Aqdas* to the One who would be His immediate successor, but by implication He, in that same book, anticipated the institution of the Guardianship.† Although the following passage in the *Kitáb-i-Aqdas* is about Huqúqu'lláh,‡ it indicates the pattern of the unfoldment of the Faith of Bahá'u'lláh.

> The endowments dedicated to charity revert to God, the Revealer of Signs. No one has the right to lay hold on them without leave from the Dawning-Place of Revelation. After Him the decision rests with the Aghṣán (Branches), and after them with the House of Justice—should it be established in the world by then—so that they may use these endowments for the benefit of the Sites exalted in this Cause, and for that which they have been commanded by God, the Almighty, the All-Powerful. Otherwise the endowments should be referred to the people of Bahá, who speak not without His leave and who pass no judgment but in accordance with that which God has ordained in this

* Bahá'ís often refer to the passing of Bahá'u'lláh as His ascension. This signifies the ascension of His Spirit to the spiritual realms of God.

† For more information about the institution of the Guardianship see *The Will and Testament of 'Abdu'l-Bahá*, and Shoghi Effendi, *The Dispensation of Bahá'u'lláh*.

‡ see p. 73n.

Tablet, they who are the champions of victory betwixt heaven and earth, so that they may spend them on that which has been decreed in the Holy Book by God, the Mighty, the Bountiful.[5]

The word Aghṣán (plural of Ghuṣn), literally means 'branches'. This word was exclusively used by Bahá'u'lláh to refer to His male descendants. In the above passage this word is used in the plural which indicates that there would be more than one Ghuṣn in His Dispensation who would become the Centre of the Cause. It turned out to be two, 'Abdu'l-Bahá and Shoghi Effendi, the Guardian of the Faith. In this passage there is a striking indication that there will be a break in the line of the Aghsán. It also makes provision for the eventuality that this line might end before the House of Justice had been instituted—a situation which actually took place after the passing of Shoghi Effendi in 1957. For a little over five years the Hands of the Cause of God managed the affairs of the Bahá'í community as custodians of the Faith, and in 1963 the Universal House of Justice came into being and took over the reins of the Cause of God.

There is a moving passage in the *Kitáb-i-Aqdas* addressed to Bahá'u'lláh's unfaithful half-brother Mírzá Yaḥyá. He had been brought under the shadow of the Faith of the Báb at an early age by Bahá'u'lláh. He was cared for by Bahá'u'lláh at every stage of his youth, so that he might serve the Cause of God with devotion and sincerity. But, alas, his lust for leadership induced him to break the Covenant of the Báb and rise up in opposition against the Supreme Manifestation of God. We have already described in previous volumes his rise and fall, as well as the unbearable sufferings that he inflicted upon Bahá'u'lláh.

In spite of the harrowing afflictions that the Blessed Beauty suffered at the hand of this half-brother, He, in the *Kitáb-i-Aqdas*, reminds Mírzá Yaḥyá of the early days of his life when

He, as a token of His bounty, nurtured him so that he might become a worthy instrument for the service of the Cause. He asks him to call to mind the times when he used to be summoned to stand before Bahá'u'lláh and take down the verses of God which were revealed by Him, counsels him to return to God after his shameful rebellion against His Manifestation, and assures him that God would forgive all his iniquities should he now repent and beg forgiveness from Him.

These words fell on deaf ears, and Mírzá Yaḥyá, in spite of losing the support of his master, Siyyid Muḥammad-i-Iṣfahání, remained unrepentant. He outlived Bahá'u'lláh by several years and after witnessing the rising prestige of the Faith of Bahá'u'lláh and the diffusion of its light in the Western world, he died ignominiously on the island of Cyprus in 1912.

One of the most important teachings of Bahá'u'lláh, perhaps the most important, is that He has strictly forbidden His followers to interpret His words. In the *Kitáb-i-Aqdas* He reveals:

> Whoso interpreteth what hath been sent down from the heaven of Revelation, and altereth its evident meaning, he, verily, is of them that have perverted the Sublime Word of God, and is of the lost ones in the Lucid Book.[6]

In other Tablets too He has clearly indicated that no one has the right to interpret, modify or alter His words. As we have already stated, 'Abdu'l-Bahá is the authoritative Interpreter of Bahá'u'lláh's words and so is Shoghi Effendi. The reason that this is the most important teaching of Bahá'u'lláh is that every schism in older religions was caused, in the first place, by differences of interpretation among their leaders.

In an attempt to highlight some of the distinguishing features of Bahá'í teachings, especially those which are not to be found in other religions, the outstanding Bahá'í scholar Mírzá Abu'l-Faḍl outlines nine teachings and briefly dwells on each, presumably in their order of importance. The first two relate to this subject. This is a translation of his words:

> First, a command which is particularly a feature of the Bahai religion and is not found in the other religion is 'abstaining from crediting verbal traditions.' It is well known to men of learning that it was verbal tradition which divided the Jews into two great sects. Such traditions are the basis of the book of Talmud, and caused the division of that one nation . . .
>
> Similarly in the Christian religion the main cause of schism and division were these verbal traditions which were termed 'authoritative'. Each one of the Christian churches, such as the Catholic, the Orthodox, the Jacobite, the Nestorian and others consider it obligatory to follow these traditions inherited from and handed down by the fathers of the Church, as the very text of the Holy Book . . .
>
> Likewise in the religion of Islam, claiming these verbal traditions which were related of the Founder of that religion, subsequent to His death, was the cause of the division and separation into various of the principal sects.
>
> Each of these hold to a set of traditions considered as authentic by their own sect.
>
> But BAHA'O'LLAH closed to the people of the world this door which is the greatest means for sedition; for He has clearly announced that 'in the religion of God all recorded matters are referable to the Book and all unrecorded matters are dependent upon the decision of the House of Justice.' Thus all narrations, relations and verbal traditions have been discredited among the Bahai people and the door of dissension, which is the greatest among the doors of hell, has been closed and locked.
>
> Second: One of the laws and ordinances peculiar to the Bahai religion is the law prohibiting the interpreting of the Word of God. For interpretation of the Words and exposition of personal opinion has been one of the greatest means of dissension in the former religions, the cause of darkening of the horizon of faith and concealing the real meaning of the Book of God.
>
> It is an evident fact that learned men differ in their minds,

and the natural gifts of sagacity and intelligence or the lack of understanding and comprehension vary in degrees among them. Thus when the door of interpretation and perverting of the Words from their outward meaning is opened, strange opinions and curious contradictory interpretations will result and different sects will arise among the one people and one religious community.

Consequently BAHA'O'LLAH has explicitly commanded His followers to wholly abandon the door of interpretation and follow the Words revealed in the Tablets according to their outward meaning, so that the events which have transpired among the past nations should not recur among the Bahai people and the unwelcome happenings which appeared among the various sects due to difference in mentality and viewpoint should not become manifest in this new auspicious day, which is the day of the glorious Lord.[7]

Our Part in the Covenant

The progress of the Cause of Bahá'u'lláh is dependent upon the actions of the believers. Every pure deed attracts the confirmations of Bahá'u'lláh which in turn bring victory to the Cause. But without the individual taking the step, God's assistance cannot reach the Bahá'í community This is one of the irrevocable laws of the Covenant of God. This Covenant has two sides, God's and man's. God's part of the Covenant cannot be confused with man's part. God pours out His bounties and grace upon man, but man must make the necessary move to receive them. Without him opening his heart and submitting himself, the gifts and bounties of God cannot reach him. In the *Hidden Words* Bahá'u'lláh has laid down the law of this Covenant in these words:

> Love Me, that I may love thee. If thou lovest Me not, My love can in no wise reach thee. Know this, O servant.[8]

It may be said that in this Dispensation God has given us two things out of His bounty. One is the Revelation of

Bahá'u'lláh; the other, derived from the former, is the person of 'Abdu'l-Bahá who became the repository of that Revelation, the Centre of the Covenant, as well as Shoghi Effendi, the Guardian of His Cause. These two, the gifts of God to man in this age, constitute the side of the Covenant pertaining to God. It is through these two sources that God's bountiful favours are bestowed upon humanity in this age.

The part that man has to play is to recognize Bahá'u'lláh as the Manifestation of God, then obey His Teachings. When the individual achieves this, he has fulfilled his side of the Covenant with God. It is then that his faith, his obedience to the commandments of God and his living the life as a Bahá'í will attract bountiful confirmations from on high; such a person will bring victory to the Cause of God. His words will become creative and his deeds will reflect the teachings and commandments of Bahá'u'lláh, he will influence the souls and move the hearts of people.

Ḥájí Mírzá Ḥaydar-'Alí, that great man of insight and understanding, writes:

> By nature, human beings are ignorant, weak, sinful, rebellious and wrongdoers, whereas authority, power, sovereignty, forgiveness, lordship, beauty, grandeur, majesty and perfection all revolve around the will of God and His Word. To the extent that we may, through the will of God and His bounties, place ourselves under the shadow of His boundless favours, will our inherent shortcomings, our animal characteristics, passions, and ignorance be transformed into perfections and divine qualities, bestowing upon us a measure of holiness, of knowledge, of power and all the gifts of the Kingdom . . .[9]

Indeed, the greatest source of strength for a Bahá'í is to draw from the power of Bahá'u'lláh. It is the only way through which the believer can effectively promote His Cause. The essential prerequisite for gaining access to this limitless source of spiritual energy is to have faith in Bahá'u'lláh and to believe wholeheartedly that this power exists. Without a sincere belief that Bahá'u'lláh is the Manifestation of God for this age and that He, and He alone, is the source of all creative energies destined to vivify the souls of all men, a Bahá'í cannot succeed in tapping this mighty reservoir of celestial strength. It is the same in nature; how can a person utilize some form of energy without knowing its source? To have certitude in the Faith* is the first condition for success in drawing on the power of Bahá'u'lláh.

The second condition is to become humble and consider oneself to be as utter nothingness in relation to God and His Manifestation. To appreciate this, let us turn to the laws of nature, for the laws and principles of this physical world are similar to those of the spiritual world. This is because God's creation, both physical and spiritual, is one entity. The laws of the lower kingdom exist in the higher kingdom but they are applied on a higher level. Energy can be generated between two points where there is a difference of levels. Water can flow from a higher plane on to a lower one. Electrical energy may be generated when there is a difference of potential between two points in the circuit.

Similarly, to draw on the power of Bahá'u'lláh, the believer must assume the position of lowliness in relation to Bahá'u'lláh's station of loftiness. Bahá'u'lláh may be likened to the summit of a mountain, and the believers to the valley below. In the same way that water pours from the mountain top into the valley, the energies of the Revelation of Bahá'u'lláh and the tokens of His power and might can reach a Bahá'í who turns to Him in a spirit of true humility and servitude. The Writings of the Central Figures of the Faith bear abundant testimony to this basic principle which governs the relationship of man to his Creator. In the *Hidden Words* Bahá'u'lláh prescribes: 'Humble thyself before Me, that I may graciously visit thee . . .'[10] When the believer assumes the position of humility and utter nothingness towards his God,

* For further information on this subject see vol. 2, pp. 216–21.

he will long to commune with Him in a spirit of prayer, a prayer which is without desire and 'transcends the murmur of syllables and sounds', a prayer of praise and glorification of God.

To have faith, to become humble and to raise one's voice in prayer and glorification of God, are not sufficient prerequisites for drawing on the power of Bahá'u'lláh. There is yet another vital condition which the individual must fulfil, namely, to arise to serve the Cause. If he does not act, the channels of grace will remain closed, and no amount of devotion to Bahá'u'lláh and humility before Him can release the powers from on high. The very act of arising in itself is bound to attract the confirmations of Bahá'u'lláh. In many of His Tablets, Bahá'u'lláh has assured His followers that if they arise with faith and devotion to promote His Cause, the unseen hosts of His confirmations will descend upon them and make them victorious. The following passage gleaned from the *Kitáb-i-Aqdas* is one such statement among many:

> Verily, we behold you from Our realm of glory, and shall aid whosoever will arise for the triumph of Our Cause with the hosts of the Concourse on high and a company of Our favoured angels.[11]

The belief that the power of Bahá'u'lláh by itself can accomplish the promotion and establishment of the Faith throughout the world, without the believers fulfilling their obligations in teaching and building up the institutions of the Cause, is unfounded and completely against the laws of the Covenant of God. Indeed, the hands of Bahá'u'lláh are tied if the individual does not arise to serve His Cause. In some of His Writings as far back as in the days of 'Akká, Bahá'u'lláh has stated[12] that if all the believers had fully carried out His teachings in their daily lives, the great majority of the peoples of the world would have recognized Him and embraced His Cause in His days.

The Báb has stated[13] that every Revelation from God in the past was endowed with the potency to become a world religion. The reason that they did not was due to the fact that the believers in each Dispensation did not live up to the teachings of their Prophets. He mentions Islám and Christianity as examples. That neither of these religions spread through the discovered world of those days, that both failed to bring mankind in its entirety under their shadow, was because their followers did not faithfully practise their teachings. All this indicates that the Revelation of God, mighty and penetrating as it is, needs a worthy carrier to plant it in the hearts of men. The power to quicken and create a new spirit in souls comes from the Revelation of God. The believer acts as a channel designed to transmit the vivifying forces of the Faith of God to his fellow human beings.

Although the greater part of the human race did not embrace the Cause of Bahá'u'lláh in His days, for the reasons already stated, yet He has clearly prophesied that ultimately, His Message is destined to envelop the whole world, illumine the hearts of its peoples and unite them under the influence of one common religion—His Faith. In the *Lawḥ-i-Dunya* Bahá'u'lláh reveals these assuring words:

> How vast is the tabernacle of the Cause of God! It hath overshadowed all the peoples and kindreds of the earth, and will, ere long, gather together the whole of mankind beneath its shelter.[14]

In another Tablet He states:

> Grieve thou not at men's failure to apprehend the Truth. Ere long thou shalt find them turning towards God, the Lord of all mankind. We have indeed, through the potency of the Most Sublime Word, encompassed the whole world, and the time is approaching when God will have subdued the hearts of all that dwell on earth. He is in truth the Omnipotent, the All-Powerful.[15]

In a Tablet[16] to Shaykh Káẓim-i-Samandar,* 'Abdu'l-Bahá refers to a prophecy of Bahá'u'lláh made towards the end of His life, to the effect that soon God would raise up holy and detached souls for the spreading of His Cause throughout the World. Bahá'u'lláh has promised that these souls will be like stars in the heaven of guidance and the light of the morn of truth. They will burn as torches lighted by the hand of God, and as lamps shedding their lustre upon a dark world. These souls will not rest for a moment, nor will they become attached to the things of this world. They will spend their time in teaching the Cause and the diffusion of divine fragrances. Their faces will shine with the light of God's Revelation and their hearts will be filled with His love. They will disperse throughout the world, travel to every country, speak every language, proclaim His Message in every assembly, reveal the divine mysteries, diffuse His light, and promote His teachings among the peoples of the world. 'Abdu'l-Bahá in this Tablet ardently prays that these souls, as promised by Bahá'u'lláh, may soon arise so that through the staunchness of their faith, the loftiness of their deeds, the potency of their detachment and the breaths of the Holy Spirit, they may bring victory to the Cause of Bahá'u'lláh.

Today a vast number of dedicated believers from all over the world, and of every conceivable background, have arisen with vigour and devotion to promote the Cause of God as Bahá'í pioneers and teachers. Indeed, with the rising of these detached and holy souls, the initial stage of this promise of Bahá'u'lláh has already been realized. The Faith of Bahá'u'lláh has now reached all parts of the world; through their self-sacrifice, their detachment and their faith, these men and women, drawing on the power of Bahá'u'lláh, have succeeded in erecting the framework of the divinely-ordained institutions of the Faith everywhere. The embryo of a new world order is now growing within the old, and for this reason the world will never be the same again.

* see p. 88.

'We Are With You at All Times'

From the beginning of this Dispensation up to the present time, every victory that the Faith of Bahá'u'lláh has achieved is due to His confirmations and assistance. The power released from on high has been responsible for the progress of the Cause and the building of its embryonic institutions. With very insignificant resources, handicapped by the lack of facilities and manpower, and often devoid of much knowledge and learning, thousands of men and women have scattered throughout the world and pioneered into the most inhospitable areas of the globe. And yet, in spite of their powerlessness and inadequacy, these souls have won astounding victories for the Cause of Bahá'u'lláh. All these people who arose with devotion have experienced the unfailing confirmations of Bahá'u'lláh reaching them in miraculous ways, enabling them to teach the Faith and build its institutions in spite of great and at times seemingly insurmountable obstacles.

The outpouring of confirmations pledged in the *Kitáb-i-Aqdas* is clearly conditional upon the activity of the individual believer. It depends upon one action which may be summed up by the single magic word: 'Arise.' It is to the believer's inner urge to teach the Faith, and his act of 'arising', that God responds, releasing His powers from on high to sustain and strengthen him in his efforts to promote the word of God. Through the mere act of stepping forward to serve the Cause, great bounties will flood the soul, transforming its weakness into strength and its ignorance into wisdom and understanding.

In many of His Tablets Bahá'u'lláh makes similar promises. For example, He utters these assuring words:

> By the righteousness of God! Whoso openeth his lips in this Day and maketh mention of the name of his Lord, the hosts of Divine inspiration shall descend upon him from the heaven of My name, the All-Knowing, the All-Wise. On

him shall also descend the Concourse on high, each bearing aloft a chalice of pure light. Thus hath it been fore-ordained in the realm of God's Revelation, by the behest of Him Who is the All-Glorious, the Most Powerful.[17]

From 'Abdu'l-Bahá, in many Tablets, have come similar assurances, as in this one:

> By the Lord of the Kingdom! If one arise to promote the Word of God with a pure heart, overflowing with the love of God and severed from the world, the Lord of Hosts will assist him with such a power as will penetrate the core of the existent beings.[18]

And Shoghi Effendi, too, reaffirmed these overwhelming promises. Through his secretary he wrote:

> . . . Today, as never before, the magnet which attracts the blessings from on high, is teaching the Faith of God. The Hosts of Heaven are poised between heaven and earth, just waiting, and patiently, for the Bahá'í to step forth, with pure devotion and consecration, to teach the Cause of God, so they may rush to his aid and assistance. Let those who wish to achieve immortality step forth and raise the Divine Call. They will be astonished at the spiritual victories they will gain.[19]

There is another passage in the *Kitáb-i-Aqdas* in which Bahá'u'lláh refers to His ascension and assures His followers of His unfailing support at all times:

> Be not dismayed, O peoples of the world, when the day-star of My beauty is set, and the heaven of My tabernacle is concealed from your eyes. Arise to further My Cause, and to exalt My Word amongst men. We are with you at all times, and shall strengthen you through the power of truth. We are truly almighty. Whoso hath recognized Me, will arise and serve Me with such determination that the powers of earth and heaven shall be unable to defeat his purpose.[20]

In this passage, Bahá'u'lláh states, 'We are with you at all times, and shall strengthen you through the power of truth.' Many of His disciples in His day became assured of this and literally saw with their own eyes that He was with them at all times. We cite two examples: one is a story recounted in detail by Ḥájí Muḥammad-Ṭáhir-i-Málmírí.* It concerns an incident which occurred in the course of his journey to 'Akká, and the words that Bahá'u'lláh addressed to him when he was ushered into His presence for the first time.

From his native city of Yazd, Ḥájí Muḥammad-Ṭáhir went to Kirmán on his way to 'Akká. There he met a devoted believer, Ḥájí Muḥammad-Khán-i-Balúch, a high-ranking personality of Balúchistán, who was going to 'Akká too. They decided that they would travel together. In his memoirs Ḥájí Muḥammad-Ṭáhir writes:

> After a stay of three months in Kirmán we went to Sírján and stayed there for forty days. Muḥammad-Khán was dressed in the garb of a dervish and had flowing hair. Because of this, the dervishes of Sírján used to come to him every night and he had to entertain them and give them food. I suggested to him that he had better cut his hair short and change his head-dress, so that we would get rid of the dervishes in the city.† He agreed with my suggestion and changed his attire. After this, whenever the dervishes came, they were told that the leader had gone, and so we were left alone. While in Sírján, a certain believer, Áqá Muḥammad-'Alí . . . asked Muḥammad-Khán to take him as his personal servant on the journey. This offer was accepted by the Khán . . . and he accompanied us to 'Akká . . . We set off for the port of Bandar-i-'Abbás . . . There we met about one hundred Muslim pilgrims who were natives of Balúchistán and were on their way to Mecca for pilgrimage. When these people heard that the Khán had arrived in the port, they

* see p. 40n.

† The dervishes considered Muḥammad-Khán, who was rich and influential, as a religious guide.

assumed that he was also going to Mecca. So they all came to him, enquired about the details of his journey to Mecca and expressed their happiness that they would travel with him . . . *Muḥammad Khán then intimated to me that we were now trapped and had no alternative but to accompany the pilgrims to Mecca, perform the rites of pilgrimage, and from there proceed to 'Akká which is a shorter way than the alternative route of going to Jedda (via Bombay) and Port Said.

I told the Khán that I would not go to Mecca. He again emphasized that it would be a much shorter journey, but I refused. He explained that he had had no intention of going to Mecca either, but circumstances had forced him this way. If he did not go to Mecca on this journey, the news would reach home and it would cause embarrassment for his family . . . I reiterated my position and said that in my conscience . . . I could not bring myself to go to Mecca on pilgrimage. I suggested that we part company, that I would proceed via Bombay and the Khán via Mecca in the company of his people . . . In refusing to go, however, I was not being obstinate or bearing a grudge against the Khán. Indeed I was very bothered to have to disagree with his wishes. I also knew that our journey via Mecca would be shorter, but my heart could not accept such a course of action . . . Our stay in Bandar-i-'Abbás lasted for eleven days, and every night the Khán spoke about this and insisted that I change my mind. But I was immovable in my opinion. I used to tell him: 'My intention on this journey is to attain the most holy presence of Bahá'u'lláh, not to go on pilgrimage to Mecca and become a Ḥájí.' †

Eventually the Khán gave in and advised his people to proceed to Mecca on their own.

. . . After these people left, the Khán and myself set off

* In those days Bahá'ís did not disclose their faith to the general public. These people did not know that Muḥammad-Khán was a Bahá'í and was travelling to 'Akká. It would have been most unwise for the Khán to disclose to them his real intentions on this journey; and so he had to pretend that he was on his way to Mecca.

† Title given to those who perform the rites of pilgrimage in Mecca.

towards the court of the presence of the Beloved. We journeyed to Haifa via Bombay, and on arrival we introduced ourselves as Bahá'ís. We were taken to the home of Áqá Muḥammad-Ibráhím of Ká<u>sh</u>án, the coppersmith. This believer was directed by Bahá'u'lláh to make his residence in Haifa, to handle the distribution of letters and to give assistance and hospitality to Bahá'í pilgrims. When Bahá'u'lláh was informed that the three of us had arrived, He advised us, through Mírzá Áqá Ján . . . that in 'Akká I should stay with my brother Ḥájí 'Alí.* We were driven from Haifa to 'Akká in 'Abdu'l-Bahá's carriage . . . that day I was most happy. Joy and ecstasy filled my soul.†

The third evening of their arrival, the three pilgrims were summoned to the presence of Bahá'u'lláh and were received by Him with loving-kindness. Ḥájí Muḥammad-Ṭáhir writes about his first meeting with Bahá'u'lláh:

> When I attained His presence, I prostrated myself at His feet. After showering His bounties upon me, He said, 'Well done! May God bless you! People were going to Mecca and you did not go there for the love of God. Instead, you considered coming to the Most Great Prison to be of prime importance. Truly your understanding was correct. Pilgrimage to Mecca can have the same reward as in the past‡ only if it is carried out with Our permission; otherwise, it has no value.§[21]

* See *The Bahá'í World*, vol. IX, pp. 624–5, article on Ḥájí 'Alíy-i-Yazdí.

† For further detail of Ḥájí Muḥammad-Ṭáhir's arrival in 'Akká see vol. 1, pp. 131–2.

‡ 'Past' means during the period of the validity of the Faith of Islám, i.e. up to 1844, the date of the appearance of the Báb. For more information on the subject of the period of validity of a religion see p. 277.

§ When Ḥájí Muḥammad-Ṭáhir was leaving 'Akká on his way home, Bahá'u'lláh directed him to proceed to Mecca and perform all the rites of pilgrimage. So he became a Ḥájí by Bahá'u'lláh's permission. It should be noted also that the above quotation does not record the exact words of Bahá'u'lláh.

These words of Bahá'u'lláh describing the episode of Bandar-i-'Abbás were the first signs of His all-encompassing knowledge which were revealed to these three pilgrims, and left them awestruck. These words helped to further confirm them in their faith and enabled them to believe with absolute certitude that, as testified by Him in the *Kitáb-i-Aqdas* and many other Tablets, He was indeed with them at all times.

Muḥammad-Khán rendered great services to the Faith. Having recognized the Supreme Manifestation of God, he could not sit idle. He conveyed the glad tidings of the Revelation of Bahá'u'lláh to his friends and associates, among them Mírzá Yúsuf Khán, the Mustawfíyu'l-Mamálik, who at one stage was Prime Minister of Persia. 'Abdu'l-Bahá relates the story of Muḥammad-Khán (whom he refers to as 'the Ḥájí') when he embraced the Faith, and describes his enthusiasm and his meeting with Mírzá Yúsuf Khán in these words:

> Thus at the very moment when he heard the call from the Kingdom of God, he shouted, 'Yea verily!' and he was off like the desert wind. He travelled over vast distances, arrived at the Most Great Prison and attained the presence of Bahá'u'lláh. When his eyes fell upon that bright Countenance he was instantly enslaved. He returned to Persia so that he could meet with those people who professed to be following the Path, those friends of other days who were seeking out the Truth, and deal with them as his loyalty and duty required.
>
> Both going and returning, the Ḥájí betook himself to each one of his friends, foregathered with them, and let each one hear the new song from Heaven. He reached his homeland and set his family's affairs in order, providing for all, seeing to the security, happiness and comfort of each one. After that he bade them all goodbye. To his relatives, his wife, children, kin, he said: 'Do not look for me again; do not wait for my return.'
>
> He took up a staff and wandered away; over the mountains he went, across the plains, seeking and finding

the mystics, his friends. On his first journey, he went to the late Mírzá Yúsuf Khán (Mustawfíyu'l-Mamálik), in Ṭihrán. When he had said his say, Yúsuf Khán expressed a wish, and declared that should it be fulfilled, he would believe; the wish was to be given a son. Should such a bounty become his, Yúsuf Khán would be won over. The Ḥájí reported this to Bahá'u'lláh, and received a firm promise in reply. Accordingly, when the Ḥájí met with Yúsuf Khán on his second journey, he found him with a child in his arms. 'Mírzá,' the Ḥájí cried, 'praise be to God! Your test has demonstrated the Truth. You snared your bird of joy.' 'Yes,' answered Yúsuf Khán, 'the proof is clear. I am convinced. This year, when you go to Bahá'u'lláh, say that I implore His grace and favour for this child, so that it may be kept safe in the sheltering care of God.'[22]

'Abdu'l-Bahá in one of His Tablets[23] states that when Bahá'u'lláh was informed of this request He directed Muḥammad-Khán to go home via Ṭihrán especially to meet Mírzá Yúsuf Khán, give him a sugar plum to eat and convey to him the assurance that God would give him a son. It was on his final return to the Holy Land that Muḥammad-Khán saw with his own eyes the fulfilment of that promise.

Muḥammad-Khán was a devoted believer on fire with the love of Bahá'u'lláh. When he embraced the Faith and later attained Bahá'u'lláh's presence, he became an entirely new creation. The honour and high esteem in which he was held by his people and the comfort and prosperity he enjoyed in his life were now utterly worthless to him. His greatest desire was to relinquish his all and become a servant of Bahá'u'lláh as a doorkeeper. He attained his wish and for some years was a servant in the household of Bahá'u'lláh.

'Abdu'l-Bahá has recounted his story as follows:

> Ḥájí Muḥammad then went to the blissful future martyr, the King of Martyrs, and asked him to intercede, so that he, the Ḥájí, might be allowed to keep watch at the doorway of Bahá'u'lláh. The King of Martyrs sent in this request by

ḤÁJÍ MUḤAMMAD KHÁN-I-BALÚCH

An eminent personality who chose to work as a servant of Bahá'u'lláh

MÍRZÁ MUḤAMMAD ENTITLED NA'ÍM

A great Bahá'í poet and teacher of the Faith

letter, after which Ḥájí Khán duly arrived at the Most Great Prison and made his home in the neighbourhood of his loving Friend. He enjoyed this honour for a long time, and later, in the Mazra'ih garden as well, he was very frequently in Bahá'u'lláh's presence. After the Beloved had ascended, Ḥájí Khán remained faithful to the Covenant and Testament, shunning the hypocrites. At last, when this servant was absent on the journeys to Europe and America, the Ḥájí made his way to the travellers' hospice at the Ḥaẓíratu'l-Quds; and here, beside the Shrine of the Báb, he took his flight to the world above.

May God refresh his spirit with the musk-scented air of the Abhá Paradise, and the sweet savours of holiness that blow from the highest Heaven. Unto him be greetings and praise. His bright tomb is in Haifa.[24]

Concerning this ever-present supernatural knowledge, Bahá'u'lláh addressing Mullá Muḥammad-i-Qá'iní, Nabíl-i-Akbar, reveals these words in the *Lawḥ-i-Ḥikmat* (Tablet of Wisdom):

Thou knowest full well that We perused not the books which men possess and We acquired not the learning current amongst them, and yet whenever We desire to quote the sayings of the learned and of the wise, presently there will appear before the face of thy Lord in the form of a tablet all that which hath appeared in the world and is revealed in the Holy Books and Scriptures. Thus do We set down in writing that which the eye perceiveth. Verily His knowledge encompasseth the earth and the heavens.

This is a Tablet wherein the Pen of the Unseen hath inscribed the knowledge of all that hath been and shall be—a knowledge that none other but My wondrous Tongue can interpret.[25]

The other story is that of Mírzá Muḥammad, entitled Na'ím, a believer of remarkable faith and devotion and a poet of outstanding calibre. The following story is his spoken chronicle and demonstrates the truth of the words of

Bahá'u'lláh when He said: 'We are with you at all times':

> After my arrival in Ṭihrán, I was once reading the *Epistle to the Son of the Wolf*, and I came across a very beautiful and penetrating prayer revealed by Bahá'u'lláh and quoted in that book. I immediately wished in my heart that these resplendent words had been revealed from the Pen of the Most High for me, this insignificant servant. Some time passed when one day I received a message from Ḥájí Mírzá 'Abdu'lláh-i-Ṣaḥíḥ-Furúsh ... who was a well-known figure among the Bahá'ís and a channel of communication with the Holy Land. In this message he told me that a Tablet in my name had arrived from the Realm of Glory and that I should call in person at his office in Sabzih-Maydán and collect it. I hastened to his office where I received an exalted Tablet ... as a result of this I was moved to the depth of my emotions. I worked out carefully that at the same moment that I had made a wish in my heart to have the above prayer revealed for me, the bounties of Bahá'u'lláh had been directed toward me in Ṭihrán. He had re-revealed the same prayer at that very moment in my name and He sent it to me. The time that it normally took for communications to arrive in Ṭihrán from the Holy Land was the same as that between my making a wish in my heart, and the arrival of the Tablet. Glorified be God, the Lord of Grandeur and Majesty! Although sufferings and tribulations had encompassed the Realm of Glory from every direction, yet the bounties of Bahá'u'lláh were being vouchsafed to His most insignificant servants, and this demonstrates the truth of the words: 'Nothing whatsoever keepeth Him from being occupied with any other thing.'*[26]

This is the text of the prayer that Na'ím had wished for:

> Glory to Thee, O my God! But for the tribulations which are sustained in Thy path, how could Thy true lovers be recognized; and were it not for the trials which are borne for

* For an explanation of these words of the *Qur'án* see vol. 1, pp. 262–3; vol. 2, p. 416.

love of Thee, how could the station of such as yearn for Thee be revealed? Thy might beareth Me witness! The companions of all who adore Thee are the tears they shed, and the comforters of such as seek Thee are the groans they utter, and the food of them who haste to meet Thee is the fragments of their broken hearts. How sweet to my taste is the bitterness of death suffered in Thy path, and how precious in my estimation are the shafts of Thine enemies when encountered for the sake of the exaltation of Thy Word! Let me quaff in Thy Cause, O my God and my Master, whatsoever Thou didst desire, and send down upon me in Thy love all Thou didst ordain. By Thy glory! I wish only what Thou wishest, and cherish what Thou cherishest. In Thee have I, at all times, placed My whole trust and confidence. Thou art verily the All-Possessing, the Most High.[27]

In His Tablet to Na'ím, Bahá'u'lláh addresses him in words of loving-kindness, states that He has re-revealed the prayer as a token of His favours, and affirms that although it had been previously written for someone else, He had again revealed it for him especially, so that he might chant it with the melody of the birds of heaven and be of those who have achieved their heart's desire.

It is obvious that after having such an experience, the believer reaches the summit of certitude in his faith and this in turn gives birth to a courage which no earthly man can ever exhibit. This is the courage of the martyr and the hero and nothing but the power of God can produce it in a believer.

Na'ím was a truly devoted servant of Bahá'u'lláh. As a result of embracing the Faith, he suffered great persecutions in his native village of Sidih near Iṣfahán. By order of the clergy, he and four other believers had their arms tied to their bodies; they were then tied closely together with a rope and paraded barefoot through the village. Crowds had gathered from neighbouring villages to watch them being tortured. For about fourteen hours the victims were alternately beaten with sticks by the officials. Their bare bodies, painted in different colours, were exposed to the severe winter cold and were so badly battered that many spectators were horrified to witness them. After some time in prison in Iṣfahán, they were exiled from their homes. In the case of Na'ím, his wife was taken from him and married to another man without any divorce proceedings.

Na'ím and his fellow believers left Iṣfahán on foot. They were penniless and suffered great hardships on the way until they arrived in Ṭihrán. Na'ím, to earn a living, at first occupied himself with transcribing the Writings of Bahá'u'lláh which were usually bought by the believers at a modest price, as there were no printing facilities available at that time. His income was so inadequate that he lived in the utmost poverty for some time. Later, however, through his literary talents he secured a prestigious post as a teacher and became prosperous.

Neither in poverty nor in prosperity did Na'ím ever fail in his devoted services to the Cause, services that he rendered with the utmost devotion and self-sacrifice. He occupied most of his free time with teaching the seekers after truth, and deepening the Bahá'ís, until the end of his life. Noteworthy among his activities was a special class he conducted for several years, teaching and deepening a limited number of Bahá'í youth, most of whom became very prominent teachers of the Cause.

Na'ím's contribution to the literature of the Faith is outstanding. His poetry, deservedly regarded as brilliant, was only matched by his deep understanding of the Faith of Bahá'u'lláh and other religions. Among his works is an enchanting book of proofs in verse which is a brilliant exposition of the truth of the Cause of Bahá'u'lláh. This book has been used in many study circles in Persia for deepening in the knowledge of the Faith and understanding the significance of many abstruse passages in the Holy Books of older religions (especially the *Qur'án*), demonstrating the truth of the Cause of Bahá'u'lláh and proving the authenticity of its divine origin.

The poems of Na'ím, those gem-like verses that this highly

gifted believer has left to posterity, will no doubt be for all time a source of teaching material for seekers of truth, and a well-spring of inspiration for the believers.

The *Kitáb-i-Aqdas*, the Most Holy Book, stands out as the mightiest testimony to the sovereignty of Bahá'u'lláh. To any Bahá'í who deeply meditates on this book, Bahá'u'lláh appears as the ruler of all mankind. In the words of Shoghi Effendi, He will be acclaimed by posterity in the same way that He is already recognized by his followers as:

> the Judge, the Lawgiver and Redeemer of all mankind, as the Organizer of the entire planet, as the Unifier of the children of men, as the Inaugurator of the long-awaited millennium, as the Originator of a new 'Universal Cycle', as the Establisher of the Most Great Peace, as the Fountain of the Most Great Justice, as the Proclaimer of the coming of age of the entire human race, as the Creator of a new World Order, as the Inspirer and Founder of a world civilization.[28]

There is no doubt that when the station of Bahá'u'lláh is universally recognized, posterity will look at the story of His life with awe and wonder. People in the future will be amazed at the blindness of man in His days, and astonished at the treatment that was meted out to Him. When the glory of his station is unveiled to the eyes of humanity, it will be hard to imagine that the Lord of Hosts was made to live in the most desolate of the cities, the Heavenly Father held as a captive by a perverse generation and the King of Kings confined in a small room unfit to be a dwelling. And yet in that small room devoid of all the luxuries of life and not even properly furnished, the *Kitáb-i-Aqdas* described by Him as His 'weightiest testimony unto all people'[29] was revealed. It is a staggering thought that in such a room, in an obscure corner of a prison city, unknown to the world, such a mighty instrument as the *Kitáb-i-Aqdas*, the great Charter for future world civilization, should have been born.

Indeed, there can be no greater tragedy than God manifesting Himself in all His glory, and mankind being blind to His Revelation. And there can be no greater feeling of loss than realizing this fact when it is too late. Bahá'u'lláh in the *Kitáb-i-Aqdas* states:

> The peoples of the world are fast asleep. Were they to wake from their slumber, they would hasten with eagerness unto God, the All-Knowing, the All-Wise. They would cast away everything they possess, be it all the treasures of the earth, that their Lord may remember them to the extent of addressing to them but one word. Such is the instruction given you by Him Who holdeth the knowledge of things hidden, in a Tablet which the eye of creation hath not seen, and which is revealed to none except His own Self, the omnipotent Protector of all worlds. So bewildered are they in the drunkenness of their evil desires, that they are powerless to recognize the Lord of all being, Whose voice calleth aloud from every direction: 'There is none other God but Me, the Mighty, the All-Wise.'
>
> Say: Rejoice not in the things ye possess; tonight they are yours, tomorrow others will possess them. Thus warneth you He Who is the All-Knowing, the All-Informed. Say: Can ye claim that what ye own is lasting or secure? Nay! By Myself, the All-Merciful. The days of your life flee away as a breath of wind, and all your pomp and glory shall be folded up as were the pomp and glory of those gone before you. Reflect, O people! What hath become of your bygone days, your lost centuries? Happy the days that have been consecrated to the remembrance of God, and blessed the hours which have been spent in praise of Him Who is the All-Wise. By My life! Neither the pomp of the mighty, nor the wealth of the rich, nor even the ascendancy of the ungodly will endure. All will perish, at a word from Him. He, verily, is the All-Powerful, the All-Compelling, the Almighty. What advantage is there in the earthly things which men possess? That which shall profit them, they have utterly neglected. Ere long, they will awake from their slumber, and find themselves unable to obtain that which

hath escaped them in the days of their Lord, the Almighty, the All-Praised. Did they but know it, they would renounce their all, that their names may be mentioned before His throne. They, verily, are accounted among the dead.[30]

Those who recognized the station of Bahá'u'lláh in His days and were numbered among His followers often availed themselves of the opportunity to have their names mentioned in His presence, and this was considered an inestimable privilege. They often requested a pilgrim who was on his way to the presence of Bahá'u'lláh, to mention their names to Him. Sometimes the pilgrim would write their names on a list and hand it to Mírzá Áqá Ján, Bahá'u'lláh's amanuensis, for presentation to Him. In all these cases, Bahá'u'lláh conferred a measure of His loving-kindness and bounties upon these believers. This He did either verbally, or in many cases in His Tablets. There were also many who wrote to Bahá'u'lláh and in the course of the letters, mentioned the names of some of the believers. In such cases, the Tablet revealed in reply to, and in honour of, the writer contained passages addressed to those whose names were given.

The mere act of Bahá'u'lláh in remembering a believer and vouchsafing His bounties upon him was sufficient to endow his soul with boundless blessings. This was a heavenly favour, and if the individual was able to play his part in living the life and in promoting the Cause with purity of motive, he could become a spiritual giant and a devoted servant.

One of the inestimable privileges which Bahá'u'lláh has conferred upon His followers is that He has summoned them to serve His Cause. In older Dispensations, the Cause of God was usually administered by a few, the religious leaders or clergy. The rest of the people did not have the same opportunity. But in this Dispensation every human being who recognizes the station of Bahá'u'lláh and is enlisted in His Faith, whether young or old, learned or unlettered, rich or poor, can render services to the Cause of God. In many of His Tablets Bahá'u'lláh urges the believers to arise and promote the Faith of God. In the *Kitáb-i-Aqdas* too there are several references to this. There is no limit to serving the Cause. One need not be educated or have influence and standing in society to serve. Often it is the simple people of the world, sometimes illiterate, who rise to great heights of service in the Faith of Bahá'u'lláh.

There can be no greater bounty in this life than serving the Cause, provided one's motive is pure. If service is rendered in the hope of securing fame, influence and other personal gains in this world or even in the next,* then such a service becomes a great burden on the soul. It fills one's life with sadness and frustration and as Bahá'u'lláh has declared in His Writings, it will not be pleasing to God, for nothing but pure deeds and pure motives can be acceptable in His sight.

The Cause of God revealed in this day is very great, and so must be human effort in its determination to promote and serve it with devotion and self-sacrifice. To the extent that a believer recognizes the exalted station of Bahá'u'lláh will he be able to purify his motive in the service of the Cause, and to the same extent he will be rewarded spiritually. Bahá'u'lláh often proclaimed the stupendous character of His Revelation. In the *Kitáb-i-Aqdas* He reveals these moving words:

> O peoples of the earth! God, the Eternal Truth, is My witness that streams of fresh and soft-flowing waters have gushed from the rocks, through the sweetness of the words uttered by your Lord, the Unconstrained; and still ye slumber. Cast away that which ye possess, and, on the wings of detachment, soar beyond all created things. Thus biddeth you the Lord of creation, the movement of Whose Pen hath revolutionized the soul of mankind.
>
> Know ye from what heights your Lord, the All-Glorious is calling? Think ye that ye have recognized the Pen wherewith your Lord, the Lord of all names, commandeth

* For a discussion of attachment to the next world see vol. 2, pp. 36–43.

> you? Nay, by My life! Did ye but know it, ye would renounce the world, and would hasten with your whole hearts to the presence of the Well-Beloved. Your spirits would be so transported by His Word as to throw into commotion the Greater World—how much more this small and petty one! Thus have the showers of My bounty been poured down from the heaven of My loving-kindness, as a token of My grace; that ye may be of the thankful.[31]

Some of the disciples of Bahá'u'lláh had reached this summit of faith and discovered for themselves the loftiness of the station of Bahá'u'lláh. When these embodiments of detachment attained His presence, they were carried away to other realms beyond this world. They wanted to express the depth of their devotion to their Lord. But words were not adequate to describe their feelings of utter dedication and self-effacement. Above all, the majesty of Bahá'u'lláh was such that they were unable to utter a word in His presence, unless He empowered them to do so. Therefore, each person demonstrated the measure of his love and his readiness to lay down his life in His path by some act. Some went down on their knees in His presence, others prostrated themselves at His feet, yet others stood in silence rapt in spiritual communion with Him. Here is a story of Ḥájí Mírzá Ḥaydar-'Alí, in the presence of Bahá'u'lláh in 'Akká, as he himself recounts:

> One day I attained His presence. I was standing and the Blessed Beauty was pacing up and down the room. The ocean of His utterance was surging, and the sun of His bounteous favours was shedding its luminous rays upon my soul. The thought occurred to me, as I found myself in His presence, that I should throw myself on His blessed feet and kiss them,* as this had been one of my cherished desires for a long time. Every time He walked towards me, I found myself pinned motionless like a painting to the wall. But

* To prostrate oneself at someone's feet and kiss them was considered by the people of the Orient to be the profoundest expression of humility.

when He turned away, I moved one, two or three steps forward with the intention of prostrating myself at His feet. Then as He turned back and walked toward me, the awe and majesty of His glorious person drove me back to the wall where I stood motionless. Three or four times I went forward in this way and then back to the wall. His Blessed Person noticed this and, smiling, said: 'What happens to you? You keep taking a step forward and then retreating.' He then signalled to me with His hand to stay in my place.

Although it was the greatest ambition of my life and the most cherished desire of my soul to throw myself at His feet, an act which I was prevented from carrying out, and I should have been disappointed and sad, yet the few words that He uttered and the movement of His hand created in me such joy that till eternity I shall remain in a state of happiness and feel greatly honoured by what happened on that day.[32]

The *Kitáb-i-Aqdas* is truly like an ocean and it is difficult to describe every subject revealed in that book. We have so far referred to some of its major themes. References have also been made previously to some of Bahá'u'lláh's teachings and prophecies in the *Kitáb-i-Aqdas*. These subjects include the appearance of the next Manifestation of God,* the praising of the learned in the Faith,† Bahá'u'lláh's summons to the kings and rulers and ecclesiastics,‡ the signs of the maturity of mankind§ and other topics.ø

The spiritual truths revealed in the *Kitáb-i-Aqdas* are fathomless. No one in this life can ever claim to have fully appreciated the potentialities hidden within each one of its revealed words. For (with the exception of its laws which are to be followed literally) the *Kitáb-i-Aqdas* is full of hidden

* See vol. 1, p. 280.
† See vol. 2, p. 265.
‡ See vol. 2, pp. 304–5.
§ See p. 157.
ø For some other topics in the *Kitáb-i-Aqdas* see vol. 1, pp. 47, 124, 212, 301; vol. 2, pp. 122, 240, 355; and the discussions in this volume.

significances. Bahá'u'lláh reveals these words in the *Kitáb-i-Aqdas*:

> Immerse yourselves in the ocean of My words, that ye may unravel its secrets, and discover all the pearls of wisdom that lie hid in its depths. Take heed that ye do not vacillate in your determination to embrace the truth of this Cause—a Cause through which the potentialities of the might of God have been revealed, and His sovereignty established. With faces beaming with joy, hasten ye unto Him. This is the changeless Faith of God, eternal in the past, eternal in the future. Let him that seeketh, attain it; and as to him that hath refused to seek it—verily, God is Self-Sufficient, above any need of His creatures.
>
> Say: This is the infallible Balance which the Hand of God is holding, in which all who are in the heavens and all who are on the earth are weighed, and their fate determined, if ye be of them that believe and recognize this truth. Say: Through it the poor have been enriched, the learned enlightened, and the seekers enabled to ascend unto the presence of God. Beware, lest ye make it a cause of dissension amongst you. Be ye as firmly settled as the immovable mountain in the Cause of your Lord, the Mighty, the Loving.[33]

In one of His Tablets,[34] 'Abdu'l-Bahá states that when Bahá'u'lláh was engaged in formulating the teachings and revealing the verses of God which streamed from His pen, the power which was released by the revelation of the Word* created such a thrill in His heart that He could not eat His meals. Sometimes He used to eat very little and there were days when He could not eat at all.

* For more information on the manner of the revelation of the Word of God see vol. 1, ch. 3.

18

Last Days Within the Citadel

The promulgation of the *Kitáb-i-Aqdas*, which according to Shoghi Effendi may well rank as the most significant act of the ministry of Bahá'u'lláh, should be regarded as a potent source for the regeneration of mankind. The mysterious forces which the revelation of this Book released in the world may be said to have been a major factor in turning the tide of the fortunes of the Faith and its Author in 'Akká.

We recall, as we survey the history of those days, how Bahá'u'lláh and His companions were engulfed in a sea of tribulations as a result of the murder of the three followers of Mírzá Yaḥyá, a reprehensible act which had cast a shadow upon the community of the Most Great Name. Now, a year later, the gloom was beginning to lift and the prestige of the Faith had begun to rise. All the believers who had been put in gaol, with the exception of the seven actually responsible for that heinous act, were released. Once again confidence was restored among the inhabitants of the city towards the company of exiles whose integrity and uprightness had dispelled all the false accusations which had temporarily tarnished their good name.

The marriage of 'Abdu'l-Bahá to Munírih Khánum* took place in the same year that the *Kitáb-i-Aqdas* was revealed. 'Abbúd, Bahá'u'lláh's next-door neighbour, who had through fear earlier on reinforced the partition between the two houses, was now moved to open a room from his own house to Bahá'u'lláh's in order to provide accommodation for 'Abdu'l-Bahá and His bride. And then the partition between the houses

* see vol. 2, pp. 204–9.

was removed and 'Abbúd left his house to Bahá'u'lláh and went to live elsewhere. In this way more accommodation became available for Bahá'u'lláh and His family.

Bahá'u'lláh Himself moved into a more spacious room with a veranda facing the sea and 'Abdu'l-Bahá moved into the room which Bahá'u'lláh had occupied up until then. Compared to the old one, the new room of Bahá'u'lláh was a delightful place. Here He could see the sea as He walked on the veranda. Also the believers could attain His presence in more comfortable and brighter surroundings.

It was in this room that for some years the pilgrims from Persia came to His presence, and it was here that many important Tablets were revealed.

Bahá'u'lláh often walked on the veranda in front of His room where He could be in the open air and gaze out to sea. Usually he did this in the afternoon. The believers from 'Akká who had shared His imprisonment and sufferings with the greatest joy and fortitude and were now living and working in different parts of the city were immensely delighted by this new development.

Ḥájí Mírzá Ḥaydar-'Alí, an eye-witness to the events of those days, has left for posterity these reminiscences:*

> There were about one hundred believers in 'Akká consisting of those who resided there and the visitors. Most of these people were engaged in some trade or business. There was tremendous love and unity among these souls. They derived great joy from associating with each other and were very proud to have the privilege of serving one another. All this made them feel that they were living in paradise.
>
> It had become Bahá'u'lláh's established practice to summon some of the believers to attain His presence. This usually took place from three hours before sunset up to two or three hours after sunset. Therefore, all the believers would leave their work three hours before sunset and

* This account relates to the year 1877, a few months before Bahá'u'lláh left the house of 'Abbúd and took up residence in Mazrá'ih. (A.T.)

assemble in the street outside the house of Bahá'u'lláh. Some would walk around the house, others would stand and some would sit in groups. There were those who were inside the reception room of 'Abdu'l-Bahá as they had some duties to perform . . .

The believers were thus able to see their Lord as He walked on the veranda of the house. Many a time through His bounty and loving-kindness, He would, with His blessed hand, signal to some to come up to His presence . . . The unity which existed among the believers was such that they were as one body; each one was ready to sacrifice his life for the other. And when one individual or a group was summoned in this way, the joy which flooded their hearts was indescribable. The person would run inside with such speed that even the door and the walls vibrated with excitement. He would be so thrilled at that moment that he could not recognize anybody, and if someone talked to him, he could not hear it. He would be on his way to meet his Lord, to reach the paradise of Divine Presence which is much more glorious than paradise itself, a paradise which cannot be seen or felt or heard by those who have not experienced it. And, after being dismissed from Bahá'u'lláh's presence, the individual was so carried away that it would take him some time to regain consciousness, when he would be able to recognize his friends and talk to them. Only one out of many could perhaps recount, in a very inadequate way, the words that he had heard in His presence. But no one was ever able to describe the spiritual experiences of his meeting with his Lord.[1]

The devotion and love which Bahá'u'lláh's companions had for Him were beyond measure. There was a believer in 'Akká, Mírzá Muḥammad-Hádiy-i-Ṣaḥḥáf (bookbinder), who wanted to make sure that the eyes of Bahá'u'lláh would not fall on any unclean sight when He emerged from His room on to the veranda. Although he was an outstanding artist engaged in illuminating the Books and Tablets of Bahá'u'lláh, he nevertheless took upon himself the task of cleaning and

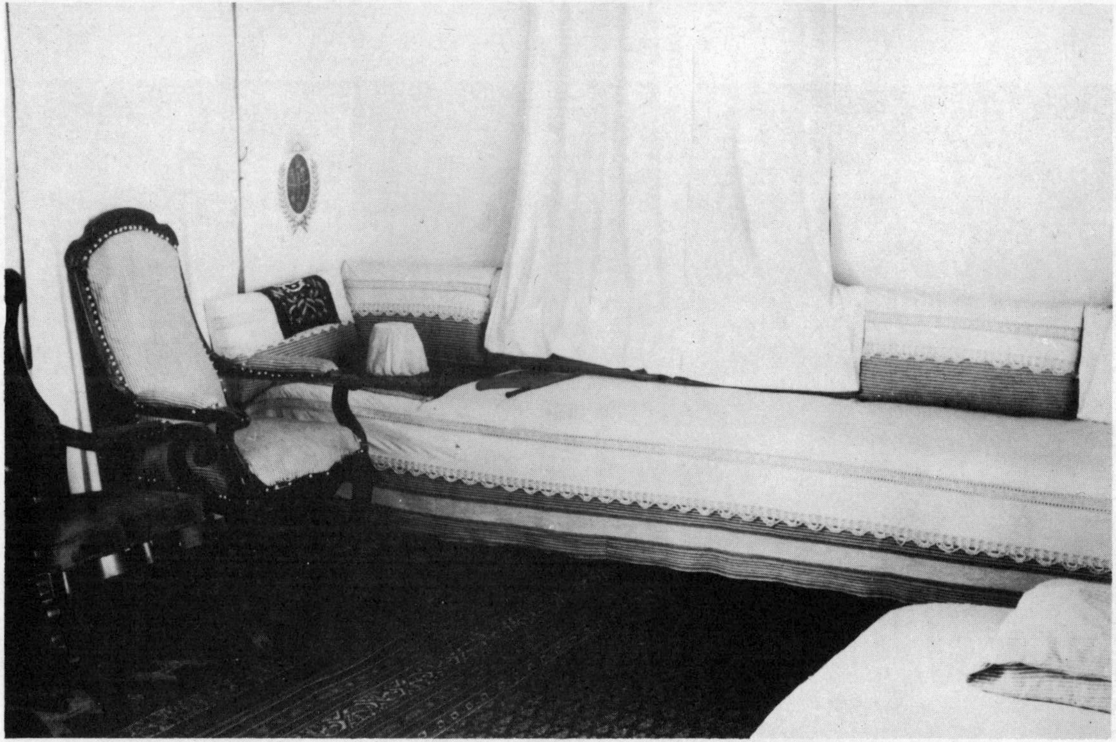

THE ROOM OF BAHÁ'U'LLÁH IN THE HOUSE OF 'ABBÚD

Bahá'u'lláh's head-dress has been placed in the corner of the divan where He usually sat

A VIEW OF THE AQUEDUCT

Restored to use at Bahá'u'lláh's request, the aqueduct brought fresh water to 'Akká

sweeping* the area around the house of 'Abbúd. 'Abdu'l-Bahá has written his story in these words:

> . . . among those who emigrated and came to settle near Bahá'u'lláh was the bookbinder, Muḥammad-Hádí. This noted man was from Iṣfahán, and as a binder and illuminator of books he had no peer. When he gave himself up to the love of God he was alert on the path and fearless. He abandoned his home and began a dreadful journey, passing with extreme hardship from one country to another until he reached the Holy Land and became a prisoner. He stationed himself by the Holy Threshold, carefully sweeping it and keeping watch. Through his constant efforts, the square in front of Bahá'u'lláh's house was at all times swept, sprinkled and immaculate.
>
> Bahá'u'lláh would often glance at that plot of ground, and then He would smile and say: 'Muḥammad-Hádí has turned the square in front of this prison into the bridal-bower of a palace. He has brought pleasure to all the neighbours and earned their thanks.'
>
> When his sweeping, sprinkling and tidying was done, he would set to work illuminating and binding the various books and Tablets. So his days went by, his heart happy in the presence of the Beloved of mankind. He was an excellent soul, righteous, true, worthy of the bounty of being united with his Lord, and free of the world's contagion . . .
>
> He was a man short of stature, lofty of station and mind. His heart was pure, his soul luminous. During all those days when he served the Holy Threshold, he was loved by the friends and favoured by God. From time to time, a smile on His lips, the Blessed Beauty would speak to him, expressing kindness and grace[2] . . .

The extraordinary love and devotion that the companions of

* The streets of 'Akká were covered in earth. There was no proper system of refuse collection at the time, and people often threw litter into the streets. This is why many householders would sweep the approaches to their houses, and sprinkle the ground with water.

Bahá'u'lláh entertained in their hearts for Him, and their enthusiasm to attain His presence as described by Ḥájí Mírzá Ḥaydar-'Alí were mainly due to two things. One was the staunchness of their faith in Bahá'u'lláh as the Supreme Manifestation of God, and the other their complete surrendering of their own wills to His. To the extent that His disciples acquired these two qualities were they able to draw near to Him. There were also believers who gained admittance into the presence of Bahá'u'lláh, witnessed the outpourings of His Revelation, were awed at His majesty and were filled with the spirit of faith. But as they were not detached from the things of this world and could not subdue their self and ego, they remained remote from His bountiful favours.

In one of His Tablets[3] Bahá'u'lláh states that there were some believers who attained His presence day and night,* and yet did not draw nigh to Him because they were spiritually remote. And there were those who never attained His presence outwardly, but enjoyed nearness to Him spiritually.

In this Tablet Bahá'u'lláh declares that the reward which God has destined for a sincere and pure-hearted believer who has attained His presence is far greater than the reward for all the good deeds in the world put together. Indeed, the reward for such a bounty, He testifies, cannot be described in words. Only God is aware of it.

Bahá'u'lláh states in this Tablet that even those who visit the land in which the throne of the Manifestation of God is established will be bountifully blessed in the world to come, how much more will be the reward of those who actually have attained His presence.

To subdue one's self and to surrender one's will to the will of the Manifestation of God may prove to be the most difficult task for man to achieve. When the individual achieves this exalted goal of submitting himself to God, he becomes the

* Mírzá Áqá Ján is an example of this. He was in Bahá'u'lláh's service most of the time, but at the end he became a Covenant-breaker and destroyed a forty-year life of service to Bahá'u'lláh.

recipient of His boundless favours.

All living creatures submit themselves in a physical sense to the forces of nature. A tree shows no resistance to the rain and the rays of the sun. It receives their life-giving energies and as a result it grows and flourishes. In a spiritual sense, man must do the same if he is to receive the bounties of God. The only difference is that whereas other living creatures submit themselves involuntarily to the forces of nature, man has free will to decide his options.

'Abdu'l-Bahá in one of His Tablets[4] states that the highest degree of sacrifice in the path of God for a believer is to surrender his will entirely to the will of God, and become a true servant of the loved ones of the Blessed Beauty. For God, in His essence, is exalted above man's servitude to Him. Therefore to become a servant of God, one must serve His loved ones. 'Abdu'l-Bahá in this Tablet reiterates His station of servitude stating that in His innermost heart, He considers Himself to be the lowliest servant of the believers, and that His greatest ambition is to be able to render devoted service to each and every one of the friends.

The story of 'Abdu'l-Bahá's servitude is widely acknowledged by those who came in contact with Him. His Writings also bear ample testimony to his unique life of service to all the human race. As the 'perfect Exemplar' of the teachings of Bahá'u'lláh, 'the embodiment of every Bahá'í ideal', and 'the incarnation of every Bahá'í virtue',[5] 'Abdu'l-Bahá's life has already inspired many, and will continue to inspire countless generations of the future in their endeavour to become selfless and live a life of humility and servitude.

Dr Yúnis Khán-i-Afrúkhtih* served the Master for some years in 'Akká. His love for 'Abdu'l-Bahá and His constant association with Him left an abiding impression upon his life. He became one of the spiritual giants of this Faith, a magnetic personality and an illumined soul endowed with great humour

* see p. 361.

and talent. He has written a great deal in His memoirs about the Master. In them he states that after the passing of Bahá'u'lláh, the Covenant-breakers arose in opposition against 'Abdu'l-Bahá. They did everything in their power to discredit Him and belittle His station as the Centre of the Covenant of Bahá'u'lláh. The reaction of the steadfast believers was to exalt the station of the Master to the point of exaggeration. This displeased Him immensely, for He always considered Himself to be only a servant. The following is a translation of Dr Yúnis Khán's thoughts and recollections concerning 'Abdu'l-Bahá's station of servitude.

> As the Covenant-breakers intensified their campaign of trouble-making for the Master and went on belittling His station, many of the steadfast believers, due to their enormous love for Him, exaggerated His station. Eventually all this resulted in a situation that if a believer was moved, for instance, to compose a poem about 'Abdu'l-Bahá's servitude, he would assuredly become the recipient of the Master's unbounded favours and bounties. But if, on the contrary, he would sing His praises and exalt His name, He would be displeased, and even ask the writer to repent and beg forgiveness.
>
> The only station that He retained for Himself was that of the appointed Interpreter of the Writings of Bahá'u'lláh. And this He did so that if a person ever sought to glorify His station by referring to the many exalted titles* by which Bahá'u'lláh had designated Him, He then would merely say, 'I am the Interpreter of the Words of God and my interpretation of all these designations is 'Abdu'l-Bahá (Servant of Bahá'u'lláh)' . . . At one stage He wrote many Tablets and prayers concerning His own station of servitude. Among them was a prayer which is now used as a Prayer of Visitation for 'Abdu'l-Bahá. Concerning this prayer He wrote, 'Whoso reciteth this prayer with lowliness and fervour will bring gladness and joy to the heart of this servant; it will be even as meeting Him face to face.'
>
> In this prayer He describes His station of servitude in

* see vol. 2, pp. 395–6

such lowly terms: 'Lord! Give me to drink from the chalice of selflessness; with its robe clothe me, and in its ocean immerse me. Make me as dust in the pathway of Thy loved ones, and grant that I may offer up my soul for the earth ennobled by the footsteps of Thy Chosen ones in Thy path, O Lord of Glory in the Highest.'

O dear reader! Most of the believers know this prayer by heart and are in the habit of reciting it every morning. This is why this servant has not quoted its full text here. My appeal to you now is to recite this prayer* first and then read the following which is entitled:

The story of a bitter-sweet experience

In those days when the friends in Persia were aflame with the fire of love, and at the same time, with a spirit of forbearance, burning in that fire of envy and hatred, of calumny and slander, created by the people of malice and the Covenant-breakers, Bahá'í poets and people of letters in that country used to write poems in praise and glorification of 'Abdu'l-Bahá. In laudatory and most eloquent language they used to acclaim His exalted station.

But we, the resident Bahá'ís of 'Akká, the spot round which the Concourse on High† circle in adoration, were very careful not to breathe a word about the station of sovereignty and lordship of the blessed Person of 'Abdu'l-Bahá. We knew well that He had often advised the poets that instead of singing His praise they ought to exalt His station of servitude and utter self-effacement.

During this time, one day I received a letter from one of the handmaidens of God‡ . . . This letter, composed in verse, and laudatory in its tone, was addressed to 'Abdu'l-Bahá in the form of a supplication to the holy presence of God. I handed the poem to the Master as He was coming down the steps of the house in front of the sea. I thought it

* 'Tablet of Visitation' of 'Abdu'l-Bahá, in most Bahá'í prayer books. (A.T.)

† See p. 180n. (A.T.)

‡ Bahá'u'lláh often designated the male believers as 'servants of God' and the female as 'handmaidens of God'. (A.T.)

was the right moment to give it to Him. He had hardly read one or two lines when He suddenly turned His face towards me and with the utmost sadness and a deep sense of grief said: 'Now even you hand me letters such as this! Don't you know the measure of pain and sorrow which overtakes me when I hear people addressing me with such exalted titles? Even you have not recognized me! If you have not appreciated this, then what can be expected of others? . . . Don't you see all that I do day and night, and everything I write in my letters . . . I swear by Almighty God that I consider myself lowlier than each and every one of the loved ones of the Blessed Beauty. This is my firm conviction . . . Tell me if I am wrong. This is my greatest wish. I don't even wish to make this claim, because I dislike every claim. He then turned towards the Qiblih and said, 'O Blessed Beauty, grant me this station' . . .

'Abdu'l-Bahá spoke angrily in this vein with such vigour that my heart almost stopped. I had a sensation of choking, my whole body became numb. Truly, I felt that life was going out of me. Not only was the power of speech taken from me, but energy for breathing seemed to have gone also. I wished the earth would open and swallow me up so that I might never again see my Lord so grief-stricken as this. Truly for a moment I was not present in this world. Only when the Master resumed His walking down the stairs, the sound of His shoes jolted me. I quickly followed Him. I heard Him say: 'I told the Covenant-breakers that the more they hurt me, the more will the believers exalt my station to the point of exaggeration . . .'

Now that the blame was removed from the believers and placed on the Covenant-breakers, I somewhat regained consciousness and a little life. I listened carefully to His words, but my thoughts were elsewhere. I now understood that it was the iniquities and transgressions perpetrated by these ruthless Covenant-breakers which had produced a strong reaction among the believers who could not control their feelings and sentiments.

This bitter experience of mine was ended now. The Master was pacing up and down the hall and speaking more about the machinations of the Covenant-breakers. But I was not in a position to think properly or meditate deeply. I was very perturbed that I had brought such grief upon the Master, and I did not know what to do. Then I heard Him say: 'This is in no way the fault of the friends. They say these things because of their steadfastness, their love and devotion . . .' Again my thoughts were directed to His words. Then I heard Him say to me: 'You are very dear to Me, etc . . .'"* From these utterances I realized that it was always the Master's way never ever to allow a soul to be hurt. And now this was a time for giving me comfort and encouragement. The pressure in my heart was now released. All the anguish pent up in me was gone. I burst into tears which flowed in great profusion upon my cheeks and I listened more carefully. I heard His utterances as He showered His bounties upon me in such heartwarming and affectionate terms that they went far beyond the normal limits of encouragement. So much loving kindness and favour He bestowed upon me that when I considered my limited capacity and worth, I could not bear to hear Him; therefore I never allowed those words to enter into my memory. Nevertheless, I was filled with such an indescribable joy and ecstasy that I wished the doors of heaven would open and I could ascend to the Kingdom on high.

When He dismissed me from His presence I went towards the Pilgrim House in such a state of intoxication and excitement that I walked all around the streets of 'Akká, not knowing where I was going!

And now, my dear reader, you can see how a bitter experience turned into a sweet one, and how it all ended. The earth did not open up to swallow me, neither did the heavens open to let me go up! And, so I can write down the stories of those days and in memory of His radiant countenance may say to you: 'Allah'u'Abhá!' †[6]

* It is obvious that through his modesty and humility Dr Yúnis Khán does not wish to reveal all the praise and encouragement which the Master had showered upon him.

† Literally: God is most glorious.

During the time that Bahá'u'lláh resided in the house of 'Abbúd, His fellow exiles had fully settled down in the city of 'Akká, and most of them were successful in their humble professions. During the governorship of Aḥmad Big Tawfíq, they enjoyed relative peace in their work. But with the arrival of a new Governor, 'Abdu'r-Raḥmán Pá<u>sh</u>á, the situation changed. For he proved to be one of the most hostile Governors towards Bahá'u'lláh and His companions. He was very covetous and when his designs to extract money from the company of exiles failed, he submitted an inflammatory report to the authorities in Istanbul. He complained that instead of imprisonment, all the Bahá'ís in 'Akká were free and working. The response from the Sublime Porte—the office of the Grand Vizír in Istanbul—was that the edict of the Sulṭán must be obeyed, that they were prisoners and had no right to work.

Ḥusayn-i-Á<u>sh</u><u>ch</u>í has given a detailed account of this episode in his memoirs. It must be noted that Áqá Ḥusayn was at the time serving a sentence in prison because of his part in the slaying of the three Azalís in 'Akká, but through the goodwill of some of the authorities, he was allowed to go every morning to the house of Bahá'u'lláh where he used to work as a cook and return to the prison at night. The following is a summary of his notes:

> When 'Abdu'r-Raḥmán Pá<u>sh</u>á received the note from the Sublime Porte condemning the exiles to imprisonment, it boosted his arrogance. He decided to use it as a means of extracting some money for himself . . . Having failed to do this, one evening he called on <u>Sh</u>ay<u>kh</u> 'Alíy-i-Mírí, the Muftí* of 'Akká who was an admirer of 'Abdu'l-Bahá, and shared with him his plan of arresting the Bahá'ís in the morning. His plan was to arrest them as they came to open their shops and send them to prison. He also planned to restrict 'Abdu'l-Bahá's freedom of movement in the city. He solicited the support of the Muftí in this plan . . . That

* The religious leader of the city who usually wielded greater influence and authority than a governor.

same night the Muftí went to 'Abdu'l-Bahá, told him the news and strongly urged the Master to bribe the Governor, as otherwise everyone would be arrested in the morning. Disapproving the Muftí's solution, 'Abdu'l-Bahá assured him that God was compassionate and merciful, and that He would leave this matter in the hand of God. He advised him to go home and to rest assured of the outcome. It was late and Bahá'u'lláh had just retired. Nevertheless, 'Abdu'l-Bahá went to Him and gave Him the news. Bahá'u'lláh ordered that the believers be advised not to go to work in the morning. Everyone was informed and they all assembled in the reception room of 'Abdu'l-Bahá in the morning.

I was, at the time, confined to prison . . . but each morning was permitted to go to the house of Bahá'u'lláh where I worked as a cook and at night I returned to prison. On that morning, on my way, I noticed that the shop of Áqá Muḥammad-Ibráhím, the coppersmith, was closed and so were other shops belonging to the believers. I was very surprised and wondered what had happened. I hastened to the house of Bahá'u'lláh where I found all the shopkeepers assembled in the reception room. I was told the news and went into the kitchen to work. It was approximately two hours after sunrise when a man pushed aside the curtain in front of the door with his walking stick. I looked up and it was Iskandar Effendi, the head of the telegraph office. He was in great haste but signs of joy could be detected in his appearance. He wanted to see the Master who was upstairs at the time. I went up and found that He was in the presence of Bahá'u'lláh. I told the Master that Iskandar Effendi had come to see Him and he was in a happy mood. The Blessed Beauty smiled and said 'Go downstairs, Áqá!* He has good news. No one can frustrate God in His purpose.'

'Abdu'l-Bahá went to the reception room where He was shown a telegram just received containing the order of dismissal of 'Abdu'r-Raḥmán Páshá.† After a few minutes

* The Master, one of 'Abdu'l-Bahá's titles given to Him by Bahá'u'lláh. He usually addressed 'Abdu'l-Bahá as Áqá.

† It was not unusual for a telegraph office to share such news with people, as there were no other news media. The fact that 'Abdu'l-Bahá received

He went hurriedly upstairs. Halfway up, I asked Him if he could tell me the news. He smiled and said in a loud voice, 'God has struck a severe blow at the Pásh͟há.' He then went to convey the news to Bahá'u'lláh.

As to 'Abdu'r-Raḥmán Pásh͟há, in the morning, accompanied by a few soldiers, he went to arrest the believers at their shops and send them to prison. To his surprise he found the shops were closed. At first he thought the late opening was perhaps due to the month of Ramaḍán when people were going late to work. Soon after, he went to the Police Station where he waited for the shops to open up. During this time he was unaware of God's intervention . . . The above telegram was addressed to S͟hayk͟h 'Alíy-i-Mírí, the Muftí of 'Akká, who communicated its content to the Pásh͟há . . . The Muftí had been truly astonished by this event. For it was late in the evening when the Governor's scheme had come to light, and in the morning the telegram arrived. He considered this incident to have been a miracle. He said to the Master, 'I am almost on the verge of losing my mind over this episode. Please tell me, what did Bahá'u'lláh say late that evening when you informed Him of the plot?' 'Abdu'l-Bahá responded by saying that the Blessed Beauty ordered the believers not to open their shops in the morning and advised them to leave their affairs in the hand of God. Bahá'u'lláh also declared that when a person leaves his affairs to God, he ought not to take any other measures himself, otherwise he could frustrate the plan of God.[7]

In a Tablet[8] Bahá'u'lláh describes 'Abdu'r-Raḥmán Pásh͟há as an embodiment of Satan, one who ruled over God in 'Akká. He asserts that God assisted him in his evil schemes for some time, until suddenly He took hold of him with might and power. Admonishing the ousted Governor, Bahá'u'lláh states that he was unable to prevent God from executing His will, and reminds him that men greater than him did not succeed in frustrating His purpose. He also refers to the fate of other

---

the news before the Governor shows the deep regard some officials had for the Master.

hostile governors and officials who were either dismissed or stricken with disease through the power of God.

Other Governors who followed ‘Abdu’r-Raḥmán Pás͟há were friendly. First Asa‘d Effendi was dispatched to ‘Akká. He was Acting Governor for a short time and was especially commissioned to investigate the condition of the exiles. Although Bahá’u’lláh did not usually give interviews to anyone outside the circle of His followers, He gave permission to Asa‘d Effendi to see Him. This was a result of repeated requests by Asa‘d Effendi and the intercession of ‘Abbúd. Asa‘d Effendi was so impressed by the glory of Bahá’u’lláh’s countenance that he knelt before Him and when he was leaving, he kissed the hem of His garment.

The next Governor was Fayḍi Pás͟há to whom we have referred previously.* During his short stay of about two months in ‘Akká as Governor, he became one of the ardent admirers of ‘Abdu’l-Bahá. One day he noticed that some religious leaders, including the Muftí of ‘Akká, were taking part in religious discussions in the Mosque. He conveyed to them his displeasure at seeing that ‘Abdu’l-Bahá was not there to conduct such classes. He was told that the reason was the order of the Sulṭán which prohibited such an activity. On another occasion, when he noticed that ‘Abdu’l-Bahá did not leave the city boundaries, he sent word that He should feel free to visit other localities outside ‘Akká. Fayḍí Pás͟há was a man of action. His admiration for and support of ‘Abdu’l-Bahá boosted the prestige of the community. This is a summary of Ḥusayn-i-Ás͟hc͟hí’s memoirs concerning Fayḍí Pás͟há:

> One day the Master was in the presence of Bahá’u’lláh and was talking about Fayḍí Pás͟há. I was present on that occasion when the Master was recounting in detail some of the activities of the Governor and praising his steadfastness, his services and his sincerity. Bahá’u’lláh said, ‘Áqá! this Pás͟há is a great personality. A man as great as he will not be

* see p. 25.

allowed to remain here very long. You will find that he will be summoned to Istanbul suddenly by a telegram. If there were a few personalities such as this among the Ottoman rulers, the Government would have made good progress.'

Then 'Abdu'l-Bahá left and went to the reception room downstairs. It did not take more than one hour and a half before a telegram arrived from the Sublime Porte directing Fayḍí Pás͟há to go to Istanbul. The telegram was first shown to the Master by the chief of the telegraph office and then was taken to the Governor . . . When he came to say farewell, he particularly offered his help if in his absence any difficulties should be created for the company of exiles. He told us to send him a telegram and he would do his best to assist. He was a very influential man. He treated us with loving-kindness and in various gatherings he spoke highly of the community.[9]

After Fayḍí Pás͟há, Ibráhím Pás͟há, who was friendly, was installed as Governor, and after him Muṣṭafá Ḍíyá Pás͟há, who was so impressed with 'Abdu'l-Bahá and the whole community that, although it was against the edict of the Sulṭán, he indicated that Bahá'u'lláh was free to pass through the gates of the city. However, Bahá'u'lláh declined his suggestion and remained in the House of 'Abbúd until June 1877 when the Muftí of 'Akká, as we shall see, literally fell on his knees and begged Him to leave 'Akká.

For almost nine years since His arrival in 'Akká, Bahá'u'lláh had not left the confines of His residence. Although, as we have already stated, the water supply was brought in, the air purified and the brackish water of the wells changed into fresh water, yet the city, devoid of all greenery, was a gloomy prison in itself. From the Writings of Bahá'u'lláh we have learned that the Manifestation of God abides in a spiritual realm far from the ken of men. In that station, imprisonment and calamities have no effect on Him. But the human part feels pain and suffering.

When we survey events in the ministry of Bahá'u'lláh, these nine years spent in the city of 'Akká can be regarded as the most depressing in His earthly life. For He was, from a human point of view, extremely enamoured of the beauty of nature. He loved oriental gardens with their perfumed flowers and shrubs. In His youth, before the birth of the Bábí Revelation until He was deprived of all His possessions at the time of Síyah-Chál,* He spent much of His time during spring and summer in the open countryside. In His ancestral home in the village of Tákur, in the district of Núr, He lived in beautiful surroundings. For days He used to tarry in gardens of exquisite beauty. And when the Bábí Faith was born, He used to entertain the believers on His regal estates.

'Abdu'l-Bahá in a Tablet[10] describes the beauty of the scenery of a summer residence where Bahá'u'lláh stayed one summer. This was in one of the villages in the area of Shimírán close to the Alburz mountain near Ṭihrán. This place had beautiful gardens and a lake. A huge stone platform was built in the middle of the lake. Upon it a tent was pitched surrounded by flowers. This was in the early days of the Bábí Faith and the believers used to come there, sometimes a hundred and fifty of them. Enchanted by the presence of Bahá'u'lláh, they would all sit around and chant the divine verses amid the charm of the surroundings. This is just an example of how He loved to spend His days in the countryside.

In Baghdád too, where Bahá'u'lláh lived an austere life for many years, He was free to walk along the banks of the Tigris in the open air, or to pitch his tent in certain of the garden parks outside the city, and stay there for some time. And in Adrianople there were occasions when Bahá'u'lláh was able to spend some time in gardens which He rented. But in 'Akká for nine years He did not see even a blade of grass to rejoice His heart. Once He had made a remark to this effect and 'Abdu'l-Bahá knew that through the creative power of His Father's

* see vol. 1, pp. 7–11.

words, it was time for Him to move out of 'Akká. 'Abdu'l-Bahá tells the story of how Bahá'u'lláh's confinement came to an end:

> Bahá'u'lláh loved the beauty and verdure of the country. One day He passed the remark: 'I have not gazed on verdure for nine years. The country is the world of the soul, the city is the world of bodies.' When I heard indirectly of this saying I realized that He was longing for the country, and I was sure that whatever I could do towards the carrying out of His wish would be successful. There was in 'Akká at that time a man called Muḥammad Páshá Ṣafwat, who was very much opposed to us. He had a palace called Mazra'ih, about four miles north of the city, a lovely place, surrounded by gardens and with a stream of running water. I went and called on this Páshá at his home. I said: 'Páshá, you have left the palace empty, and are living in 'Akká.' He replied: 'I am an invalid and cannot leave the city. If I go there it is lonely and I am cut off from my friends.' I said: 'While you are not living there and the place is empty, let it to us.' He was amazed at the proposal, but soon consented. I got the house at a very low rent, about five pounds per annum, paid him for five years and made a contract. I sent labourers to repair the place and put the garden in order and had a bath built. I also had a carriage prepared for the use of the Blessed Beauty. One day I determined to go and see the place for myself. Notwithstanding the repeated injunctions given in successive firmans that we were on no account to pass the limits of the city walls, I walked out through the city gate. Gendarmes were on guard, but they made no objection, so I proceeded straight to the palace. The next day I again went out, with some friends and officials, unmolested and unopposed, although the guards and sentinels stood on both sides of the City Gates. Another day I arranged a banquet, spread a table under the pine trees of Bahjí, and gathered round it the notables and officials of the town. In the evening we all returned to the town together.
>
> One day I went to the Holy Presence of the Blessed Beauty and said: 'The palace at Mazra'ih is ready for you,

and a carriage to drive you there.' (At that time there were no carriages in 'Akká or Haifa.) He refused to go, saying: 'I am a prisoner.' Later I requested Him again, but got the same answer. I went so far as to ask Him a third time, but he still said 'No!' and I did not dare to insist further. There was, however, in 'Akká a certain Muḥammadan Shaykh, a well-known man with considerable influence, who loved Bahá'u'lláh and was greatly favoured by Him. I called this Shaykh and explained the position to him. I said, 'You are daring. Go tonight to His Holy Presence, fall on your knees before Him, take hold of His hands and do not let go until He promises to leave the city!' He was an Arab . . . He went directly to Bahá'u'lláh and sat close to His knees. He took hold of the hands of the Blessed Beauty and kissed them and asked: 'Why do you not leave the city?' He said: 'I am a prisoner.' The Shaykh replied: 'God forbid! Who has the power to make you a prisoner? You have kept yourself in prison. It was your own will to be imprisoned, and now I beg you to come out and go to the palace. It is beautiful and verdant. The trees are lovely, and the oranges like balls of fire!' As often as the Blessed Beauty said: 'I am a prisoner, it cannot be,' the Shaykh took His hands and kissed them. For a whole hour he kept on pleading. At last Bahá'u'lláh said, 'Khaylí khub (very good)' and the Shaykh's patience and persistence were rewarded. He came to me with great joy to give the glad news of His Holiness's consent. In spite of the strict firman of 'Abdu'l-'Azíz which prohibited my meeting or having any intercourse with the Blessed Perfection, I took the carriage the next day and drove with Him to the palace. No one made any objection.[11]

This episode alone demonstrates the spiritual supremacy of Bahá'u'lláh, His majesty and greatness. Although the decree of the despotic Sulṭán condemning Him to solitary life imprisonment was still in force, it was the highest dignitary of the city of 'Akká who with great humbleness knelt before Him and insisted that He leave the prison city and take up residence wherever He wished. 'Abdu'l-Bahá describes this event as one of Bahá'u'lláh's greatest miracles. These are the words of the Master:

> For the Most Great Name was held prisoner and confined nine years in the fortress-town of 'Akká; and at all times, both in the barracks and afterward, from without the house, the police and farráshes had Him under constant guard. The Blessed Beauty lived in a very small house, and He never set foot outside that narrow lodging, because His oppressors kept continual watch at the door. When, however, nine years had elapsed, the fixed and predetermined length of days was over; and at that time, against the rancorous will of the tyrant, 'Abdu'l-Ḥamíd, and all his minions, Bahá'u'lláh proceeded out of the fortress with authority and might, and in a kingly mansion beyond the city, made His home.
>
> Although the policy of Sulṭán 'Abdu'l-Ḥamíd was harsher than ever; although he constantly insisted on his Captive's strict confinement—still, the Blessed Beauty now lived, as everyone knows, with all power and glory. Some of the time Bahá'u'lláh would spend at the Mansion, and again, at the farm village of Mazra'ih; for a while He would sojourn in Haifa, and occasionally His tent would be pitched on the heights of Mount Carmel. Friends from everywhere presented themselves and gained an audience. The people and the government authorities witnessed it all, yet no one so much as breathed a word. And this is one of Bahá'u'lláh's greatest miracles: that He, a captive, surrounded Himself with panoply and He wielded power. The prison changed into a palace, the jail itself became a Garden of Eden. Such a thing has not occurred in history before; no former age has seen its like: that a man confined to a prison should move about with authority and might; that one in chains should carry the fame of the Cause of God to the high heavens, should win splendid victories in both East and West, and should, by His almighty pen, subdue the world. Such is the distinguishing feature of this supreme Theophany.[12]

Shoghi Effendi, the Guardian of the Bahá'í Faith, has also

referred to the same subject. Citing some passages from the words of Bahá'u'lláh and 'Abdu'l-Bahá, he writes:

'Sulṭán 'Abdu'l-'Azíz,' Bahá'u'lláh is reported by one of His fellow-exiles to have stated, 'banished Us to this country in the greatest abasement, and since his object was to destroy Us and humble Us, whenever the means of glory and ease presented themselves, We did not reject them.' 'Now, praise be to God,' He, moreover, as reported by Nabíl in his narrative, once remarked, 'it has reached the point when all the people of these regions are manifesting their submissiveness unto Us.' And again, as recorded in that same narrative: 'The Ottoman Sulṭán, without any justification, or reason, arose to oppress Us, and sent Us to the fortress of 'Akká. His imperial farmán decreed that none should associate with Us, and that We should become the object of the hatred of everyone. The Hand of Divine power, therefore, swiftly avenged Us. It first loosed the winds of destruction upon his two irreplaceable ministers and confidants, 'Álí and Fú'ád, after which that Hand was stretched out to roll up the panoply of 'Azíz himself, and to seize him, as He only can seize, Who is the Mighty, the Strong.'

'His enemies,' 'Abdu'l-Bahá, referring to the same theme, has written, 'intended that His imprisonment should completely destroy and annihilate the blessed Cause, but this prison was, in reality, of the greatest assistance, and became the means of its development.' '. . . This illustrious Being', He, moreover, has affirmed, 'uplifted His Cause in the Most Great Prison. From this Prison His light was shed abroad; His fame conquered the world, and the proclamation of His glory reached the East and the West.' 'His light at first had been a star; now it became a mighty sun.' 'Until our time,' He, moreover, has affirmed, 'no such thing has ever occurred.'

Little wonder that, in view of so remarkable a reversal in the circumstances attending the twenty-four years of His banishment to 'Akká, Bahá'u'lláh Himself should have penned these weighty words: 'The Almighty . . . hath transformed this Prison-House into the Most Exalted Paradise, the Heaven of Heavens.'[13]

The sufferings of Bahá'u'lláh during the nine years of His confinement within the walls of the prison city of 'Akká and especially the two years in the barracks, were the most grievous of His ministry. Yet it was in this period that some of the most momentous Writings were revealed by His Pen. The *Kitáb-i-Aqdas*, the Mother Book of the Dispensation of Bahá'u'lláh, described by Shoghi Effendi as the 'brightest emanation of the mind of Bahá'u'lláh', was revealed, as we have noted, at this time of great afflictions and sorrows. The proclamation of His Message to the kings and rulers of the world reached its final consummation during this period. And it is significant that most of His summons to the crowned heads of the world were delivered from within the confines of that prison city. It was also in this period that the foundations of the Bahá'í community in the land of its birth were greatly strengthened, on the one hand by the heroism and self-sacrifice of its martyrs such as Badí', and on the other by the appearance of dedicated and highly gifted teachers of His Cause, among them the learned apologist Mírzá Abu'l-Faḍl.

And, significantly, it was during these calamitous years, and as a direct result of the afflictions and sufferings which were heaped upon the Supreme Manifestation of God in this Most Great Prison, that enormous spiritual forces were released causing humanity to be freed of all fetters which had been placed upon it in the course of past ages and centuries. As testified by Bahá'u'lláh in the following Tablet, revealed in 'Akká, He had consented to be bound in chains so that generations yet unborn might find themselves freed from the curse of oppression and injustice and be enabled to live a noble life in real freedom and peace.

> The Ancient Beauty hath consented to be bound with chains that mankind may be released from its bondage, and hath accepted to be made a prisoner within this most mighty

Stronghold that the whole world may attain unto true liberty. He hath drained to its dregs the cup of sorrow, that all the peoples of the earth may attain unto abiding joy, and be filled with gladness. This is of the mercy of your Lord, the Compassionate, the Most Merciful. We have accepted to be abased, O believers in the Unity of God, that ye may be exalted, and have suffered manifold afflictions, that ye might prosper and flourish. He Who hath come to build anew the whole world, behold, how they that have joined partners with God have forced Him to dwell within the most desolate of cities![14]

APPENDIX I

The Transfer of the Remains of the Báb

The remains of the Báb and His disciple Mírzá Muḥammad-Alíy-i-Zunúzí who was martyred with Him were taken to the edge of the moat outside the gate of the city of Tabríz on the evening of the day of martyrdom, 9 July 1850, and ten sentinels were posted to guard them.

The person who became instrumental in removing the remains of the Báb and His companion from the edge of the moat was His courageous and faithful follower Ḥájí Sulaymán Khán, the son of an officer in the service of the father of Muḥammad Sháh. He was a highly influential man. Amír Niẓám, the Prime Minister of the time, was induced to spare his life, in spite of the fact that many of his fellow believers were being put to death.

However, two years after the death of his Master, he too died as a martyr in a spirit of jubilant heroism, and shed a great lustre upon the infant Cause of God. It was he in whose body several incisions were made and burning candles inserted. He chanted the praises of His Lord as he was being paraded in the streets of Ṭihrán prior to his martyrdom with blood pouring all over his body and his flesh sizzling with the flame of the candles.*

The following words, uttered prior to his martyrdom and when he was informed that his life could be spared if he recanted his faith, are indicative of the courage and devotion of one who had set off from Ṭihrán for Tabríz with the intention of rescuing the Báb from the imminent danger that threatened His life. Having arrived two days too late, he instead had

* For details of his martyrdom see *The Dawn-Breakers*, pp. 610–21.

carried out the dangerous and most difficult task of removing the remains of the Báb from the hands of the enemy:

> 'Never, so long as my life-blood continues to pulsate in my veins, shall I be willing to recant my faith in my Beloved! This world which the Commander of the Faithful* has likened to carrion will never allure me from my heart's Desire.' He was asked to determine the manner in which he wished to die. 'Pierce holes in my flesh,' was the instant reply, 'and in each wound place a candle. Let nine candles be lighted all over my body, and in this state conduct me through the streets of Ṭihrán. Summon the multitude to witness the glory of my martyrdom, so that the memory of my death may remain imprinted in their hearts and help them, as they recall the intensity of my tribulation, to recognise the Light I have embraced. After I have reached the foot of the gallows and have uttered the last prayer of my earthly life, cleave my body in twain and suspend my limbs on either side of the gate of Ṭihrán, that the multitude passing beneath it may witness to the love which the Faith of the Báb has kindled in the hearts of His disciples, and may look upon the proofs of their devotion.'[1]

He died exactly as he had wished.

Only a few hours after his arrival in Tabríz, Ḥájí Sulaymán Khán, with the help of the Mayor of the city (who was a personal friend) succeeded in planning his strategy for the rescue of the remains of the Báb. The Mayor called on the venturous Ḥájí Alláh-yár, a courageous and daring man, to render this service to his friend. In the middle of the night Ḥájí Alláh-yár took some of his men accompanied by two Bábís from Milán (a town in the province of Adhirbáyiján) to the spot where the remains of the Báb and His disciple lay. The soldiers guarding the bodies did not dare to challenge the Ḥájí's men, and in the morning they had no choice but to announce that the wild beasts at night had devoured the bodies!

* Imám 'Alí. (A.T.)

The sacred remains were wrapped in the *'abá** of one of the believers and delivered to Ḥájí Sulaymán Khán who with the help of Ḥusayn-i-Mílání took them to the silk factory of Ḥájí Aḥmad, a believer of Milán. Ḥusayn-i-Mílání (who was one of the two believers accompanying Ḥájí Alláh-yár on that historic night) was later martyred in Ṭihrán on the same day that Ḥájí Sulaymán Khán laid down his life in the path of his Beloved. For two days the remains were left in the silk factory. They were wrapped in shrouds and hidden under the bales of silk. They were then placed in a special casket and transferred to another place of safety. Ḥájí Sulaymán Khán communicated the news to Bahá'u'lláh and awaited His instructions.

It is important to realize that the arrival of Ḥájí Sulaymán Khán at Tabríz was an act of providence directed by Bahá'u'lláh Himself. As soon as He was informed that the martyrdom of the Báb was imminent, Bahá'u'lláh had summoned Ḥájí Sulaymán Khán to His presence and instructed him to proceed immediately and speedily to Tabríz.

Now, when the latest news reached Him, He directed His faithful brother, Mírzá Músa (entitled Áqáy-i-Kalím) to send a trusted person to Tabríz and bring the casket to Ṭihrán. This was done and the sacred remains were taken via Zanján (where they were kept for one night) to Ṭihrán. The casket arrived at a time when Bahá'u'lláh had departed from Ṭihrán for Karbilá. According to His instructions the casket containing the remains of the Báb and His companion was delivered to Áqáy-i-Kalím who placed it in the Shrine of Imám-Zádih Ḥasan† in a safe location. The only other person who was involved in this mission was Mírzá 'Abdu'l-Karím-i-Qazvíní, known as Mírzá Aḥmad.

From there they transferred it after some time to the house of Ḥájí Sulaymán Khán in Ṭihrán; later it was placed in the Shrine of Imám-Zádih Ma'ṣúm. It was concealed in a northern corner of the shrine and a wall was constructed in front of it.

* Cloak worn by Persian men at the time.

† A Muslim shrine in Ṭihrán.

No one except these men knew its whereabouts. But Mírzá 'Abdu'l-Karím and Ḥájí Sulaymán Khán were both martyred in Ṭihrán in 1852 during the great massacre of the Bábís following an attempt on the life of Náṣiri'd-Dín Sháh. The only person left who knew of its exact whereabouts was Áqáy-i-Kalím.

The sacred casket remained concealed in Imám-Zádih Ma'ṣúm until AH 1284 (1867–68). From Adrianople, Bahá'u'lláh directed Mírzá Áqá of Káshán (entitled Muníb*) to transfer the remains to another place. Áqáy-i-Kalím briefed him as to its exact location, but Muníb failed to find it. Bahá'u'lláh then addressed a Tablet to Mullá 'Alí-Akbar-i-Shahmírzádí, known as Ḥájí Ákhúnd,† and Jamál-i-Burújirdí‡ instructing them to remove the casket immediately. The details of its whereabouts were again furnished by Áqáy-i-Kalím.

The transfer of the remains proved to be an act of providence directed by Bahá'u'lláh. For very soon after, the custodians of the Shrine of Imám-Zádih Ma'ṣúm carried out extensive reconstruction work which would have definitely revealed the secret of that precious trust reposing behind one of the walls of the Shrine. Such a discovery could have had disastrous consequences for the protection of the sacred remains.

Ḥájí Ákhúnd and Jamál succeeded in finding the casket and removing it from the Shrine of Imám-Zádih Ma'súm. They carried it to a village outside Ṭihrán in which stands the celebrated shrine of Sháh 'Abdu'l-'Aẓím. Finding conditions unsatisfactory for depositing the casket in that area, they moved towards the village of Chashmih-'Alí. On the way they came upon the Mosque of Máshá'u'lláh, an old and dilapidated building which was not commonly visited by people. They waited there until sunset. Ḥájí Ákhúnd opened the casket and

* see vol. 1, pp. 283–7.

† He was appointed later as a Hand of the Cause of God. We shall refer to his life and services in the next volume.

‡ He was an outstanding teacher of the Faith who later became a Covenant-breaker, see vol. 2.

in the dim twilight gazed upon the remains of the Martyr-Prophet of the Faith. What feelings of awe, reverence and grief must have descended upon his soul and what emotions must have erupted in his heart at that time, no one can tell. But knowing the degree of his faith and devotion to the Cause and the vibrant nature of his personality we can imagine the impact of such a mighty event on his soul. It is said that he found a flower which had dried up placed on the old shroud, probably a symbol of loving devotion by Ḥájí Sulaymán Khán.

Ḥájí Ákhúnd and Jamál wrapped yet another silken shroud around the remains and closed the casket. They placed it in a niche in a wall and bricked it up with old bricks which could be found in plenty in that dilapidated building.

That night the two returned to a village near by. The next morning they decided to visit the place on their way to the capital. Upon arrival at the spot they discovered to their consternation that someone had opened up the section of the wall and broken the casket. But soon they were relieved to find that the remains were untouched. This was the work of some men who must have seen the two placing the casket inside the old mosque and thought it was treasure of some sort, leaving it alone when they discovered it to be otherwise. Immediately Ḥají Ákhúnd and Jamál closed the casket and took it away. Both were riding on donkeys; one of the men held the casket in front of him and in this way proceeded towards Ṭihrán.

In those days guards were placed at the gates of the cities and used to search people entering. Ḥájí Ákhúnd and Jamál were extremely worried in case the officials might attempt to open the casket. But Providence played its part in this episode. As the two approached the city gate, a severe gale unexpectedly arose, heavy rain began to pour and gusty winds blew it hard in every direction. Crowds of people ran through the city gate to find shelter and with them went Ḥájí Ákhúnd and Jamál.

They took the sacred casket to the home of Mírzá Ḥasan-i-Vazír, a believer of note. Ḥájí Ákhúnd rented that house and lived in it as a custodian of that sacred trust. For about fourteen months it was kept in that house, but after some time its whereabouts were no longer a secret. Believers used to come from all over the country to visit the house and pray at the threshold of the room in which it was kept. Alarmed at the possible consequences of this discovery, Ḥájí Ákhúnd reported the matter to Bahá'u'lláh who by that time was imprisoned in the barracks of 'Akká. On receiving the news, Bahá'u'lláh ordered His Trustee Ḥájí Sháh-Muḥammad to proceed immediately to Ṭihrán and remove the holy remains to another place of safety.

Soon after this Ḥájí Sháh-Muḥammad arrived in Ṭihrán. He handed to Ḥájí Ákhúnd a Tablet of Bahá'u'lláh addressed to him. In that Tablet Bahá'u'lláh had directed Ḥájí Ákhúnd to hand over the sacred casket to Ḥájí Sháh-Muḥammad. The emphasis was on secrecy and Bahá'u'lláh had bidden Ḥájí Ákhúnd not to question the bearer of that sacred trust as to the place of its safe keeping. Once Ḥájí Ákhúnd had consigned the casket to the Trustee of Bahá'u'lláh, he did not even look to see in which direction it was carried.

Ḥájí Sháh-Muḥammad, assisted by one of the believers, succeeded in burying the casket beneath the inner sanctuary of the Shrine of Imám Zádih Zayd, where it remained for about sixteen years.

In the year AH 1301 (1884–85) Bahá'u'lláh instructed Mírzá Asadu'lláh-i-Iṣfahání,* one of the believers resident in Ṭihrán, to remove the remains from Imám Zádih Zayn and take it to another place of safety. The exact location of the casket was charted by Bahá'u'lláh and the chart sent to Mírzá Asadu'lláh. It must be borne in mind here that the act of burying a casket in an Islámic shrine without anyone seeing it, and later removing it in similar circumstances, called for great wisdom, caution

* He had married the sister of Munírih Khánum (the wife of 'Abdu'l-Bahá). Dr. Faríd was their son whose contemptible behaviour brought much sorrow to the heart of 'Abdu'l-Bahá and who was eventually announced as a Covenant-breaker. Mírzá Asadu'lláh himself also defected towards the end of his life.

and courage. There is no doubt that all those who were charged by Bahá'u'lláh to carry out this important mission were assisted by the invisible forces of divine Providence.

Mírzá Asadu'lláh succeeded in removing the casket from the Shrine. He first took it to his own house and kept it there for some time, then he transferred it to other localities including the houses of Ḥusayn-'Alíy-i-Iṣfahání (entitled Núr) and Muḥammad Karím-i-Aṭṭár where it remained hidden till the year AH 1316 (1899).

The manner in which the remains of the Báb were taken to these homes is interesting. It demonstrates that those who were charged with their protection carried out their task with great caution and wisdom.

The following is the translation of the spoken chronicle of Mírzá Ḥusayn 'Alíy-i-Iṣfahání concerning the transfer of the remains of the Báb to his house:

> It was about the year 1269 (AH solar) (AD 1891) that Mírzá Asadu'lláh-i-Iṣfahání accompanied by his wife came to stay with me at my home in Ṭihrán . . . After a few days they intimated to me that they were on their way to the Holy Land, and wished to entrust me with a case containing some important items. They indicated that they would collect it on their return home. But they emphasized that I should pay great attention to its safe keeping. I agreed. The next day, he and his wife brought a wooden case and with much reverence placed it in a room near the entrance to the house. He requested that the room be locked and no one enter it for a day or two. We locked the room and he took the key.
>
> The following day Mírzá Asadu'lláh and his wife brought an empty steel case. They went into the room and pulled the curtains across. No one could see what they were doing inside. For about four hours they stayed inside the room. Then they opened the door and called me in and said 'This is the trust which is given to your care.'
>
> I saw the steel case, which was new, placed in the middle of the room, padlocked and sealed; a strong scent of attar of rose had filled the room. We placed the case inside an alcove

in the room and one of the Bahá'í youths who was a bricklayer closed it in with bricks.*

The protection and safekeeping of any trust is a difficult task, especially if one suspects that the items he is entrusted with are Tablets and Holy Writings in the handwriting of the Báb and Bahá'u'lláh.

This is why after Mírzá Asadu'lláh's departure, I committed myself wholeheartedly to the safekeeping of his trust. At night I used to stay in that room for hours to guard it. For some time I used to sleep in that room, but after a while I gave up sleeping there.

About two years had passed when the enemies of the Faith in Ṭihrán renewed their persecution against the Bahá'ís and imprisoned certain believers . . . There were rumours that the houses of the friends could be plundered.

This news caused us great anxiety as we were afraid that the enemies might attack the house and take away the case which was entrusted to us. Therefore we held a family consultation and decided that it should be hidden in a safer place. Immediately we transferred the case into another room . . . We made an opening in one of the walls, placed the case vertically in the middle and re-built the wall in front of the case and plastered it during the night. We even lighted a big fire inside the room so that by morning the plaster had dried and it did not look different from the rest of the wall. That day I wrote a lettter to Mírzá Asadu'llah-i-Iṣfahání informing him of the disturbances in Ṭihrán where the fanatical mob and the ruffians were threatening to harm this innocent community and if they found it possible they might attack and plunder the homes of the believers . . . Therefore I suggested to him to return to Ṭihrán as soon as possible and take away his trust.

Some time passed and a reply came from Mírzá Asadu'lláh saying that at an appropriate time he would mention the situation to the Master, and when permission was granted he would return to take away the case. He

* It was common practice by the believers in those days to place the Holy Writings in a steel case and bury it in the ground or place it inside a cavity in the wall and close it in with bricks, or other material.

arrived in Ṭihrán about one year later, and came to our house. We took out the case from the wall and handed it to him. After careful examination of the case, he took it away and deposited it in the house of another believer, Áqá Muḥammad-Karím-i-Aṭṭár.

About six months passed by when I received a letter from Mírzá Asadu'lláh thanking me for all my efforts in protecting the case which had been entrusted to me for about four years. He went on to say that the trust which had been kept in my house was so precious that even my descendants in the future would pride themselves on its safekeeping in that house . . . He then revealed to me that the case contained the sacred remains of the blessed Báb! . . .

Immediately after reading this letter I invited some of the believers to the house and read the letter to them. We had such a glorious meeting, the like of which has seldom been experienced . . . The lovers of that Beloved of the world were ecstatic. They prostrated themselves at that holy place and chanted joyous melodies and prayers.

The remains of the Báb were kept in the house of Áqá Muḥammad-Karím-i-Aṭṭár until the year AH 1316 (AD 1899). As directed by 'Abdu'l-Bahá, Mírzá Asadu'lláh, together with a number of other believers who did not know what the case contained, transported the sacred remains to the Holy Land via Baghdád, Damascus and Beirut. They arrived safely in 'Akká on 31 January 1899.

For ten years the sacred remains were secretly kept in the Holy Land, for a time in the home of 'Abdu'l-Bahá in 'Akká and later in a place on Mount Carmel. In the meantime 'Abdu'l-Bahá, in spite of great difficulties and in the midst of disturbances created by His enemies and misrepresentations by the Covenant-breakers, succeeded in building six rooms for the Shrine of the Báb on Mount Carmel at a site chosen by Bahá'u'lláh Himself.* 'Abdu'l-Bahá asked the Bahá'ís of

* We shall refer to this in greater detail in the next volume when describing Bahá'u'lláh's visit to Mount Carmel.

Rangoon to order the construction of a marble sarcophagus. This was done and the sarcophagus was presented to 'Abdu'l-Bahá as a gift. It was carved out of solid stone and had the Greatest Name in the handwriting of Mishkín-Qalam* engraved on its sides. This together with a casket made of hardwood arrived in Haifa by sea. As there were no vehicles for its transportation, the crate containing the sarcophagus was placed on wooden rollers and dragged by men from the pier all the way up the mountain.

Shoghi Effendi, the Guardian of the Faith, describes the historic and moving occasion when 'Abdu'l-Bahá laid to rest the sacred remains of the Báb and His companion in the Shrine He had built on Mount Carmel:

> Finally, in the very year His royal adversary lost his throne, and at the time of the opening of the first American Bahá'í Convention, convened in Chicago for the purpose of creating a permanent national organization for the construction of the Mashriqu'l-Adhkár, 'Abdu'l-Bahá brought His undertaking to a successful conclusion, in spite of the incessant machinations of enemies both within and without. On the 28th of the month of Ṣafar 1327 AH, the day of the first Naw-Rúz (1909), which He celebrated after His release from His confinement, 'Abdu'l-Bahá had the marble sarcophagus transported with great labour to the vault prepared for it, and in the evening, by the light of a single lamp, He laid within it, with His own hands—in the presence of believers from the East and from the West and in circumstances at once solemn and moving—the wooden casket containing the sacred remains of the Báb and His companion.
>
> When all was finished, and the earthly remains of the Martyr-Prophet of Shíráz were, at long last, safely deposited for their everlasting rest in the bosom of God's holy mountain, 'Abdu'l-Bahá, Who had cast aside His turban, removed His shoes and thrown off His cloak, bent low over the still open sarcophagus, His silver hair waving

* see vol. 1, pp. 26–8.

about His head and His face transfigured and luminous, rested His forehead on the border of the wooden casket, and, sobbing aloud, wept with such a weeping that all those who were present wept with Him. That night He could not sleep, so overwhelmed was He with emotion.

'The most joyful tidings is this,' He wrote later in a Tablet announcing to His followers the news of this glorious victory, 'that the holy, the luminous body of the Báb . . . after having for sixty years been transferred from place to place, by reason of the ascendancy of the enemy, and from fear of the malevolent, and having known neither rest nor tranquillity has, through the mercy of the Abhá Beauty, been ceremoniously deposited, on the day of Naw-Rúz, within the sacred casket, in the exalted Shrine on Mt. Carmel . . . By a strange coincidence, on that same day of Naw-Rúz,* a cablegram was received from Chicago, announcing that the believers in each of the American centres had elected a delegate and sent to that city . . . and definitely decided on the site and construction of the Mas͟hriqu'l-Ad͟hkár.'[2]

* see vol. 1, p. 268, for another important incident on that day. (A.T.)

APPENDIX II

Mírzá Abu'l-Faḍl of Gulpáygán

The conversion of Mírzá Abu'l-Faḍl to the Faith of Bahá'u'lláh is described in Chapter 5. He was to become the foremost scholar of that Faith.

The teaching activities of Mírzá Abu'l-Faḍl began soon after he embraced the Faith. Almost all his Bahá'í career, stretching over a period of well-nigh forty years, was spent in teaching the Cause to members of the public and in deepening the Bahá'ís in the verities of the Faith.

About five years after Mírzá Abu'l-Faḍl joined the ranks of the believers, Bahá'u'lláh in a Tablet[1] commanded him to arise in His Name and invite the peoples of the world to come to him so that he might recount to them the news of the 'Most Great Announcement', might show them the vista of the 'Most Exalted Horizon' and might enable them to hearken to the 'Voice of God' in this day.

This Tablet and the command of Bahá'u'lláh exerted a galvanizing influence upon Mírzá Abu'l-Faḍl. Some time later, quoting this Tablet and knowing that the confirmations of Bahá'u'lláh would surround him from every direction he wrote these challenging words addressed to the peoples of the world:

> And lately this servant who considers himself to be the most insignificant among the servants of the Lord of creation, and one who has quaffed only a drop from the ocean of certitude, is prepared, bearing in mind the auspicious utterances of the Lord of Lords quoted above,* to inform

* A reference to the Tablet of Bahá'u'lláh which had been revealed for him.

> any person of any nationality in the world of the truth of this great Cause, and to prove to him its authenticity based on the clear proofs by which the truth of that person's religion is also established. If he be of the people of philosophy and logic, to prove by intellectual and rational proofs, and if he belongs to the people of controversy and contention, to convince and silence him by adducing compelling and binding proofs. This is in order that the right path may be distinguished from the path of error, truth from falsehood and health from disease. And, in what we say, we rely entirely upon God, exalted be He.[2]

They were not mere empty words that this great and godly man wrote and published in the *Fara'id*, one of his outstanding works. He lived up to everything he said. Not only did he hold discourses with countless souls of different backgrounds and religions, and converted hundreds of them to the Cause, but he also left for posterity the fundamentals of Bahá'í proofs from every point of view, that generations yet unborn might learn from them and deepen their knowledge and understanding of the Faith of Bahá'u'lláh.

Mírzá Abu'l-Faḍl was renowned for his knowledge. His name 'Abu'l-Faḍl' which he had adopted when he was a Muslim, means the father of knowledge. 'Abdu'l-Bahá in a Tablet addresses him as the father of knowledge, its mother and its brother. But those who knew him have testified that as far as his knowledge and understanding were concerned there was a vast difference before and after he was a Bahá'í. He himself has testified that before his coming in contact with the Faith of Bahá'u'lláh he was the embodiment of vain imaginings and idle fancy and his vision was obscured by these. Ḥájí Mírzá Ḥaydar-'Alí writes of him:

> His honour, the dearly loved Abu'l-Faḍl, . . . has adorned the city of Iṣfahán with his presence. Since formerly he was a student in Iṣfahán, he is well known by the scholars and men of learning here. These men have met him and have realized

> that he is not the same person as in the past. They confess that his vast knowledge, learning and power of utterance puts him in the forefront of all. In the past he was as a drop, now he is as a billowing sea. He was then as a mere atom and now he shines as a brilliant star . . .[3]

Soon after embracing the Faith of Bahá'u'lláh Mírzá Abu'l-Faḍl was forced to leave his post as head of a theological college in Ṭihrán. The high esteem and honour in which he was held by the public as well as in government and ecclesiastical circles up till then, turned into abasement and persecution. He was twice imprisoned, the last time for about twenty-two months. He lived very modestly and earned a small income, often working as a scribe.* His attachment to Bahá'u'lláh knew no bounds. But he was as detached from this world as he was attached to His Lord, and this alone conferred upon him all his powers and virtues. Prayer and meditation were the cornerstone of his life and through them he polished the mirror of his heart so perfectly that he radiated the light of the Faith of Bahá'u'lláh to those who came into contact with him.

When he was in Egypt, he did not disclose his faith at first. This was suggested to him by 'Abdu'l-Bahá. A great many scholars and professors of the famous University of Al-Azhar and others recognized the depth and profundity of his knowledge and were attracted to his person. Since they did not suspect him of being a Bahá'í there was no prejudice and they congregated around him in great numbers. So earnest was their quest for the outpouring of spiritual knowledge from his lips that they sat spellbound at his feet and some of them were enraptured with his explanations of the verities of the *Qur'án* and other spiritual subjects.

To cite one example of the homage that men of learning paid

* In those days people who were illiterate would engage the services of a scribe to write letters for them. Mírzá Abu'l-Faḍl also used to earn a small sum of money by transcribing Bahá'í holy books, which were in great demand by the believers.

to Mírzá Abu'l-Faḍl, the following is a tribute by 'Abdu'r-Raḥmán-i-Baraqúqí, a learned scholar and journalist of the time:

> About eight years ago we heard that a learned man from Persia by the name of Abu'l-Faḍl was living in Cairo. We were told that he had become a point of adoration for scholars and a centre of pilgrimage for those who yearn after knowledge and understanding. We sought his abode and went to see him. There we saw a man of slender build and of medium height. He was old, more than seventy years of age, but from the point of view of vitality, zest, intelligence and keenness of insight he looked like a man of thirty . . . He captivated our minds through the magic of his words and the sweetness of his utterances. Soon we became his devoted disciples in such wise that there was nothing more enjoyable than to sit at his feet and no story could be found sweeter than that which was recounted by him. The more we associated with him and examined his person, the more we respected him and became conscious of his exalted station.[4]

Among those scholars who venerated Mírzá Abu'l-Faḍl there were some who went as far as to believe that he was endowed with divine powers which are bestowed only upon God's chosen ones. One such person was a certain Shaykh Badru'd-Dín-i-Ghazzí who later became an ardent believer, as about thirty other scholars did when they learned that Mírzá Abu'l-Faḍl was a Bahá'í.

Shaykh Badru'd-Dín describes how he was enraptured by listening to Mírzá Abu'l-Faḍl's discourses. After some time he came to the conclusion that Mírzá Abu'l-Faḍl was one of the chosen ones of God, possessed of a great spiritual station and exalted above other men. In a spoken chronicle to a number of friends, he said:

> I asked him about his station and he said that he did not have any. One day I told him plainly: 'O Master, why do you hide from me? If you are a chosen one of God and have a

station, please tell me, for I will accept and follow you.' He laughed at this statement and deferred the answer to this mystery to a later time. Time passed and I had to depart for Palestine. He then bade me attain the presence of 'Abdu'l-Bahá while there. I obeyed, attained His presence and discovered the truth of the Cause.

Some years passed and I did not see Mírzá Abu'l-Faḍl. When I returned to Egypt, I met him there, and said to him: 'When in the past I came in contact with you, I considered you to be a unique person and one without a peer in this world, but when I attained the holy presence of the Master, I realized that you are no more than a drop in relation to that billowing ocean.' Hearing this, Mírzá Abu'l-Faḍl became filled with joy, and in a state of ecstasy threw his arms around me and said: 'Now I know that you have recognized the truth.'[5]

A striking feature of the life of Mírzá Abu'l-Faḍl was his absolute submission to the will of his Lord. His steadfastness in the Covenant and obedience to the wishes of Bahá'u'lláh and the Master knew no bounds. He would rather die than contemplate even a small deviation from the words and teachings of the Cause. The following story recounted by a certain believer, Ḥusayn-i-Rúḥí Effendí, who knew Mírzá Abu'l-Faḍl, illustrates this point clearly.

When I was in 'Akká, I procured a copy of a Tablet of 'Abdu'l-Bahá known as *Lawḥ-i-Dukhán* which is written in honour of Muḥammad-Ḥusayn-i-Vakíl . . . When I arrived in Egypt I shared the contents of this Tablet which disapproved of smoking* with Mírzá Abu'l-Faḍl.

I had not yet finished the reading of the Tablet for him when he took his cigar case, threw it out in the street and said that this was the end of smoking for him, although he

* This Tablet in the West is known as the 'Tablet of Purity' and is published in 'Abdu'l-Bahá, *Selections*, pp. 146–50. Smoking is not forbidden in the Bahá'í Faith, but 'Abdu'l-Bahá has discouraged it for the sake of health and cleanliness.

was a chain-smoker. He used to roll his own cigarettes by hand, light a new one with the old, and smoke non-stop from morning till evening. He said to me: 'O Rúḥí Effendi, I have been smoking for fifty-five years and I am addicted to it. And, soon you will see that because of the effect of nicotine a member of my body will be paralysed.

It did not take very long until one of his arms was paralysed and he could not move it. This lasted for two years. The doctors strongly urged him to resume smoking but he refused, saying, 'I prefer to die than to disobey 'Abdu'l-Bahá.'[6]

The following is an extract from the *Lawḥ-i-Dukhán*:

Observe how pleasing is cleanliness in the sight of God, and how specifically it is emphasized in the Holy Books of the Prophets; for the Scriptures forbid the eating or the use of any unclean thing. Some of these prohibitions were absolute, and binding upon all, and whoso transgressed the given law was abhorred of God and anathematized by the believers. Such, for example, were things categorically forbidden, the perpetration of which was accounted a most grievous sin, among them actions so loathsome that it is shameful even to speak their name.

But there are other forbidden things which do not cause immediate harm, and the injurious effects of which are only gradually produced: such acts are also repugnant to the Lord, and blameworthy in His sight, and repellent. The absolute unlawfulness of these, however, hath not been expressly set forth in the Text, but their avoidance is necessary to purity, cleanliness, the preservation of health, and freedom from addiction.

Among these latter is smoking tobacco, which is dirty, smelly, offensive—an evil habit, and one the harmfulness of which gradually becometh apparent to all. Every qualified physician hath ruled—and this hath also been proved by tests—that one of the components of tobacco is a deadly poison, and that the smoker is vulnerable to many and various diseases. This is why smoking hath been plainly set forth as repugnant from the standpoint of hygiene . . .

My meaning is that in the sight of God, smoking tobacco is deprecated, abhorrent, filthy in the extreme; and, albeit by degrees, highly injurious to health. It is also a waste of money and time, and maketh the user a prey to a noxious addiction. To those who stand firm in the Covenant, this habit is therefore censured both by reason and experience, and renouncing it will bring relief and peace of mind to all men. Furthermore, this will make it possible to have a fresh mouth and unstained fingers, and hair that is free of a foul and repellent smell. On receipt of this missive, the friends will surely, by whatever means and even over a period of time, forsake this pernicious habit. Such is my hope.

As to opium, it is foul and accursed. God protect us from the punishment He inflicteth on the user. According to the explicit Text of the Most Holy Book, it is forbidden, and its use is utterly condemned. Reason showeth that smoking opium is a kind of insanity, and experience attesteth that the user is completely cut off from the human kingdom. May God protect all against the perpetration of an act so hideous as this, an act which layeth in ruins the very foundation of what it is to be human, and which causeth the user to be dispossessed for ever and ever. For opium fasteneth on the soul, so that the user's conscience dieth, his mind is blotted away, his perceptions are eroded. It turneth the living into the dead. It quencheth the natural heat. No greater harm can be conceived than that which opium inflicteth. Fortunate are they who never even speak the name of it; then think how wretched is the user . . .

Make ye then a mighty effort, that the purity and sanctity which, above all else, are cherished by 'Abdu'l-Bahá, shall distinguish the people of Bahá; that in every kind of excellence the people of God shall surpass all other human beings; that both outwardly and inwardly they shall prove superior to the rest; that for purity, immaculacy, refinement, and the preservation of health, they shall be leaders in the vanguard of those who know. And that by their freedom from enslavement, their knowledge, their self-control, they shall be first among the pure, the free and the wise.[7]

And, finally, the writings of Mírzá Abu'l-Faḍl are the best proof that his person was assisted by the powers and confirmations of Bahá'u'lláh. It is no exaggeration to claim that apart from the Holy Writings and those of Shoghi Effendi, the Guardian of the Faith, his are the most inspiring, the most informative, the most challenging and the most voluminous, in the literature of the Faith of Bahá'u'lláh. He may be described as the most able spiritual diver who immersed himself in the ocean of the Revelation of Bahá'u'lláh and brought out in profusion pearls of infinite preciousness—truths and mysteries which lay hidden in its depths and filled the pages of his numerous books with their verities. Almost all the Bahá'í teachers in the East have used his writings as a basis for deeper study of religion in general, and proofs of the Faith of Bahá'u'lláh in particular. His explanations and profuse quotations from the Holy Scriptures of the past, as well as the apologies he has written in defence of the Faith have been used by scholars and writers of both East and West.

It is beyond the scope of this book to enumerate the vast range of his writings or write in appreciation of them. Suffice it to say that from the literary point of view alone his writings have been acclaimed by critics of the time as superb, while their contents have, on the one hand, inspired the friends and the fair-minded, and on the other, discomfited and silenced the enemies. Indeed, one of his great contributions to the promotion and protection of the Faith of Bahá'u'lláh is his voluminous *œuvre* in defence of the Cause. Whenever the enemies opposed or misrepresented the Faith, his pen was ready to defend it with a vigour and assertiveness that confounded the enemy and strengthened the friends. The book of *Fará'id*, over 800 pages, written without revising or improving his original draft, from which it was printed, is the best example.

In praise of those who arise to defend His Faith, Bahá'u'lláh declares:

If any man were to arise to defend, in his writings, the Cause of God against its assailants, such a man, however inconsiderable his share, shall be so honoured in the world to come that the Concourse on high would envy his glory. No pen can depict the loftiness of his station, neither can any tongue describe its splendour. For whosoever standeth firm and steadfast in this holy, this glorious, and exalted Revelation, such power shall be given him as to enable him to face and withstand all that is in heaven and on earth. Of this God is Himself a witness.[8]

APPENDIX III

The Burial of the Purest Branch and the Mother of 'Abdu'l-Bahá

from an article by Rúḥíyyih Rabbani[1]

The garden is dark. Twilight has fallen on Mount Carmel and the veils of dusk have deepened over the bay of 'Akká. A group of men stand waiting by the gate, beneath the steps. Suddenly there is a stir, the gardener runs to illumine the entrance and amidst the white shafts of light a procession appears. A man clothed in black rests the weight of a coffin on his shoulder. It is the Guardian of the Cause and he bears the mortal remains of the Purest Branch, Bahá'u'lláh's beloved son. Slowly he and his fellow bearers mount the narrow path and in silence approach the house adjacent to the resting place of the Greatest Holy Leaf. A devoted servant speeds ahead with rug and candelabra from the Holy Shrines and swiftly prepares the room. The gentle, strong face of the Guardian appears as he enters the door, that precious weight always on his shoulder, and the coffin is laid temporarily to rest in an humble room, facing Bahjí, the Qiblih of the Faith. Again those devoted servants, led by their Guardian, return to the gate and again remount the path with another sacred burden, this time the body of the wife of Bahá'u'lláh, the mother of the Master.

What a wave of joy seems to come onward with those simple processions! A joy indefinable, touched with deep tenderness and pathos. Like a great white pearl the marble temple marking the grave of Bahíyyih Khánum glows in the light of its reflectors, seeming afire on the dark mountain side, lighting up and watching over those two approaching the scene of their last resting place.

When we enter to pay our respects to those beloved, revered and long since departed ones, their presence seems to fill the room. At last, after seventy years, that saintly mother lies reunited beside her son of whom Bahá'u'lláh wrote: 'He was created of the light of Bahá.' Side by side, facing 'Akká, the sweet fumes of attar of rose with which they have been anointed by the Guardian filling the room, they lie. And above them, lit by the flickering lights of the sentinel candles, the picture of The Greatest Holy Leaf hangs, her beautiful eyes, so full of love and that purity which is goodness itself, looking out over her mother and brother. What cause for joy and gratitude!

That tender youth, born to affliction, reared in exile, died in prison, buried in solitary haste! Here he lies, raised up from the earth by the hands of the Guardian of his Father's Faith, removed from the lonely isolation of the Arab cemetery where he had been interred so long ago and placed beside his illustrious sister and holy mother, that mother who was affectionately known as 'Búyúk Khánum' or 'Great Lady.' Slender, stately, lovely to look on with white skin and blue eyes and dark hair; she who, when Bahá'u'lláh was thrown into the dungeon of Ṭihrán, was abandoned by friend and foe alike and who purchased food for her children by selling the gold buttons of her robes; she who was forced to leave this same son, then a delicate child of four, behind her when she followed Bahá'u'lláh into exile; she whose tender hands, unaccustomed to work, bled as she washed the clothes of her family; who remained patient, devout, serene and selfless to the end of her life, and who was laid to rest near 'Akká in a cemetery away from her son, now lies beside him, so to remain forever more.

As we meditate beside those two eloquent coffins, covered with woven cloths, strewn with jasmine from the Threshold of the Báb's Tomb, so all pervading is the presence of their spirits—or maybe it is their memory, as perfume lingers when the flower is withered—that the very room they rest in for so short a while becomes itself filled with the sweet peace of a shrine.

Not only has the Guardian raised them to rest in their

rightful graves, put them where the whole world may see their honor and their glory, but in some mysterious way he has given them back to us. So long ago they passed away, so quietly, in days of such turmoil and oppression, were they laid to rest, that their places, at least to us of the West, were on written pages of the history of our Faith. But now their places are in our hearts. The veil of time and obscurity separating us has been rent asunder, and we find, to our joy and astonishment, two glowing and holy figures drawing nigh to us, entering into our lives, and ready to help us on that path which leads to their Lord and ours, Bahá'u'lláh . . .

Bahá'u'lláh asked of His dying son if he desired to live, but he replied that his sole desire was that the gates of the prison should be opened so that the believers might visit their Lord. Bahá'u'lláh granted that youth's earnest wish and sat beside His youngest son as they made him ready for the grave, and it was in those tragic circumstances that He revealed the following: 'At this very moment My son is being washed before My face after Our having sacrificed him in the Most Great Prison . . . ' 'Glorified art Thou, O Lord, My God! Thou seest Me in the hands of Mine enemies, and My son blood-stained before My face!' Such sentences as these were wrung from the heart of the Blessed Beauty as He gazed upon His child. But then thundering forth came these marvelous words: 'I have, O My Lord, offered up that which Thou has given Me, that Thy servants may be quickened and all that dwell on earth be united.' The tremendous significance of these words is inescapable; Bahá'u'lláh designates to His own child the *rôle* of blood offering in order that the unity of all men which He has proclaimed may come about. The sacrifice of Isaac by Abraham is accomplished.

After, in secrecy, poverty, and haste, the Purest Branch had been interred, his gentle mother, the victim of so many sorrows and deprivations, saddened and wept unceasingly. Bahá'u'lláh on learning of her plight came to her and assured her she had no cause for grief for God had accepted this precious son as His Ransom to draw not only the believers nigh unto their Lord but to unify all the sons of men. After hearing these words that saintly soul was greatly comforted and ceased to mourn her heavy loss.

And who was such a mother? Not merely a holy and faithful woman, willing in the path of God to sacrifice her all, but she of whom Isaiah, in his 54th chapter, says:* 'For thy Maker is thy husband; the LORD of hosts is his name; and thy Redeemer the Holy One of Israel; the God of the whole earth shall he be called.' 'For the mountains shall depart, and the hills be removed; but my kindness shall not depart from thee, neither shall the covenant of my peace be removed, saith the LORD that hath mercy on thee.' And she to whom Bahá'u'lláh revealed the following: 'Hear thou Me once again, God is well pleased with thee . . . He hath made thee to be His companion in every one of His worlds and hath nourished thee with His meeting and presence so long as His name and His remembrance and His kingdom and His empire shall endure.'

How fleeting and priceless the days that this mother and son lie side by side in that small room! To be privileged to draw close—in that strange and pitiful closeness one feels to a coffin in which all that remains of dear ones after the soul has flown rests, a token and reminder of our common mortality and immortality—is something never to be forgotten. Thousands will read these Prayers and Tablets of Bahá'u'lláh and 'Abdu'l-Bahá forever immortalizing them. They will supplicate those radiant spirits to intercede on their behalf. They will seek humbly to follow in their noble footsteps. But it will never, so it seems to me, be as sweet and touching as to see them lying there together under the watchful eyes of Bahíyyih Khánum.

Whilst their tombs were still in process of excavation from the solid rock of the mountain, the Guardian had learned that the Covenant-Breakers were protesting against the right of the Bahá'ís to remove the Mother and brother of 'Abdu'l-Bahá to new graves, actually having the temerity to represent to the government their so called claim as relatives of the deceased. As soon, however, as the civil authorities had the true state of facts made clear to them—that these same relatives had been the arch-enemies of the Master and His family, had left the true Cause of Bahá'u'lláh to follow their own devices, and had been

* The authority for this statement is the words of 'Abdu'l-Bahá Himself in *Tablets of 'Abdu'l-Bahá*, vol. 1, p. 107. (R.R.)

denounced by 'Abdu'l-Bahá in His Will and Testament—they approved the plan of the Guardian and immediately issued the necessary papers for the exhumation of the bodies. Without risking further delay Shoghi Effendi, two days later, himself removed the Purest Branch and his mother to Mount Carmel where, watched over by the loving devotion of the believers, and safeguarded from any danger of insult or injury, they could await, close to Bahíyyih Khánum's shrine, their reinterment.

The last stone is laid in the two vaults, the floors are paved in marble, the name plates fixed to mark their heads, the earth smoothed out, the path that leads to their last resting place built, but storm and rain sweep unceasingly over the crest of the mountain postponing the final arrangements until the day before Christmas dawns, bright and clear, as if a sign that this is the appointed time. At sunset we all gather in that humble, twice blessed house. We hear the voice of one of the oldest and most devoted believers of the Near East raised, at the command of his Guardian, in prayer. Tremulous, faint, yet filled with a poignant faith and love hard to describe but never to be forgotten, he prays. As voice follows voice, one of them that of the Guardian himself, it seems as if one could almost hear the refrain of those prayers sung in triumphant joy by an invisible concourse on high.

And now, again on the shoulder of the Guardian, they are borne forth to lie in state in the Holy Tomb of the Báb. Side by side, far greater than the great of this world, they lie by that sacred threshold, facing Bahjí, with candles burning at their heads and flowers before their feet. It is the eve of the birth of Christ. She who was foretold of Isaiah, he who was the son of Him of Whom Jesus said: 'Howbeit when he, the Spirit of truth, is come, he will guide you into all truth,' rest quietly here their last night before the earth hides them forever more from the eyes of men.

The following sunset we gather once again in that Holy Shrine. The Guardian chants the Tablet of Visitation, first in the Tomb of the Báb, then in the Tomb of the Master. The privileged friends who have been able to make the pilgrimage to Haifa for this sacred occasion enter with the Guardian a second time the Báb's Shrine. Slowly, held aloft on the hands of the faithful, led by Shoghi Effendi, who never relinquishes his precious burden, first the mother of 'Abdu'l-Bahá and then the Purest Branch are ushered from that Holy Spot. Once they circumambulate the Shrines, the coffin of beloved Miḥdí, supported by the Guardian, followed by that of the Master's mother, passes us slowly by. Around the Shrine, onward through the lighted garden, down the white path, out onto the moonlit road, that solemn procession passes. High, seeming to move of themselves, above the heads of those following, the coffins wend their way. They mount the steps and once again enter that gate leading to Bahíyyih Khánum's resting place. They pass before us, outlined against the night sky, across whose face fitful clouds make sport of the full moon. They approach, the face of the Guardian close to that priceless burden he bears. They pass on towards the waiting vaults.

Now they lay the Purest Branch to rest. Shoghi Effendi himself enters the carpeted vault and gently eases the coffin to its preordained place. He himself strews it with flowers, his hands the last to caress it. The mother of the Master is then placed in the same manner by the Guardian in the neighbouring vault. Not six feet apart they rest. The silent faces of the believers in the brilliant light of the lamps, form a waiting circle. Masons are called to seal the tombs. Respectfully and deftly they fulfil their task. Flowers are heaped upon the vaults and the Guardian sprinkles a vial of attar of rose upon them. The pungent scent is caught up on the breeze and bathes our faces. And now the voice of Shoghi Effendi is raised as he chants those Tablets revealed by Bahá'u'lláh and destined by Him to be read at their graves.

Surely this is a dream? It cannot be I that stand here gazing at these new-made graves, laid in the breast of ancient Carmel! Beneath me stretches an endless vista. 'Akká gleams white across the bay, that onetime prison city where these two were so long captives, near which they were once buried. The reaches of the sea and plain lie before me, opening out to where the moon silvers the rims of the mountains of the Holy Land, the Land of the Prophets, the Land of the loved ones of God, the Land chosen to be the Seat of the Ark of God in this most glorious Day. Forever and increasingly about the resting place of this mother, sister, brother of 'Abdu'l-Bahá, the life-giving activities of their Faith will gather. Close to them, focused on their shrines, great institutions will rise to strengthen the soul and body of mankind. And forever interwoven with those institutions will be the memory and example of these three holy persons. Their way has become our way and they lead us on before, heading the ranks of Bahá'u'lláh's followers.

BIBLIOGRAPHY

'ABDU'L-BAHÁ. *Makátíb-i-'Abdu'l-Bahá* (Letters of 'Abdu'l-Bahá). Vol. 3, Cairo: 1921; Vol. 4, Iran: BE 121 (AD 1965); Vol. 8, Iran: BE 134 (AD 1978).

—— *Memorials of the Faithful.* Translated from the original Persian text and annotated by Marzieh Gail. Wilmette, Illinois: Bahá'í Publishing Trust, 1971.

—— *Selections from the Writings of 'Abdu'l-Bahá.* Compiled by the Research Department of the Universal House of Justice; translated by a Committee at the Bahá'í World Centre and by Marzieh Gail. Haifa: Bahá'í World Centre, 1978.

—— *Tablets of Abdul-Baha Abbas.* 3 volumes. First published 1909–16. New York: Bahá'í Publishing Committee, 1930.

—— *Tablets of the Divine Plan, revealed by 'Abdu'l-Bahá to the North American Bahá'ís.* Wilmette, Illinois: Bahá'í Publishing Trust, rev. edn. 1977.

—— *A Traveller's Narrative written to illustrate the episode of the Báb.* Translated by E. G. Browne. 1930, RP Amsterdam: Philo Press 1975.

—— *Will and Testament of 'Abdu'l-Bahá.* Wilmette, Illinois: Bahá'í Publishing Committee, 1944.

ABU'L-FAḌL, MÍRZÁ. *The Bahai Proofs.* Chicago: Grier Press, undated.

—— *The Brilliant Proof.* Syria: 1911.

—— *Kitábu'l-Fará'id.* An apologia. Cairo, undated. Written in AH 1315 (AD 1899).

—— *Risáliy-i-Iskandaríyyih.* (Unpublished treatise.)

AFRÚKHTIH, DR YÚNIS KHÁN. *Kháṭirát-i-Nuh-Sáliy-i-'Akká*

(Memories of Nine Years in 'Akká). Written in the year BE 99 (AD 1942). Ṭihrán, undated.

BÁB, THE. *Selections from the Writings of the Báb*. Compiled by the Research Department of the Universal House of Justice and translated by Habib Taherzadeh with the assistance of a Committee at the Bahá'í World Centre. Haifa: Bahá'í World Centre, 1976.

Bahá'í Education: A Compilation. The Research Department of The Universal House of Justice. Wilmette, Illinois; Bahá'í Publishing Trust, 1977.

Bahá'í World, The. An International Record. Vol. III. 1928–30. New York, Bahá'í Publishing Committee, 1930.

Vol. VIII. 1938–40. Wilmette, Illinois: Bahá'í Publishing Committee, 1942.

Vol. IX. 1940–44. Wilmette, Illinois: Bahá'í Publishing Committee, 1945.

Bahá'í World Faith. Selected Writings of Bahá'u'lláh and 'Abdu'l-Bahá. Wilmette, Illinois: Bahá'í Publishing Committee, 1943.

Bahá'í Writings on Music. Compiled by the Research Department of The Universal House of Justice. Oakham, England: Bahá'í Publishing Trust, undated.

BAHÁ'U'LLÁH. *Áthár-i-Qalam-i-A'lá* (The Traces of the Supreme Pen). A compilation of the Writings of Bahá'u'lláh. Ṭihrán: Bahá'í Publishing Trust. Vol. 1, BE 120 (AD 1963); Vol. 4, BE 125 (AD 1968).

—— *Epistle to the Son of the Wolf*. Trans. by Shoghi Effendi. Wilmette, Illinois: Bahá'í Publishing Trust, rev. edn. 1953.

—— *Gleanings from the Writings of Bahá'u'lláh*. Trans. By Shoghi Effendi. Wilmette, Illinois: Bahá'í Publishing Trust, 1935; rev. edn. 1952. London: Bahá'í Publishing Trust, 1949.

—— *The Hidden Words*. Trans. by Shoghi Effendi with the assistance of some English friends. First published in England 1932. London: Bahá'í Publishing Trust, 1949. Wilmette, Illinois: Bahá'í Publishing Trust, rev. edn. 1954.

—— *Ishráqát* (A compilation of the Tablets of Bahá'u'lláh). India: AH 1310 (AD 1892–3).
—— Kitáb-i-Aqdas. Extracts translated by Shoghi Effendi in *Synopsis and Codification of the Kitáb-i-Aqdas, the Most Holy Book of Bahá'u'lláh*. Haifa: Bahá'í World Centre, 1973.
—— *Kitáb-i-Íqán. The Book of Certitude*. Translated by Shoghi Effendi. Wilmette, Illinois: Bahá'í Publishing Trust, rev. edn. 1974.
—— *Majmú'iy-i-Alváḥ* (A compilation of the Tablets of Bahá'u'lláh). Cairo, 1920.
—— *Prayers and Meditations by Bahá'u'lláh*. Translated by Shoghi Effendi. Wilmette, Illinois: Bahá'í Publishing Trust, 6th RP 1974.
—— *The Proclamation of Bahá'u'lláh to the Kings and Leaders of the World*. Haifa: Bahá'í World Centre, 1967.
—— *Qad Iḥtaraqa'l-Mukhliṣún. The Fire Tablet*. London: Bahá'í Publishing Trust, 1980.
—— *Tablets of Bahá'u'lláh revealed after the Kitáb-i-Aqdas*. Compiled by the Research Department of the Universal House of Justice and translated by Habib Taherzadeh with the assistance of a Committee at the Bahá'í World Centre. Haifa: Bahá'í World Centre, 1978.
BALYUZI, H. M. *Bahá'u'lláh. The King of Glory*. Oxford: George Ronald, 1980.
Consultation: A Compilation. Extracts from the Writings and Utterances of Bahá'u'lláh, 'Abdu'l-Bahá, Shoghi Effendi, and The Universal House of Justice. Compiled by the Research Department of the Universal House of Justice. Wilmette, Illinois: Bahá'í Publishing Trust, 1980.
ESSLEMONT, J. E. *Bahá'u'lláh and the New Era*. London: Bahá'í Publishing Trust, rev. edn. 1974.
FÁḌIL-i-MÁZINDARÁNÍ, ASADU'LLÁH, MÍRZÁ. *Amr Va Khalq* (Revelation and Creation). Ṭihrán: Bahá'í Publishing Trust. vol. 3, BE 128 (AD 1971).
—— *Asráru'l-Áthár*. A glossary of Bahá'í terms. Ṭihrán:

Bahá'í Publishing Trust. 5 Vols., BE 124–9 (AD 1967–72).

FAIZI, MUḤAMMAD-'ALÍ. *L'álíy-i-Darakhshán.* A commentary on some of the Writings of Bahá'u'lláh. Ṭihrán: Bahá'í Publishing Trust, BE 123 (AD 1966).

ḤAYDAR-'ALÍ, ḤÁJÍ MÍRZÁ. *Bihjatu'ṣ-Ṣudúr.* Reminiscences and autobiography. Bombay: 1913.

Individual and Teaching, The. Raising the Divine Call. Extracts from the Writings of Bahá'u'lláh, 'Abdu'l-Bahá, and Shoghi Effendi. Compiled by the Research Department of The Universal House of Justice. Wilmette, Illinois: Bahá'í Publishing Trust: 1977.

ISHRÁQ KHÁVARÍ, 'ABDU'L-ḤAMÍD. *Raḥíq-i-Makhtúm.* A commentary on a letter of Shoghi Effendi. 2 vols. Ṭihrán, Bahá'í Publishing Trust, BE 103 (AD 1946).

—— *Risáliy-i-Ayyám-i-Tis'ih.* The history of the nine Bahá'í Holy Days together with a compilation of relevant Tablets. Ṭihrán: Bahá'í Publishing Trust, BE 103 (AD 1946); 3rd RP BE 121 (AD 1964).

IVES, HOWARD COLBY. *Portals to Freedom.* London: George Ronald, 1967.

Koran, The. Translated by George Sale. London: Frederick Warne & Co., undated.

Má'idiy-i-Ásamání. A compilation of Bahá'í Writings. Compiled by 'Abdu'l-Ḥamíd Ishráq Khávarí. 9 vols. and one index volume. Ṭihrán: Bahá'í Publishing Trust, BE 129 (AD 1972).

MALIK KHOSROVÍ, MUḤAMMAD-'ALÍ. *Táríkh-i-Shuhadáy-i-Amr* (The History of the Martyrs of the Faith). Vol. 3, BE 130 (AD 1974).

MEHRÁBKHÁNÍ, RÚḤU'LLÁH. *Sharḥ-i-Aḥvál -i-Mírzá Abu'l-Faḍl-i-Gulpaygání* (Biography of Mírzá Abu'l-Faḍl of Gulpaygán). Iran: BE 131 (AD 1975).

MU'AYYAD, DR. ḤABÍB. *Kháṭirát-i-Ḥabíb* (Memoirs of Ḥabíb). Ṭihrán: 1961.

MUḤAMMAD-ṬÁHIR-I-MÁLMÍRÍ, ḤÁJÍ. History of the Faith in the Province of Yazd. Unpublished.

NABÍL-I-A'ẒAM (Muḥammad-i-Zarandí). *The Dawn-Breakers.* Nabíl's Narrative of the Early Days of the Bahá'í Revelation. Wilmette, Illinois: Bahá'í Publishing Trust, 1932.

OLIPHANT, LAURENCE. *Haifa, or Life in the Holy Land* 1882–1885. Jerusalem: Canaan Publishing House, rev. edn. 1976.

Prayer, Meditation and the Devotional Attitude. Extracts from the Writings of Bahá'u'lláh, 'Abdu'l-Bahá, and Shoghi Effendi. Compiled by the Research Department of The Universal House of Justice. Wilmette, Illinois: Bahá'í Publishing Trust, 1980.

Principles of Bahá'í Administration. London: Bahá'í Publishing Trust, rev. edn. 1976.

Qur'án, see *Koran.*

SAMANDAR, SHAYKH KÁẒIM. *Táríkh-i-Samandar* (The History of Samandar). Ṭihrán: Bahá'í Publishing Trust, BE 131 (AD 1974).

SHOGHI EFFENDI. *The Advent of Divine Justice.* First published 1939. Wilmette, Illinois: Bahá'í Publishing Trust, rev. edn. 1963.

—— *Bahá'í Administration.* 5th rev. edn. Wilmette, Illinois: Bahá'í Publishing Trust, 1968.

—— *God Passes By.* Wilmette, Illinois: Bahá'í Publishing Trust, 1944.

—— *Messages to America.* Selected Letters and Cablegrams Addressed to the Bahá'ís of North America 1932–1946. Wilmette, Illinois: Bahá'í Publishing Committee, 1947.

—— *The Promised Day is Come.* First published 1941. Wilmette, Illinois: Bahá'í Publishing Trust, rev. edn. 1961.

—— *The World Order of Bahá'u'lláh.* First published 1938. Wilmette, Illinois: Bahá'í Publishing Trust, rev. edn. 1955.

SULAYMÁNÍ, 'AZÍZU'LLÁH. *Maṣábiḥ-i-Hidáyat.* Biography of some of the early Bahá'ís. Ṭihrán: Bahá'í Publishing Trust, Vol. 7, BE 129 (AD 1972).

THE UNIVERSAL HOUSE OF JUSTICE. *Messages from The Universal House of Justice 1968–1973.* Wilmette, Illinois:

Bahá'í Publishing Trust, 1976.

ZARQÁNÍ, MÍRZÁ MAḤMÚD-I-. *Kitáb-i-Badáyi'u'l-Á<u>th</u>ár*. Diary of 'Abdu'l-Bahá's travels in Europe and America, written by His secretary. Bombay: Vol. I, 1914: Vol. II, 1921.

REFERENCES

Full details of authors and titles are given in the Bibliography.

CHAPTER 1: BAHÁ'U'LLÁH'S ARRIVAL AT 'AKKÁ

1. Bahá'u'lláh, quoted by Shoghi Effendi, *God Passes By*, p. 185.
2. Unpublished Tablet of Bahá'u'lláh.
3. Arabic no. 4.
4. Quoted by Shoghi Effendi, *Advent*, p. 67.
5. Bahá'u'lláh, quoted by Shoghi Effendi, *God Passes By*, p. 184.
6. *God Passes By*, pp. 183–4.
7. Quoted by Ishráq Khávárí, *Raḥíq-i-Makhtúm*, vol. 2, p. 771.
8. Reported in Fáḍil-i-Mázindarání, *Asráru'l-Áthár*, vol. 4, p. 349.
9. Quoted in *Raḥíq-i-Makhtúm*, vol. 1, p. 367.
10. Quoted by Shoghi Effendi, *God Passes By*, p. 186.
11. Unpublished Tablet of Bahá'u'lláh.
12. *Fará'id*, pp. 523–4, translated by Kházeh Fanánápazir.
13. Unpublished memoirs.
14. *Gleanings*, CXXXIX, 6.
15. *Synopsis*, p. 27.
16. *Asráru'l-Áthár*, vol. 1, p. 103.
17. *Gleanings*, XIII, 1.

CHAPTER 2: 'THE CAUSE OF GOD WILL FLOURISH THROUGH PERSECUTION'

1. Unpublished.
2. *Gleanings*, XVII, 5.
3. Unpublished Tablet of Bahá'u'lláh.
4. Unpublished Tablet of Bahá'u'lláh.
5. *Gleanings*, XVI, 3.
6. *Má'idiy-i-Ásamání*, vol. 5, p. 156.
7. *The Hidden Words*, Persian no. 57.
8. Unpublished memoirs, translated by Habib Taherzadeh.

9. Unpublished.
10. Unpublished, except for the last part, a prayer translated by Shoghi Effendi, *Prayers and Meditations of Bahá'u'lláh*, no. 153.
11. *Qur'án*, ii. 154–5.
12. Quoted by Shoghi Effendi, *Advent*, p. 67.
13. *God Passes By*, p. 324.
14. *Will and Testament*.
15. Quoted by Shoghi Effendi, *Bahá'í Administration*, pp. 21–2.

CHAPTER 3: THE PRISONER

1. Published in Ishráq Khávarí, *Risáliy-i-Ayyám-i-Tis'ih*, p. 313.
2. *Gleanings*, CXXIV, 2.
3. 27 October 1914, reported by Mu'ayyad, *Kháṭirát-i-Ḥabíb*, pp. 171–2.
4. Unpublished memoirs.

CHAPTER 4: TRUSTEES OF BAHÁ'U'LLÁH

1. *Memorials of the Faithful*, p. 46.
2. *The Proclamation of Bahá'u'lláh*, p. 22.
3. *Tablets of Bahá'u'lláh*, p. 219.
4. Zarqání, *Badáyi'u'l-Áthár*, vol. 2, pp. 395–7.
5. *Tablets of Bahá'u'lláh*, p. 83.

CHAPTER 5: *LAWḤ-I-FU'ÁD*

1. Quoted by Shoghi Effendi, *The Promised Day is Come*, p. 63.
2. *Gleanings*, CLIV, 1.
3. *Synopsis*, pp. 15–16.
4. Quoted by Samandar, *Táríkh-i-Samandar*, p. 204.
5. *Kitáb-i-Íqán*, p. 3 (Brit.), p. 3 (US).
6. From a treatise known as *Risáliy-i-Iskandaríyyih*.
7. From Ḥájí Mírzá Ḥaydar-'Alí's unpublished biography of Mírzá Abu'l-Faḍl.
8. *Synopsis*, p. 14.
9. *The Bahá'í World*, vol. IX, p. 858.
10. Quoted by Mehrábkhání, *Sharḥ-i-Aḥvál-i-Mírzá Abu'l-Faḍl-i-Gulpáygání*, p. 342.
11. *The Bahá'í World*, vol. IX, p. 856.
12. *ibid*. p. 860.
13. *Bahá'í Proofs*, pp. 244–5.

CHAPTER 6: THE WORLD'S MOST POWERFUL RULERS

1. Quoted by Shoghi Effendi, *God Passes By*, p. 212.
2. Quoted by Shoghi Effendi, *The Promised Day Is Come*, p. 28.
3. *ibid.* pp. 29–30.
4. pp. 52–3.
5. *Gleanings*, CLVIII.
6. *Epistle to the Son of the Wolf*, p. 55.
7. *The Proclamation of Bahá'u'lláh*, pp. 83–5.
8. *The Promised Day Is Come*, pp. 55–6.
9. *Proclamation*, pp. 27–8.
10. *ibid.* p. 29.
11. *ibid.* p. 27.
12. Unpublished memoirs.
13. *Proclamation*, p. 33.
14. *ibid.* p. 34.
15. *Gleanings*, CXIX, 3.
16. 'The Unfoldment of World Civilization', *The World Order of Bahá'u'lláh*, pp. 162–3.
17. *Gleanings*, CXX.
18. *ibid.*
19. 'The Goal of a New World Order', *The World Order of Bahá'u'lláh*, pp. 33–4.
20. *Tablets of Bahá'u'lláh*, p. 222.
21. *Qur'án*, viii. 63.

CHAPTER 7: *SÚRIY-I-HAYKAL*

1. Quoted by Shoghi Effendi, *The Promised Day Is Come*, pp. 47–8.
2. Quoted by Fáḍil-i-Mázindarání, *Asráru'l-Á<u>th</u>ár*, vol. 5, p. 277.
3. Quoted by Shoghi Effendi, 'The Dispensation of Bahá'u'lláh', *The World Order of Bahá'u'lláh*, p. 109.
4. *Gleanings*, XIV, 16.
5. Quoted by Shoghi Effendi, 'Dispensation', *idem*, pp. 109–10.
6. *ibid.* p. 110.
7. *ibid.* p. 109.
8. *ibid.* p. 138.
9. *ibid.* p. 107.
10. *ibid.* p. 117.
11. *ibid.*

12. Quoted by Shoghi Effendi, *God Passes By*, p. 250.
13. *ibid.* pp. 101–2.
14. Quoted by Shoghi Effendi, 'Dispensation', *The World Order of Bahá'u'lláh*, p. 109.
15. Quoted by Shoghi Effendi, *Advent*, p. 66.
16. Quoted by Shoghi Effendi, 'Dispensation', *The World Order of Bahá'u'lláh*, p. 113.
17. *ibid.* p. 97.
18. Quoted by Shoghi Effendi, 'The Unfoldment of World Civilization', *The World Order of Bahá'u'lláh*, p. 169.

CHAPTER 8: KINGS AND ECCLESIASTICS

1. *Synopsis*, pp. 17–19.
2. *ibid.* p. 20.
3. *ibid.* p. 21.
4. *ibid.* p. 19.
5. Quoted by Shoghi Effendi, 'Unfoldment', *The World Order of Bahá'u'lláh*, p. 178.
6. *Synopsis*, p. 21.
7. 'Unfoldment', *idem*, pp. 173–6.
8. *Synopsis*, pp. 20–21.
9. *Gleanings*, CXVIII, 6.
10. Quoted by Shoghi Effendi, *The Promised Day Is Come*, p. 72.
11. *ibid.*
12. *Tablets*, p. 28.
13. Quoted by Shoghi Effendi, *The Promised Day Is Come*, p. 76.
14. *ibid.* p. 73.
15. *Synopsis*, p. 19.
16. Unpublished memoirs.
17. Unpublished memoirs.
18. Quoted by Shoghi Effendi, *The Promised Day Is Come*, p. 91.
19. *Synopsis*, pp. 22–3.
20. *ibid.* pp. 26–7.
21. Quoted by Shoghi Effendi, *The Promised Day Is Come*, pp. 85–6.
22. *ibid.* pp. 76–7.
23. *Qur'án*, xxiii. 14.
24. From the memoirs of Mírzá 'Azíz'u'lláh-Ja<u>dh</u><u>dh</u>áb, quoted by Sulaymání, *Maṣábíḥ-i-Hidáyat*, vol. 7.

CHAPTER 9: THE PRIDE OF MARTYRS

1. Translated and quoted by Balyuzi, *Bahá'u'lláh The King of Glory*, p. 299.
2. Quoted in Faizi, *L'álíy-i-Darakhshán*, p. 396.
3. *Áthár-i-Qalam-i-A'lá*, vol. 1, p. 166.
4. *ibid.* p. 169.
5. *ibid.* p. 189.
6. *Bihjatu'ṣ-Ṣudúr*, p. 243.
7. *ibid.* p. 244.
8. *ibid.* p. 245.
9. Quoted by Malik Khosroví, *Táríkh-i-Shuhadáy-i-Amr*, vol. 3, p. 368.
10. Translated by Balyuzi, *Bahá'u'lláh The King of Glory*, pp. 304–9.
11. *Má'idiy-i-Ásamání*, vol. 4, pp. 175–6.
12. Unpublished History.
13. *The Dawn-Breakers*, pp. 245– 8.
14. *Áthár-i-Qalam-i-A'lá*, vol. 1, p. 208.
15. *Má'idiy-i-Ásamání*, vol. 4, p. 34.
16. Quoted by Faizi, *L'álíy-i-Darakhshán*, pp. 411–12.
17. *Má'idiy-i-Ásamání*, vol. 4, p. 34.
18. *Ishráqát*, a compilation, p. 247.
19. Unpublished memoirs.
20. *Áthár-i-Qalam-i-A'lá*, vol. 1, pp. 189–91.
21. Quoted by Muḥammad'-'Alíy-i-Faizi, *L'álíy-i-Darakhshán*, p. 191.

CHAPTER 10: THE DEATH OF THE PUREST BRANCH

1. Unpublished memoirs.
2. *ibid.*
3. Quoted by Shoghi Effendi, 21 December 1939, 'The Spiritual Potencies of that Consecrated Spot', *Messages to America*, p. 34.
4. *God Passes By*, p. 188.
5. Letter to the believers in the East, 25 December 1939.
6. Letter to the believers in the East, Riḍván 89 (= April 1933).
7. Quoted in *Messages to America*, p. 34.
8. 25 December 1939.
9. *Messages to America*, pp. 32–3.
10. Quoted in *Messages to America*, pp. 33–4.

11. Quoted by Ḥájí Mírzá Ḥaydar-'Alí, unpublished biography of Mírzá Abu'l-Faḍl, p. 150.
12. *Tablets of Bahá'u'lláh*, p. 126.
13. *ibid.* p. 257.
14. *ibid.* p. 88.

CHAPTER 11: THE WRONGED ONE OF THE WORLD

1. *Qad Iḥtaraqa'l-Mukhliṣun* (The Fire Tablet).
2. *ibid.*
3. Quoted in *Ishráqát*, a compilation, p. 15.
4. *Gleanings*, CXXX.
5. Quoted by Shoghi Effendi, *The Promised Day Is Come*, pp. 42–3.
6. *ibid.* p. 47.
7. Unpublished.
8. *God Passes By*, pp. 189–91.
9. *Synopsis*, p. 22.
10. p. 190.
11. *Gleanings*, XXXVI.
12. Quoted by Fáḍil-i-Mázindarání, *Asráru'l-Áthár*, vol. 2, pp. 164–5.
13. *Qur'án*, vi. 59.
14. *ibid.* xix. 18.
15. *ibid.* iii. 183.
16. *Risáliy-i-Iskandaríyyih*, a treatise by Mírzá Abu'l-Faḍl.
17. *Bihjatu'ṣ-Ṣudúr*, p. 158.
18. *Má'idiy-i-Ásamání*, vol. 7, pp. 236–8.

CHAPTER 12: FIRST CONVERTS OUTSIDE THE MUSLIM COMMUNITY

1. *The Dawn-Breakers*, pp. 100–101.
2. *ibid.* pp. 147–8.
3. *Má'idiy-i-Ásamání*, vol. 4, p. 362.
4. *Memorials of the Faithful*, p. 8.
5. 'History of the Faith in the Province of Yazd', unpublished.
6. *God Passes By*, pp. 93–4.
7. *Táríkh-i-Samandar*, p. 348.
8. Unpublished.
9. *A Traveller's Narrative*, p. 34.
10. *Majmú'iy-i-Alváḥ*, p. 259.
11. *Gleanings*, CVI.
12. Quoted in *The Promised Day Is Come*, pp. 79–80.

CHAPTER 13: *KITÁB-I-AQDAS.* 1. THE LAW OF GOD

1. Quoted by Shoghi Effendi, *God Passes By*, p. 216.
2. *ibid.*
3. Quoted by Fáḍil-i Mázindarání, *Amr Va Khalq*, vol. 1, p. 8.
4. *ibid.* p. 10.
5. *Synopsis*, pp. 3–5.
6. *God Passes By*, p. 214.
7. Quoted in *Principles of Bahá'í Administration*, p. 7.
8. Letter of 23 February 1976.
9. *Synopsis*, p. 6.
10. *ibid.* p. ix.
11. Quoted in *Principles of Bahá'í Administration*, pp. 6–7.
12. *Má'idiy-i-Ásamání*, vol. 7, p. 119.
13. *Synopsis*, p. 11.
14. *ibid.* pp. 11–12.
15. 'The Unfoldment of World Civilization', *The World Order of Bahá'u'lláh*, p. 199.
16. *Synopsis*, p. 11.
17. *Tablets of Bahá'u'lláh*, p. 164.
18. *The Hidden Words*, Arabic no. 2.
19. *Lawḥ-i-Maqṣúd*, in *Tablets of Bahá'u'lláh*, p. 164.
20. *Má'idiy i-Ásamání*, vol. 7, pp. 119–25.
21. *Synopsis*, p. 12.
22. *ibid.* p. 17.
23. *ibid.* pp. 24–5.
24. Unpublished memoirs.
25. *ibid.*
26. Unpublished memoirs.
27. *ibid.*
28. Mr. 'Ali-Akbar Furútan, Hand of the Cause of God, heard this story from Siyyid Miḥdí several times and recorded it in one of his reminiscences.
29. *Synopsis*, p. 18.
30. The Báb, *Selections*, pp. 6–8.
31. *Má'idiy-i-Ásamání*, vol. 2, p. 79.
32. Quoted in *Selections from the Writings of the Báb*, pp. 6–7.

CHAPTER 14: *KITÁB-I-AQDAS.* 2. A NEW WORLD ORDER

1. *Synopsis*, p. 27.

2. 'The Unfoldment of World Civilization', in *The World Order of Bahá'u'lláh*, p. 190.
3. Quoted by Shoghi Effendi, *ibid*. p. 202.
4. Quoted by Shoghi Effendi, 'The Goal of a New World Order',*The World Order of Bahá'u'lláh*, p. 33.
5. Quoted by Shoghi Effendi, *The Promised Day Is Come*, p. 121.
6. 'The Unfoldment of World Civilization', *The World Order of Bahá'u'lláh*, pp. 168–9.
7. *The Promised Day Is Come*, pp. 128– 9.
8. *Synopsis*, p. 13.
9. Lawḥ-i-Maqṣúd, in *Tablets of Bahá'u'lláh*, p. 168.
10. *Consultation: A Compilation*, p. 3.
11. *ibid*.
12. *ibid*. p. 9.
13. *ibid*. pp. 8–9.
14. Shoghi Effendi, *God Passes By*, p. 332.
15. *Tablets of Bahá'u'lláh*, pp. 128–9.

CHAPTER 15: *KITÁB-I-AQDAS*. 3. DIVINE EDUCATION

1. *Prayer, Meditation and the Devotional Attitude*, p. 1.
2. *Synopsis*, p. 27.
3. *ibid*. pp. 15–16.
4. *Makátíb-i-'Abdu'l-Bahá*, vol. 3, p. 333.
5. *Tablets of Bahá'u'lláh*, pp. 51– 2.
6. *ibid*. p. 68.
7. *Bahá'í Education*, p. 2.
8. *Selections*, pp. 126–7.
9. *ibid*. p. 127.
10. *ibid*.
11. *Bahá'í Education*, p. 52.
12. From a letter written on his behalf, 7 June 1939, quoted in *Bahá'í Education*, p. 70.
13. See *Synopsis*, pp. 43–6.
14. *Makátíb-i-'Abdu'l-Bahá*, vol. 8, p. 51.
15. pp. 18–34.
16. *Gleanings*, CLVIII.
17. *Tablets of the Divine Plan*, p. 51.
18. *Bahá'í Administration*, p. 66.
19. Quoted by Fáḍil-i-Mázindarání, *Amr va Khalq*, vol. 3, p. 121.

20. *Bihjatu'ṣ-Ṣudúr*, p. 257.
21. *Portals to Freedom*, pp. 39–40.
22. *ibid.* pp. 54–9.

CHAPTER 16: *KITÁB-I-AQDAS.* 4. WORSHIP AND DAILY LIFE

1. *Bahá'í Writings on Music*, p. 3.
2. *ibid.*
3. Quoted in *The Bahá'í World*, vol. III, pp. 159–63.
4. Quoted by Fáḍil-i-Mázindarání, *Amr Va Khalq*, vol. 4, p. 92.
5. *ibid.* p. 93.
6. Bahá'u'lláh, *Tablets*, p. 26.
7. *Má'idiy-i-Ásamání*, vol. 4, p. 33.
8. *Tablets*, p. 71.
9. *ibid.* p. 24.
10. *ibid.* pp. 24–5.
11. *Synopsis*, p. 24.
12. Persian no. 24.
13. Persian no. 25.
14. Persian no. 35.
15. Letter of 8 June 1948.
16. Unpublished memoirs.
17. *Kháṭirát-i-Nuh-Sáliy-i-'Akká*, p. 336.
18. Quoted by Shoghi Effendi, *The Promised Day Is Come*, pp. 26–7.
19. *ibid.* p. 25.
20. *Synopsis.* p. 17.
21. *Selections*, p. 117.
22. *ibid.* p. 118.
23. *Bahá'í Writings on Music*, p. 3.
24. *Bahá'í World Faith*, p. 378.
25. *Synopsis*, p. 25.
26. Arabic no. 68.
27. Persian no. 48.

CHAPTER 17: *KITÁB-I-AQDAS.* 5. THE COVENANT OF BAHÁ'U'LLÁH

1. Quoted by Shoghi Effendi, *God Passes By*, p. 221.
2. *Synopsis*, p. 27.
3. *ibid.* p. 24.
4. *ibid.* p. 16.
5. Quoted by The Universal House of Justice, 7 December 1969.

6. *Synopsis*, p. 23.
7. *The Brilliant Proof*, pp. 24–6.
8. Arabic no. 5.
9. *Bihjatu'ṣ-Ṣudúr*, pp. 242–3.
10. Arabic no. 42.
11. *Synopsis*, p. 16.
12. Lawḥ-i-Ṭibb (Tablet of Medicine) in *Majmú'iy-i-Alváh*.
13. *Panj Sha'n*.
14. *Tablets*, p. 84.
15. *ibid.* pp. 263–4.
16. Unpublished.
17. *Gleanings*, CXXIX, 3.
18. *Tablets of Abdul-Baha*, p. 348, quoted in *The Individual and Teaching*, p. 9.
19. 28 March 1953, quoted in *The Individual and Teaching*, p. 32.
20. *Synopsis*, p. 14.
21. Unpublished memoirs.
22. *Memorials*, pp. 92–3.
23. *Má'idiy-i-Ásamání*, vol. 5, p. 280.
24. *Memorials*, p. 93.
25. *Tablets*, pp. 148–9.
26. *Qur'án*, iv. 29. This spoken chronicle is published in *Gulzár-i-Na'ím*, p. 19.
27. Bahá'u'lláh, *Epistle to the Son of the Wolf*, p. 95.
28. *God Passes By*, pp. 93–4.
29. *ibid.* p. 216.
30. *Synopsis*, pp. 14–15.
31. *ibid.* pp. 16–17.
32. *Bihjatu'ṣ-Ṣudúr*, p. 249.
33. *Synopsis*, pp. 27–8.
34. *Má'idiy-i-Ásamání*, vol. 9, p. 26.

CHAPTER 18: LAST DAYS WITHIN THE CITADEL

1. *Bihjatu'ṣ-Ṣudúr*, pp. 156–7.
2. *Memorials*, pp. 67–9.
3. *Má'idiy-i-Ásamání*, vol. 1, pp. 59–60.
4. *Makátíb-i-'Abdu'l-Bahá*, vol. 4, p. 14.
5. Shoghi Effendi, 'The Dispensation of Bahá'u'lláh', *The World Order of Bahá'u'lláh*, p. 134.

6. *Khâṭirát-i-Nuh-Sáliy-i-'Akká*, pp. 331–6.
7. Unpublished memoirs.
8. *Má'idiy-i-Ásamání*, vol. 8, p. 63.
9. Unpublished memoirs.
10. A Tablet to Bashíru's-Sulṭán.
11. Quoted in Esslemont, *Bahá'u'lláh and New Era*, pp. 34–5.
12. *Memorials*, pp. 26–7.
13. *God Passes By*, pp. 195–6.
14. *Gleanings*, XLV.

APPENDIX I: THE TRANSFER OF THE REMAINS OF THE BÁB

1. Nabíl-i-A'ẓam, *The Dawn-Breakers*, pp. 617–18.
2. *God Passes By*, p. 276.

APPENDIX II: MÍRZÁ ABU'L-FAḌL OF GULPÁYGÁN

1. Quoted in *Kitábu'l-Fará'id*, p. 424.
2. *ibid*. p. 429.
3. Unpublished biography of Mírzá Abu'l-Faḍl.
4. Article in *Majillatu'l-Bayán*, a magazine, months of Shavvál and Dhíqa'dih, AH 1313.
5. Mehrábkhání, *Sharḥ-i-Aḥvál-i-Mírzá Abu'l-Faḍl-i-Gulpáygání*, pp. 16–17.
6. *ibid*. pp. 328–9.
7. 'Abdu'l-Bahá, *Selections*, pp. 147–50.
8. *Gleanings*, CLIV, 1.

APPENDIX III: THE BURIAL OF THE PUREST BRANCH AND THE MOTHER OF 'ABDU'L-BAHÁ

1. Printed in *The Bahá'í World*, vol. VIII, pp. 253–8.

INDEX

Part I of this index consists of the titles of Tablets and Writings of Bahá'u'lláh described or mentioned by the author, including a few which were revealed after 1877. Part II contains all other entries. Titles of Tablets and books are italicized. Footnotes are indicated by the abbreviation n. after the page number; if the name or subject occurs both in the text and in a note, this is indicated by 'p. – and n.'. Principal themes are shown by bold figures.

I. TABLETS AND WRITINGS OF BAHÁ'U'LLÁH

Bishárát (Glad-Tidings), quoted, 353

Epistle to the Son of the Wolf, 390

Hidden Words, quoted, 10, 35, 325, 356, 370, 378

Ishráqát (Splendours), 270 n.; quoted, 219, 319

Kalimát-i-Firdawsíyyih (Words of Paradise), quoted, 352–3

Kitáb-i-'Ahdí (The Book of My Covenant), 81, 371

Kitáb-i-Aqdas (Most Holy Book), 108, 147, 240, **275ff.**, 400; Charter of world civilization, 294, 393; circumstances of revelation, 279, 393; laws of, **276ff., 281**, 292–4, 295–8; their implementation, 282, 286; Mother Book, 147, 164, 275; relation to World Order, 281, 294; *Synopsis and Codification of*, 284; translation of, 283–4; Writings of the Báb quoted, 305–7, **Statements by Bahá'u'lláh**: enjoins amity with followers of all religions, 369; on chastity, 364; on cleanliness, 363; forbids confession of sins, 353; forbids contention and violence, 369; on His Covenant and succession, 371–3; on education of children, 91, 326–7, 344; on healing and medicine, 357; on Houses of Justice, 316; on Huqúq'u'lláh, 372; denounces hypocrisy in religion, 355; on inheritance, 330; forbids interpretation by followers, 374; addresses kings and rulers: 147–8, 156; Francis Joseph, 150; William I, 148–9; Presidents of American Republics, 155–6; on language, international auxiliary, 157; on liberty, 298–9; on saintly life and character, 356–7; on next Manifestation of God, 398; on marriage, 365–6; forbids mendicancy, 352; forbids monasticism, 352–3; on Most Great Infallibility, 300; on music, 368; on Nineteen Day Feast, 352; on obligatory prayer, 348; on pride, 369–70; prophecies, 398, future Bahá'í sovereigns, 159; World Wars, 149–50; on reciting verses of God, 323–4; in Mashriqu'l-Adhkár, 343–4; addresses religious leaders, 163–5, 240; on responsibility of parents towards children, 326–7, 366;

II. GENERAL INDEX